W9-DGZ-779

DATE DUE

MAY 3 1 1995			
	MAR 0 1 1996		
MAY 1 5 1995	MAY 0 3 1996		

SOCIAL SCIENCE STUDIES

DIRECTED BY THE SOCIAL SCI-
ENCE RESEARCH COMMITTEE
OF THE UNIVERSITY OF CHICAGO

NUMBER XXXII

T HE SOCIAL SCIENCE STUDIES are an expression of community of interests of the social sciences. The publication of these Studies is one of the results of a comprehensive program of research which has been undertaken by a group or conference of departments. The formation of this conference is an outgrowth of the belief that the social sciences should engage more actively and systematically in co-operative consideration of their problems and methodology. This does not imply any diminution of interest in the development of their special fields. The Studies, therefore, are to include the results of scientific investigations usually associated with the fields of each of the participating departments. But they will also include the results of joint investigations of several or all of these departments as well as studies in related fields.

SOCIAL SCIENCE RESEARCH COMMITTEE

CHARLES E. MERRIAM
WILLIAM F. OGBURN
ROBERT REDFIELD
LOUIS WIRTH
DONALD SLESINGER, *Chairman*

NEGRO POLITICIANS

THE UNIVERSITY OF CHICAGO PRESS
CHICAGO, ILLINOIS

—

THE BAKER & TAYLOR COMPANY
NEW YORK

THE CAMBRIDGE UNIVERSITY PRESS
LONDON

THE MARUZEN-KABUSHIKI-KAISHA
TOKYO, OSAKA, KYOTO, FUKUOKA, SENDAI

THE COMMERCIAL PRESS, LIMITED
SHANGHAI

NEGRO POLITICIANS

THE RISE OF NEGRO POLITICS
IN CHICAGO

By HAROLD F. GOSNELL

Associate Professor of Political Science
University of Chicago

WITH AN INTRODUCTION BY
ROBERT E. PARK

THE UNIVERSITY OF CHICAGO PRESS
CHICAGO · ILLINOIS

PREFACE

Many studies have been made of urban politics in the United States and there is a growing body of printed materials on American party bosses and machines. There is also a great mass of published data on the Negro in American civilization; in fact, there are several excellent books on different phases of the Negro life in Chicago. However, as far as I know, there is no detailed account of the political struggles of a minority group in an American metropolitan community such as the present volume furnishes.

The political process may be studied by comparing the techniques used in the struggle for political power by political parties and other groups in different countries or by an intensive analysis of the political behavior of a single group in a given time and place situation. I endeavored to make a comparative study of certain aspects of political behavior in my *Why Europe Votes* (Chicago, 1930). Comparative studies must necessarily be extensive and distributive. I discovered only a few of the necessary intensive studies of politics have been made in different countries to furnish the data for a real comparative politics. Such concepts as political power, political equilibrium between groups, superordination and subordination, command and obedience, group loyalty and patriotism, political symbolization, and authority can be given meanings only by concrete materials. It is hoped that the present study furnishes some of these data, and that when combined with other intensive analyses it may play some small part in the building up of a science of politics.

Before I started the present study some five years ago I had already demonstrated my interest in the political behavior of minority groups in urban communities. In our study, *Non-Voting: Causes and Methods of Control* (Chicago, 1924), Professor Charles E. Merriam and I analyzed the interest in the voting process shown by different racial and ethnic groups in

vii

the city of Chicago. In my *Getting Out the Vote* (Chicago, 1927) I continued this analysis by means of an attempt to measure experimentally the influence of a non-partisan mail canvass upon the voting behavior of different minority groups in Chicago. In connection with these studies it became clear that the patterns of behavior of the Negro in Chicago politics furnished fascinating materials for the understanding of the rôle of minority groups in urban politics.

The choice of the Negro group for a detailed study of the political process meant that I had to acquire some familiarity with the field of race relations. I soon found out that this was a field where it was easy to make mistakes and impossible to please all the parties concerned. In fact, one of the first things I discovered was that in my previous publications I had made the egregious error of not capitalizing the word "Negro." I found out that this usage, which is not common among political scientists, is looked upon by some Negroes as a symbol of fair-mindedness. This is just one illustration of what was brought home to me time after time during the past few years. Language and behavior which aroused no emotional response in one racial group may arouse a storm of protest and indignation in the other. Furthermore, within the white world and within the colored world there is considerable variation in the sensitiveness of individuals to given stimuli. Because of the nature of the material, I must make in this Preface the usual confessions of guilt for sins of omission and commission.

Another discovery that I made was that the materials regarding the Negro in politics were scattered and woefully incomplete. After piecing together, cataloguing, and indexing data gleaned from the white press, the colored press, national, state, and local documents, books, and pamphlets found in the libraries of Chicago, New York, and Washington, D.C., there still remained many wide gaps in the account. No Negro who has been active as a leader in Chicago politics has published his memoirs, no legislative investigations of the Negro in politics

have been made in Illinois, and the group in general is not aware
of the importance of preserving records.

Most of the information which is presented in this book cannot be found in other printed sources. It has been laboriously
collected by means of direct observation, interviews, and informal conversations. For a period of five years, Republican,
Democratic, and Communist meetings in the "Black Belt" have
been faithfully attended and recorded, the work of a party headquarters has been observed at first hand, the "drawings" in
gambling houses have been witnessed, the conduct of elections
has been watched, police squad cars have been ridden in, and
legislative bodies, courts, churches, and funerals have been attended. When taking notes I have sometimes been glared at,
and one of my research assistants was nearly arrested when
watching a picketing line.

The direct observations furnished valuable clues which had
to be followed up by interviews. By one device or another it
was necessary to win the confidence of persons who were carrying the information around in their heads and to persuade them
that it was important for them to impart some of that information. While no formal schedules were prepared, special ques-
tionnaires were worked out for particular individuals and a
number of forms were used to check the completeness of the information. The interviews were usually short, but some persons
were questioned at intervals over a period of several months.
During some of the interviews, stenographic notes were taken,
but this procedure was not advisable in all cases. Among the
officials, past and present, who were interviewed, were mayors
of the city of Chicago, Illinois congressmen, judges, state legislators, aldermen, ward committeemen, state's attorneys, coroners, sheriffs, city clerks, United States district attorneys,
policemen, firemen, postal workers, teachers, and social service
workers. Among the persons interested in or acquainted with
politics who were seen were white and colored ministers, lawyers, bondsmen, precinct captains, gambling-house keepers,
bootleggers, funeral directors, business men, leaders of women's

clubs, small shopkeepers, and officials of fraternal orders. The farther that one proceeds in a study like the present one the clearer it becomes that it is impossible to separate the study of politics from sociology, economics, and the other social sciences.

No one method has been followed in presenting the materials which have been collected. Although I am a firm believer in the use of quantitative methods in the social sciences, I have tried to cut down the number of statistical tables presented. The statistical method is only one of many methods that can be used to study political behavior, and the interpretation of numbers always calls for logical inference and general familiarity with the materials. From the many tables in my files I have selected those which I regarded as most significant. Extracts from life-history documents are also presented which illustrate different aspects of the group life. These documents have been checked against the official records, the press, all available published sources, and the testimony of other individuals.

It is obvious that a study of the present sort could not be completed by a single academic person with pedagogical obligations in a period of five years without generous assistance. The work was done under the auspices of the Social Science Research Committee of the University of Chicago, and I am greatly indebted to the co-operation of the members and staff of that committee. I am particularly indebted to my colleague, Professor Robert E. Park, of the Department of Sociology, for his contribution to this volume and for his sound advice and encouragement during different stages of the work. My colleagues, Professors C. E. Merriam, Quincy Wright, L. D. White, H. D. Lasswell, L. Wirth, and F. L. Schuman, and Professor Charles S. Johnson of Fisk University, have also been very generous of their time in reading the manuscript. The suggestions of those who looked at the manuscript were invaluable, but for one reason or another they were not followed in every case. The following graduate students have been research assistants at one time or another during the past five years, Professor Solly A. Hartzo, 1929–30; Miss Mary Herrick, Summer, 1930; Miss

Frances Williams, 1930–32; Miss Myra Logan, Summer, 1931; and Mr. Horace R. Cayton, 1931–33. Mention should also be made of the investigating work done by Mr. Truman K. Gibson, student at the University of Chicago Law School, Mr. Daniel Swinney, and Miss Dorothy Blumenstock, graduate students. All of these and a number of other persons made the present volume possible. However, none of them are responsible for the mistakes and lapses which may have been made by the author. Several of the investigators happen to belong to the race which is described in the pages that follow. They have disagreed with some of my interpretations.

The purpose of the present volume is to describe in realistic fashion the struggle of a minority group to advance its status by political methods. It is not to give support to any particular race theory or to collect information for any reform organization. Where the facts presented might injure the reputation of certain white and colored politicians, names and places are omitted. However, in my files every bit of evidence may be identified as to person referred to, source of information, name of interviewer, date and place of interview.

Another purpose of the present volume is to examine dispassionately some of the beliefs held by white people regarding the civic consciousness of Negroes. The Chicago Commission on Race Relations, which was appointed following the race riot of 1919, listed some of the common beliefs concerning Negroes and gave among the secondary beliefs the following:

That they are lacking in civic consciousness. Absence of community pride and disregard for community welfare are alleged to be the common failing of Negroes. It is pointed out that the "Black Belt" has been allowed to run down and become the most unattractive spot in the city. To this fact is attributed the tolerance of vice in this region. Negroes generally, it is still believed, can be bought in elections with money and whiskey. They are charged with having no pride in the beauty of the city, and with making it unbeautiful by personal and group habits.

Some of the beliefs concerning the civic pride of Negroes are investigated in the present work, but it is clear that this is a

subject with so many ramifications that a project of a different
sort would be required to cover it. I am using the term "politics" to include voting, campaigning, bargaining for jobs and
special favors, and office-holding. If I had gone into a full discussion of the kind of governmental services secured by the
Negroes as a result of their political activities or lack of such
activities, much more time and a larger investigating staff would
have been necessary.

I wish to acknowledge the courtesy of the editors of the *National Municipal Review*, the *American Journal of Sociology* and
the *American Political Science Review* in permitting me to use
in this volume materials which appeared as separate articles in
these journals.

Harold F. Gosnell

March, 1935

INTRODUCTION

I

Some twenty-five years ago, in the summer of 1910 to be exact, Booker T. Washington conceived the notion that he would like, for once, to get quite away from the United States and see what this America, in which he had been so long and so actively immersed, looked like from the outside. Accordingly, he took seven weeks out of a very busy life to visit and see Europe.

What made this journey unique was the fact that, though he visited most of its capitals, he did not, in the sense of the ordinary traveler, see Europe at all. So far from visiting the historical shrines and seeing the customary sights he sedulously avoided them, limiting his observations to the life and labor of what he described as "the man farthest down." His purpose was, so far as possible in the time at his command, to meet and make the acquaintance of the classes in Europe which, in respect to their opportunities, their handicaps, and their conditions of life generally, were comparable, not, to be sure, with the élite, but with the masses of the Negro people in the United States.

What Washington wanted to see abroad, and from the distance and point of view of Europe, was America, and not America merely but the American Negro. He therefore visited in preference the slums of London instead of the art galleries; hunted out the abandoned ghettos of Prague and Cracow; explored the sulphur mines of Sicily and discovered in remote villages returned Polish or Italian immigrants. Eventually he published his observations in a volume to which he gave the title, suggested by his own description of the object of his journey, *The Man Farthest Down*.

Booker Washington's conception of "the man farthest down," it perhaps needs to be said, was not racial. He did not, at any

xiii

rate, think of him either as a man foredoomed to be a hewer of wood and drawer of water, nor as one whom the oppression of a more favored class had reduced to a position of hopeless inferiority. On the contrary, with an optimism characteristic of other self-made Americans, Washington was disposed to believe that all men were predestined to rise and that those who found themselves behind were, in all probability, merely those who, like the Negro, had started late and were now, or would soon be, on their way.

In any case, the backwardness of peoples seems to be, on the whole, a historical and not a biological phenomenon. So conceived it loses some of the tragic interest ordinarily attributed to it. The Negro's case was not at that time and is not now as exceptional as it has sometimes seemed. There are, for example, in the Appalachian Mountains, on the high plains of New Mexico, and in the swamps of southern Louisiana, other peoples who have not yet emerged, or are just beginning to emerge, from their ancient isolation. They are, like the "Habitants" of Quebec, the "Pennsylvania Dutch" of Pennsylvania, and the so-called "Cajuns" of southern Louisiana, what Benton McKaye calls "the indigenous and colonial" as contrasted with "metropolitan" peoples. They are, in short, the provincial peoples who have not yet left home to try their fortune in cities and centers of civilization.[1]

America and, perhaps, the rest of the world, can be divided between two classes: those who reached the city and those who have not yet arrived.

Now it happens that since Booker Washington went to Europe twenty-five years ago in quest of the man farthest down, there has been a great migration of the Negroes from the plantation and small towns of the South to the manufacturing cities and metropolitan centers of the North. This migration has brought about, for good and for all, a great change in the condition and in the outlook of the Negro people in America—a change that Washington, who assumed that Negroes were destined to re-

[1] Benton MacKaye, *The New Exploration: A Philosophy of Regional Planning* (New York, 1928).

main for an indefinite period in the rural South—could not have foreseen.

In the cities rural Negroes have become involved in a competition—biological and economic—more intense and pervasive than they had ever known. On the other hand, in this stimulating environment the Negro has developed an intellectual life and produced a literature for which otherwise and elsewhere there would have been neither the occasion nor the opportunity. Finally, in the city the masses of the Negro have gone into politics.

When in January, 1901, George H. White, the last Negro member of Congress from the southern states, delivered his valedictory speech, the incident, although it attracted little attention at the time, marked the end of an epoch. Since that time the public—the public at any rate that gets its politics from the press—has become accustomed to the notion that the Negro was, humanly speaking, out of politics, if not for good and all, at least for an indefinite period.

The public was therefore surprised and a little disconcerted when in 1928 Republicans of the First Congressional District of Illinois elected a Negro to Congress. Still more surprising, six years later, a Negro was elected from the same district on the Democratic ticket to succeed a Republican. This shattered all traditions.

What makes this the more interesting and significant is that both Republican and Democratic congressmen were presumably elected by the votes of Negro migrants from the South, voters who at home had been effectively dispossessed of the franchise. The First Congressional District includes Chicago's First and Second wards, where Negroes constitute 58 per cent of the population, most of them comparatively recent arrivals.

It is still true of the Negro in America, as it once was of the serfs in Europe, that city air makes men free, and this is true in more ways than are ordinarily conceived of. The great cities are now what the frontier and the wilderness once was, the refuge of the footloose, the disinherited, and all those possessed by that undefined *malaise* we call social unrest.

This volume, if I might characterize in a word, is at once a chapter in the local history of Chicago and at the same time an account of the way in which the rural Negro, "the man farthest down," came to the city and got into politics.

II

The motives which, since 1914, have turned the faces of the Negro people cityward have been primarily economic rather than political. However, the prospect of regaining in the North some measure of the political power they had lost in the South undoubtedly did speed up the exodus. There are, besides, historical reasons why the ballot should have for Negroes a sentimental and symbolic significance, quite out of proportion to any positive value it may have had in the past or is likely to have in the future.

The Negro's first experience in politics was gained during the anti-slavery agitation which—so far as Negroes participated in it—may be said to have begun with the publication in 1829 of *Walker's Appeal*, an anti-slavery pamphlet which General Giles of Virginia referred to at the time as "a seditious pamphlet sent from Boston." Coming as it did as few years after the Denmark Vesey conspiracy in Charleston in 1822 and just before the Nat Turner insurrection in Virginia in 1830, its influence upon public opinion, North and South, was profound.

In the course of the anti-slavery struggle, which began at this time and in this way, Frederick Douglass, who had been a fugitive slave before he became an anti-slavery orator and journalist, played a leading rôle. It is probably the prestige he gained at that time, rather than the prominence he achieved afterward during the period of reconstruction, that has made him the one outstanding figure in Negro politics.

It was unfortunate in some respects, but not in others, that Negroes got their introduction to politics in connection with a radical and more or less revolutionary movement. It was inevitable that the abolition crusade should have created expectations that could not, at the conclusion of the Civil War, be suddenly and miraculously fulfilled. The failure of reconstruction to realize the millennial hopes it had inspired was the first and most tragic disillusionment which emancipation brought to the Negro.

It has been customary to refer to Negro politicians of the reconstruction period as if they deserved the contempt that a partisan public opinion has bestowed upon them. The fact seems to be that very few of them were the downright rascals they are sometimes described to be. Politicians are rarely either as noble or as despicable as their contemporaries conceive them to be, and Senator Tom Reed's saying, "a statesman is a politician who is dead" is quite as likely to be true of black men as of white.

Not all Negro office-holders under the reconstruction governments were either as ignorant or as incompetent as they have been represented to be. Among them were, for example, men like John Mercer Langston, who graduated in 1844 from Oberlin College, and Robert Brown Elliott, born in Boston and educated in England, who seems to have been, of all the twenty-two Negro members of Congress, the one man who could be described as brilliant.

Of the two colored United States senators elected at different times from Mississippi, Blanch K. Bruce had been a school teacher in Missouri, and Hiram Revels, after graduating from Knox College, Galesburg, Illinois, had been a preacher and lecturer before he got into politics.

Men such as these, who had succeeded either at the cost of a long and desperate struggle, or by the grace of some unusual good fortune, in getting any kind of superior education, were disposed to take themselves seriously and to be, if anything, a little too conscious of their responsibilities. In fact, if I might base an opinion upon men of that period whom I have known I should say it was characteristic of them that they put too high an estimate upon their respectability, and were rather more ambitious than would be true of the Negro intelligentsia of today to behave correctly and in what James W. Garner describes as "an Anglo-Saxon manner."

It was said of John R. Lynch, who was a member of the

legislature of Mississippi in 1872, that he presided over the deliberations of the House with a dignity and unpartiality to which, upon his retirement, even his political opponents bore testimony.[2]

Another reconstruction legislator, Hannibal Thomas, a Negro carpet-bagger from Ohio, was so shocked by what he heard and saw after he went South, of the life of the Freedman, that he was impelled to write a book describing "the insensate follies of a race blind to every passing opportunity."

The book is mainly interesting now as an evidence of the idealism of the politicians of the reconstruction era. It is characteristic of idealists that they expect too much of human nature and are hence likely to become embittered and pessimistic when they discover how far ordinary human beings fall short of what they expected of them.[3]

There were at the time, and there have been since, among Negro leaders those who shared the misgivings with regard to the future of the Negro in America which Hannibal Thomas has so candidly expressed, but they have not, as one might expect, been effective leaders of the masses. They have not been successful politicians.

Not all of the Negro politicians of the reconstruction shared the illusions of the anti-slavery crusaders. There were men like Isaiah Montgomery, the founder of the Negro town at Mound Bayou, who was born, reared, and educated on the plantation which he, his father, and his brother later purchased and conducted.[4] Isaiah Montgomery was the only colored man to participate in the constitutional convention of 1890, which adopted a constitution which effectively disfranchised the Negroes in that state.

In that convention he made a notable speech in defense of his race, which was so moderate, wise, and realistic in tone that it

[2] James W. Garner, *Reconstruction in Mississippi* (New York, 1901).

[3] William Hannibal Thomas, *The American Negro: What He Was, What He Is, and What He May Become* (New York, 1901).

[4] The famous Hurricane Plantation, located on the river below Vicksburg and owned by Joseph Davis, brother of Jefferson, President of the Confederacy.

attracted wide comment at the time and was regarded of sufficient importance to be printed in full in the New York World.

The Negro politicians described in this volume are perhaps· not as moderate and as considerate of white folks as they should be. They have very few illusions, however, in regard to the people they seek to represent. On the other hand, they are making no apologies for them either.

III

Reconstruction in the South seems to have passed through most of the characteristic phases of other revolutionary movements. There was a brief period of violence and exaltation, when the new order was introduced, followed by a longer period of adjustment, disillusionment, and general deflation.

Probably no one expected the Negro would be permitted, without a struggle, to enjoy all his newly acquired civil rights; but it was hoped that, having the ballot, he would at least be able to enforce in the new social and political order a consideration that he had not received in the old.

As it turned out, the interests of race and caste triumphed over the interests of class and party. With the rise of the so-called Solid South, at any rate, Negroes lost their representation not only in southern legislatures but in congress. They continued to share, to be sure, in the federal patronage, but they ceased to participate, in any effective way, in local politics.

Meanwhile, in the ensuing struggle to enforce the Negro's civil rights and to prevent a more or less complete nullification of the reconstruction legislation, by interpretation, qualification, and legal chiseling, the battle-ground shifted from the legislatures to the courts.

It is not enough, it seems, that laws, like New Year's resolutions, be solemnly proclaimed and inscribed on the statute books. They must, eventually, be enforced. In no other way can they be so effectively incorporated in the habits of a people and in the customs of a country as to be, relatively at least, self-enforcing. The courts must complete the work of the legislature, and until the law, as interpreted and enforced, has brought about what the psychologists might describe as a "reconditioning" of the people for whom it was enacted, one cannot say that the political process is complete.

The task of securing the enforcement of the Negro's civil rights was eventually taken up by the emerging Negro intelligentsia, led by men like Burkhardt Du Bois, supported by the Society for the Advancement of Colored People, of which he was the founder. This society inherited the idealism and the radicalism of the abolitionists, but radicalism, at this time, amounted to no more than an insistence that the Negro should have, here and now, the rights which the new order promised but in practice postponed.

Meanwhile the masses of the Negro people, where they were permitted to vote at all, continued to support the Republican party. In this way they were acting in accordance with, if not in response to, the admonition of their number one political leader, Frederick Douglass. "The Republican party," he once told them, "is the ship. All else is the open sea."

The migration to the northern cities, caused by the shortage of labor during the World War, has resulted in a renaissance in Negro politics. The character of this new Negro politics seems to have been largely determined by the fact that, like other immigrants, Negroes moving northward settled first where they encountered least opposition, either in the way of high rents or social prejudice, namely, in the slums.

In Chicago, for example, the first Negro settlement was on Dearborn Street in close proximity to the old red-light district of the First Ward. From there they moved southward, along State Street, and eastward, into more spacious and respectable quarters, in the direction of Lake Michigan. In New York Negroes were mainly settled in Greenwich Village as late as 1880. Later they were numerous in and around West Fifty-third Street and the San Juan Hill district, notorious for the riots which occurred there in 1900. At present the largest Negro settlement in New York is in Harlem, from north of 110th Street. Negro Harlem has been adequately characterized in

Carl Van Vechten's novel, *Nigger Heaven*, and in Langston Hughes' volume of poems, *The Weary Blues*.

The slums of cities, where people live ordinarily from necessity rather than from choice, are in many respects the most democratic of all the territorial units into which the urban complex finally, resolves itself. Here, where neighbors are mostly strangers, there is likely, if anywhere, to be some sort of equality and a general disposition to live and let live not characteristic of more highly organized communities. It was in the slums and the adjoining territories into which the Negro migrants moved that Negroes first achieved a voting preponderance that made them a political power to be reckoned with.

It is significant, also, that the migration of the Negroes to the northern cities took place at a time when urban residents were abandoning their homes in the center of the city for the more spacious suburbs. As these suburbs multiplied the abandoned and the so-called "blighted" area surrounding the central business core steadily expanded. These areas are now largely occupied by immigrants and Negroes. The result has been that by a singular turn of fortune the southern Negro, lately from the "sticks"—the man politically farthest down—now finds himself living in the center of a great metropolitan city where his vote is not only counted but where, in various ways and for various reasons, it counts.

IV

Not all Negro politicians of the new era got their political education in the slums. Some of them have merely held office and kept out of the dirt. But in the crowded Negro quarter, where most of the voters live, there is always a good deal of vice and disorder, and the men who owe their influence in politics to the fact that they have been able to get out the vote are likely to be on such intimate terms with the underworld that they are not received in colored society.

Some of them, like "Mushmouth" Johnson and "Teenan" Jones in Chicago, and R. R. Church, Sr., of Memphis, the boss

of Beale Street, where the "blues" come from, who seem to
have been political personalities before Negro politics achieved
an organization, never quite emerged from the underworld in
which they grew up.

Men who succeed in the jungle politics of a city slum are
likely to be a hard-bitten, disillusioned, and cynical sort, not
overscrupulous about police regulations, but faithful, on the
whole, to their friends and respected by their enemies. Politics
in the wards and among the lowly is more than elsewhere organized on a personal and a feudal basis.

In the case of Negroes, however, ward politics has assumed at
times a dignity and importance it would not otherwise have had
because it has been associated with the Negro's struggle for
fundamental civil and political rights.

In any case, men of the sort here described, accustomed to the
freedom and democracy of the city, are of a type different from
the politicians of the reconstruction era, who grew up on the
tradition of the anti-slavery movement and under the influence
of the missionary schools.

They are, for one thing, not inhibited by the necessity of
living at the same time in two different worlds, the world of the
white man and the world of the black. Ward politicians are
likely, in any case, to understand and feel at home among the
people of whom they are the political shepherds.

If Negro politicians of the reconstruction era were, by temperament and training, idealists, the men who have recently
come to power are realists. They are realists, for one reason, if
not for others, because they are the products of the struggle
to survive and live in a free and competitive world such as did
not exist for most Negroes before emancipation. In this world,
where every man is on his own, he is expected—whatever he
may eventually do for the general good—at least to make an
individual success.

From the Yankee school-ma'ams, who came South after the
war to complete in the schools the emancipation of the Freed-
men, Negroes learned, among other things, that they, like other
Americans, were destined and expected to rise.

In the early days of freedom, when Negro schools and Negro colleges were springing up in every part of the South, General O. O. Howard, who as head of the Freedman's Bureau was more or less responsible for many if not most of them, visited Atlanta University. In concluding an address to the students he asked them what message he might take to the benefactors and well-wishers of the school in the North. Thereupon a small voice piped up: "Tell 'em," it said, "we'se aris'n."

The story, which has been repeated so often that it has become legendary, owes its wide currency at the time and since to the fact that it so aptly expresses the faith with which the Yankee teachers, more or less consciously, inspired their colored pupils.

"We'se aris'n" is, like the Declaration of Independence, an expression of the American spirit—the spirit most conspicuously manifest in the personalities, from Benjamin Franklin to Andrew Carnegie, of our so-called self-made men.

Nowhere has this American spirit—its optimism and its individualism—found a more complete embodiment than in the philosophy and the career of the author of *Up From Slavery*. At any rate, it is probable that no American was ever more convinced than Booker Washington that the main business of life was to rise and succeed. The future of the Negro—that was the substance of his teaching—rests finally on the ability of the individual Negro, each for himself, to make his way in the world. Only out of the struggle to rise will the race get the discipline that will make it master of its fate.

The secret of success for the man farthest down, is, as he put it, "to take advantage of his disadvantages."

The Negro politicians described in this volume, are, on the whole, men like that. They are, so to speak, self-made politicians. They are no longer obsessed with a sense of their dependence on Washington and the central government. They no longer regard themselves as the wards of the Republican party. They cherish no vain hopes and, like Margaret Fuller, they "accept the universe."

There is among the members of the Negro intelligentsia in

New York and elsewhere a radical school of thought that gets its inspiration from Moscow. During the depression communist propaganda has made deep inroads in the ranks of the Negro proletariat. But the Negro politicians of Chicago are no more likely than Tammany Hall to go radical or indulge in romantic dreams about the future either of the country or the race.

The older generation of Negro politicians were very largely the descendants of old free Negro families, who have constituted, and still do, a colored aristocracy within the Negro race. But like most aristocracies they have been jealous of their privileged position, both within and without the race, and have been mainly interested in maintaining it.

Meanwhile, there has emerged a robust and vigorous middle class, men of the mental type of Booker Washington, and of the men of the Negro Business League which he organized. These men have more or less the attitudes of pioneers, men who have grown up on an advancing frontier—in this instance a racial frontier.

The Negro politicians who have risen in ward politics, as distinguished from those who still take their cue from Washington, seem to be, in most every case, of this type. They are not infrequently men of superior education and are active in promoting the interests of the race as they see them, but they act on the principle that the best way to solve the problem of the race as a whole is for each member to solve the problem as an individual. They are, in short, "We'se Arisers," who as a result of their conflict and competition with the white man have become race, rather than class, conscious.

What seems to be taking place in Negro politics, then, not only in Chicago but elsewhere, is a transfer of political power. A new generation and a new type of man has arisen within the ranks of the race, occupying a position between the traditional leaders and the masses of the Negro. It is upon this middle class that Negro political leadership has descended.

In sketching, by way of introduction to this study of Negro politics in Chicago, the story of the Negro's political adventures in the United States, I have sought, incidentally, to indicate the relation of Negro politics to some other aspects of Negro life which though significant are not so obvious and open to observation. In doing this I have been moved by the conviction that for most readers this volume might have a double interest: First, because it illuminates the obscure region of local and racial politics; and second, because it adds another chapter in the career of the Negro race in America—a career which for sheer human interest, at any rate, is not equaled by that of any other element of our population, except the Jew.

Robert E. Park

TABLE OF CONTENTS

LIST OF TABLES

LIST OF ILLUSTRATIONS

CHAPTER I

THE NEGRO IN AMERICAN POLITICS

The rôle of an ethnic minority in the politics of a given locality is closely related to the total situation in which the group finds itself. Before discussing the Negro in the politics of a northern metropolitan community, it is therefore necessary to review the history of Negro participation in American politics. It is also necessary to consider in what direction this group is going.

JOHN R. LYNCH

The trend of American political development has been toward the wider and wider participation of all elements of the population in the affairs of government. Property, religious, sex, and racial qualifications for voting and office-holding have gradually been eliminated or liberalized. These changes have been made in accordance with the ideology of democracy which calls for political equality in the form of universal suffrage and freedom of choice. However, when these dogmas have been applied to a people which is struggling to rise from an inferior status, friction and conflict have resulted. This friction between ethnic groups arising out of the application of democratic principles has not been peculiar to the relations between white and colored peoples.

From the very beginning of the United States as a separate nation there existed minority white as well as colored peoples whose presence gave rise to political problems. The Irish who came to this country to escape harsh criminal laws, illiberal laws against Catholics, discrimination against their political advancement, absentee landlordism, and famine conditions, found that they were not liked here because of their Irish brogue, their

1

poverty, their illiteracy, their religion, and their genius for politics. There were anti-Irish riots near Boston in 1834, and ten years later the natives in Philadelphia were so excited that they started a riot and burned some Irish Catholic churches. The Irish were thrown back upon themselves, they developed an intense loyalty to the Democratic party, and they worked so hard to get ahead in politics that they were able to help lay the foundations of such political organizations as the Tammany machine in New York.

Another group which has had to fight its way in American politics is the Jewish group. Partly because of persecutions at different times and in different parts of Europe, Jews have been coming to America from the earliest times. At first they were not allowed to vote in some of the colonies, but gradually the suffrage was extended to them. Hostility to the Jews has increased in comparatively recent times because of the growth of nationalism and of intolerant movements. The anti-semitism of such organizations as the Ku Klux Klan is based in part on the fact that the Jews have religious and cultural traditions which are different. Living sometimes in ghetto communities, speaking often a strange language, the Jews have been isolated to a certain extent and they have been compelled to struggle for political recognition. Partly because of their success in business and politics, they have played the rôle of a scapegoat for farmer and middle-class aggressions in times of economic stress.

Since the Negroes are more conspicuous than the Irish, the Jews, or any other ethnic group that has come to the United States, the friction that has developed out of colored-white relations has been the most acute of all race frictions. Furthermore, the Negro had farther to go than the Irish or the Jews. He started farther down—as a slave. While it is difficult to define what is a Negro, in general it can be said that all noticeable mixtures of white and colored strains are regarded as colored in the United States. This attitude on the part of the whites has forced the Negroes to make their own group the center of their interests and activities. When two ethnocentric groups, both numerous, are found together in the same political unit, no common "public opinion," no "constitutional consensus" exists between them, and the conditions for a democracy are not present. The experience of South Africa, Australia, and Barbadoes, as well as that of the southern states of the American Union, shows that the ethnic group with the dominant culture will endeavor to impose a caste status upon the group without power, on the ground of its "inferior" culture. Many Negroes in the United States have refused to accept an inferior status, and consequently the relations between the white and colored groups have frequently been strained. On the other hand, lynchings, riots, bombings, and other forms of violence have from time to time belied the faith that white Americans have professed in the peaceful processes of democracy.

The conflict between the ideologies of democracy and white supremacy was clearly shown during the period of slavery. According to the United States Constitution a Negro slave was counted as three-fifths of a person for purposes of apportioning representatives in Congress among the various states. In other words, a slave was regarded as a being that was not quite a man. In between the slaves and free white persons were the free Negroes, who occupied an anomalous position since they were free but they did not have the full rights of citizenship. While in the New England states there were no race distinctions in suffrage, in all the other northern states and in the South free Negroes were deprived of the suffrage in the period preceding the Civil War. However, from time to time, free Negroes voted in states where they were disfranchised, but never in large numbers.[1] In fact, the free Negroes were only about one-tenth of the total Negro population in 1860, and it can therefore be said that the direct political importance of the Negro prior to the Civil War was very slight.

The indirect political influence of the Negro during the slave period was considerable. While the "old-time" Negro has been

---

[1] E. Olbrich, *The Development of Sentiment on Negro Suffrage to 1860* (Madison, 1912); C. P. Patterson, *The Negro in Tennessee;* G. T. Stephenson, *Race Distinctions in American Law* (New York, 1910); K. H. Porter, *History of Suffrage in the United States* (Chicago, 1918). Free Negroes could vote in North Carolina until 1835.

pictured as docile, polite, respectable, and timid, the white
planter class was afraid that some of them might develop into
revolutionary leaders on the model of those in the West Indies.
The history of the successful, ruthless, violent revolutions in
San Domingo and Haiti struck terror in the hearts of the southerners. This terror was greatly heightened by Negro insurrections, particularly the one threatened by Denmark Vesey in
1822 and the Nat Turner rebellion of 1831. Furthermore, some
of the slaves who escaped to the northern states became abolition agitators and orators. Notable among these was the mulatto, Frederick Douglass, who escaped from Maryland when he
was twenty-one years of age and a few years later became an
agent for a Massachusetts Anti-slavery Society.[2] He attracted
the attention of William Lloyd Garrison and other abolitionists
because of the eloquence, vigor, and brilliant logic which he displayed in an impromptu address made before an anti-slavery
convention. Despite many difficulties he spoke eloquently in
various parts of the United States and in England. His lectures
and publications in England played a part in the arousing of
British sentiment against the recognition of the Confederacy.

While men like Douglass were active on behalf of the cause of
emancipation and enfranchisement, it cannot be said that the
Negroes won freedom and the suffrage by their own efforts.
Emancipation was a military measure and the suffrage was
thrust upon them by the Republican party leaders who were in
desperate need of votes in the early days of the reconstruction
period. Without the Negro voters the Republicans would have
lost the presidency on two occasions.

To the southern whites Negro suffrage seemed an intolerable
punishment for losing the war. Their dismay at what happened
is illustrated by the following extract which is typical of any
number of contemporary accounts: "The maddest, most unscrupulous and infamous revolution in history has snatched the
power from the hands of the race which settled the country . . . .

---

[2] F. Douglass, *Life and Times of Frederick Douglass* (Hartford, 1882), p. 216; B. T.
Washington, *Frederick Douglass* (Philadelphia, 1907).

and transferred it to its former slaves, an ignorant and feeble race."[3]

A calmer view of the reconstruction period brings to light other aspects of the situation. At no time did the Negroes control altogether any state government, and a large proportion of those who won elective or appointive positions were free Negroes who had acquired some education in the North. An analysis of the twenty Congressmen and the two United States senators who represented the race during the reconstruction period shows that ten of them were men of college education and that the others had by self-instruction acquired a rudimentary education.[4] Of these Congressmen, all were mulattoes except three, and some of them had been educated by their white fathers.[5] The Negro Congressmen were typical of other colored elective office-holders of the period. The leading rôles were taken largely by the mixed bloods who had had some opportunities to prepare themselves for leadership during the slave period. That the Negro leaders regarded themselves as apart from the Negro masses is clearly shown by such men as William H. Thomas, a northern Negro who wrote a candid account of his experiences in the South.[6]

While many mistakes were made by these early Negro office-holders and they were made the objects of scorn, ridicule, and hatred, a number of recent interpretations of this period indicate that they were not as insolent, unprincipled, and corrupt as they have been pictured.[7] How terrifying it was for some of the southern whites to see Negroes sitting in the state house, talking

[3] *Charleston News*, June 12 and 15, 1868, cited by F. B. Simkins and R. H. Woody, *South Carolina During Reconstruction* (Chapel Hill, 1932), p. 110.

[4] A. A. Taylor, "Negro Congressmen a Generation After," *Journal of Negro History*, VII (April, 1932), 127. See also John R. Lynch, *The Facts of Reconstruction* (New York, 1913); John M. Langston, *From the Virginia Plantation to the National Capitol* (Hartford, 1894).

[5] E. B. Reuter, *The Mulatto in the United States* (Boston, 1918), p. 251.

[6] *The American Negro* (New York, 1901).

[7] Simkins and Woody, *op. cit.*; A. A. Taylor, *The Negro in South Carolina during the Reconstruction* (Washington, 1926).

loudly and easily, has been so well documented that we do not
need to go into it here.[8] The southern whites regarded impudence on the part of Negroes as a sign that the whole social order was being overturned. On the other hand, it has also been
brought out that many of the most active Negro politicians observed all the rules of racial etiquette of the pre-war period.
The wife of one of the most prominent colored leaders in South
Carolina was still a maid in the house of her white mistress and
she observed all of the proprieties of her position.[9] Isaiah Montgomery of Mound Bayou, Mississippi, was typical of those
southern Negroes who observed the etiquette and who were respected by the southern whites. He was taught with white children and trained as an accountant on the Joseph Davis plantation. In the Mississippi Constitutional Convention of 1890 he
made a plea for better relations between the races. Considering
the ignorance in which the masses of the slaves had been kept
and their general unpreparedness for freedom, the surprising
thing is that conditions were not much worse.

While the law-making product of the Negro legislators was
not outstanding, the presence of Negroes in the representative
assemblies had several lasting effects. Some Negroes acquired
parliamentary skills which they found useful in party conventions and in other connections. The race as a whole got a taste
of political power which has not been forgotten. In spite of
many bitter experiences and disappointments, hopes survived in
the hearts of many Negroes that some day their race would rise
Phoenix-like and again take an active part in government.
What the Negroes liked to remember about the reconstruction
period were such pictures as James G. Blaine gave in his *Twenty
Years in Congress* when he said that the Negro Congressmen
were "as a rule studious, earnest, ambitious men, whose public
conduct—as illustrated by Mr. Revels and Mr. Bruce in the

---

[8] C. G. Bowers, in his *Tragic Era* (Cambridge, 1929) has summarized a great deal of
this material. See also works like R. L. Morton, *The Negro in Virginia Politics, 1865–
1902* (Charlottesville, 1919); F. A. Bancroft, *A Sketch of the Negro in Politics* (New York,
1885). W. L. Fleming, *Civil War and Reconstruction in Alabama* (New York, 1905).

[9] Simkins and Woody, *op. cit.*, p. 356.

Senate, and Mr. Rapier, Mr. Lynch and Mr. Rainey in the House—would be honorable to any race."[10] In addition, the reconstruction legislatures left a permanent impress upon the statute books and the administrative practices. Steps were taken to establish a free universal compulsory school system and a new importance was given to educational institutions in the South.

When the federal troops were withdrawn from the South in 1877, the rôle of the Negro in politics was greatly diminished. Violence, intimidation, legal obstacles, and arbitrary administrative practices were used to keep the Negroes from the polls. However, these methods were not immediately successful in all parts of the South. For more than twenty years a representative or two was sent to Congress from such states as Mississippi, Virginia, and the Carolinas. Negro political leaders from other sections of the South turned their attention to fields which were still open to them, namely the federal administrative system and the Republican party hierarchy.

Beginning with the first administration of President Grant a number of federal appointive positions of more or less importance were open to Negroes. An astute politician like Frederick Douglass preferred a federal appointment to an elective position in a reconstructed state government. He was successively commissioner to Santo Domingo, minister to Haiti, counsel for the government, and recorder of deeds for the District of Columbia. When the reconstructed governments collapsed in the South the Negro political leaders hastened to rebuild their shattered prestige by securing federal appointments. A number of them held such positions as register of the Treasury, consular agent, collector of internal revenue for a given city, collector of a port, collector of customs, or postmaster of a small city.[12] While the pol-

---

[10] Vol. II, p. 515. The early congressmen were, as a rule, respectable men. Their very respectability made it difficult for some of them to understand their own people. They were more interested in their own status at times than in the status of the race.

[11] The methods used are fully described in P. Lewinson, *Race, Class and Party* (London and New York, 1932).

[12] *Republican Campaign Text Book* (1900), p. 149.

icy of different national administrations has varied as to what positions should be filled by Negroes, all presidents, Republican and Democratic alike, have continued the precedent set by President Grant of appointing some Negroes to important federal posts. In the South it has become increasingly difficult to appoint Negroes to local federal positions with considerable power and prestige,[13] but in other parts of the federal service the Negroes have forged slowly ahead.

Another field of political activity that has remained open to Negroes is found in the councils of the Republican party. Beginning with the Republican National Convention of 1868, Negro delegates have been sent to Republican nominating conventions ever since. In the convention of 1884, former Congressman John R. Lynch, a Negro delegate from Mississippi, was chosen as temporary chairman over the opposition of the Republican National Committee. Generally speaking, the Negro delegates have been with the administration forces and in a crucial convention like the 1912 convention they held the balance of power.[14] When a Democratic president has occupied the White House, the colored delegates have usually supported that faction of the Republican party which appeared to be wealthiest and strongest. This was the situation in 1896 when Mark Hanna came to the convention with the southern delegations committed to the candidacy of William McKinley.[15] The fact that the southern states polled so few Republican votes gave rise to agitation to change the basis for apportioning delegates. Since 1916 delegates to Republican national conventions have been roughly apportioned according to Republican votes and this has meant a reduction in the number of Negro delegates.[16] Colored aspirants for Republican party leadership in the South have also had to face the rise of "lily-white" movements which were

[13] W. F. Nowlin, *The Negro in American National Politics* (Boston, 1931), pp. 112–24.

[14] *Official Report of the Proceedings of the Fifteenth Republican National Convention, Chicago, 1912* (New York, 1912), p. 402–403.

[15] *Official Proceedings of the Eleventh Republican National Convention, St. Louis, 1896,* p. 123. See also H. Croly, *Marcus Alonza Hanna* (New York, 1912), p. 175.

[16] *Negro Year Book, 1916–1917,* p. 37; *ibid., 1931–1932,* p. 93.

given considerable encouragement by recent Republican presidents.[17] In the meantime, however, the number of Negro delegates from northern states has been slowly increasing and some of the southern Republican colored leaders have displayed surprising political vitality.

Booker T. Washington once shrewdly remarked that there "are other ways of getting into politics than by holding office."[18] This outstanding leader of his people illustrated in his own career that it was not necessary to hold office in order to exercise considerable influence upon political affairs. On many matters relating to Negroes and race relations in the South, he was called upon to give advice by a number of presidents. He was especially close to President Theodore Roosevelt, regarding whom he wrote: "Shortly after Mr. Roosevelt became established in the White House I went there to see him and we spent the greater part of an evening in talk concerning the South. . . . . After discussing many matters, he finally agreed to appoint a certain white man, whose name had been discussed, to an important judicial position."[19] Following Washington's death, Robert Moton, the new head of Tuskegee Institute, became an important adviser of presidents on race matters. Like his predecessor, he was recognized because he was one of the leaders of the Negro race.

While Booker T. Washington held the view that voting and office-holding were not the only ways of being in politics, he made it clear that he did not believe that personal influence was a substitute for the ballot. On this point he said, "It ought to be clearly recognized that, in a republican form of government, if any group of people is left permanently without the franchise, it is placed at a serious disadvantage."[20] A recent study of Negro suffrage in the South has borne out this view. In the sections where the Negro has been most completely disfranchised,

[17] A lily-white Republican organization is one which excludes Negroes. On the origin of the term, see Lewinson, *op. cit.*, p. 110.

[18] *My Larger Education* (Garden City, 1911), p. 163.

[19] *Ibid.*, pp. 170, 174.

[20] *The Story of the Negro* (New York, 1909), p. 370.

he receives a small share of the public funds, whether for education or for such basic improvements as water, street lighting, and paving.[21] The exact extent to which this treatment is a result of disfranchisement it is impossible to tell, but when a few Negroes actually participate in an election as in the Atlanta bond issue election, the group as a whole is given greater recognition.[22]

The struggle of the Negro for political status has been most successful in the last fifty years in the border states and in northern cities. First the Negro regained some of the importance which he had enjoyed as a voter during the reconstruction period. Where the margin between the Republican and the Democratic parties was small or the Republican party was strong, the Republican leaders could usually rely upon the loyalty of the Negro voters, and made every effort to poll the full Negro vote. If the colored voters supported machine candidates, their behavior in no way differed from that of other ethnic groups which tended to vote in bloc fashion. Where the Democrats were found in overwhelming numbers, as in the city of New York and in some of the border cities, many Negroes deserted their traditional Republican allegiance and voted with the Democrats. A minority group which is seeking governmental protection cannot afford to be on the losing side all of the time.

Since the Negro migrants to the urban centers tended to be concentrated in certain areas, they soon found that they could control the election of representatives from these areas. They then demanded candidates of their own, and in the seventies and eighties a few Negro legislators began to appear in northern law-making bodies. The period of heavy migration which began in 1914 made it possible for the Negroes within a few years to send representatives to at least nine state legislatures.[23] Similar progress has been made by the race in selecting municipal coun-

[21] Lewinson, *op. cit.*, pp. 125, 127.

[22] E. R. Embree, *Brown America* (New York, 1932), p. 186.

[23] M. N. Work (ed.), *Negro Year Book*, volumes for 1914–15, 1916–17, 1918–19. See also L. A. Pendleton, *A Narrative of the Negro* (Washington, 1912).

cilors. Not only has the race retained and increased its legislative representation but it also secured legal appointments, clerkships, teaching positions, jobs on the police and fire forces, and various other positions in the national, state, and municipal services. In the past ten years three municipal judgeships have also been won by the race, in the United States as a whole.[24]

The city of Chicago has been one of the places where this general cultural process has been going on. The materials in the following chapters show how in a given time and place situation an unpopular group strives to gain status. The events in Chicago during the first third of the twentieth century furnish excellent data on this process. The Negroes in Chicago have achieved relatively more in politics during this period than have the Negroes in other cities of the United States. They have been more aggressive along political lines than have the Negroes in New York City, they have been more experienced than the Negroes in Detroit, they have been more adventuresome than the Negroes in Cincinnati, and they have been more united than have the Negroes in St. Louis.

What the Negroes have achieved in Chicago cannot be measured by any absolute standard, since it is relative to what they started with and to what they aimed at. The struggle of the Negro to get ahead has been described by one keen observer to be at once an inspiration and a discipline. To quote,

What is more, it has given him a cause and a career, the influence of which upon his intellectual life can hardly be overestimated, for intelligence and intellectual life are incidents of action that give individuals or races the courage and the *élan* that is necessary to rise from a lower to that higher cultural level of intellectual life which is the standard in the modern world.[25]

It is hoped that the material in the following pages will throw light upon a number of hypotheses that might be formulated regarding the rôle of minority groups in the democratic process. To be more specific, it is hoped that the data presented when

[24] One in Chicago and two in New York. There have been colored municipal judges in Washington, D.C., for a much longer time, but these judges have been appointed, not elected.

[25] R. E. Park, "Mentality of Racial Hybrids," *American Journal of Sociology*, XXXVI (1931), 551.

compared with similar materials which might be collected for other areas will help answer such questions as the following: What difference does the possession or non-possession of the suffrage make in the social status of a racial minority in a society which extends the suffrage freely to the racial majority? When members of a minority who have been deprived of political privileges in one area migrate to another area where they are given political privileges, do they tend to prize these privileges more highly than do other groups? When a persecuted minority increases its political power and influence, does this bring increased opposition from the majority group? Will the opposition of the majority take non-violent or violent forms? To what extent does a submerged group which is furnishing competition become a scapegoat for class antagonisms? Is there likely to be a lag between the rate of increase of the voting power of an ethnic minority and the rate of increase of its representation in law-making bodies? To what extent are the political preferences of a racial minority influenced by feelings of race consciousness or solidarity? Must a minority act together in order to secure recognition? To what extent is the rise of an oppressed group accompanied by revolts against all kinds of authority?

CHAPTER II

THE "BLACK BELT" AS A POLITICAL BATTLE-GROUND

The Negro population of the city of Chicago has increased so rapidly during the last two decades that the Negro voters have come to be an important factor in local politics. Since most of the colored migrants came from southern states where they were virtually deprived of the right to vote, their political behavior in their new environment presents a number of interesting questions. How soon would the migrants, many of whom were ignorant of city ways and used to occupations open to common laborers in a rural section, become politically assimilated in the urban electorate? What interest would they show in voting and in attending political meetings and functions? How would they distribute themselves geographically over the various election districts? What attitudes would they take toward the party alignments in the city and in the nation? A partial answer to these questions may be found in the recollections of some of the migrants of their experiences in the South, in their opinions regarding their treatment in Chicago, in the attitude of national and state political leaders toward race relations, in the election returns for the areas where they lived, and in the character of Negro leadership which was developed in the new situation.

The story of the Negro in Chicago starts about 1779 with the figure of Jean Baptiste Point de Saible, a Negro from Santo Domingo, who was the first known settler on the site of the city.[1] The de Saible tradition has been used by a number of societies of colored persons in the city interested in building up

---

[1] M. M. Quaife, *Checagou* (Chicago, 1933); A. T. Andreas, *History of Chicago, from the Earliest Period to the Present Time* (Chicago, 1884), I, 70. In the *Mississippi Historical Review*, XV (June, 1928), 89–92, is printed the bill of sale and invoice of de Saible's goods at Chicago dated May 7, 1800. The amount was 6,000 livres and the invoice shows that de Saible had quite an establishment on the north bank of the Chicago River.

race consciousness and civic pride.[2] When Illinois became a
state in 1818 it was regarded as fairly liberal, since its compromise constitution forbade perpetual slavery, although indenture
for twenty-five years of service was permitted. As the constitution granted the suffrage only to male white inhabitants,[3] free
Negroes were denied the right to vote. When the Fugitive Slave
Law was passed in 1850 a convention of colored people met and
resolved "not to fly to Canada but to remain and defend themselves." A resolution was passed by the city council a few days
later to the effect that the city police should not be required to
aid the recovery of slaves. A convention of colored citizens held
six years later protested against the disfranchisement of Negroes in the state, against the denial of the right to testify in
court against a white man, and against the barring of colored
children from the public schools.[4] At this time there were less
than a thousand colored persons in the city. Five years after
the Civil War, Negroes in the state were given the right to vote
by both the federal and state constitutions, and colored children
were admitted to the public schools by law in 1874. A Civil
Rights Act, which forbade discrimination in restaurants, hotels,
theaters, railroads, street cars, and in other places of public accommodation and amusement, was passed in 1885.[5]

At this time the colored population of the city was relatively
small, the some ten thousand Negroes constituting about 1 per
cent of the total population of the city. However, the number
was increasing at a rapid rate, and by 1900 the World's Fair and
other attractions had brought the ratio to nearly 2 per cent.

During the first decade of the twentieth century the rate of
growth of the colored population of the city slowed down to a
certain extent,[6] but during the next ten years it turned sharply

[2] de Saible Association, *A Souvenir of Negro Progress in Chicago* (Chicago, 1925). See
also *Chicago Whip*, December 22, 1928, regarding plan for a memorial.

[3] Article 2, section 27.

[4] Proceedings of the *State Convention of Colored Citizens of the State of Illinois held in
the City of Alton, November 13, 14 and 15, 1856* (Chicago, 1856).

[5] For a discussion of Illinois civil-rights cases, see Chicago Commission on Race Relations, *The Negro in Chicago* (Chicago, 1922), pp. 232–38.

[6] A chart of the growth of the Negro population in Chicago is given by E. F. Frazier,
The Negro Family in Chicago (Chicago, 1932), p. 87.

upward. The cutting-off of immigration after the start of the World War, the increased demand for labor in the city, the diffi-culties in agricultural production in the South because of the ravages of the boll weevil, and the appeals made by the militant colored weekly, the *Chicago Defender*, and other agencies ad-vertising the advantages of the city, were among the factors which brought tens of thousands of Negroes to the city in the years 1914–20. The changed immigration policy of the national government, the agricultural depression in the South, and the stories about opportunities for work and political advancement in Chicago kept on attracting Negroes from the South to the city after 1920 in spite of memories of the race riot of 1919.

One of the motives for migration as soon as migration was economically possible was the desire to live in a free community. In connection with the Race Commission investigation a great many migrants testified that they liked Chicago and the North because of "freedom in voting and conditions of colored people here."[7]

Like the immigrants who came from foreign countries, the Negroes who came to Chicago from the South were predomi-nantly in the prime of their lives. Consequently, there were relatively fewer Negroes in the city who had not reached voting age than there were native whites. Unlike the foreign-born im-migrants, practically all the colored migrants were citizens of the United States. As a result of these conditions, the relative importance of the Negro vote was greater than the mere popu-lation figures might indicate. This is clearly brought out in Table I, which shows the percentage that the Negroes were of the total population and of the total eligible vote.

The relative importance of the potential Negro vote in Chi-cago trebled in the first three decades of the twentieth century. The huge increment in the absolute number of the estimated eligible colored voters between 1910 and 1920 was due largely to the adoption of woman suffrage in 1913 and to the flood of newcomers after 1914. The increase in the next decade was the result of the continued migration of many colored persons of voting age. The net result of these factors was that in 1930 the

[7] Chicago Commission on Race Relations, *op. cit.*, pp. 98, 100, 169.

city of Chicago had the second largest colored population of any
city in the world. Only Greater New York, which is composed
of five counties, some of which are not contiguous, has a larger
colored population, and Manhattan Island alone has fewer Negroes than Chicago.[8] When it is considered that one in every
twelve of the adult citizens of Chicago is a Negro, it is clear that
here is a factor of great political significance.

TABLE I

TOTAL POPULATION AND ESTIMATED ELECTORATE IN
CHICAGO BY COLOR, 1900–1930*

YEAR	ALL CLASSES		NEGRO			
			Number		Per Cent	
	Total Population (1)	Total Adult Citizens (2)	Population (3)	Adult Citizens (4)	Column 3 of Column 1 (5)	Column 4 of Column 2 (6)
1900†.......	1,698,575	424,424	30,150	12,414	1.8	2.9
1910†.......	2,185,283	491,793	44,103	17,845	2.0	3.6
1920........	2,701,705	1,367,515	109,594	81,872	4.1	6.0
1930........	3,376,438	1,906,366	233,903	165,959	6.9	8.7

* Figures compiled from the population volumes of the thirteenth, fourteenth, and fifteenth censuses.
† Adult male citizens only.

The increasing size of the Negro population raised the question as to what rôle the group would play in the politics of the
city and the state. What interest in voting would these invaders
show? Would the fact that they were new to urban life and un-
familiar with the racial attitudes of the northern whites tend to
make them timid about going to the polls? On the average, it
takes a foreign-born white person ten years to complete the
naturalization process. How soon would the colored migrants
take advantage of the privileges of citizenship?

An analysis of the voting figures shows that the Negroes take
about as much interest in voting as do the white citizens of

[8] In 1930, Manhattan Borough had 224,670 Negroes and Greater New York,
327, 706.

similar economic and social status. If a liberal allowance is made for the factor of mobility, the Negroes have shown a higher participation in elections than have most of the whites. On the basis of figures for the Second Ward, which over a period of time has had the highest proportion of Negroes, it was estimated that 72 per cent of the eligible Negro voters were registered in 1920 as compared with 66 per cent for the entire city, and that ten years later the respective rates were 77 and 68.[9]

The apologists for the virtual disfranchisement of the Negro in the South usually state that the Negroes do not vote because they have lost interest in politics. Some of the Negroes themselves complained about the political apathy of the colored people in the South.[10] If it can be shown that a large proportion of the colored voters in Chicago came from the far South where the participation of Negroes in politics is very slight, then it is reasonable to conclude that the migrant Negro leaves his political apathy behind when he comes north or else he was not as apathetic as he was reported to be. In order to study this question a special tabulation was made from the election registers of the place of birth of nearly ten thousand persons living in districts which were overwhelmingly colored. These data are presented in Table II, which shows that the migrants were born for the most part in the agricultural states of the South, where the smallest proportion of the Negro population exercised the franchise. Nearly one-half of them were born in the East South Central states, and Mississippi alone was the birth place of one-sixth of them. According to an additional tabulation of these data by length of residence in Cook County, it was discovered that about one-fourth of those born in Georgia, Alabama, Mississippi, and Louisiana had been in the city for less than five years and less than 15 per cent for more than fifteen years. Of those born in the North, or in such border states as Maryland and Kentucky, where colored people voted freely, over half had been in the city for more than fifteen years. This clearly shows that these new Chicago voters came largely from rural districts

[9] See Table XVI in Appendix I for figures and calculations.

[10] P. Lewinson, *Race, Class and Party* (London and New York, 1932), pp. 107, 124ff.

where they had had few opportunities for voting experience. The attitude of the migrants toward voting is shown by the following case:

Mr. Edwards, a young laborer in the stockyards, was anxious to "get on in politics." He had attended a rural school in Mississippi up to the fourth grade and had been enthusiastic about living in the North long before the time of his migration in 1922. As soon as he arrived in Chicago, he had talked with the party workers and was eager to work with the party organizers. Mrs. Edwards, his wife, became of age about the time she arrived in Chicago. She was very anxious to vote "because her parents had never had the chance."[11]

TABLE II

PLACE OF BIRTH OF 9,834 NEGRO REGISTERED
VOTERS IN CHICAGO IN 1930*

	Number	Per Cent of Total
South Atlantic..........................	1,663	17.0
East South Central...................	4,565	46.3
West South Central....................	1,693	17.3
Middle Atlantic, East North Central, (omitting Illinois)..................	628	6.4
Illinois..............................	628	6.4
New England..........................	33	0.3
West North Central, Mountain Pacific, (omitting Missouri).................	218	2.2
Missouri.............................	363	3.7
Washington, D.C......................	43	0.4
Total............................	9,834	100.0

* Data from 1930 registration books of 24 selected precincts located in 19 census tracts which contained 81.1–98.9 per cent Negro population according to *Census Data of Chicago, 1930.*

While some of the migrants may have been timid about starting to vote, their political education proceeded rapidly. To some of the race-conscious Negroes the ballot box is the symbol of emancipation, a guaranty of equality of opportunity. In the South the ballot box is a token of class stratification based upon color. To the southern whites the symbols of democracy have a revolutionary significance as far as race relations are concerned. When a Negro migrates from the South to the North, he goes through a transformation. He must find a new job, a new place

[11] C. E. Merriam and H. F. Gosnell, *Non-Voting* (Chicago, 1924), p. 83.

to live, new friends, and new amusements. One of the badges of
his changed life is the ballot box. Of course, the great interest in
voting which the new migrants display is partly the result of
efficient political organization,[12] but the background and experiences of the migrants make them responsive to the appeals
of the party workers. Colored women from the South shared
with their men folks an intense interest in politics. A canvass
in selected districts in Chicago showed that there were relatively fewer colored women who were antisuffragists than there
were white women who took this position.[13]

Another reason for the great interest shown by the Negroes of
Chicago in politics is the strong racial solidarity which they have
developed. This solidarity is based in part on the operation of
race prejudice in the North. No matter how divided they may
be among themselves on issues which do not affect their general
place in society, they are united in facing the white world when
it presents a hostile front. In theory the state of Illinois does
not permit race discriminations in places offering services to the
public, but in practice, Negroes are sometimes limited in choosing their places of abode, in finding places to eat, and in selecting their amusements. When seeking homes in Chicago, the
colored migrants were not forced by law to settle in certain parts
of the city, but like the Jews who formed their ghettos and like
the Italians who formed their immigrant colonies, they settled
in communities which were largely their own. Because of this
liking for their own people and because of difficulty in finding
satisfactory places elsewhere, there grew up on the South Side
of the city the so-called "Black Belt," not as a matter of law but
as a matter of fact. The Negroes formed this community as
an accommodation to the northern urban environment. The
boundaries of this area were never clearly drawn, and during the
last twenty years they have shown a slight tendency to reach
outward from the center of the city. The radial growth of the

---

[12] See below, pp. 137 ff.

[13] See Table XVII in Appendix I for a special unpublished tabulation in connection
with the *Non-Voting* study of the reasons for not voting given by women who have never
voted in their lives.

Negro population has not been as rapid as that of some of the foreign-born groups because there is greater resistance to the dispersion of colored residents. In 1910 the main Negro community extended in a narrow line for about six miles south of the center of the city.[14] Twenty years later the community extended in a much broader strip of territory for about eight miles.[15] White persons may still be found living in the heart of this region, but the great bulk of the population is now colored. Less than 10 per cent of the total population is white in the three census community areas that comprise the principal part of the "Black Belt."[16]

While the South Side Negro community contains persons of widely divergent interests and backgrounds, its compactness has facilitated economic, social, and political solidarity. Between 85 and 90 per cent of the total colored population of the city live within a relatively short compass. This means that around 200,-000 colored persons are in fairly close touch with each other. The shape of the area and of that of other colored settlements is indicated in Figure 1, which is based on the 1930 census. On the west, the main community is bounded by a railroad, on the north by the business section of the city, on the east by railroad and industrial property, the lake, a park and resistant white communities, and on the north by industrial and railroad property. Several lines of communication unite the different parts of the district. The South Side elevated runs through the center as a main artery, and the State Street, Indiana, Wentworth, and Cottage Grove surface lines, and the bus lines furnish the minor arteries. Large numbers of colored persons have automobiles, telephones, and according to the census about 44 per cent have radios.[17] The community also has its weekly newspapers. As compared with white communities within the city the Negro

---

[14] *The Negro in Chicago*, p. 107.

[15] There were a few Negroes in the Woodlawn area in 1910. In 1930, the main South Side community and the Woodlawn community were practically continuous.

[16] For definition of census communities, see *Census for Illinois*.

[17] 19,342 radios out of 44,097 families in census tracts 80 per cent or more colored in 1930. Figures compiled from *Census Data of Chicago* (1930).

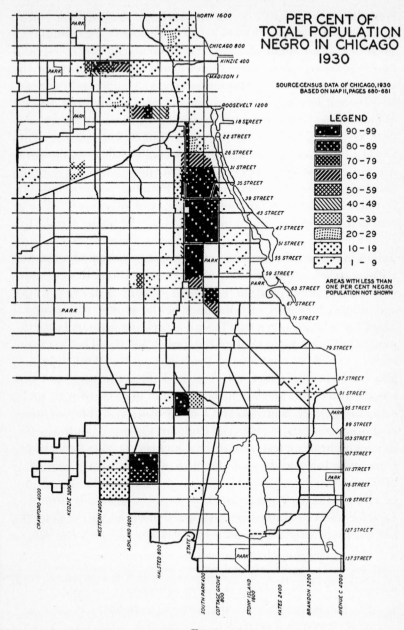

FIG. 1

community does not have superior physical means of communication but it uses the devices it has more largely for community purposes. The smaller colored settlements on the West and North sides are more isolated and hence more backward in the development of group consciousness.

Although the Negroes living in the South Side area are not homogeneous from the standpoint of cultural attainments,[18] they are forced together by the persistent hostility of the white world. In the colored community, unskilled laborers, domestic servants, gamblers, policemen, prostitutes, clerical workers, bootleggers, teachers, mail carriers, Pullman porters, lawyers, business men, physicians, clergymen, and others are all surrounded by a wall of prejudice erected by the white world. Because the Negro world is smaller than the white world, an individual in it has a wider range of acquaintanceships through the various social, economic, and other stratifications than a white person in a similar position in his own world.[19] A discriminatory act or threat against any member of the group, whatever his standing may be, is regarded as an attack upon the entire community. As one young colored attorney put it, "The Negro on the South Side is conscious of the Negro on the West Side, and all over Chicago, in fact, all over the United States. Some day I hope to see the time when the wrong of one Negro will be the concern of every Negro in the United States."[20] The exclusive race organizations, such as the Pullman Porters' Union, the colored churches, the fraternal orders, and the various social clubs, sometimes furnish channels through which this race solidarity finds expression.

The politicians have found that in the South Side area it is easy for them to reach a large proportion of the voters at political meetings, easy to spread a rumor about the racial attitudes

[18] Frazier, *op. cit.*, has ably demonstrated that succession is taking place within the Negro community and that individual members may be differentiated on the basis of occupation, color, education, home ownership, literacy, and many other factors.

[19] As far as the number of people and the area covered is concerned the Negro world in Chicago is smaller than the white world. In the Negro world there is also less inequality of wealth than in the white world.

[20] Interview.

of a given candidate, easy to engage in conversation about politics, easy to find persons interested in the details of registration
and voting, and easy to demonstrate that on election day the
popular thing to do is to vote. There may be many in the district who have had limited opportunities for schooling and some
of the older ones may neither read nor write, but they are kept
informed regarding political matters by a variety of face-to-face
contacts. In church, at a lodge meeting, on the street corner, in
their place of employment, at a restaurant, at home with their
children who have just come from school, or at a place of amusement, they learn about the political issues and the candidates of
the day.

Some of the same factors which have developed among the
colored citizens of Chicago an intense interest in voting have
also determined their actual choices on election day. Whether
or not the new voters would vote in accordance with the traditional loyalty of their race to the Republican party has depended upon the length of their stay in the South before coming
northward, the extent of the recognition which they received
from the Republican party during and after the reconstruction
period, their social position in the Negro group before coming
to the city, the treatment which they received at the hands of
the Democrats in the South, the recency of their arrival in the
city, the attitude of the local politicians toward them, the policies of the national administration on matters of race interest,
and the recommendations of their own leaders. How partisan
choices may have been affected by some of these conditions can
be illustrated by a number of individual cases.

A direct connection between loyalty to the Republican party
and reconstruction in the South can be traced in the case of a
number of Chicago citizens. One of the picturesque figures is
the "old warrior," former Congressman John R. Lynch, who at
the age of eighty-seven is still active at his law practice and
whose advice is still sought in political matters. Lynch was born
a slave in Louisiana and had only limited opportunities for formal education. He came to Chicago in 1912 after a political
career in the state of Mississippi which lasted more than twenty-

five years. During this time he had served as justice of the peace, state representative, speaker of the state legislature, congressman, temporary chairman of the Republican National Convention of 1884, chairman of the Republican Central Committee of Mississippi, and Auditor of the Treasury for the Navy Department. All of these positions he felt he owed to the Republican party. He also witnessed the virtual disfranchisement of the members of his race by the Democratic party in his own state. When Secretary Lamar offered him the position of special agent of public lands under the first Cleveland administration if he would refrain from embarrassing the administration, he refused the appointment out of loyalty to the Republican party. Eight years later when Secretary Gresham under the second Cleveland administration offered to continue him as Auditor of the Treasury for the Navy Department on the condition that he would say he was in sympathy with the main purpose of the administration he again refused and remained faithful to the Republican party.[21] During the Spanish-American War he served as a paymaster with the rank of major in the United States volunteers, and after the war he served in the regular army, retiring in 1911.

In Chicago politics Major Lynch has not taken an active part because of his age and his former military position, but he has gone to the polls regularly, voted faithfully as Republican, and on three or four occasions has made political speeches. He did not urge the election of a Negro Congressman from Chicago until the Republican organization placed one in nomination, and then he discouraged the candidacy of independents on the ground that the Negro vote might be split.[22] In a personal interview, the white-haired veteran said that he was a Republican by conviction in national elections, but in local elections he voted for the man. "The colored voters cannot help but feel that in voting the Democratic ticket in national elections they will be voting to give their indorsement and their approval to every wrong of which they are the victims, every right of which

[21] J. R. Lynch, *Facts on Reconstruction* (New York, 1914), pp. 238, 279.

[22] *Chicago Tribune*, April 20, 1928; *Chicago Whip*, June 9, 1928.

they are deprived, and every injustice of which they suffer."[23]
The Republicans have deserted the Negro in many ways but the
Democrats persecute him. The Republicans are the least of two
evils. Major Lynch represents the type of Negro whose memories of the early recognition received by the Republican party
still remain vivid.

Many of the migrants have brought with them bitter memories of the life which they lived in the South. One of the most
militant of these was the late Mrs. Ida Wells-Barnett, a woman
of powerful frame, whose eyes gleamed with an inner fire. She
was born in Holly Springs, Mississippi, in 1868, of parents who
had been slaves. When she was fourteen years of age her parents
died leaving her with five younger brothers and sisters. She had
been attending one of the schools maintained by the Freeman's
Aid Society of the Methodist Episcopal Church and she thought
she would try to get a job teaching school. After teaching a
country school for a few years she went to Memphis, where she
attended school a little more and began teaching in the city.
In the meantime, she became a contributor to one of the local
newspapers. One of her articles concerning the teachers' moral
qualifications caused her dismissal from the school system. This
forced her into journalistic work, where she soon acquired a
reputation for fearless writing. When two of her friends who
ran a store just outside the city limits were lynched because
they defended themselves against what they regarded a hostile
attack, she fled to Oklahoma and continued her editorial work
by mail.

One of her editorials brought such a storm of protest among
the whites in Memphis that a mob destroyed her printing plant
and threatened death to anyone who attempted to publish the
paper again.[24] Mrs. Wells-Barnett began a career as a lecturer
on lynching, traveling extensively in both England and the
United States. Typical of her vigor of expression is the following passage on the value of the franchise.

[23] *Oklahoma Eagle*, October 15, 1932.

[24] Ida Wells-Barnett, *Southern Horrors: Lynch Law in All Its Phases* (New York Age
Print, 1892).

With no sacredness of the ballot there can be no sacredness of human life itself. For if the strong can take the weak man's ballot, when it suits his purpose to do so, he will take his life also. . . . . The mob says: "This people has no vote with which to punish us or the consenting officers of the law, therefore we indulge our brutal instincts, give free rein to race prejudice and lynch, hang, burn them when we please."[25]

Coming to Chicago at the time of the World's Fair in 1893, Mrs. Wells-Barnett became active in movements for racial justice. She achieved a wide reputation as a social worker, an agitator for woman suffrage, a promoter of colored women's clubs, and a Republican party organizer. In 1909 she took an active part in urging Governor Charles S. Deneen to take vigorous action against the sheriff of Alexander County in whose jurisdiction a Negro had been lynched.[26] Although there have been several race riots, no lynchings have occurred in Illinois since that time. Mrs. Wells-Barnett's burning zeal for Negro rights and her untiring energy devoted to the cause of greater political power for her people were the products in part of her experiences in the South.

Some of the citizens of the South Side feel that under no circumstances should the party to which they have been attached by tradition be deserted. Or, to put it negatively, in no election, national or state, should a Negro vote for a Democratic candidate. In the mayoralty election of 1923 some of the colored leaders urged their followers to support the Democratic ticket. Mayor William Hale Thompson was not a candidate for reelection and the Republican nominee, Arthur Lueder, the postmaster of Chicago, was supported by newspapers and political factions which some of the colored politicians regarded as unfriendly. Stories were circulated on the South Side to the effect that Lueder had been unfair in his treatment of Negroes in the post-office and that he was receiving support in the campaign from the Ku Klux Klan.[27] In the churches and in political rallies Lueder was openly denounced because of the aid which he re-

[25] Wells-Barnett, *How Enfranchisement Stops Lynching* (*Original Rights Magazine*, June, 1910, Charles Lenz, New York).

[26] *Chicago Daily News*, March 25, 1931.

[27] *Chicago Tribune*, March 17, 1923. See below, pp. 43–44, 177.

ceived from the *Chicago Tribune*.[28] The Democratic candidate
was pictured as a man who would be fair to the race. In spite of
this active campaign of propaganda designed to change their
traditional Republicanism for a special occasion only, many refused to move an inch. A young laborer from Alabama told an
investigator at the time that he could never vote for a Democrat as long as he kept his memory.[29] The Democrats he knew
in Alabama were the "imps of Satan." A woman from Georgia,
who had lived in the city for seventeen years, did not like the
attitude of the colored people in voting for the other party candidate. She thought that anyone who lived in the South should
forever hate the Democratic party, "not because all Democrats
are bad, but because the party keeps its foot on the black man."
An elderly man, who had lived in the city for six years, said that
he had cast his first ballot at the presidential election in 1880 in
a Tennessee village. He voted regularly there until disqualified
by the "grandfather clause." He began again after the repeal
of the "Dortch law" and voted until he came to Chicago. He
has always voted the straight Republican ticket and always
will. He thought that the colored people who voted for a Democratic candidate would be "putting their heads in the lion's
mouth."

What do the election returns show about the number of migrants whose loyalty to the Republican party was of the sort
which has just been described? In presidential elections the
figures show that the Republican party has received anywhere
from 70 to 95 per cent of the votes cast in the sections inhabited
largely by Negroes.[30]

In 1916 and in 1920 over four-fifths of the colored voters reg-

[28] *Chicago Defender*, March 24, 1923, and *Chicago Whip*, March 31, 1923.

[29] This and the two following cases are adapted from C. E. Merriam and H. F. Gosnell, *op. cit.*, pp. 139–40.

[30] In order to obtain data for the last five presidential elections which were as nearly
comparable as possible, selected voting precincts were matched with census tracts
whose population was 80 per cent or more colored in 1920. The proportion of Negroes in
these areas was less in 1916 and greater in the years following 1920. According to the
1930 census these same areas were 90 per cent or more colored. If the mayoralty election of 1935 is any indication, it looks as though the Negroes would vote Democratic in
1936.

istered a protest against a Democratic national administration by voting for the Republican candidate for president. In 1912 Woodrow Wilson had expressed "his earnest wish to see justice accorded to Negroes" but his first administration was regarded as extremely disappointing by Negro leaders.[31] Contrary to the precedent set by President Cleveland, President Wilson failed to appoint Negroes to such positions as Register of the Treasury and Minister to Haiti. The administrative departments in Washington, D.C., also introduced a practice of segregating the colored civil service employees. The 95 per cent Republican vote cast by the Negro voters in 1920 was in part a protest against the Democratic administration. Before Harding became president of the United States it was hoped that he would become a second McKinley in his attitude toward race relations. At any rate, a Republican national administration was to be greatly preferred to a Democratic one. During the campaign, the *Chicago Whip*, a colored weekly, commented at length upon the "failure of Woodrow Wilson":

The President has attempted to formulate public opinion in favor of international arbitration and a League of Nations, against labor disorders and strikes, against the high cost of living, against Irish slavery, against the Armenian and Polish treatment of Jews. . . . . Mr. Woodrow Wilson has not taken an open stand against the maltreatment of Negroes. He has not taken a militant stand against mob violence and lynchings. He has not taken an open stand against the segregation and political slavery of 12,000,000 Americans. . . . .

Would a stand against these evils hurt Mr. Wilson and the Democratic party? We think the answer is self-evident, it would. Southern opinion is addled, rankled and conjured by the infernal imps of his Satanic Majesty, the Devil; the South has a mono-mania and that is Negro hatred. The mind of the South is one-sided. The Negro has no rights that white men must respect; this is a Southern slogan. In order to be friends with the South, you must keep the Negro down, and segregate and discriminate him. The Democratic party must crush the Negro to keep its foothold below the Mason-Dixon. If Mr. Wilson defends Negroes, the South would be enraged. The Democratic party would be injured and Mr. Wilson's political life would wane into oblivion.[32]

In the election of 1924, there was a slight falling off in the size of the Republican vote in the districts inhabited largely by

[31] *The Crisis,* No. 5 (1912), p. 75, and No. 13 (1916), pp. 16–17.

[32] September 11, 1920.

Negroes. Three-fourths of the 4 per cent decrease in the Republican vote went to the Progressive party and one-fourth to the Democratic party. President Coolidge was compelled to carry the load of his predecessor's unpopular racial policies. President Harding's speech in Birmingham in October, 1921, was viewed with great alarm by colored leaders[33] and his official actions showed that he agreed with the Taft policy of insisting that Negroes appointed to federal positions in the South were acceptable to the white communities.[34] Shortly after becoming president by reason of Harding's death, Coolidge appointed Bascom Slemp of Virginia as his private secretary. This appointment was criticized by the *Chicago Whip* because Slemp had been active in organizing a "lily-white" Republican party in the South.[35] However, as the 1924 election drew near, the *Whip* declared its preference for Coolidge over Davis or La Follette:

> For three paramount and for innumerable subsidiary reasons, Mr. Calvin Coolidge should be supported by the black Americans in the coming presidential election. Mr. Coolidge is a New Englander, he was born in the "cradle of liberty" and because of traditions, contacts and environment he cannot regard a black man as the men of the south regard him. . . . .
>
> Because wealth and capital, essential industries and monied men are behind Coolidge, the black people are compelled at this time to countenance their desires. To do other would be stupid and perhaps disastrous. Our flight north has put us at the mercy of the great mill and factory magnates, we are dependent upon them for work and opportunity to survive. . . . .
>
> Coolidge is clever. A clever Republican at this instance will do nothing to alienate the affections of the black people. . . . . Coolidge has catered to us and in his cleverness he seeks to square the party with us. This writer believes that Coolidge will be fairer than most of his predecessors and at all hazards will do nothing to crush our hopes and defile our ideals.[36]

Four years later, a considerable proportion of the colored voters abandoned their traditional Republicanism. Herbert Hoover received in 1928 about 15 per cent less of their votes than Coolidge did in 1924. Although Hoover had won favor when he abolished segregation in the Department of Commerce,

---

[33] *Chicago Whip*, November 5, 1921.

[34] *Negro Year Book* (1912), p. 30.   [35] August 25, 1923.

[36] October 11, 1924. This editorial shows a high degree of sophistication.

and although his supporters in Ohio had chosen a colored delegate-at-large for the national convention, his friends on the Republican National Committee were unfavorable to the Negro delegates from the South. In the pre-convention campaign it was apparent that the Hoover forces were trying to encourage the "lily-white" Republican organizations in the South. Among the Southern colored Republicans not recognized was Simuel D. McGill from Jacksonville, Florida, the brother of Nathan K. McGill, who was the business manager of the *Chicago Defender* at the time. During the campaign the *Defender* came out openly against Hoover in an editorial which stated that the Republican party had allied itself with the Ku Klux Klan and with racial and religious bigots.[37] After the convention the control of Hoover's campaign in the South was in the hands of Colonel Horace Mann who believed that the South could be carried under white leadership. Hoover's speech at Elizabethton, Tennessee, showed that he himself entertained this point of view.[38] In this and in other ways, he gave all Negroes the plain understanding he had the election won and did not need the Negro vote. In Chicago, the Republican national leaders did nothing to placate colored leaders like Alderman Louis B. Anderson, and the result was that on the eve of the election Anderson said in a public meeting: "The Republican party has shown us the gate. Now let all the colored people walk out of this gate."[39] The fact that Hoover received 75 per cent of the vote in these areas in spite of the agitation against him shows the strength of the Republican tradition.

Although the economic depression, which began in 1929, had a disastrous effect upon Hoover's popularity with the white voters of Chicago, it did not appear to have any immediate influence upon the voting behavior of the Negroes. In the sections of the city which were inhabited largely by white persons, on the average 12 per cent less of the voters supported Hoover in 1932 than in 1928.[40] In the areas of Negro concentration the

---

[37] November 3, 1928. See also issues of October 20 and 27, 1928.

[38] *Chicago Defender*, October 20, 1928.   [39] *Chicago Tribune*, October 31, 1928.

[40] Difference between the means for 147 subsections of the city.

percentages for Hoover were about the same in both elections. Aside from the economic conditions, there were other reasons why some of the Negro voters might have deserted their Republicanism. The fact that the solid South was broken in 1928 made the Republican managers all the more determined to build up a "lily-white" movement in the southern states, and the Hoover administration started out by trying to eliminate certain colored leaders in the South. While Perry Howard, Republican National Committeeman from Mississippi, was acquitted by a federal jury of the charge of patronage-selling made against him, he was deprived of the federal patronage.[41] Other acts of the Hoover administration were looked upon with great disfavor by colored citizens. The appointment of two southerners to cabinet positions, Hurley of Oklahoma and Doak of Virginia, was protested against by colored leaders.[42] Particularly objectionable was the nomination to the United States Supreme Court of Judge John J. Parker of North Carolina, who was quoted as having said in 1920: "The Negro as a class does not desire to enter politics. The Republican party of North Carolina does not desire him to do so."[43] The rejection of this nomination by the United States Senate was regarded as a deserved rebuke to the Hoover administration. Protests were also registered at the segregation of the gold-star mothers in their trip to France[44] and at the failure of Hoover to appoint colored men to certain administrative posts and important commissions.[45] In the Republican convention of 1932 the Hoover administration forces again made determined efforts to recognize the "lily-white" delegations from the southern states wherever this was possible. In spite of all these disappointments, the Negro voters in the main were about as loyal to Hoover in 1932 as they had been in 1928.

[41] The situation was investigated by the United States Senate Subcommittee of the Committee on Post Offices and Post Roads, 70th Congress, 2d Session, Influencing Appointments to Postmasterships, *Hearings*, pts. and *Report*, Washington, 1929, 1930.

[42] Doak belonged to a union which excluded Negroes. See *Crisis*, November, 1932.

[43] *Chicago Defender*, May 31, 1930.   [44] *Ibid.*, March 1, 1930.

[45] *Ibid.*, February 15, 1930; January 10 and 17, March 14, April 18, 1931.

Why is it that in presidential elections the loyalty of the Negro voters to the Republican party has been so well maintained under such adverse conditions? Some light on this question is thrown by a consideration of the alternatives open to the Negroes. The Democratic party as a national organization contained elements in 1932 which race-conscious Negroes could not very well defend. The Hoover leaders were hard on some of the southern delegations, but the Democrats in 1928 elected no colored delegates, and the few colored alternates in the Houston convention were separated from the others by chicken-wire. In 1932 the colored alternates were better treated, but there were no colored delegates. The Afro-American leaders received poor treatment at the hand of the Democratic resolutions committee, and Franklin D. Roosevelt's record was open to criticism, because he had been a member of the Wilson administration which segregated colored employees.[46] Even harder to explain than Roosevelt's record was the presence of a southerner on the ticket, "Cactus" John Garner, from Uvalde, Texas, a town which was said to ban the presence of Negroes.[47] If the Democratic ticket should be elected, and if something should happen to Roosevelt, then the South with its proscriptive policies toward Negroes would be in the saddle.

Some of the colored voters who supported the Democratic ticket in Chicago were undoubtedly influenced by local considerations. In New York City, where the Democratic party with rare exceptions controls all the local patronage, there are many inducements offered to Negroes to forsake their customary allegiance to the Republican party.[48] In Chicago, on the other hand, the margin between the two major parties has been a close one until recently, and the colored voters are just now finding it necessary to change their views regarding the party of Lincoln, the emancipator, in order to be on the winning side. In 1915, about the time that the migration began to assume large proportions, the Republican party was in control of the

[46] On President Wilson's failure to take a stand against segregation, see *Chicago Whip*, September 11, 1920.

[47] *Chicago Defender*, September 3, 1932.

[48] Colored Citizens Non-Partisan Committee for Re-election of Mayor Walker, *New York City and the Colored Citizens* (1929).

state government and of most of the local offices in Chicago. However, in certain parts of the city determined efforts were made by the Democrats to win over some of the colored voters. In a Democratic stronghold like the First Ward, jobs, protection against police interference, and strong-arm methods were used with considerable success. On the West Side of the city, in the Twenty-eighth Ward, similar methods were employed, but in the wards inhabited largely by colored voters more emphasis was placed upon jobs than upon police protection. In 1930 there began a series of Democratic victories which could not help but attract the attention of the South Side citizens. First, the Democrats won many important county positions, then they gained the mayor's office, and soon after they triumphed in the nation and the state. At first the great mass of colored voters in the city remained impervious to these shifts in party power, but in the 1933 and subsequent elections they deserted the Republican fold in large numbers.

Even before the New Deal was inaugurated there were some younger colored migrants to the city who did not feel themselves particularly bound by the traditions connected with the early history of the Republican party. They looked at politics in a realistic fashion. Among these was B., who held an appointive position in the Democratic administration of the city of Chicago before Franklin Roosevelt was elected president. Before he came to Chicago some eleven years ago, B. had practiced law in Mississippi and had taught in a Negro college in Texas. In Chicago he joined the Democratic party and became a precinct captain. Regarding his political attitudes he said:

In Texas where I lived for a good length of time there is no difference between the Republican and Democratic parties. Under Coolidge and Hoover régimes the lily-whites have taken over the Republican party and treat Negroes the same as the Democrats. The Negro can't vote in the Democratic primary but the Republicans hold their county and state conventions in hotels where a Negro can't go unless he's wearing the hotel uniform. We must face conditions here and not let the southern situation get the best of us. The outstanding abolitionists in Illinois have been associated with the Democratic party. We in the northern states will have to stop knocking the Democratic party and get in it and help elect senators and governors. Those senators will protect our people in the south. We can put forth some effort on the senators

from the inside which we can't from the outside. If a senator from Georgia
starts something obnoxious to our people, all we have to do is get our senator
from Illinois on the wire and he will bring pressure on the fellow from Georgia.[49]

How common the attitude expressed by B. became after the
presidential election of 1932 is shown by Table III, which gives
the economic status and the voting record of the three census
communities in Chicago having the largest number of Negroes.

TABLE III

SOCIAL CHARACTERISTICS AND DEMOCRATIC PERCENTAGE
OF THREE SOUTH SIDE CENSUS COMMUNITIES

	CENSUS COMMUNITY		
	35	38	40
Northern and Southern boundaries*	26–39 St.	39–51 St.	51–63 St.
Median rental in 1930*	$35.28	$44.48	$57.50
Homes owned in 1930 (per cent)*	10.8	9.8	8.1
Unemployed in 1930 per 1,000*	41.09	36.58	25.16
Percentage Negro in 1930*	89.1	94.9	92.2
Percentage of total vote cast for Democratic candidate†			
For mayor in 1927	6.5	6.4	29.6
For president in 1928	29.3	24.6	29.8
For U.S. Senator in 1930	27.6	22.6	26.9
For mayor in 1931	16.2	12.1	11.4
For president in 1932	25.0	20.0	22.0
For Congressman-at-large in 1934	34.6	43.6	44.9

* *Census Data of Chicago* (1933).
† The election returns by precincts were fitted as closely as possible to the census communities.

It is usually said that the relief program of the national administration has been the most important factor in winning over the
colored voters to the Democratic party. Table III does not give
much support to this theory. Greater gains were made by the
Democratic party in 1934 in the outlying areas (Community 40)
where unemployment was less and rents were higher than in
depreciated areas (Community 35) where there were the largest
number of relief cases.[50] The Democratic vote doubled in the

[49] Personal interview, 1931.

[50] Community 40 had more whites in 1927 than in 1930. Census Community 35
would be regarded as a low rental area. Dividing the entire city into 147 units (excluding census tracts 20 per cent or more Negro) it was found that the average of the median
rentals was $47.50 with a standard deviation of $18.50. Housing conditions were crowd-

areas inhabited by Negroes south of Thirty-ninth Street, but it increased less than one and a half times in the areas north of that boundary. The struggle to save Congressman DePriest from defeat may have kept some of the colored voters in the latter area loyal to the Republican party. At any rate, there were many Negroes on relief who were not stampeded to vote the Democratic ticket.

A comparison of the voting behavior of Negroes in Chicago with that of citizens in other parts of the city shows that the Negroes are atypical in a number of respects. In connection with a study of election returns which the author has made, the city was divided into some 166 units.[51] These figures show that the districts inhabited largely by Negroes have a larger percentage of Republican votes, a larger ratio of straight Republican ballots, and a higher percentage of favorable votes on a bond issue and on a prohibition repeal measure than any other part of the city. Until recently, this attachment of the Negro voters to the Republican party has not been affected by landslides, economic depressions, or by other influences that seem to sway the voters in other parts of the city. The Democratic party has been most successful in attracting Negro voters in the isolated Negro communities and in the depreciated residential areas that border on the main Negro community. However, in some respects, the behavior of the Negro voters was similar to that of the white voters in the city. The Negroes in those districts where there were high ratios of home owners and of women voters tended to vote dry and to oppose bond issues that might increase taxes. In the areas where there were high percentages of straight-party voters, the Negroes tended to vote wet and to favor bond issues. This was typical of tendencies in other parts of the city.

---

ed in the areas inhabited by Negroes. In 1931 the average percentage of the 1930 workers who were unemployed was 28.3 for the 147 units (white population) and 47.4 for the 19 units which were 20 per cent or more Negro.

[51] The 19 units in which the Negro population was 20 per cent or more of the total were so atypical that they destroyed the normality of many of the distributions. Consequently, they were not used in the calculations of coefficients of correlation. The study referred to is based upon *Census Data of Chicago 1930*, and the election returns for the years 1927, 1928, 1930, 1931, 1932.

While the Negroes who vote the Democratic ticket are multi-
plying rapidly in Chicago, the South Side has been regarded as
Republican territory. Since this is so, the size of the Negro vote
becomes a factor of added importance when it is considered in
connection with Republican primaries rather than in connection
with general elections. While only 8.7 per cent of the total adult
citizens were Negro in 1930, it is probable that about 11 per cent
of the Republican primary voters were Negro in that year.[52] In-
asmuch as there have been many bitter factional quarrels in the
Republican party of Cook County, the faction which could
count on a large share of the vote from the "Black Belt" was in
a favored position. In the Republican primaries before 1934
this area was the great political battle-ground.

The foregoing paragraphs have indicated something about
the political attitudes and behavior of the thousands of Negroes
who have migrated to Chicago. What has been taking place in
Chicago has been typical of what is going on in many northern
cities of the country. In the case of the older generations the
tradition of Abraham Lincoln as the emancipator, and the bitter
disappointment at the collapse of the reconstruction régimes,
have conditioned them against any association with the Democratic party. Disfranchisement, lynchings, Jim-Crow laws, the
cropping system, and other social and economic practices are
laid at the door of the Democratic party. On the other hand,
many in the younger generation are not moved by Republican
traditions. They see a new Republicanism which cuts down the
representation of the southern states in national conventions
and they see the Democrats firmly in power. Whether Democratic or Republican, the Negro in Chicago shows a great interest in exercising the franchise. While this interest is partly the
result of party organization, it is also the product of a high eval-
uation put upon the election process because of disfranchisement in the South and high expectations in the North.

[52] On the basis of the Second Ward, it is estimated that 74 per cent of the adult Negro
citizens are registered. Applying this ratio to the city, there were about 120,000 registered Negroes in 1930. The Republican primary vote in 1930 was 526,000. Assuming
that about 50 per cent of the Negro voters took part in the Republican primary, this
would give a figure of about 60,000 primary voters, or about 11 per cent of the total.

CHAPTER III

MAYOR THOMPSON, THE "SECOND LINCOLN"

What white politicians were to profit from the large block of new colored voters who streamed into the city of Chicago? On the South Side of Chicago there were two main Republican factions which contended for the colored vote. One of these factions was led by Charles S. Deneen, who was governor of the state from 1905 to 1913 and United States Senator from 1925 to 1931. While a master at compromise and combination, Deneen was regarded as a cold figure personally, and his faction directed many of its appeals to the so-called respectable elements of the Republican party. As one prominent South Side citizen put it, his organization always seemed to be made up of pseudo-aristocrats and it was whispered about that Deneen was prejudiced and that he acted as though he were not particularly anxious to appeal to Negroes.[1] However, as governor of the state, he won the praise of the colored citizens because of his support of the Illinois anti-lynching bill and because of his prompt and vigorous action in the Cairo lynching affair.[2] As state's attorney for Cook County, as governor, as United States senator, and as the leader of an important Republican faction, he did not hesitate to appoint Negroes to important political offices. Many colored persons were also included in the primary slates which his faction offered to the Republican voters. In a cool and calculating fashion he followed the general rule of Illinois politics that all racial, linguistic, religious, economic, and neighborhood groups should be recognized on a balanced ticket. In the period under discussion, the Deneen faction was at a disadvantage because it had no control over the city government. To some extent this situation was the result of a combination of circumstances over

[1] In 1926 the picture of William S. Braddan, colored candidate for county commissioner, was omitted from the pamphlet issued by the Deneen faction. This was unfavorably commented upon. See *Chicago Tribune*, April 13, 1926.

[2] Ida Wells-Barnett, *How Enfranchisement Stops Lynching*.

which the faction had little control. Deneen was defeated for re-election as governor in 1912 because of the split in the ranks of the Republican party caused by the Progressive movement. If he had been governor in 1915 it is possible that Harry Olson, his preference for the Republican nomination for mayor, would have won in that year. As it was, the faction still had some county patronage and the defeat of Olson in the primary came as a great surprise.[3] Without the city patronage, without leaders who could make dramatic appeals to the common man, and without the support of the most prominent leaders of the South Side community, the Deneen faction had hard sledding with the colored voters.

The man who defeated Olson in the Republican mayoralty primary of 1915 belonged to a faction which had cultivated assiduously all the minority elements in the city, including the Negroes. This man was William Hale Thompson, a member of the faction that was once led by William Lorimer. The methods and tactics of this faction cannot be understood apart from the career of its one time leader, the late Senator Lorimer, the placid blond boss, whose name aroused conflicting emotions and animosities.[4] In the eyes of some of the citizens of Chicago, Lorimer was a statesman, a trusted friend, a self-made business man, a benefactor, who was persecuted by the "trust press" and other powerful enemies. In the eyes of others, he was a disreputable gang politician, a tool of selfish interests, a sinister influence in public life, and a demagogue of the lowest level. As a constable, as superintendent of the water department, as a congressman, and as a faction leader, Lorimer played the game of politics that is based upon profitable personal loyalties. Jobs, special favors, and friendship were his chief stock in trade. He was faithful to his friends and ruthless in his attacks upon his enemies. When mud was thrown at him in a political campaign,

---

[3] As one prominent politician put it, "Deneen had the Negro vote when he had the state patronage." This election is discussed by L. Lewis and H. J. Smith, *Chicago: A History of Its Reputation* (New York, 1929), p. 372.

[4] Lewis and Smith, *op. cit.*, pp. 244, 353–64; C. H. Wooddy, *The Case of Frank L. Smith* (Chicago, 1930), pp. 146–56.

he responded by throwing mud at his opponents regardless of the facts. After his election to the United States Senate in 1909, Lorimer was bitterly assailed by a hostile press. Following two investigations of bribery charges in connection with his election, he was finally unseated by the Senate in 1912. The crowd which greeted him when he returned to Chicago contained William Hale Thompson and, among others, several prominent colored citizens. Among the latter was a minister who had stood by Lorimer in the trying days at Washington, D.C.[5] There is no evidence that Lorimer himself was particularly clever in dealing with colored voters, but the rules of politics which he taught others who were familiar with some of the intricacies of race relations seemed to work in the Negro communities in Chicago. In such specialized fields as showmanship and patronage distribution, the mayor-elect of 1915 was an apt pupil of the Lorimer school.

Like his former associate, William Hale Thompson aroused conflicting impressions. As mayor of the city from 1915 to 1923 and from 1927 to 1931, he was hailed as "Big Bill, the Builder," Chicago's greatest booster, the defender of the weak, the champion of the people, while at the same time in certain newspapers the word "Thompsonism" came to be a symbol for spoils politics, police scandals, school-board scandals, padded pay-rolls, gangster alliances, betrayal of the public trust, bizarre campaign methods, and buffoonery in public office. He was a master showman and a firm believer in the idea that bad publicity was better than none. He was also a follower of the Lorimer tradition that

[5] The name of this minister was Rev. Archibald J. Carey. Rev. Carey was also a friend of Thompson's, as the following paragraphs indicate. Lorimer's political bailiwick was on the West Side of the city and not on the South Side. At the time when Lorimer was a congressman there were practically no colored people in his district. In his speech before the United States Senate, when he was fighting for his political life, Lorimer made a reference to Booker Washington which showed that he was not particularly free from racial prejudice. The remark was, "Theodore Roosevelt could enjoy a luncheon with Booker Washington, but could not afford to dine in the same room with William Lorimer." Mayor Thompson, Congressman Madden, and State Senator George F. Harding, all South Side leaders, have not been caught making statements like this. However, there was a real feeling of friendship between Lorimer and Rev. Carey as is shown by Lorimer's appearance and remarks at the funeral of Bishop Carey.

aggressive campaigning is the most effective. "If your opponent calls you a liar, call him a thief." His slight to General Joffre during the war, his expedition to photograph the tree-climbing fish, his rat show at which he tried to discredit two former associates,[6] his slogan, "Kick the snoot of King George out of Chicago," and his campaign properties such as a halter, a burro, and a donkey, started reports that went around the world. As one political observer put it, "His genius for the spectacular made him an international figure. He might produce dismay and ridicule, but he was a force to be reckoned with."[7] In a more critical vein, another writer said: "The truth regarding Mr. Thompson can be stated in a few words: he is indolent, ignorant of public issues, inefficient and incompetent as an administrator, incapable of making a respectable argument, reckless in his campaign methods and electioneering oratory, inclined to think evil of those who are not in agreement or sympathy with him, and congenitally demagogical."[8] Such were some of the unfavorable opinions about the man whose faction controlled the city hall in the years when the Negro population of the city was rapidly increasing.

An examination of the election returns shows that the favorable views regarding Mayor Thompson predominated among the citizens of the near South Side. Here his failings did not loom up in such a glaring fashion. Here his crudeness, his mistakes in judging men, his disregard for details, and his opportunistic political policies were offset by other considerations. Was Thompson persecuted by certain newspapers? So were the Negroes, and they understood what persecution meant. Especially in Republican primary elections the name of William Hale Thompson had great drawing power among the colored voters. In the four primary elections at which he was a candidate for mayor he received over 80 per cent of the total Republi-

[6] Thompson brought a cage with two rats in it on the platform and addressed remarks to it regarding his former associates.

[7] Phillip Kinsley, in the obituary which was removed from the *Chicago Tribune* office and used in Thompson's campaign pamphlet for the 1931 mayoralty election.

[8] Victor S. Yarros, "Presenting Big Bill Thompson of Chicago," *Independent*, November 5, 1927.

can primary vote cast in the Second Ward, the ward which contained the largest proportion of Negro voters.[9] In the crucial primary of 1915, when he was starting out as a factional leader, the plurality which he received in the Second Ward was largely responsible for his nomination.[10] Without it he would have gone down to defeat. In 1927 he received 94 per cent of the Republican primary vote in the Second Ward, in spite of the fact that the former colored ward leader was against him. In the 1931 primary he received 91.7 per cent of the Republican vote in the Second Ward and 83.3 per cent in the Third Ward. These ratios gave him a plurality in these two wards of over 25,000, which was over one-third of his plurality for the entire city. In this primary, as in every other mayoralty primary at which he was a candidate except the one in 1927, the plurality which he piled up in the wards inhabited largely by Negroes was decisive in winning the nomination.[11]

In securing Negro primary votes for his white associates, Thompson has been equally successful. The choice of his faction for governor of Illinois, Len Small, received over three-fourths of the vote in the Second Ward in the four primaries at which he was presented, beginning with the one in 1920. As in the case of Mayor Thompson, the unfavorable publicity which Len Small received was balanced by other considerations. The Supreme Court may have held Small liable for the interest on public funds unlawfully retained when he was state treasurer,[12] but on racial matters Small's record was regarded as better than that of his opponents. The favorites of the Thompson faction for United States senator at six different primaries received over

[9] The percentages were calculated from figures obtained from the *Chicago Daily News Almanac* and from the official returns in the office of the Board of Election Commissioners for Chicago.

[10] The Republican primary vote for the city was: Olson, 84,825; Hey, 4,283; Thompson, 87,333. In the Second Ward: Olson, 1,870; Hey, 47; Thompson, 8,633.

[11] Thompson's plurality percentages for the city at large in the four primaries in date order were: 1.4, 17.6, 35.7, and 10.7. By 1920 the Negro vote in the entire city made up at least 10 per cent of the Republican primary vote. A shift of 10 per cent of the voters from one candidate to another would mean a plurality change of 20 per cent.

[12] *People* v. *Small*, 319 Ill. 437.

60 per cent of the Republican vote cast in the Second Ward. On three of these occasions the candidate was Frank L. Smith, the senator-elect of 1926, whose credentials were turned down by the United States Senate because that body held them to be tainted with fraud and corruption. The action regarded as improper by the senators was Smith's acceptance of large campaign funds from Samuel Insull and other officers of public utility corporations operating in Illinois while at the same time he was chairman of the Illinois Commerce Commission.[13] In the 1928 primary, when Smith ran to vindicate himself, he lost the city and the state at large, but he received 79 per cent of the Republican vote in the Second Ward. In similar fashion the voters of this ward were held in line for the Thompson primary candidates for county, sanitary district, and municipal offices.[14]

Some of the minor candidates on Thompson's slates have been less fortunate than the major candidates, but the cases have been rare. One example occurred in the 1932 fight for the ward committeemanship in a mixed South Side ward. The incumbent had at one time been identified with the Thompson faction but when a split occurred in 1931 he left with the dissenting wing. He was opposed for re-election in the 1932 primary by several candidates, among whom was one backed by former Mayor Thompson. Thompson campaigned in the area and denounced the ward official vigorously.[15] In spite of this, the committeeman polled more votes in the section of the ward inhabited by Negroes than any of his opponents, including the one endorsed by Thompson. His success in combating Thompson's influence was the result of a number of factors. He had had long experience in dealing with Negro voters; he was backed by a large

[13] See C. H. Wooddy, *op. cit.*

[14] In some of the district primaries, where racial candidates ran against the organization candidates who were white, the Thompson faction has had difficulty in keeping the voters in line. This was the case in 1928 in the First Congressional District where Dawson (colored) opposed the organization candidate, Martin B. Madden (white). This primary is described below, chap. iv.

[15] At a meeting in the ward, March 11, 1932, Thompson said: "Mr. L., I hope to God you'll do for him what he's done to you. He was part of the program to sell Bill Thompson out."

campaign fund; he had the advantage of the state patronage; and in his fundamental policies he was little different from the Mayor himself. In the same primary, Len Small carried the part of the ward containing most of the Negroes.

In elections, as contrasted with primaries, the Republican candidates nominated by the Thompson faction have invariably received over 70 per cent of the combined Democratic and Republican votes cast in the Second Ward. Upon a number of occasions the pluralities received in the districts inhabited largely by Negroes have been decisive. Without these pluralities Thompson could not have defeated his Democratic opponents in the mayoralty elections of 1919 and 1927.[16] In the latter year, when Thompson ran against Mayor Dever, he received 91.2 per cent of the vote cast in the Second Ward. The influence of the Republican tradition when it was united with the popularity of the Thompson faction proved to be, among the colored voters, an unbeatable combination. It was unmoved by political landslides, economic depressions, graft revelations, and other ground swells that affected the voters in other parts of the city. The native white and the foreign-born voters might shift with the changing tide but the black voters stood firm as an island in the sea.[17]

The real test of control over a block of votes is the power to swing it in a given direction contrary to political traditions. One important test of the Thompson influence over the colored voters was the mayoralty election of 1923 at which "His Honor" was not a candidate. The resistance offered by some of the black voters to suggestions that they change their party for this election has already been commented upon.[18] The Republican nominee, Arthur C. Lueder, the Postmaster of Chicago, belonged to a faction which was usually opposed to the Thompson

[16] His plurality percentages in the city at large were 3.1 and 8.3.

[17] The Negro vote constituted only a small part of Thompson's majority. Thompson also won many votes in areas where the proportion of foreign-born persons was high, where the rents were low, where the ratio of straight-party voting was high, and where Hearst newspapers were relatively popular.

[18] See above, p. 26.

faction. His candidacy was heralded as the political downfall of William Hale Thompson[19] and if he had been elected it might have been possible for his faction to build up a powerful organization to combat the Thompson machine. In the Second and Third wards, the colored leaders were divided in their support of the mayoralty candidates. Edward H. Wright, the Republican ward committeeman, was ostensibly for Lueder but in reality the Republican organization gave some support to the Democratic candidate, William E. Dever. Two sub-chieftains in the organization, Alderman Louis B. Anderson and ex-Alderman Oscar DePriest were designated for this work and they came out openly for Dever, who received 60 per cent of the vote cast in the rock-ribbed Republican Second Ward. These leaders, like Thompson, looked for a return to power at the next election. In this remarkable shift of political sentiment, Thompson did not come out openly against Lueder, but all the signs indicated that he secretly maneuvered in this direction. Lueder was denounced as the candidate of the *Chicago Tribune*, an anti-Thompson paper whose treatment of race news was very irritating to Negroes. He was also identified by means of a whispering campaign with the Klan, and his administration of the Chicago post-office was criticized.[20] If Lueder had been a member of the Thompson faction, this type of campaigning would have not been effective.

Thompson's confidence in his power to control the Negro vote was so great that he at times overshot the mark.[21] In the Republican primary of 1930 he supported the candidacy of Mrs. Ruth Hanna McCormick for United States Senator against Charles S. Deneen. Mrs. McCormick was nominated and shortly after the primaries repudiated Thompson's support. Embittered by this action, Thompson endeavored to swing the votes of some of his friends to James Hamilton Lewis, the Democratic

[19] *Chicago Defender*, March 31, 1923.

[20] *Whip*, March 10 and 31, 1923.

[21] This campaign is analyzed in Frances Williams McLemore's *The Rôle of the Negroes in Chicago in the Senatorial Election, 1930* (University of Chicago Master's dissertation, 1931).

nominee. He started in the Black Belt where a float representing Uncle Tom, Little Eva, and Abraham Lincoln appeared on a Sunday morning to distribute ballots marked for Lewis.[22] Police officers were also stationed outside the colored churches to hand out the same literature. Thompson had gone too far and he had underestimated the importance of certain things to the Negro. Many colored ministers registered protests. Unlike the Dever election, this was a national election and the Negro leaders could not forget their Republicanism so easily. Congressman DePriest came back from Washington to state that he would remain loyal to Mrs. McCormick. His position as a Republican in the national capitol, his personal gratitude to Mrs. McCormick because of the steps she had taken to prevent any embarrassment when he first took his oath of office,[23] and his solicitude regarding his own re-election all dictated this choice. Besides, Lewis was a vulnerable candidate as far as the Negroes were concerned. He was born in Virginia and raised in Georgia, a fact which identified him with the southern Democrats.[24] In 1920, when he was a candidate for governor of Illinois, he was reputed to have said, "This is a white man's country."[25] This statement stirs up active resentment among most Negroes, since it means to them that they are not citizens, but Negroes, persons

[22] The selection of Uncle Tom and Little Eva for this float was a tactical error on Thompson's part as Negroes interpret this story differently from whites. Negroes regard Uncle Tom as a subservient type.

[23] See below, pp. 183–84.

[24] These facts were mentioned frequently by speakers addressing audiences in the Second and Third wards during the campaign.

[25] *Chicago Defender*, October 30, 1920, carried the following: "TO A DEFENDER REPORTER he gave the following statement when questioned as to the truth of the newspaper quotations: 'I never said what was attributed to me. What I did say was, This is a white man's government, and as long as I have voice or power to protest I will never permit the criminal, lawless Negro to over-run the righteous, law-abiding Negro or drive the white man from the polls or prevent Christian citizenship, black or white, from having their rights under the law, at the ballot box or elsewhere.' "

"HE SAID BY 'WHITE MAN'S COUNTRY' he meant the whites were in the majority; therefore, it was a white man's country. True they are in the majority, but why single out the Negro any more than the Jew, the Irish, the French, the Italian or any other group that are now component parts of this great 'free' country. And what about the criminal white man?"

to whom only limited rights are given and whose status is inferior to that of whites. As one orator put it during the campaign, "To tell you the truth, this country belongs to the American Indians. If it doesn't belong to them, it belongs to all of us. It belongs to the American Negro. Tell J. Ham Lewis that fifteen million of us said so. The Negro put in 250 years of toil without pay. America belongs to the people who sawed the forests and tilled its soil."[26] Thompson soon saw that he could not control the situation and be began to back water. A mayoralty primary was in sight and he could not afford to alienate the colored leaders. He did not take away DePriest's patronage and he distributed campaign funds as usual. At the next election the colored leaders were again with him. The fact that Thompson could extricate himself so easily from this situation is an indication of his skill in handling racial matters. The South Side leaders did not resent his actions because, from past experience, they knew that his stand was a matter of tactics and not his estimate of the group. The Negroes were loyal to him personally, but he found that he could not regard their vote as a personal possession. There were signs that DePriest and his associates were glad to show that they were in some matters independent of Thompson. When loyalty to a friend conflicted in such a clearcut fashion with loyalty to the Negro group, the group loyalty won out.

Within limits, then, the name of William Hale Thompson was a powerful factor in the "Black Belt" on primary and election days. What has been the secret of Thompson's popularity among the Negro voters? This is a complex question which does not have a single answer. Thompson's showmanship, bombastic style of oratory, ready platform wit, geniality, and practical ethics appealed to many Negroes as well as to many whites. At a crowded political mass meeting in the Black Belt, when the bugles announced the arrival of "Big Bill" and the huge form came lumbering down the center aisle with a cowboy hat and a cordial greeting for everybody, there was no mistaking the en-

[26] Miss Nannie Burroughs at the Eighth Regiment Armory mass meeting, November 2, 1930.

thusiasm expressed by the audience. He was "Big Bill," the mayor, who did not hesitate to stand up for their rights. Thompson talked a language which they knew and understood. His lapses into grammatical errors were very convincing. He used the simple device of presenting himself as an ill-used man. Judge Olson was a meddling, self-appointed savior of this and that civic institution.[27] His other opponent was a scratcher and a nagger. At a later primary, his opponent was a southern "cracker"; he discriminated against Negroes; he was supported by "the dirty lying sheet, the *Chicago Tribune*."[28] Bill Thompson, your mayor, was not like that. Thompson drawled his words and pounded his fist emphatically. His illustrations were taken from the cattle range, the saloon, the football field, the race track, the Bible, and from some of the homely incidents of city life. There was clearly a friendly feeling between the chief executive of the city and his listeners. To have a friend in a powerful position who could wrest benefits from a hostile community—that was something worth having. Who else was more deserving of their support?

A few words about an actual Thompson meeting in the "Black Belt" will show more concretely how he dealt with colored audiences. On the Sunday before the mayoralty primary in 1931, Thompson addressed a mammoth meeting at the Eighth Regiment Armory. Early in the afternoon every seat in the hall was filled. As Thompson made a triumphal entry down the center aisle, the entire audience stood up and cheered lustily. The police quartet sang "Happy Days" and "Big Bill the Builder." After a laudatory introduction by State Senator Roberts, Mayor Thompson began to speak in his usual thick voice: "Mr. Chairman, the representatives of the church and my good friends: As Senator Roberts, your chairman, said, the

[27] *Chicago Tribune*, February 17, 1919. The eye-witness reporting the meeting wrote: "For skillful demagoguery, flawlessly perfect to the time and occasion, I have never seen anything finer than the easy, fluent, winning, don't-give-a-damnery of Mr. Thompson's achievement before the audience at the Eighth Regiment Armory yesterday afternoon. . . . . He made them laugh, he made them listen, and he made them mad—always mad in his behalf—and he seemed to do it all without half trying."

[28] Speech at Baptist Church, Walnut and Leavitt, February 21, 1931.

Mayor cannot and does not have to brag about his black mammy."[29] Thompson clearly understood the unpopularity of this sort of reference among Negroes in Chicago.[30] He continued: "But it might be well for you to know that when I was a cub in politics and just beginning (they nominated aldermen in those days in convention—the different ward conventions) and when I was to be nominated who do you suppose nominated Bill Thompson? Did a white man arise to do this job? No sir, a Negro, your now Senator Del Roberts (applause), is the man that arose in that ward aldermanic convention and put your Mayor in politics." Thompson usually tried to link the beginning of his speech with some personage present. He went on with a reference to the *Daily News* and the *Chicago Tribune*, both of which have offended colored people by some of their articles.[31] "Were the *News* and the *Tribune* with me then? They were not. They opposed me then as they do now. Were you with me then? You were, as you are now." (Applause.)

Thompson now turned to attack his opponent in the primary election. "But there's one thing that encourages me as we go along in political life. I think the *Tribune* is getting crazier every election. (Laughter and applause.) They have gotten so insane that they think they can beat Bill Thompson for Mayor with a Tennessee cracker. (Cheers and applause.) Well, they've got another guess coming." Here was a direct appeal to racial antipathies. He continued: "I was very much interested at a meeting where a Negro woman arose and made to me a magnificent speech. It wasn't so much up there, it was right down here where it counts, my friends." Thompson fell into the lingo of the prize ring. He quoted her as follows: "We've got a great world's fair coming on. Well, you better re-elect your friend,

[29] The excerpts are taken from a stenographic report of his speech of February 22, 1931.

[30] C. O. Johnson, *Carter H. Harrison I* (Chicago, 1928), p. 98, tells how Mayor Harrison I, a Democrat, used to make such an appeal in the eighties.

[31] The *Home Coverage* study made by the *Chicago Daily News* in 1933 shows that the home coverage of the Hearst *Herald and Examiner* was larger and that of the *Chicago Daily News* smaller in an area of Negro concentration than the average for other selected areas.

Bill Thompson, Mayor, if you want to go in the front gate because if you elect that cracker you'll go in the back gate." (Applause and cheers.)

Thompson next referred to the attempt on the part of the opposition to attract voters by offering hams to the needy. He explained his code of ethics in such matters as follows:

When a great general is fighting for his country with his soldiers, strategy counts for much. Well, if you can capture the supplies and the ammunition of the enemy, your army can eat the supplies and they certainly can't shoot with the ammunition that you capture. (Applause.) Well, if hams are to be the ammunition, be a great general. You are going to vote for Thompson, but go get the ham too. (Laughter and applause.) Now, the more hams you get the less they'll have to tempt the weak-minded with. (Laughter.) Before we get through with them and their hams they better get a fleet of trucks from where the Negro lives to the stock yards because we'll take those hams as fast as they can haul them over. (Laughter and applause.)

His confidence in his popularity with his listeners was so great that he said, "Why should I talk to you about voting for Bill Thompson? If I talked here two hours I couldn't make a vote because every damn one of you were for me when you came in the door." (Cheers and applause.) There were some in the audience who resented this boast, but the great mass did not take offense.

Thompson's personality and platform technique do not in themselves explain fully the overwhelming character of his popularity. As indicated in the speech just quoted, he began cultivating the Negro vote as far back as 1900, when he was a candidate for alderman in the Second Ward. In the colored sections of his ward he stressed the part that his father had played in the Civil War under Farragut. Among his campaign assistants was a young colored preacher, Rev. Archibald J. Carey, who had been interested in politics in Georgia before he came to Chicago in the late nineties. The Rev. Mr. Carey was known as a great church organizer and a very effective platform speaker. Thompson has described this episode in his own picturesque language:

This meeting tonight takes me back a number of years when I was a candidate for alderman. I was a poor struggling youngster. A minister helped me a lot in that campaign. That minister was a poor struggling youngster, too, just starting his chosen career. We fought together, this minister and I. The minister was Archibald Carey. It is a coincidence, but I am going to Quinn Chapel tonight when I leave this meeting.[32]

When I got the ordinance for the first kiddies' playground, Bishop Carey got me to put it across the street from his church at 24th and Wabash. I got the ordinance. Thompson was responsible for that and the Negroes got the playground and Bishop Carey was responsible for that. In other words, the first Municipal playground for kiddies in the world, and which started a world-movement, was built where the Negroes had the most show. White people from near-by came over and said they wanted it in their neighborhood. I said to this, "I see you have a fine house and yard with fences around them and nice dogs but no children; I'll build a playground for children and not poodle dogs."[33]

After his election as alderman Thompson continued his cultivation of the Negro community. The Rev. Carey helped to elect him Cook County commissioner in 1902. In 1913 Thompson secured Carey's appointment as orator at the Centennial Celebration of Perry's victory at Put-in-Bay.[34] In the 1915 mayoralty primary Thompson reaped the benefit of the many contacts that he had made in the South Side community. In the early part of the campaign he had the support of Mrs. Ida Wells-Barnett, the militant crusader whose anti-lynching agitation, woman suffrage activities, and social work has already been described.[35] Six months before the election her organization of women was active in securing pledges for Thompson. When Olson came out for mayor she was in a dilemma because she was a Deneen office-holder. She then ceased her work for Thompson, but what she had already accomplished could not

[32] Political meeting, April 7, 1932.

[33] Political meeting, March 25, 1931. See also Carey's speech in the *Defender*, February 5, 1927.

[34] In an interview Thompson said: "I found out that Perry's crew was made up in part of Negroes. So I said we should have a Negro speaker. The group said they didn't want a Negro. I said, 'Perry wanted them.' They consented and wanted Booker T. Washington. I had nothing against Mr. Washington but I thought here was a chance for me to reward my friend Carey. Mr. Washington was made—it would have meant nothing to him— but to Rev. Carey it would mean something. Though I had gotten the appropriation they would not trust me and sent a committee to investigate. I took them to Carey's house and Carey captivated them. Carey made the best speech that was made and Taft took him to his room afterwards and kept him four hours."

[35] See above, p. 25.

very well be undone. Thompson also had the aid of the master Negro political organizer, ex-County Commissioner E. H. Wright, who went about his work systematically. Incidentally, it is significant to note that Oscar DePriest's election as the first colored alderman coincided with Thompson's first election as mayor.

On the platform and in the pulpit one of the most active campaigners for Thompson was Bishop Carey. Shortly after the mayor's first inauguration, he, together with E. H. Wright and others, promoted an ambitious mass meeting at the Coliseum to celebrate the fiftieth anniversary of the passage of the Thirteenth Amendment to the United States Constitution, which abolished slavery in this country. It was estimated that fifteen thousand colored people jammed into the building. The occasion was an auspicious one. Mayor Thompson, the principal speaker and the guest of honor, had made some appointments of Negroes that had been commented upon adversely in the press. Bishop Carey rose to introduce the Mayor:

Whatever Mayor Thompson has done, whatever he will do, he will do not out of sympathy for the descendants of a race once enslaved, but for American citizens who have earned their position. By these appointments Mayor Thompson is merely recognizing the worth of a people.

There are three names which will stand high in American history—Abraham Lincoln, William McKinley and William Hale Thompson. (Cheers interrupted the speaker.)

William Hale Thompson may not be elected president in 1916, but I'm sure he will be in 1920. I helped elect him alderman; I helped elect him county commissioner; I helped elect him mayor; and my work will not be completed until I have helped elect him president. (There was further cheering.)

I present to you (continued Mr. Carey, as soon as he could make himself heard at all) your friend and my friend, the biggest man in all Chicago, the biggest man in all Illinois, and the best mayor Chicago ever had—William Hale Thompson. (Then the storm broke!)[36]

The constant repetition of encomiums of this sort year after year had its effect upon the popular imagination. After Bishop Carey's death, Rev. J. C. Austin became prominent as a speaker for Thompson. The following excerpts from Austin's speech of April 5, 1931, show how he continued the tradition:

[36] *Defender*, September 18, 1915.

Let us follow the leadership of a man who knows nothing but forward and upward in the person of William Hale Thompson. . . . . We know that our mayor received all like a man. . . . . We saw Big Bill go down out of the confidence of the people, out of the love of the people. . . . . He struggled in the grave. . . . . The *Tribune* wrote an obituary. I went back again and looked upon the grave. . . . . But thank God, before the primary I heard the grave crack, the tombstone fall and saw William Hale Thompson rise (applause) and stand over his enemies and say "I am on the side of truth, of right, of justice." (Big applause.)[37]

The very name of Mayor Thompson carried a halo which the most pious of the opposition could not remove.

The Mayor's white associates were a great asset to him in winning and holding the Negro voters. They understood the methods of attracting the various immigrant groups that came to the metropolis. A master hand at group compromise was Fred Lundin, former Lorimer associate, who called himself the "poor Swede" in order to remind the ward henchmen that he belonged to a minority group. It was ex-Congressman Lundin who managed the pledge-card campaign for Thompson prior to the 1915 mayoralty primary. When he started out in business as a huckster of soft drinks he used colored entertainers to attract crowds.[38] When he began the work of "selling" the candidacy of Thompson for mayor in 1915 he had his agents in all parts of the city, including the Negro community. Here, as elsewhere, his chief sales arguments were promises of jobs and favors.

In the immediate neighborhood of the "Black Belt" the white leaders of the Thompson faction were long noted for their skill in handling the colored voters. George F. Harding, a close per-

[37] This was a large meeting. At some of the smaller meetings held in churches, the minister was sometimes more extravagant. The following is an account of a meeting held in a church on March 29, 1931: "God made just one William Hale Thompson and forgot the mould. Truth, courage, consecration, ideas of right, ideas of justice, let there be right, righteousness. Let it come to earth. Call it William Hale Thompson. . . . . I would call him Napoleon, I would call him Abraham Lincoln. When history is written, they will write in the blue sky high above all of them the name of William Hale Thompson, not only the Mayor of the World's Fair, but fitted and suited to be United States Senator. It would be the joy of the world. William Hale Thompson ought to have the vote of every Negro outside of Dunning."

[38] *Chicago Tribune*, January 27, 1923.

sonal friend of the Mayor and a fellow-sportsman,[39] had extensive real estate holdings in the sections where the Negroes were penetrating and he managed to reap profits out of the panic which seized some of the white property owners when they saw the approaching hordes of black people. An inheritor of considerable wealth, which his own shrewdness increased, Harding could afford to become interested in politics. Like Thompson, he served as alderman of the Second Ward. Regarding his record in this office, the *Chicago Defender* said:

> He owns in the ward two or three hundred houses. When he was alderman for ten years our Race could always reach him at his home and he often at night in the cold got up and went to the police stations and in the mornings to the courts to bail our people out and to secure their release, and he never charged a single cent.[40]

Harding had what seemed to be an inexhaustible campaign barrel[41] and his friends claimed that he was free from all race prejudice. As a young man he enjoyed playing cards with Negro laborers, and later on he helped finance the prize-ring career of Jack Johnson. Harding was generous in helping South Side citizens who were in trouble, very liberal in paying for workers at the polls, and careful in rewarding faithful supporters. When Harding split with Thompson in the mayoralty primary of 1931 he found that he could not keep the colored voters from supporting Thompson, but this was long after the ward machines had been taken over by the Negroes and long after the Mayor's reputation had been firmly established.[42] When Thompson and

---

[39] J. B. Wood, in his pamphlet *The Negro in Chicago* (1916), p. 29, states that Congressman Martin B. Madden was the first to capitalize the colored vote. However, in 1915 Madden was more interested in national than in local politics. He tended to his fences in Chicago from time to time and he helped furnish campaign funds, but he left most of the details to others. His relation to his constituents is discussed in the next chapter.

[40] February 16, 1918.

[41] J. B. Wood, *op. cit.*, p. 29.

[42] There were other factors which accounted for Harding's failure to win more colored voters for his candidate, Judge Lyle, than he did. Judge Lyle was not especially popular among colored people. He was a vulnerable target for Thompson's campaign darts. Harding got a little support from the colored ward organizations, but Thompson forced the big ward leaders to come out in the open for him.

Harding were together on the South Side the opposing factions
found it wise to look elsewhere for votes.

Another one of the Mayor's white associates in the area of
Negro penetration was Samuel A. Ettelson, whose law partner
was retained by the Insull utility interests. Ettelson served
as state senator from the Third Senatorial District from 1905
to 1924, when he resigned in order to make way for the first
colored state senator. Keenly aware of the discrimination that
is sometimes practiced against his own people, the Jews, armed
with ample funds from the Insull group, occupying a key office
in the Thompson administration, he was in a position to help
consolidate the power of the Thompson faction in his bailiwick.

Because of the ineptitude of their opponents, especially the
Democratic politicians, the task of the Mayor and his associates was rendered much easier than it might have been. The
Democrats failed to see the danger of raising the race issue in a
local campaign. Especially in the mayoralty campaign of 1927
the Democrats practically drove the Negro voters into the
Thompson fold. Early in the campaign Thompson held a huge
rally in the Black Belt, at which he promised the colored citizens
jobs and protection. Democratic orators used this meeting as a
means for arousing race prejudice among the white voters.
When some of the Dever supporters sent calliopes through the
streets piping the strains of "Bye, Bye, Blackbird," and spreading a circular which displayed a trainload of Negroes headed
from Georgia with Thompson as pilot of the train, and the caption: "This train will start for Chicago, April 6, if Thompson is
elected,"[43] the obvious answer of the colored leaders was:

[43] R. J. Bunche, "The Thompson-Negro Alliance," *Opportunity*, VII (March, 1929),
79. The *Defender*, March 26, 1927, carried the following: " 'All the Negroes are for
William Hale Thompson. Will you place yourself on the level of a Negro?' This is the
battle cry, printed on plain white cards, scattered over the North Side this week, with
which opponents of "Big Bill" waged their campaign for the mayor's chair. It was a
campaign based on the most dangerous appeal a candidate could make—the appeal to
the evil, smouldering passions of race hate." See also the *Whip*, April 16, 1927. This type
of Negro baiting is very common in the South. See Lewinson, *op. cit.* The Negro is
made a scapegoat for middle-class antagonisms. This appeal was not successful in 1927
in Chicago because the Negro minority was small and concentrated in one part of the
city. Furthermore, Thompson had many supporters who were not alarmed by the
situation.

"Elect Big Bill or it's going to be bye-bye blackbirds in Chicago."[44]

In race matters Thompson had wise advisers and his own intuition stood him in good stead. He and his faction were extolled because of the appointments made.[45] So many Negroes were appointed to municipal offices that one of his Republican factional opponents called the City Hall "Uncle Tom's Cabin." When campaigning in the Black Belt Thompson used this charge with great effectiveness. As in one meeting he would say, "When I gave what was due you, Brundage and the *Tribune* called the City Hall 'Uncle Tom's Cabin!'" At once there were shouts of "Yes, yes" and "That's the truth."[46] The news of the appointment of E. H. Wright as assistant corporation counsel at a salary of $5,000, and of the appointment of Carey to a position in the same office, was featured in the colored press of 1915.[47] Mayor Thompson did not hide his colored appointees in the back rooms but he gave them the regular places to which their positions entitled them. As the size of his majorities in the Black Belt increased at each successive election, so the amount of recognition he gave this section in the form of patronage also increased.[48]

Thompson also showed great adroitness in handling race situations. One form of race discrimination which has persisted in Illinois in spite of the Civil Rights Acts is the virtual barring of Negroes from certain places to eat. On a number of occasions Mayor Thompson championed the cause of the Negro leaders against the prejudices of many white politicians. Shortly before a big political banquet at a downtown hotel someone told "Big Bill" that certain men in the organization and some hotel people were not willing to let the Negroes sit down. Thompson arose and said to the entire group, "I have many friends here tonight and I want to make the statement that

[44] *Chicago Tribune*, March 26, 1927.

[45] For a discussion of colored public employees, see chapter x.

[46] Report of political meeting, April 7, 1932.

[47] *Defender*, August 7, 1915.

[48] Thompson did not appoint a Negro as a member of the Board of Education. A Negro received such an appointment in New York under a Democratic administration.

those friends who are not friends of my friends are not friends of mine."[49] Within a short time the colored leader present was one of the most popular men in the hall. When the Republican National Convention met in St. Louis, Thompson took a similar stand on behalf of the colored delegates. The Mayor also attended the funerals of important colored leaders. At the funeral of Bishop Carey he appeared on the program not only as a personal friend of the deceased but as a public official. He said in part: "This is one of the saddest occasions in my life. As mayor of a city of three and a half million people, I extend the sympathy of the city to the family. . . . . Bishop Carey laid down his life for his friends."[50] He spoke in a dignified, almost reverential tone of voice and no one could question the genuineness of his feeling. Here was a kind recognition which the colored people did not receive from the leaders of the other Republican factions of the city.[51]

The sporting group was favorable to the Thompson organization when it controlled the important law-enforcing agencies or was likely to gain control of them. Some of the minor leaders of the Deneen group had alliances with the colored underworld. If the vice, liquor, and gambling kings are to continue in business, under the existing legal system, they must make their arrangements with those in power. Some administrations are easier to deal with than others. When Thompson ran for alderman in 1900 he spent money liberally in the saloons. As he put it:

[49] Personal interview with participant.

[50] When Bishop Carey died he was under indictment for receiving bribes for favors in connection with his work as civil service commissioner. In addition to the remarks quoted above, Thompson said at the funeral: "As Jesus Christ carried his cross to the grave, so Bishop Carey had to carry his cross to the grave. He has been persecuted and unjustly accused." The writer was present at the occasion. See also report in *Chicago Defender*, March 28, 1931.

[51] It is difficult to say what Thompson's actual feelings on racial matters were. In private conversation with whites it is said that he uses such terms as "nigger," "darkie," "pickaninny," and "coon." These words may appeal to his desire to use strong language. The usual explanation that these words are an indication of an attitude of contempt or derision may not be true as far as Thompson is concerned. Negroes in private conversations with Negroes and also with white friends who are well within the fold have been known to use these terms with interesting shades of meaning.

"There were 270 saloons in the ward. I spent $175 a day, wore out two pair of shoes, and gained fourteen pounds; but we won."[52] In the 1915 election he talked about enforcement to the reform elements and about beer to the working classes. As mayor he issued the famous Sunday closing order in compliance with the state law regulating saloons, but some of the lesser lights in his administration eased the application of this order. In his third administration Thompson appointed a lieutenant of Al Capone to an important city office. In 1927 the alliance between the Thompson faction and the colored underworld was openly revealed. Daniel M. Jackson, the notorious colored "gambling king," was deliberately selected as the leader of the Thompson forces in the Second Ward.[53] For many years it had been publicly known that Jackson was the head of a gambling syndicate operating on the South Side.[54] During the campaign Big Bill made the most of the police raids that had taken place in the Black Belt during the Democratic administration. He would remove the offending police captains, he would stop the breaking-in of homes and the "fanning of mattresses for pints"; he would end the persecution of the colored people; he would open ten thousand joints.[55] After he had been elected mayor, some of these promises were carried out. In Chicago history, the period has been called that of the "Big Fix."[56]

It is natural that the official acts of a person in office as long as Thompson was would be displeasing at times to certain minority elements. There were occasions when the Negroes found fault with what the Mayor did or failed to do. During his first administration complaints were made about his failure to take more vigorous action against the showing of the film, "The Birth of a Nation," which was regarded as vicious by many col-

[52] Interview.

[53] It is probable that Mayor Thompson knew Dan Jackson for many years. Thompson used to live on Prairie near Twenty-eighth. Dan Jackson's place was on Twenty-eighth Street.

[54] *Chicago Daily News*, August 6, 1921; June 5, 1922; January 9, 1923; April 30, 1923; June 15, 1923.

[55] *Defender*, March 19, 1927.   [56] C. E. Merriam, *Chicago* (New York, 1929).

ored people.[57] Complaints were also made about the segregation of the colored employees of the fire department.[58] In 1919, the year of the race riot, the Negroes had many criticisms to make of Thompson's shortcomings. His failure to stop the bombings of Negro real estate owners before and after the riot brought forth many bitter comments.[59] During the riot itself the conduct of the police received much adverse criticism from the Negroes. The police force was inadequate to deal with the situation and the Mayor was accused of being dilatory in calling the aid of the state militia.[60] It was not until considerable pressure was brought to bear upon him that he finally asked help from the state troops. A delegation of colored leaders joined with others in bringing the Mayor to this decision.[61] This same delegation asked the Mayor to appoint a commission to investigate the riot but the governor and not the Mayor took action on this suggestion.[62] The Mayor did not present himself to the voters

[57] *Defender*, February 19, 1916.

[58] *Ibid.*, April 22, 1916, and in many subsequent issues.

[59] *Chicago Daily News*, June 4, 1919; *Defender*, February 21, 1920; *Chicago Tribune*, May 14, 1921.

[60] In a signed article, Patrick B. Prescott, Jr., commented as follows in the *Chicago Whip*, February 19, 1927: "Why, it has even been advanced that William Hale Thompson committed a grave offense by not calling out the militia during the riots of 1919. First, the mayor couldn't 'call out' the militia. He could only ask the governor to do so. But it has never been told that when members of Caucasian people called upon William Hale Thompson and demanded that he ask for the militia, he sent for a committee of colored leaders to seek their advice. And it was these leaders who, remembering the riots of Springfield, Atlanta, and East St. Louis, when the National Guardsmen, called upon to restore peace, turned their guns upon colored men and women and children, said 'No!' It was colored men who told William Hale Thompson that they would rather take their chance with the police force under his control, than with the militia under the control of General Dickson. And the militia was not asked for." This is substantially the explanation given by Mayor Thompson himself. However, it should be pointed out that Prescott's father-in-law, Bishop Carey, was one of the citizens who urged Thompson to call the militia on July 30, 1919 (*Chicago Tribune*, July 31, 1919). The Chicago Commission on Race Relations, *op. cit.*, p. 599, states that when the troops were finally summoned their conduct was good and order was restored. As far as the statement which the writer made in the text above is concerned, the main point to remember is that Thompson was criticized for his handling of this situation.

[61] *Chicago Tribune*, July 31, 1919.

[62] Chicago Commission on Race Relations, *op. cit.*

until nearly eight years after the riot. During his third administration as mayor, the Granady episode created a very unfavorable impression on many Negroes. Octavius Granady was a colored attorney who ran for ward committeeman in the "bloody Twentieth" ward against Morris Eller, Thompson's city collector. On the day of the primary, Granady was shot down in cold blood by a gang of hoodlums engaged in a campaign of terrorism. Eller was indicted for conspiracy but the prosecution failed. In the fall election the Negro voters were urged to cut Eller's name from their ticket.[63]

Mayor Thompson, like many other politicians, relied upon the short memories of the great mass of the voters. He knew that the specific incidents which were displeasing at the time would be forgotten by the following election day. However, he was confronted with a more or less permanent opposition among the colored citizens. This opposition was small, as the vote shows, but it was active enough to throw doubt on some of the mythical qualities which the most ardent Thompson supporters attached to their idol. The anti-Thompson group was composed in part of clergymen, lawyers, journalists, retired public employees, and disappointed office-seekers. Some of the opposition group had no direct interest in politics other than as citizens, but a few received patronage from the Deneen faction of the Republican party. A few examples will show how the opposition tried to undermine the popularity of Thompson with counter-propaganda of their own.

There were several types of argument that were made against Mayor Thompson. He was frequently attacked because of the vice conditions which were tolerated in the Black Belt during

[63] *Chicago Daily News*, October 31, 1928. Two years later the N.A.A.C.P. protested the appointment of one of Eller's henchmen to a city position. See *Chicago Bee*, November 9, 1930. When a delegation of colored citizens from the Twentieth Ward came to Mayor Thompson asking for more recognition and complaining about the treatment which they received from the Republican organization in the ward, Thompson referred them to their ward committeeman, Morris Eller. In this instance, Thompson put ward politics above his regard for a minority race. In the campaign of 1931 the Eller incident was used against Thompson by the colored Democrats. Report on meeting of April 5, 1931.

his administrations. In 1919 one of the colored weeklies presented a number of questions, some of which were as follows: "Is vice immunity the only plum that Negro aldermen can secure in the way of patronage? . . . . Would the voters of the Second Ward prefer to have open and protected vice to playgrounds and free milk stations? . . . . Is the average voter satisfied to see Civil Service perverted to the patronage system of politicians?"[64] In a later issue this same paper said: "His [Mayor Thompson's] black friends permitted and most likely converted the once fashionable south side into the city's cesspool. It reflects on the Mayor. His Black friends with their boon companions have betrayed the Mayor."[65] This is typical of some of the criticism leveled at the Mayor. He was not attacked personally, but his organization was criticized.[66] Another weekly expressed its disgust with the Thompson régime in the following words: "In return they [the Thompson leaders] have turned over the Negro communities of Chicago to the vice lords, policy kings, bootleggers and racketeers, and have foisted upon their people crooked political leaders who have given the city, county and state the worst administrations in all the history of Illinois."[67] This type of appeal was sometimes heard from the pulpits of certain colored churches.[68]

Ridicule was another weapon in the hands of the anti-Thompson forces. During the primary of 1931 when Thompson was campaigning with a halter, a mule, an elephant, and a burro, one of the outstanding Chicago colored attorneys in a public address said:

When a man takes a mule and an elephant and uses that as an argument, I wonder what's wrong with me. Thompson brought that elephant and cowboy

[64] *Chicago Whip*, December 13, 1919.

[65] *Ibid.*, February 10, 1923.

[66] As one prominent colored official put it, "Thompson is a fine man, but some of the Negroes he had around him, I wouldn't invite into my house."

[67] *Chicago Bee*, November 9, 1930.

[68] L. K. Williams and W. S. Braddan, both pastors of Baptist churches. On October 26, 1930, Rev. Braddan said in effect that Mayor Thompson was responsible for the great number of thieves in Chicago and for the great number of bandits, also for the prostitution of many women.

hat and said vote for me on my record. Is that his record? I think when a man
is giving the biggest fool argument given any man in any place and expects to
get your votes, it depends on how intelligent you are whether you are insulted.[69]

The anti-Thompson forces were far weaker than the Thompson forces. They were not strong enough in numbers and
wealth, nor determined enough in their zeal, to carry their counter-propaganda into precincts to the individual voters over a
long period of time. Thompson's personality was an important
factor in the situation. The favorable reports of his racial attitudes and actions outweighed the unfavorable, and there was
no Republican leader in the opposition who stood out as he did.
On the platform, on the screen, over the radio, in the city hall, at
political banquets, in the pre-primary conferences, at national
conventions, at party celebrations, on election day, in times of
sorrow and in times of joy, Mayor Thompson was their friend.
The lasting character of his personal popularity among Negro
voters is shown by the fact that in 1931, in the areas with a population 75 per cent or more Negro, he polled over 83 per cent of
the total vote cast.[70] In the areas of highest rentals and in those
of lowest rentals, in the Second Ward and in the "Bloody Twentieth," among the employed and among the unemployed, Mayor
Thompson was their choice. After sixteen years of pitiless publicity he emerged triumphant in the "Black Belt" in an election
at which he went down to defeat in the city at large.

Great as Mayor Thompson's personal popularity was among
Negroes, it is probable that another man from his faction might
have built up a similar reputation if he, rather than Thompson,
had come into power at the proper time. Thompson represented
a system, a set of traditions that are firmly rooted in Illinois
politics. He was the "product of his times and of the forces
which pushed him on."[71] He came into power when the Negro
migration was assuming large proportions. Many of the Negroes who voted for Thompson appreciated his shortcomings

[69] Fourth Ward mass meeting for Judge John H. Lyle, February 20, 1931.

[70] See Appendix I for table.   [71] Kinsley, *loc. cit.*

but they felt that no other candidate running was as acceptable as he.[72] On some occasions Thompson overestimated his personal popularity, but most of the time the organization to which he belonged came much nearer to satisfying the demand of the group for status than did any other faction. By furnishing them with new jobs, by protecting them against mishandling by the police, by recognizing them as citizens, by fitting its appeals to the various groups found within the Negro community, the faction created a situation in which colored preachers could refer to Thompson as the "Second Lincoln" and win applause.

[72] One very prominent young Negro organization leader said on May 2, 1932: "Thompson was the Negro's greatest handicap. The Negro leaders had made Thompson and Thompson for a while thought he made the Negro but he had found out that he had not. He tried to break Oscar like he had broken other Negro leaders but he failed."

CHAPTER IV

RACIAL CANDIDATES FOR ELECTIVE OFFICE

Like the other minority groups Negroes have not been satisfied with voting on issues—they have wanted to vote for candidates of their own choosing. The practice of democracy involves not only freedom of discussion and equal suffrage, but also freedom of candidacy. In Fascist Italy and Nazi Germany there is no freedom of candidacy. Only those who are hand-picked by the ruling clique are permitted to run for public office. In the southern states of the United States, where Negroes are virtually deprived of the right to vote, the right to run for public office is confined to whites. When Negroes came North, they first exercised the right to vote and then they began thinking about running candidates of their own.

ROBERT R. JACKSON

Colored candidates for elective positions which they had a chance to win were desirable for a number of reasons. The Negroes had an issue which was not recognized by the parties. They were a pressure group like the prohibitionists. The prestige of the entire race was raised when a member of the group was elected to an important political position. The power of this member depended primarily upon black votes and not upon the favor or success of a given party faction. He was in a measure independent of the white bosses and of their financial resources.[1]

---

[1] "Unless we are diligent in fighting our own cause, we cannot expect to leave the job to somebody else. We believe that these successes and victories are but the first steps to real power and a voice in affairs at Washington, a voice unfettered by jobs held at the mercy or whim of some white political leader, but held because the man in office has a mandate from the voters of his race and of his home district to be there." *Chicago Defender*, April 5, 1924.

In Chicago, he did not fear Democratic landslides until 1934. This elected officer, no matter what his personal short-comings might be, understood the privations of an unpopular minority group better than a white man could. He might sell out his group on many matters, but on certain funda-mental race issues he could not go contrary to the deep-seated convictions of his constituents and hope to be re-elected.

It has been indicated in another connection that in 1930 some 8.7 per cent of the adult citizens in Chicago were Negroes. On a strictly proportional basis, this ratio should entitle the colored citizens to four of the fifty aldermen, five of the some fifty-seven state representatives, one of the ten Cook County commission-ers elected at large from the city, and one of the ten congressmen elected from the area. It is well known that defects in the sys-tem of representation, lack of perfect group cohesion, and the criss-crossing of economic, social, religious, factional, personal, and other currents prevent voting from following any single line, such as race, on all occasions. It is also well recognized that voting according to strictly racial considerations is deprecated in many quarters. The Negro group in Chicago is definitely a minority group, and if the whites always followed a color line in voting no black man could hope to win a city-wide office. Jeal-ousy within the group might prevent some from supporting a race candidate. It is also conceivable that the distribution of the colored vote might be such that it would be ineffective in any one election district. In Greater New York there are enough colored voters to elect a congressman, but they are so scattered that they cannot control any single congressional district. While the distribution of the Negro population has been more favor-able to representation in Chicago than in New York, the actual nomination and election of Negroes to public office has meant hard work and careful planning.

The task of electing Negroes to public office was taken seri-ously by some of the race leaders. Shortly after the race riot of 1919, when relations were still strained, the following statement was made by ex-County Commissioner Edward H. Wright, one of the foremost colored political leaders:

The Negro in the 1st congressional district constitutes the backbone of the Republican party and he desires politically what any other element of the American people desire under like conditions. The Negro is a native born American; he is 100 per cent patriotic; he is intelligent and progressive and his ambition is to reach the status of absolute equality as an American citizen.

We feel that if we bear all the burdens and responsibilities of citizenship we should be accorded all the privileges that go with it. We want no special privileges—and we want no special handicaps.

That a better understanding may be brought, the Negro should be represented in all bodies that have to do with the shaping of policies under which the people must live.

It is unfortunate that the white man's unreasoning prejudice (no matter to what party he belongs) makes it almost a necessity that the Negro should have a preponderance of the vote in a certain territory or have at least the balance of power between the parties before he is given any political recognition. This has a tendency to compel the Negro to draw racial lines as a matter of self-protection. This is all wrong on both sides.

In the program herein outlined, the enemies of the Negro will raise the cry of Negro domination wherever he is numerically in the majority. This is all rot. It is the desire and purpose of the intelligent progressive Negro to maintain the most friendly relations with the white man and to co-operate with him in all matters touching the public welfare.[2]

STATE SENATORIAL DISTRICTS

As in other cities of the North, the colored citizens of Chicago have been more successful in electing colored representatives to the various law-making bodies than they have been in electing colored administrative officers. The system of cumulative voting used for the election of the Illinois House of Representatives since 1870 was adapted to their purposes, since a group which could muster at least one-third of the votes in a senatorial district could be sure of one representative. In every district each voter had three votes which could be concentrated on a single candidate or split between two or three candidates. It was to the advantage of a candidate of a minority group to instruct his followers to cast all their three votes for him.[3]

As far back as 1876, when the colored people comprised only 1 per cent of the total population of the city, one of them, John

[2] *Chicago Daily News*, September 26, 1919.

[3] B. F. Moore, *A History of Cumulative Voting and Minority Representation in Illinois* (Urbana, 1909).

W. E. Thomas, was sent as their representative to the capitol at Springfield by the Republican voters of the Second Senatorial District in Chicago.[4] A native of Alabama, he came to Chicago when he was twenty-six and started a grocery business which was destroyed by the fire of 1873. At the time of his election to the legislature, he was a teacher by occupation, keeping a private school near the center of the city.[5] His election was in part the result of his efforts to train his colored constituents to cumulate or "plump" their votes for him. However, as he received 11,532 votes and the total colored population of the city was less than 7,000, it is obvious that a large proportion of his supporters were white.

Representative Thomas was not re-elected until 1882, but after that date there has never been a session of the Illinois General Assembly which has lacked a colored representative. For thirty-two years the colored people were not able to elect more than one member of the legislature. During this time, nine different men in addition to Representative Thomas served at Springfield.[6] Five of them served two terms each and the other four served single terms only. The list included three lawyers, a professional baseball club owner, a physician, a major in the state militia, a state office-holder, and an ex-postal employee. One of the lawyers, Edward H. Morris, who was elected for his first term in 1890 and for his second term in 1902, has made a distinguished record at the bar and is regarded as the dean of colored lawyers at the present time. Except at the very end of the period under discussion, all of the colored representatives were nominated by Republican senatorial district conventions. White leaders, like Alderman Martin B. Madden, who was later congressman, carefully cultivated the delegates from the areas inhabited by Negro voters. Under the Illinois system of cumulative voting, a nomination by one of the major parties

[4] At a meeting of the Municipal Reform Club, Mr. King moved to nominate Mr. J. W. E. Thomas to fill the vacancy in the Second District of the House of Representatives and supported this move by lengthy remarks urging the claims of Mr. Thomas. *Chicago Tribune*, November 3, 1876.

[5] *Illinois Blue Book, 1877–1878.*

[6] For a list of these representatives, see Appendix I.

was almost equivalent to election, as each party usually limited the number of nominations to the number which it was sure to elect. Prior to 1891 only party ballots were used in Illinois, and under the Australian Ballot Act of that year the party column system was adopted with the straight-ticket device. Any person, white or colored, who voted the straight Republican ticket in a senatorial district where a colored man had been nominated for representative, automatically cast one, one and a half, or three votes for that colored representative, depending upon whether the Republican convention had nominated three, two, or one candidates. The operation of this system, together with the development of a tradition that the colored people were entitled to some representation in Springfield, meant that there were no breaks in the continuity of that representation.

The last of the single colored representatives was Robert R. Jackson, who was elected from the Third Senatorial District in a close fight with two Democrats, a fellow-Republican, and a Progressive in 1912. It was not until after an election contest that Jackson was finally seated. Although two colored representatives were not sent to Springfield until 1914, the election of Jackson in 1912 clearly foreshadowed the increase in colored representation. Following the reapportionment act of 1901, the colored representative for five successive sessions was chosen from the First Senatorial District. The Negro candidate from this district in 1912 was defeated by the white Progressive party candidate. The collapse of the Progressive movement after 1912 and the success of Jackson in the Third District clearly forecast the increase in the colored delegation which came about at the next general election. The nomination of Jackson in the Third District in 1912 under the direct primary law is therefore a matter of special interest. The Republican Senatorial Committee limited the number of nominations for the party to two, as this was the greatest probable number that it thought could be elected. Jackson had the support of Congressman Madden for the position and he was very popular with his own people.[7] A

[7] R. R. Ross, "The Rise of a Newsboy to One of the Fathers of Chicago," *American Life* (Chicago, June, 1927), pp. 12–15, gives a typical view of Major Jackson. The Municipal Voters' League has said in a number of its reports that Alderman Jackson lacks in independence. See also *Broad Ax*, March 9, 1912; May 3, 1913.

native of Illinois, he had lived in Chicago practically all his life. Soon after graduating from the public schools of the city he entered the postal service, where he was employed for twenty years. In 1909 he left the postal service and became interested in the Fraternal Press, which printed laws and constitutions for lodges. The genial and pleasant "Bob" Jackson was a great fraternal man. He belonged to the Masons, the Odd Fellows, the Elks, the Knights of Pythias, the Musicians' Union, and at least fifteen other clubs. He was also well known because of his military record. Starting as a drummer in 1893, he rose to the position of major in the Eighth Illinois Infantry and saw service during the Spanish-American War. Major Jackson received more votes in the Republican primary than William Ostrom, a white man, who had already been elected to the legislature on two occasions.[8] In the final election, Major Jackson, Ostrom, and a Democratic candidate by the name of Ashton all received about the same number of votes with Jackson running fifth.[9] In the recount Jackson's vote was increased by over 1,000. This placed him third and he was declared elected.[10] The detailed analysis of the vote showed that he ran ahead of his Republican colleague in the districts inhabited largely by Negroes.

The delegation of colored representatives in Springfield was increased to three in 1918. The larger stream of migration following the World War was in part responsible for this result. Table IV shows why this additional representative came from the Third District rather than the First. The latter district contained most of the colored people in the first decade of the century but the former was nearer to the heart of the new Negro community which was rapidly increasing in numbers.

An analysis of the election of Warren B. Douglas, the additional representative chosen in 1918, illustrates how factional

[8] *Illinois Blue Book, 1913-1914*, p. 534. Ostrom received 4,889½ votes and Jackson 6,528¼.

[9] *Ibid.*, p. 605. F. E. J. Lloyd, Prog., 11,735½; John P. Walsh, Dem., 11,080; H. M. Ashton, Dem., 9,565½; William Ostrom, Rep. 9,498½; Robert R. Jackson, Rep., 9,059; A. L. Voorhees, Soc., 3,486¼.

[10] *Journal of the House of Representatives, 1913*, p. 848. F. E. J. Lloyd, 13,488; John P. Walsh, 11,312; R. R. Jackson, 10,166; H. M. Ashton, 9,602; William Ostrom, 9,566¼.

alignments may be used to the advantage of a minority group.[11] A native of Missouri, Douglas had completed high school and two years of commercial work in a Kansas college. After graduating from a night law school in Chicago in 1915 he became active in politics so as to broaden his contacts. An effective speaker and a vigorous organizer, he joined the DePriest group, which was active at the time in promoting William Hale Thompson for mayor. DePriest's temporary eclipse in 1918 made Douglas re-

TABLE IV

NEGRO POPULATION IN SELECTED SENATORIAL DISTRICTS
IN CHICAGO, 1920 AND 1930*

SENATORIAL DISTRICT	1920			1930		
	All Classes	Negro		All Classes	Negro	
		Number	Per Cent		Number	Per Cent
1................	62,328	22,521	36.1	44,036	19,776	44.9
3................	107,998	41,468	38.4	101,234	55,782	55.1
5................	183,883	17,992	9.8	214,765	98,440	45.8
Total selected senatorial districts.....	354,209	81,981	....	360,035	173,998	....

* *Census Data of the City of Chicago,* 1920 and 1930. Some minor estimates were made where tract lines and ward lines did not exactly fit.

ceptive to the overtures of the Deneen group, which offered to support him for the nomination for state representative in the Republican primary. The Thompson ticket had two candidates, Adelbert H. Roberts,[12] colored, who was replacing Major Jackson, and Herman E. Schultz, white, who was running for renomination. The cumulative system enabled the colored voters to concentrate upon the two colored candidates, some plumping for Douglas and others plumping for Roberts. Douglas also secured many white votes because of the favorable publicity which the Deneen slate received in some of the daily papers. The primary was held in September and this made possible

[11] Interview.   [12] See below, p. 71.

street-corner campaigning. Douglas had a wagon or a Ford in which he used to go around the district evenings. He and Roberts spoke in the fraternal organizations, such as the Knights of Pythias, the Masons, and the Elks, in the many Sunday evening clubs and in the churches on Sunday morning, but never from the same platform. On primary day both men had money for workers from their respective organizations. The net result of these activities was the defeat of the white candidate who had had one term's experience in the legislature.[13]

It was not until 1924 that the colored voters of the First District caught up with their neighbors in the Third and returned two representatives of their group to the state legislature. For ten years the Republican organization had supported two candidates for the House of Representatives from this district, Sheadrick B. Turner,[14] colored, and William M. Brinkman, white. Brinkman moved out of the district before the 1924 election and the organization leaders decided to send a colored man in his place. Charles A. Griffin, an insurance and real estate broker, was selected for this position. He was well known in the district as he had run for public office on four previous occasions, twice for alderman, once for Cook County commissioner, and once for state senator.[15] The large vote that he had polled in 1922 for nomination as state senator in the First District marked him as an available candidate for the House. Like Douglas, Griffin had been aligned with several of the different Republican factions in Chicago at different times. At the time of his nomination for the state legislature in 1924 he had the support of George F. Harding as the result of an arrangement between Harding and Edward J. Brundage, who was a candidate for renomination as attorney-general of the state. Turner and Griffin were nominated and elected with little difficulty.

In 1924, for the first time in the history of the state, a man of African descent was elected to the state Senate. State Senator

---

[13] *Illinois Blue Book, 1919–1920*, p. 615. Results in Third District for primary of September 11, 1918; Schultz, 2,540½; Roberts, 5,680; Douglas, 4,167.

[14] Turner was not elected in 1916.

[15] *Chicago Defender*, April 4, 1914; *Chicago Daily News*, April 8, 1922.

Samuel A. Ettelson, a former corporation counsel under Mayor Thompson, voluntarily retired in 1924 and left the field open to the local organization. Adelbert H. Roberts, who had served three terms in the Illinois House of Representatives, was the unanimous choice of the Third Ward organization for the position.[16] A native of Michigan, Roberts came to Chicago in the early nineties and attended law school while he practiced his trade as a barber. After graduating from law school he obtained an appointive position in the city, and in 1906 he was made a clerk for the newly created municipal court. Possessing a gift for words and a striking oratorical style, he gained a position of prominence in the local Republican organization. His nomination for the state Senate was backed by Ettelson, Harding, Madden, Robert R. Jackson, and Edward H. Wright, and he was unopposed in the Republican primary. His election followed as a matter of course, and he served for ten years in the state Senate.[17]

It is clear from Table IV that the election of a colored representative from the Fifth District was possible in 1928 if a uniform rate of growth of the Negro population between 1920 and 1930 is assumed. That it actually happened was the result of the organizing ability of the colored leaders. A Negro candidate who ran in the primary of 1926 received 18 per cent of the vote cast in this district with little organized effort.[18] The main contestants in the 1928 primary for the two Republican nominations were Mrs. Cheney and Mr. Lyon, both white, and Messrs. Haynes and Warfield, both colored. Warfield and Lyon had the backing of the Thompson faction. It was known that Mrs.

[16] *Chicago Daily News*, January 18, 1924.

[17] The Legislative Voters' League has made conflicting reports about Senator Roberts. In 1918, he was "exceptionally well qualified." In 1920, he had a "highly creditable record." The 1924 report said that he gave close attention to legislative work but "damaged his record by lack of independence." In 1930, he was called "an unfailing follower of Governor Small during four sessions" and it was said he had "some good intentions but little legislative ability." See *Chicago Daily News*, November 2, 1918; September 11, 1920; February 18, 1924; and January 27, 1930. Senator Roberts was defeated for renomination in the Republican primary of 1934 by William E. King.

[18] George C. Adams by name. See *Daily News Almanac* for 1927, p. 741.

Cheney with Deneen and independent backing could not be beaten. It appeared that the white leaders hoped that the colored vote would be divided and that Lyon, who had been a representative for twelve years, would be returned. Oscar DePriest, the ward committeeman for a ward partially included in the district, encouraged Warfield and showed him how to run his campaign. Warfield was a young real estate expert who had seen military service in France during the World War, and his wife was employed in DePriest's real estate office. The precinct captains were lined up in the areas populated largely by Negroes and the word was passed around that to insure the election of Warfield they should vote for him alone. The returns showed that in these areas over one-half of the voters supported Warfield.[19] Here, as in 1912 and 1918, was another demonstration of the ability of the colored voters under skilful leadership to insist upon racial representation.

In the legislative districts where a minority system of representation was in effect and where there was a racial concentration of population, it is apparent that voting tended to follow racial lines. From a single representative in the House in 1913 the colored delegation increased to five in the House and one in the Senate by 1929. Of the five additional legislators, two were nominated in a field left clear by the withdrawal of the sitting white legislators, while three defeated white organization candidates in straight fights either in the election or in the primary. While many of the Negro legislators chosen during the period belonged to the Thompson faction of the Republican party, only a small portion of the increase in the colored representation can be claimed by that faction. The delegation numbered two before the first election of Thompson as mayor, the third was elected with Deneen support, and the fifth defeated the white candidate who was favored by the white bosses. The turnover of the individual representatives has been fairly high, but the race representation quite constant. Up to the present, only two, Turner and Roberts, have been elected to the legislature more

[19] Analysis of official returns on file in Board of Election Commissioners of the City of Chicago.

than four times. In the 1932 primary, because of a factional
fight within the colored community, one of the colored representatives from the First District was displaced by a white
man.[20] Many of the colored voters may have been illiterate, but
under careful guidance they have used the Illinois system of representation to their own advantage.

Closely related to the legislative positions are the seats in
Illinois constitutional conventions. The convention of 1919–22
was composed of 102 delegates, two being elected at large from
each senatorial district. In the Republican primary preceding
the election, E. H. Morris and Bishop A. J. Carey were nominated in the Third District without opposition. Reference has
already been made to the two elections of Morris to the Illinois
House of Representatives and to the friendship between Bishop
Carey and Mayor Thompson.[21]

CHICAGO WARD ELECTIONS

Much more highly prized than a seat in the state legislature
or in a state constitutional convention is a seat in the Chicago
city council, because the local position carries a higher salary
and larger patronage powers. The total expenditures of the
state of Illinois are much smaller and are spread over a much
larger area than those of the city of Chicago. The city spends
money for functions which are close to the people. The protection of persons and property, the conservation of health, sanitation, and recreation are services to the public for which the
city fathers are responsible. The colored migrants who came to
the city were certainly in need of these services. Before 1921 the
city council was composed of seventy aldermen, two selected for
each of the thirty-five wards. Because of the powers of the city
council to pass the city budget, to create new departments, to

---

[20] George Blackwell, who belonged to the Alderman Anderson faction, was defeated
by Arthur T. Broche, white, who had some support from the DePriest faction. See
Chicago Daily News, April 13, 1932. Continued factional struggles helped renominate
Broche in the 1934 primary.

[21] See above, p. 66, and below, p. 98. Bishop Carey spoke at the Centennial Celebration of Perry's victory at Put-in-Bay. Among the other speakers present were President
Wilson, ex-President Taft, Governor Cox of Ohio, and Dr. McDonald of Toronto.

grant franchises, to reject appointments, and to pass local ordi-
nances, the aldermen are in a position to recommend certain
appointments and to supervise the administration of city affairs
within their respective wards.

/ Prior to 1915 the colored voters struggled in vain to secure an
alderman of their race. In 1910 the Second Ward under the
1901 ward lines was 27 per cent colored.[22] Edward H. Wright
claimed that he had contributed largely to the election of
Chauncey Dewey, white, as Republican ward committeeman in
the ward and he demanded that Dewey nominate a colored man
for alderman in the Republican convention of 1910. When
Dewey refused to do this a meeting of colored voters was called
and Edward H. Wright was put in the field as an independent
Republican candidate.[23] He received 18 per cent of the total
vote cast.[24] In 1914, Wright backed William Randolph Cowan
for the Republican nomination for alderman as against the
white incumbent, Hugh Norris. Cowan was prominent in the
real estate business and was well known on the South Side. He
gave Norris a close run, receiving 45 per cent of the Republican
primary vote in the ward.[25] Cowan's battle in the aldermanic
primary was so promising that Charles A. Griffin came out as
an independent candidate in the final election. In a large field
of candidates, Griffin ran second with 21 per cent of the total
vote cast.[26]

It is very likely that the Negro voters constituted a majority
of the voters of the Second Ward by 1915. According to the
census of 1920 the Second Ward under the 1911 ward lines was
70 per cent colored. George F. Harding, the senior alderman in
the ward, voluntarily retired from the aldermanic contest following his election as state senator in November, 1914. In the
Republican primary, ex-County Commissioner Oscar DePriest

[22] United States Bureau of the Census, *Thirteenth Census, 1910; Population.*

[23] Washington Intercollegiate Club of Chicago, *The Negro in Chicago, 1779–1927*, I
(1929), 136; *Broad Ax*, March 26, April 9, 16, 1910.

[24] *Daily News Almanac and Year Book*, 1911.

[25] *Chicago Defender*, February 28, 1914.

[26] *Daily News Almanac and Year Book*, 1915, p. 632; *Broad Ax*, March 14, April 4,
11, 1914.

defeated Louis B. Anderson, Charles A. Griffin, and five white adversaries.[27] After his election, DePriest became the idol not only of colored people in his ward but of the so-called "race" men in the city. Their dream of a colored alderman was at last realized. When the six-foot rugged-looking councilor appeared on the streets he was surrounded by admirers.

Upon the expiration of his term in 1917 DePriest announced that he would not be a candidate for re-election. He was indicted a month before the primary for conspiracy to permit a graft syndicate in his neighborhood and there was not sufficient time to clear his record.[28] Louis B. Anderson was nominated and elected to the position with comparatively little opposition. At the time Anderson was an assistant corporation counsel under the Thompson administration. For seventeen years prior to 1915 he had been an assistant county attorney. Shrewd, suave of manner, well versed in parliamentary law, thoroughly familiar with the methods of political organization, Alderman Anderson embarked on a career in the city council which lasted sixteen years. For eight consecutive terms of two years each he was returned to the council by the voters of the Second Ward.[29]

When the draft in 1918 showed men like Bishop Carey, who was on a draft board, that seven or eight out of every ten in the Second Ward were Negroes, pressure was brought to bear upon the Republican organization to put up a colored candidate for the second alderman in the ward. On two previous occasions Alderman Norris had been confronted with determined opposition on the part of colored candidates.[30] In 1918 he withdrew from the race. Major Robert R. Jackson, who has already been mentioned in connection with the state legislature, was nomi-

[27] *Broad Ax*, February 27, 1915; *Chicago Defender*, May 3, 1930.

[28] See chapter ix, below.

[29] The Municipal Voters' League reported adversely upon his record at the end of each term. In 1919 it said, "In his mellifluous way, quite as bad an alderman as was his predecessor, DePriest." In 1925, it said: "Ringmaster of the council under the Thompson-Lundin régime, now a mere water-carrier. Known as a friend of gamblers and dive-keepers. . . . . A 'smart guy,' but unscrupulous." See *Reports* of Municipal Voters' League, annual until 1921 and biennial after 1921.

[30] *Broad Ax*, February 28, April 11, 1914, March 18, April 8, 1916.

nated and elected to the position, defeating DePriest in both the primary and the election. On these occasions Major Jackson had the backing of Congressman Madden and State Senator Harding.[31] The same genial qualities that helped Major Jackson win elections to the state legislature have aided him in re-electing himself to the city council. His service has been continuous from his first election down to the present time.

When the ward lines were redrawn in 1921 on a fifty-ward plan with one representative from each ward, two areas were

TABLE V

NEGRO POPULATION IN SELECTED WARDS IN CHICAGO,
1920 AND 1930 (1921 WARD LINES)*

	1920			1930		
WARD	All Classes	Negro		All Classes	Negro	
		Number	Per Cent		Number	Per Cent
2	55,468	39,741	71.6	47,027	40,735	86.6
3	57,927	26,062	45.0	69,255	55,306	79.9
4	61,273	8,345	13.6	70,077	41,221	58.8

* *Census Data of the City of Chicago,* 1920 and 1930. Some minor estimates were made where tract lines and ward lines did not exactly fit.

carved out for the incumbents of the old Second Ward. According to political custom in Chicago, the sitting aldermen look after their own interests when the city is being redistricted. One of the reasons why the Negroes have held these two seats for so long is indicated by Table V.

According to Table V, the Negro voters might have elected a member of their race as alderman of the Fourth Ward in 1929 or 1931 had they chosen to do so. However, the incumbent Alderman Cronson, the nephew of Samuel Ettelson, was close to the Republican faction which the great mass of the Negroes supported and he was left in his seat. An independent colored candidate in 1929 only received 16 per cent of the total vote cast and in 1931 an independent colored candidate was practically

[31] *Ibid.,* November 3, 1917.

eliminated because his name was kept off the ballot by the unfavorable decision of the Board of Election Commissioners regarding his petition.[32] If the colored leaders had made a determined fight against Alderman Cronson on either of these occasions, they might well have caused him considerable trouble. However, as several organization leaders were employed in the office of Corporation Counsel Ettelson at the time, the organization itself did not raise the issue.

TABLE VI

NEGRO POPULATION IN SELECTED WARDS IN CHICAGO,
1930 (1931 WARD LINES)*

WARD	ALL CLASSES	NEGRO	
		Number	Per Cent
2............	82,000	78,628	95.9
3............	75,212	52,596	69.9
4............	69,909	19,552	28.0

* *Census Data of the City of Chicago*, 1930. Some minor estimates were made where tract lines and ward lines did not exactly fit.

When the ward lines were redrawn in 1931 in accordance with the city charter, the immediate possibility of a third colored alderman was removed. This is clearly indicated in Table VI.

Aldermen Anderson and Jackson were careful to see that their own bailiwicks were preserved. Alderman Jackson was compelled to move south in order to secure a legal residence in the new Third Ward.[33] Apparently no serious attempt was made to insure the concentration of the colored population in another ward which might at some time return a third colored alderman. Alderman Cronson was able to win black votes, but it is apparent that he appreciated the potential threat of the power of these votes.

[32] Edgar G. Brown was the candidate. See *Chicago Tribune*, February 8, 1931; *Whip*, February 14, 1931; for details of his attempt to get on the ballot.

[33] The new Third Ward was carved out of the old Third, Fourth, and Fifth wards. Alderman Jackson had the backing of both Democratic and Republican organizations in 1935.

FIRST CONGRESSIONAL DISTRICT

Because of its national importance, a seat in Congress was coveted by the Negroes in Chicago many years before one was available. The last colored congressman of the reconstruction days, Representative George H. White, of North Carolina, said in his farewell speech of January 29, 1901: "This, Mr. Chairman, is perhaps the Negro's temporary farewell to the American Congress; but let me say, Phoenix-like, he will rise up some day and come again. These parting words are in behalf of an outraged, heart-broken, bruised and bleeding but God-fearing people, faithful, industrious and loyal people—full of potential force."[34] The political power which the Negroes in Chicago acquired after 1915 aroused in their hearts the hope that they might be able to fulfil the prophecy of George White.

The big obstacle in the way of the election of a colored representative to Congress prior to 1928 was Martin B. Madden, representative from the First Congressional District of Illinois from 1904 to the time of his death. Table VII shows to what extent the Negro vote was concentrated in this district in 1920 and in 1930. When Congressman Madden was first elected from this district the colored population was in a distinct minority, but it is probable that in 1926 or 1928 it was in a majority. Madden had acquired a private fortune and he found pleasure in spending it in politics. He was known to be very liberal with the colored people in Chicago and to be a royal entertainer for all who came to Washington.[35] When the colored postal employees of Chicago were attacked on the floor of the House, Madden came to their defense.[36] When a colored weekly newspaper was in trouble, he was one of those who came to the rescue.[37] He did not back any particular person in Chicago, but he tried to keep harmony among all the colored leaders. An additional reason for Madden's strong position was his national importance as chairman of the Committee on Appropriations.

[34] *Congressional Record*, 56th Congress, 2d session, Vol. XXXIV, Part 2, p. 1638.

[35] Interview with associate of Madden's.

[36] *Congressional Record*, 70th Congress, 1st Session, February 2, 1928, p. 2485. See also below, chapter xiv.

[37] *Chicago Defender*, May 31, 1930; *Broad Ax*, January 3, 1914.

In accordance with the philosophy of Edward H. Wright, as shown in the quotation cited previously, the colored leaders ran several candidates of their own race against Congressman Madden. In 1922 the colored candidate received only 17 per cent of the Republican primary vote cast in the First Congressional District,[38] but in 1924, when Nathan S. Taylor, a graduate of the University of Michigan and a well-known attorney, was a candidate for the Republican nomination, he received almost 40 per cent of the total Republican primary vote.[39] This was the closest to ousting Madden that any of the colored candidates came, but in 1928 William L. Dawson made matters more uncomfortable for the Republican organization leaders, white and colored, than had any previous Negro candidate. A native of Georgia, educated at Fisk University and Northwestern University Law School, Dawson was a man who understood how to make a racial appeal. "By birth, training and experience I am better fitted to represent the district at Washington than any of the candidates now in the field," he said. "Mr. Madden, the present congressman, does not even live in the district. He is a white man. Therefore, for those two reasons, if no others, he can hardly voice the hopes, ideals and sentiment of the majority of the district."[40] At a mammoth meeting Mayor Thompson, still the idol of the colored people, said: "A Negro might go to congress and after serving there for twenty years might become chairman of the powerful finance committee—perhaps he might —perhaps." Following this remark from the great Mayor Thompson, there were hisses, howls, and the stamping of feet which drowned out his voice.[41] When the ballots were counted after the primary Dawson was accredited with 29 per cent of the Republican primary vote. Table VII shows the proportion of Negroes in the First Congressional District two years after this dramatic struggle.

[38] *Daily News Almanac,* for 1923, p. 735. Martin B. Madden, 14,193; Richard E. Parker, 2,842.

[39] *Daily News Almanac for 1925,* p. 766. Martin B. Madden, 12,796; Nathan S. Taylor, 8,258. The *Chicago Defender* came out for Madden probably in view of past favors received. See issues of April 5 and April 12, 1924.

[40] *Chicago Daily News,* March 2, 1928.

[41] *Chicago Tribune,* March 12, 1928; *New York Times,* March 12, 1928.

Congressman Madden died shortly after the 1928 primary and the filling of the vacancy on the Republican ticket was in the hands of the Congressional District Committee, which was made up of the Republican ward committeemen who had jurisdiction over any part of the district. This committee included Daniel Serritella, an associate of Al Capone, Dan Jackson, Negro gambling king, John "Dingbat" Oberta, who was later assassinated in a gang war, W. S. Finucane, and Oscar DePriest.[42] All of these men belonged to the Thompson faction of the Re-

TABLE VII

ADULT NEGRO CITIZENS IN FIRST CONGRESSIONAL
DISTRICT, 1920 AND 1930*

YEAR	ALL CLASSES	NEGRO	
		Number	Per Cent
1920.........	110,100	49,224	44.7
1930.........	94,090	54,606	58.0

* *Census Data of the City of Chicago*, 1920 and 1930. Some minor estimates were made where tract lines and ward lines did not exactly fit.

publican party. Mayor Thompson was in a position practically to dictate the nomination. His account of his position was later stated in public in the following words:

I used to come to you and say to you that Bill Thompson would be the last one who would put his hand on a Negro's head to prevent him from rising higher. Yet I used to ask you to vote for a white man for Congress—the Honorable Martin B. Madden—not because I was for a white man, but because I was for Martin B. Madden, Calvin Coolidge, Len Small, Bill Thompson; Martin B. Madden was fighting to complete the waterway. (Applause.) Why did we keep him there; because of the great work Madden was doing.

When he died there came some Judas from Washington and said to me, "We don't want a Negro Congressman. You're the man that can keep a Negro out of Congress." I said, "If I'm the one man who can keep a Negro out of Congress, then, by God, there'll be one there."[43]

The committee finally decided upon Oscar DePriest for the position. This nomination did not please some of the elements

[42] *Chicago Tribune*, April 28, 1928.

[43] Political meeting at Wendell Phillips High School, March 20, 1932, and meeting at Savoy Ballroom, April 3, 1931.

in the Negro community; so an independent Negro candidate, William H. Harrison, was also put in the field. A comparison of the votes in the district for 1926 and 1928 indicates that some of the white Republican voters cut both of the colored candidates, but their numbers were small in the district and DePriest was elected by a plurality of nearly four thousand votes over his white Democratic opponent.[44] By sheer weight of their numbers in the district, by the strength of their bargaining power with the Thompson faction of the Republican party, and by the skill of their organizers, they had secured the election of a representative to Congress and had fulfilled Congressman White's prophecy after a lapse of twenty-eight years. In some small way the Negroes all over the country shared the success of their new representative. Oscar DePriest, who had been a local politician, soon became a national figure.[45]

COUNTY AND CITY ELECTIONS AT LARGE

The elective positions held by Negroes discussed so far have all been gained from districts which were small subdivisions of the city in which the Negro population was concentrated. Negroes have also been elected to public office in Chicago from the city at large. It appears that it was easier to elect a colored man on a city-wide ticket some years ago than it is at the present time. The analysis of this change is therefore worthy of attention.

The first colored man to be elected at large from the city—in fact the first colored man elected to any public office in Cook County[46]—was John Jones, who came to the city in 1845, some twelve years after its founding. Jones was born in North Carolina of mixed parentage. His mother was a free mulatto and his

[44] The vote was: DePriest, Republican, 24,479; Baker, Democrat, 20,664; William Harrison, Independent, 5,861. The coefficient of correlation between Baker's vote in 1928 (expressed as a percentage of the total vote in each area) less Doyle's vote (the Democratic white candidate in 1926 whose vote is also expressed as a percentage of the total in each area) and the Negro percentage by census tracts was .60. This shows that the few white Republican voters in the district tended to vote for Baker, the white Democratic candidate.

[45] See chapter ix, below.

[46] *Chicago Tribune*, March 12, 1875. He was also one of the earliest elective colored officers in the north.

father a German. This established his status as a free Negro, and he was apprenticed to a tailor in Tennessee. For fear that his free status might be challenged in this state, he collected evidences of his freedom and prayed for a writ of habeas corpus that he might be brought into court and discharged. The court record made it easy for him to secure his free papers when he moved to the state of Illinois.[47] In Chicago he continued his trade, learned to write, acquired some property, entertained abolitionists, and became a leader of his race. In 1856 he was active in a convention called to petition for the rights of the colored people in the state.[48] When a unified ticket was made up for the county board following the fire of 1871, Jones was proposed by the Republicans and unanimously accepted by the Democrats. He was elected like the rest of the ticket, practically without opposition. His first term was for one year and he was re-elected for a three-year term in 1872. He ran again in 1875, but was defeated along with the other Republican candidates. In 1876 he was indicted with some of the other county commissioners, but when the case came to trial he was acquitted without difficulty, there being no evidence against him.[49] The career of John Jones seemed to forecast some of the problems and difficulties that were to confront elective officer-holders of his race in later years.

After Jones' last election in 1872 there were no colored county commissioners for twenty-two years. In 1894 a group of colored citizens determined to make a fight to get a position on the county board. They presented their claim to the Republican leaders, but they failed to secure the co-operation of the slate-makers. In the county convention itself the colored delegates were divided into two groups, those who supported Theodore W. Jones for the position and those who supported Edward H. Wright. Realizing that it would be impossible to break the slate with two candidates, Wright took the floor and withdrew

[47] He first lived in Alton, Illinois. In 1845 it took him seven days to come to Chicago, then a town of 2,000 inhabitants.

[48] *Proceedings of the State Convention of Colored Citizens of the State of Illinois, 1856.*

[49] *Chicago Tribune*, May 22, 1879.

in favor of Jones.[50] This move was successful in securing the nomination of Jones, who was elected in the following November and served one term. Theodore W. Jones was related to the pioneer John Jones and he was engaged in the moving business at the time of his election.

Edward H. Wright's action in the 1894 Cook County Convention paved the way for his own nomination for the county board in 1896. He was renominated and re-elected in 1898.[51] In this election he was the last of the Republican slate to be elected. Following Wright, the colored candidates were unsuccessful until 1904, when Oscar DePriest was elected. DePriest served two terms, and he was followed by Frank Leland in 1908. In each case the nomination was secured in the Republican county convention and the election was facilitated by the straight-ticket provision of the Illinois Ballot Law. Since only 3 per cent of the adult citizen population of Chicago was colored at the time, the election depended almost entirely upon white voters. The Negroes were such a small minority that many white voters were not aware of the presence of colored candidates on the ticket. However, the defeat of the colored candidate in 1900 was partly due to the raising of the race issue against him by white newspapers.[52]

The conditions that were favorable to the election of colored candidates from the city at large to the county board changed after 1908. The Primary Law of 1910, which provided for direct nominations by the party voters, meant that greater publicity would be given to the racial and nationalistic origins of the various candidates. The increasing size of the Negro population, the race riot of 1919, the recognition given to the Second and Third ward leaders by the Thompson administration, and the unfavorable publicity given to some of the colored leaders resulted in the developing of a more intense race consciousness on the part of the white voters. At any rate, since 1908, no colored citizen has been elected by the voters of Chicago to the Cook County

[50] Washington Intercollegiate Club of Chicago, *op. cit.*, I, 135.

[51] See below, chapter viii.

[52] Daniel Jackson was the candidate. See below, p. 131.

Board of Commissioners. On different occasions at least six have been nominated in the Republican primaries but not one of these six has been able to weather the tides of racial feelings, bi-partisan deals, and Democratic landslides in the November elections. At least four others have been submerged in the Republican primaries.[53] In 1930 the colored candidate for commissioner, who was nominated in the Republican primary, was Carrol N. Langston, the grandson of John M. Langston, well-known educator and representative to the Fifty-first Congress from the state of Virginia.[54] The Republican ticket of 1930 was buried in a Democratic landslide. The fact that the colored candidates at several recent county board elections were close to the bottom of the list indicates that some white voters draw a color line. A number of white precinct captains report that their constituents ask them who are the colored candidates on the ticket.

Negroes have been elected to legislative posts in all parts of the United States. Except as to the longer duration and fulness of the representation, the Illinois situation was not unusual in this regard. The Negroes in Chicago felt that their political position was important enough to deserve representation upon other elective bodies, administrative and judicial. The prestige enjoyed by the courts in American political and economic life is such that any group which is struggling for status desires to be represented upon the bench. In Chicago the demand for the election of a Negro judge grew out of a complex set of conditions. Comparatively little part was played by the thought that a colored judge would be fairer than the white judges in cases

[53] A few instances will show some of the influences that were at work. In 1914 there were two colored candidates nominated for commissioner, Dr. George Cleveland Hall on the Progressive ticket and Colonel Franklin A. Denison on the Republican ticket. The division within the ranks of the Republican party meant that the Democrats made a clean sweep of all the ten commissioners selected at large by the voters of the city. In 1918 and in 1926 the election returns indicate that there was some kind of a bi-partisan deal between the Republicans and the Democrats. When there were bi-partisan deals, factional quarrels, trimming, and trading, the colored candidates lost out first.

[54] See J. M. Langston, *From Virginia Plantation to the National* (Hartford, 1894). For a campaign reference to C. N. Langston's family history, see *Defender*, November 1, 1930.

involving race relations. The primary demand was for recognition. The usual connection which Negroes had with the courts was limited to attachés, deputy sheriffs, police officers, prosecutors, bondsmen, spectators, and litigants or defendants. The election of a judge would be an elevation for the Negro group.[55] It would mean that they would be participants in the administration of justice. It was assumed that everyone connected with the courts would have a slightly different conception of the Negro if there was a colored judge.

The first attempt to elect a colored judge was made in 1906, just after the creation of the new Municipal Court of Chicago. Ferdinand L. Barnett, who had been appointed as an assistant state's attorney by Charles S. Deneen in 1896, was put forward by the Deneen faction as a candidate for the municipal bench. His thirty-seven years of residence in the city, his legal training at the Chicago College of Law, and his ten years of experience in the prosecutor's office made him an available candidate. Although the white Republican newspapers urged that his name be cut, the preliminary returns seemed to indicate that he had been elected.[56] However, the final figures showed that he lost by the narrow margin of 304 votes out of a total of some 200,000 votes cast for the office. He was the only Republican candidate to be defeated, running some 20,000 votes behind the next highest man on his ticket.[57] Charges were made that he had been counted out, but the real facts in the situation are difficult to establish.[58]

After the migration had increased the size of the colored population, other serious attempts were made to elect a Negro judge.

[55] As the *Chicago Defender* expressed it in its issue of April 5, 1924: "The *Defender* has also contended for judges from our Race in the courts. We know and believe that there is plenty of material among our lawyers. Every other race has a representative on the bench but our own." See also issues of June 10, 1916, October 9, 1920, and April 1, 1922.

[56] *Chicago Daily News*, November 8, 1906; *Broad Ax*, November 10, 1906.

[57] *Daily News Almanac for 1907*, p. 360.

[58] *Broad Ax*, December 21, 1907; *Chicago Tribune*, November 5, 1924. The Democratic candidate who defeated Barnett was Thomas B. Lantry, who was said to have enjoyed the confidence of the bar and who made a good record on the bench.

In 1920 Attorney James A. Scott missed the Republican nomination by a very narrow margin.[59] Since 1920 was a Republican year in Chicago, the chances are that Scott might have been elected had he won the nomination. In 1923 the colored leaders bargained with the city bosses for a position on the ticket of the Republican party for the Superior Court bench. Nominations for this court were in the hands of the county committee made up of the ward committeemen of the city and delegates from the outlying towns. The Negro committeeman from the Second Ward threatened to embarrass Congressman Madden in the following year if a Negro was not nominated.[60] Edward H. Morris was put on the ticket but he went down to defeat in the bi-partisan arrangements made in the fall election.

In the following year the efforts of nearly two decades were rewarded by the election of Albert B. George to the Municipal Court Bench. Born in Washington, D.C., educated in the public grammar and high schools of the nation's capital city, trained also in the Spencerian Business College, he came to Chicago in the nineties on the invitation of Dr. George C. Hall, one of the leading colored physicians in the city.[61] After graduating from the Northwestern University Law School in 1897, he engaged in general law practice and, according to the Chicago Bar Association, "In twenty-six years' practice, he built up a good reputation as a lawyer deserving the confidence of the Bar and of his clients." With reference to his fitness to serve on the bench, the Bar report said: "We consider him qualified."[62] In commenting on his nomination, Judge George said:

In 1924, Mr. Wright who had absolute control of the organization of the Second Ward had so ingratiated himself with the Republican party that he was able to ask them to nominate a colored person for judge. The Republican

[59] Like Barnett, he had had experience as an assistant state's attorney, and he had practiced law in Chicago for over thirty years. Ten judges were nominated in the Republican primary and he stood eleventh in the poll, only 1,941 votes behind the tenth man. The *Chicago Defender* for October 9, 1920, bewailed the fact that Scott had been defeated by the indifference of the colored voters who failed to mark their choices on the separate judicial ballot.

[60] *Chicago Tribune*, July 22, 1923.

[61] *Broad Ax*, December 27, 1902.   [62] Report of March 25, 1924, p. 8.

leaders asked that they have the opportunity to approve the man first. They didn't want to take a chance before they gave an O.K. on Mr. Wright's choice.

He looked around the field and it was with considerable reluctance that he chose me. He wanted someone who was connected with his organization. Someone whom he could reward for services. Now up to this I had never attended a ward or precinct meeting. I had never held any sort of political office in any political organization. But evidently the other names were not suitable and he finally had to compromise on me.[63]

At the time of the 1924 primary elections there was a Democratic mayor in the city hall and the Republican factions were not as embittered as they had been on other occasions. Ex-Governor Deneen was seeking the nomination as United States senator and he secured some mild support from the Thompson faction.[64] Second Ward Committeeman Wright informed George that he thought the nomination would go over. Out of fifty candidates that were running, with twelve to be nominated, George was ninth on the list. Not a great deal of attention was paid in the white newspapers to George's color since in the campaign photographs the color of his skin was not noticeable.[65] The fall election was a Republican landslide, with Coolidge heading the ticket. George was swept into office, although he was twelfth on the list and some 114,000 votes behind the leading man on the separate judicial ballot. Still he had 66,000 votes to spare over his nearest Democratic opponent. Even the Klan took no steps to prevent the seating of the first elected Negro judge.[66]

Would the combination of events which had produced the election of Judge George be duplicated in the near future? Colored citizens asked themselves this question anxiously. Would Judge George be an asset to the bench? Would he reflect credit

[63] Interview.

[64] C. H. Wooddy, op. cit., p. 20.

[65] "He is light in color, with straight hair parted on the side and slightly graying over the temples, a handsome head, eyes sparkling with intelligence, lips compressed in a determination to make the most of this great opportunity that has come to him and to his race." Chicago Tribune, November 7, 1924.

[66] In an interview, Judge George said: "One of the daily newspapers asked me if I had received any threats from the Ku Klux Klan. I assured them that the only way for the Klan or anyone else to get rid of me was to kill me as I intended to take my seat."

upon his race? At the end of his six-year term, the Bar Association report said: "He is prompt, industrious and diligent in the dispatch of his judicial duties. He is an able lawyer. He is fearless and positive in expressing himself."[67] The report went on to say that he was impatient. Some of the members of his own race felt that they got the brunt of this impatience. Judge George refused to become a politician and to forget that he was a judge. This made him unpopular with some of the Republican ward committeemen. At a public meeting he said that the ward committeeman would not think of asking him to do anything other than follow his judicial duties.[68] A precinct committeeman in the back of the room said: "If he is no good to the ward committeeman, what good is he to me?" In spite of Judge George's refusal to play politics, he was renominated in the primary of 1930 as the eleventh man on the list.[69] In the fall election, only three Republican judges survived the Democratic landslide. Out of twelve to be elected, Judge George's name stood twenty-fourth on the final election returns. The three Republican judges who were saved in this strong Democratic year had powerful newspaper and organization support. Judge George lacked these aids and he had to fight, in addition, the growing consciousness of some of the prejudiced white voters that a colored man was on the ticket.

In 1932 the colored citizens who desired a judge of their own race faced additional obstacles as well as the same difficulties that had thwarted them in 1930. There was a struggle for political power within the colored group itself. Congressman De-Priest and Alderman Anderson were fighting each other for the

[67] *Report of March 20, 1930,* p. 11.

[68] As one colored attorney expressed it: "George was a man of ability and knew the law, but he would not do a favor for anyone. He had it in mind when anyone came to him that they were coming to him as a colored judge. When he was in the Speeders Court, DePriest sent the ticket which a cop had sent to his son, Stanton. George paid the fine and sent the slip marked 'paid' back to DePriest. George was attempting to change the whole political system of Chicago."

[69] An examination of the precinct returns for the Second and Third wards shows that he was not cut by the colored voters in spite of his unpopularity. He ran slightly ahead of any other judicial candidate in these two wards. See official returns in Election Commissioners' Office.

nomination to Congress from the First District.[70] As a result, there were three colored candidates, including Judge George, who entered the Republican primaries seeking the nomination for judge. The *Chicago Tribune* printed the pictures of these candidates under the caption, "Colored Attorneys Run for City Court."[71] Out of twelve to be nominated, no one of the three came closer than twenty-first, and Judge George stood twenty-sixth in the Republican primary. Even if a colored candidate had been nominated on the Republican ticket, his chances of election in the fall would have been small as only two Republican judges managed to survive the great Democratic sweep of the November elections.[72]

For the time being the colored citizens of Chicago have lost a judgeship. In 1930 two colored judges were elected in New York City on the Democratic ticket, not from the city at large but from judicial districts. In Chicago the election of the judges from the entire city and the identification of the Negroes with the Republican party at a time when the Democrats control nearly all the local offices prevent the colored citizens from keeping up with the voters in Harlem.[73]

TRENDS

The racial candidates discussed so far have all come from the main Negro community and from the Republican party. Colored candidates have also run in the Republican primaries in other sections of the city. In the Maxwell Street district the names of four Negroes appeared on the 1932 primary ballot as candidates for such offices as state representative, delegate to the Republican National Convention, senatorial committeeman, and ward committeeman.[74] All but one of these candi-

[70] See below, p. 187.

[71] April 5, 1932. There was also a colored candidate on the Democratic ticket, but he ran thirty-second in the primary. His name was Richard Hill, Jr. This was the first time that any colored man ran for judge in a Democratic primary.

[72] A third Republican, Samuel Heller, was later seated by a recount.

[73] One of the colored legislators introduced a bill for the election of judges by districts but it did not pass. See *Defender*, April 18, 1931.

[74] For a description of the first election of a Negro as Republican ward committeeman see below, p. 157.

dates were on the relief rolls, and as the Negroes constituted only 19 per cent of the total population in the Twentieth Ward,[75] the candidates were all defeated. The Irish, Jewish, and Italian political leaders of this area used intimidation, violence, and fraud to further reduce the importance of the Negro voters.

Following the Democratic landslide of 1932 many colored voters were induced by offers of jobs and other favors to leave the Republican party. The increase in the number of colored Democratic voters in the aldermanic elections of 1933 led to a demand for Negro candidates on the Democratic ticket in 1934. By this time the colored voters of the Third Ward already had a Democratic committeeman of their own, Michael Sneed, who had won the position with organization support in 1932. In the Democratic primary of 1934 Bryant A. Hammond, colored, was nominated for the state Senate in the Third Senatorial District, and another Negro, Arthur W. Mitchell, almost defeated Baker, the white candidate for Congress in the First Congressional District. Following the primary Baker died and Mitchell was nominated in his place by the Democratic ward committeeman for the district. Starting with the support of the white Democrats controlled by the famous First Ward boss, "Hinky Dink" Kenna, in the north end of his district, Mitchell received a sufficiently large Negro vote to defeat the veteran, Oscar DePriest, in one of the major upsets of the congressional elections of 1934.[76]

The election of Mitchell as the first Negro Democratic congressman in the history of the United States was an event of greater national than local importance. As compared with DePriest, Mitchell was a novice in Chicago politics. At the time of DePriest's first election to Congress in 1928 this little-known lawyer from Washington, D.C., who had just come to Chicago, was Republican in politics. Four years later he shifted to the Democratic party and took an active part in the Democratic national campaign.[77] The Democratic Committeeman for the Second Ward, a white man, supported him for the congressional

---

[75] According to the 1921 ward lines.

[76] The final returns were: Mitchell, Democrat, 27,963; DePriest, Republican, 24,820.

[77] *Chicago Defender*, November 26, 1932.

nomination. Mitchell's candidacy was not taken seriously and his election viewed with amazement and alarm by many Negroes in Chicago.[78] However, in the national field the election was an outstanding event. Several spells had been broken. Northern Democrats had given national recognition to the place of the Negro in their party. The Democratic caucus in the House of Representatives was compelled to admit a Negro. The Republican party could no longer claim that it had the Negro vote in its vest pocket.

Have there been racial candidates for other offices? Would the colored voters prefer candidates of their own for elective positions in general? Why have no Negroes been elected to important administrative posts? Other minority racial elements have representatives in the highest offices of the city and the state, why have the Afro-Americans been deprived of this representation? In the eighties and nineties some colored men were elected as town clerks in South Town, one of the subdivisions of the city.[79] Since 1900 no Negro has been elected to an important administrative post. The "Black Belt" has not been given the important patronage positions on the organization slates that would go to another racial minority of the same size whose visibility was much less. The German-born groups soon lose their foreign-language habits and accent and are merged in the general body politic. The Negroes retain their badge of color. In addition, they have suffered in Chicago from some of the unfavorable publicity which has been associated with the Thompson régime. Their increased political power has awakened opposition among many of the whites. It would appear

[78] *Ibid.*, November 10, 1934. A letter to the editor which referred to a Mitchell interview which appeared in the *Chicago Daily News*, November 9, 1934, said among other things: "The trend of the Congressman's interview appears to represent a desire on his part to sanction the ideas that are so prevalent in America to blame us for being free, and for insisting upon our proper citizenship right.—We have no intention of apologizing for the fight we are making to retain it, and we object to our representatives presuming to do so. We need no apologists in Congress, and if that is going to be Congressman Mitchell's attitude as representative of 15,000,000 Negroes, the defeat of Congressman DePriest was a calamity."

[79] *Chicago Tribune*, April 4, 1882. See also Washington Intercollegiate Club of Chicago, *op. cit.*, I, 135.

that among the white voters there is a growing consciousness of the color of candidates for city offices and a tendency to draw race lines. With some voters race prejudice is stronger than the theories of democracy or the common political practices among minority groups.

The elevation of members of their group to elective office has an importance to colored citizens that is not appreciated by many whites. An alderman or a municipal judge or a congressman does not enjoy, by reason of the office he holds, a position of great prestige in a wealthy community made up largely of native whites of native parentage. In a minority racial group, particularly one which is conspicuous because of color, the opportunities in the business world are limited, and a municipal judge who receives a salary of ten thousand dollars a year, who sits in a position of power, and who is part of the machinery of justice, is in a position of honor and distinction in his community. With the election of a Negro judge every colored person in the country felt that he was benefited in some way, however slight. Likewise, a Negro congressman, who sits in the national capitol and who is the sole representative of an entire racial group in the federal legislative process, is in a position of great respect in the eyes of his racial kinsmen. The election of representatives of the group to lesser political offices has paved the way for the advances made to the capitol and to the bench. It is all part of the process of the emancipated group struggling for freedom in a larger field.

CHAPTER V

THE PARTS OF THE NEGRO
POLITICAL MACHINE

The unified action of the colored voters in Republican primaries and in elections where favorite white candidates or racial
candidates were involved depended upon careful organization
and planning. As in other minority communities within the
city, a strong political organization was needed to educate the
voters regarding issues and candidates and to induce them to
perform their duties as citizens upon election day. Such an organization must have a well-trained rank and file, persons who
are willing to perform the routine tasks so necessary in politics,
such as canvassing, opening their homes for small meetings,
addressing envelopes, distributing literature, making public
speeches, and looking after the technical details of the election
process. There must also be leaders who know how to run a
campaign, to arrange for meetings, to direct publicity, and to
meet the tactics of the opposition. In addition, the organization
must have access to means of mass impression. Somewhere it
must find crowds for its speakers and readers for its literature.
It is conceivable that the elements of a political organization
which have been mentioned so far could be supplied on practically a volunteer basis. The workers and leaders might be
fired with a zeal for their cause. Crowds assembled for other
than political purposes might be addressed by the organization
speakers and general newspapers might carry political news.
However, in the great metropolitan communities of the United
States it is a well-known fact that the political organizations do
not depend upon voluntary efforts. Money furnishes the backbone of American political organizations. Certain services, such
as printing, use of the mails, newspaper advertisements, use of
auditoriums and office space, telephone service, and radio broad-
castings, are not available without large expenditures of mon-

ey. Money can buy practically every other type of political
service needed. Speakers, clerical helpers, canvassers, professional publicity men, professional organizers, legal experts on
election affairs, can all be hired for a consideration. Where in
the Negro community were the elements of a political organization to be found? How many volunteer workers were at hand?
Where would the money come from to fill the campaign chests?

In order to find out how the Negro political machine was con-
structed in Chicago it is necessary to analyze the parts. What
relation did the party organization have to the churches, to the
Negro press, to the business and professional men, to the labor
organizations, to the fraternal organizations, to the military associations, and to the underworld? What volunteer services
could be expected from these agencies? Were some of these
services peculiar to Negro communities? It is also important to
consider how necessary it was for Negro candidates for elective
office to belong to some of these organizations.

THE NEGRO CHURCHES IN POLITICS

Since the Negro churches furnished the first opportunities for
freedom of action on the part of the Negro, they have played
and continue to play an important rôle in Negro society. The
continuation of certain artificial restraints upon the social, economic, and civic life of the Negro has tended to foster a reliance
upon racial religious institutions. In Chicago the growing race
consciousness and the steady migration have resulted in a
very rapid growth in the number and membership of Negro
churches.[1] According to a recent study, there were some 344
Negro churches in the city in 1930 with an aggregate membership (persons 13 years of age and over) of about 113,000.[2] On
the basis of these figures it would be fair to say that more than
half of colored voters in the city were church members and that

[1] According to the United States Census volumes, the number of colored clergymen
increased from 76 in 1910 to 388 in 1930.

[2] B. J. Mays and J. W. Nicholson, *The Negro's Church* (New York, 1933), p. 215.
See also R. L. Sutherland, *An Analysis of Negro Churches in Chicago* (Doctor's dissertation, University of Chicago, 1930).

about a fourth attended services regularly on Sunday.[3] The politician who could reach the church membership was in an excellent position to influence votes.

The Negro churches in Chicago, like those in other parts of the country, were far from being unified. They were split into various denominations and each sect was subdivided into individual churches, some of which were entirely independent. Nearly four-fifths of the Negro churches in Chicago were store-front or house-front churches whose congregations were small. On the other hand, there were eight churches which owned large and imposing edifices and whose membership exceeded three thousand each.[4] The 1926 *Census of Religious Bodies* shows that in Illinois the Baptists comprise some 60 per cent of the total Negro church membership, the African Methodist Episcopal Church some 14 per cent, the other Methodist bodies 14 per cent, and the remaining church members were scattered among Holiness sects, independent churches, and other denominations.[5] While the Baptist churches were only loosely joined together into a Baptist association, some of the largest churches in the city were of this denomination. On the other hand, the African Methodist Episcopal churches were united in an ecclesiastical hierarchy which had some control over its entire city membership. It is not surprising, then, that the Baptist and Methodist ministers were the most active in politics.

While some white ministers have taken a conspicuous part in Chicago party politics,[6] none of them have been more active than certain colored clergymen. Negro ministers have more reasons for going into politics than have white ministers. A large proportion of the Negro churches are in debt and the congregations are almost always poor. In Chicago the purchase or

[3] About 60 per cent of the Negroes 13 years of age and over were church members. About 42 per cent of the church members attend regularly in the 12 cities analyzed by Mays and Nicholson, *op. cit.*, p. 109.

[4] Sutherland, *op. cit.*, p. 47.

[5] Bureau of the Census, *Religious Bodies: 1926*, I, 734.

[6] Mayor Thompson spoke from the pulpit of the South Park Avenue Methodist Episcopal Church at the request of Rev. Brushingham. See John Bright, *Hizzoner Big Bill Thompson* (New York, 1930), pp. 65, 186.

the building of the church edifices to house the large member-
ships has called for extraordinary efforts on the part of the ministers. In a few cases the white politicians have come to the rescue of the Negro clergymen with large gifts or loans. The loans
have sometimes run as high as $50,000 for a single church.[7]
When these same white politicians are seeking support for their
favorite candidates it is natural that they should turn to the
ministers who have accepted aid at their hands. These ministers
can speak at regular political meetings, they can rally their congregations together on special occasions, and they can open
their pulpits to the particular candidates concerned.

It is not uncommon on a Sunday morning during a primary or
election campaign to see a number of white candidates on the
platform ready to present their claims for support at the polls
as soon as the regular service is over and before the congregation
is disbanded. The congregations do not ordinarily resent their
presence. Many of the listeners are hard-working people who
do not have the time or energy to attend the evening political
meetings during the week.[8] The church is an institution which
plays an important rôle in their social life and they look to it for
advice on political matters. The members feel that they have
gained recognition because the white candidates have come to
them.

The tie that binds some Negro ministers to white politicians
is not always a loan or a gift for a church building. Sometimes a
fee is charged for opening the pulpit on Sunday to candidates.[9]
Sometimes Negro ministers seek campaign funds outright in return for the delivery of a block of votes,[10] and at other times a
Negro minister may seek advancement within the church by

---

[7] Statement of minister concerned.   [8] Statements from church members.

[9] "There is a strong feeling against any congregation as a whole or the pastor in
charge permitting the edifice in which they worship being used as a meeting place by a
crowd of cheap politicians allied with one of the many political factions. . . . . To com-
pensate for the desecration of the holy edifice the church is given a certain sum of money,
and often, too often, the pastor has a little wad slipped to him personally to gain his influence and to keep his lips closed." *Defender*, November 22, 1924.

[10] "As the city of Chicago gets ready for its primary and election of public officials,
the political hustlers are getting their old gags polished and ready for action. . . . .
Nondescripts seek to palm themselves off as influential characters, and others, who draw

displaying his power and influence in the political world.[11] Many colored ministers sincerely believe that they are expected to do something about the social problems facing the group and therefore it is logical for them to take part in political life as a means of advancing the group. They realize that the game of politics has many sordid aspects and that their participation is fraught with danger, but they feel that they must face these risks.

The rôle of the Negro churches in politics has been criticized by many citizens living on the South Side. Not every colored minister permits candidates to address his congregation[12] and there have been occasions when the Negro clergymen as a group protested against political interference.[13] The *Chicago Defender* in its editorial columns has condemned the entire practice in the following words:

From time to time we have called attention to the conduct of ministers in using their churches for purposes other than those for which they were dedicated. . . . . The ministers excuse these things on the grounds that it is their duty to direct their congregations in matters political as well as spiritual. It is strange, however, that these abuses are confined almost entirely to ministers of our group. One scarcely, if ever, hears of a white church being used for such purposes.

There is no question as to the right of a minister to hold any political view that appeals to him, but it is a piece of consummate gall on the part of the minister in trying to force his members to become the camp followers of some particular political group. There is generally some sinister reason for this action. The white politicians know how susceptible some of our people are to the urgings of the pulpit. They know that many of us are prone to take the statements of our ministers on any point as gospel truth. The ministers are aware of this attitude on the part of the political powers and take advantage of it to turn a handy penny for themselves.[14]

If the church is so important in the political life of the colored citizens, does this mean that the successful Negro candidates for

---

no water, claim that they carry thousands of votes in their vest pockets. Strange as it seems, but stranger it is true, many of our ministers, play this confidence game with deftness and despatch. They take money from all candidates and all sides." *Whip*, March 3, 1928.

[11] *Broad Ax*, May 13, 27, 1916.   [12] *Defender*, March 7, 1931.

[13] Frances Williams McLemore, *The Rôle of the Negroes in Chicago in the Senatorial Election 1930.*

[14] March 27, 1920.

elective office must in general belong to some church? Of the elective office-holders whose religious affiliations were known, one-half were Methodists, two-fifths were Baptists, and only a few were known to be non-church members. Rev. Mr. A. J. Carey was presiding elder of the African Methodist Episcopal Church at the time that he was elected to the Illinois Constitutional Convention. Important ministers like the Rev. Mr. Fisher of Olivet Baptist Church aided in the first election of Oscar DePriest as alderman.[15] Congressman DePriest joined the Congregational Church shortly after his election to the House of Representatives and he is frequently invited to talk at Baptist and other churches. In the 1932 primary DePriest's opponent for congressional nomination, Alderman Anderson, was attacked because of the fact that he was a non-church member.[16]

The Negro churches furnish opportunities for the development of leadership within the group. Have these churches produced any outstanding political leaders? Bishop Carey exercised considerable power in Republican circles but he did not consider himself primarily as a political leader. He was too busy with church and educational work to devote time to political organization.[17] It was said that he never concerned himself with the details of precinct politics. While he made political speeches and occupied such positions as member of the board of motion-picture censors, librarian in the office of the corporation counsel, member of the Constitutional Convention, and member of the Civil Service Commission, none of these activities brought him great political power. The Civil Service Commission is a very important board but it has no direct appointing powers and it cannot prevent the practice of discrimination by department heads. Bishop Carey's position on this board brought him little besides trouble.[18] Even when he gained control of the Chicago

[15] M. M. Fisher, *The Master's Slave: Elijah John Fisher* (Philadelphia, 1922), p. 161.

[16] Report of political meeting, April 3, 1932.

[17] Editorial in the *Chicago Defender*, March 28, 1931.

[18] On November 1, 1929, Bishop Carey was indicted for conspiracy and bribery to get a position through the Civil Service Commission. See Records of the Clerk of the Criminal Court, Doc. 54626 and Doc. 54627. When Bishop Carey died the cause was abated, March 27, 1931.

district of his church his influence in civic affairs was not greatly
enhanced. The African Methodist Episcopal Church had lagged
far behind the Baptist churches in its rate of increase during the
period of migration.[19] Internal dissension within the church retarded its growth.[20] Bishop Carey was criticized because of his
political activities, his preoccupation with many affairs gave the
impression of aloofness from the common people, and his name
became associated with unfavorable publicity.[21] He was a man
of superior education, keen intellect, and great oratorical powers, but his energies were not concentrated upon politics. The
constructive achievements of his political career have been summarized by his friends as follows:

> Pioneers like Bishop Carey blazed the way to the polls for us, emphasized
> the importance of the ballot and preached to his people on the power of this
> constitutional guarantee. He awoke them to the sense of their duty and the
> importance of its performance. As one of his brilliant admirers concluded in
> a burst of oratory, "He made the church articulate in the affairs of state."[22]

Another minister who might have become a political leader
was relatively ineffective in politics for another set of reasons.
Rev. Mr. William S. Braddan was a courageous crusader against
vice and corruption in politics and he ran twice for the office of
county commissioner.[23] As a chaplain with the rank of major
in the Eighth Illinois Regiment he was well-known and respected for his military record. In the immediate neighborhood of his

---

[19] *Census of Religious Bodies, 1926*, pp. 166–70.

[20] In 1920 Dr. W. D. Cook withdrew from the A.M.E. denomination to form the
People's Church of Christ and Metropolitan Community Center, and in 1922 Dr. J. R.
Harvey withdrew to form another community church. See Sutherland, *op. cit.*, p. 69.

[21] For publicity in connection with the release of Dr. L. N. Bundy, self-confessed
election corruptionist, see *Chicago Tribune*, November 26, 1917. For publicity regarding
the indictment for conspiracy, see *Defender*, October 26, 1929; *Daily News*, October 24,
1929; and *Chicago Tribune*, March 10, 1931. For over twenty years the *Broad Ax* waged
a campaign against Bishop Carey. See issues of May 10, 1902, November 28, 1903, June
11, 1904, December 20, 1913, July 25, 1914, July 28, 1923.

[22] *Chicago Whip*, March 10, 1928.

[23] In an interview he said, "Vice here has many ramifications and reaches into high
places. It gets to the 'big shots.' Men such as lawyers, preachers and business men are
controlled by it. I fought them for thirty-two years and I'll fight them for thirty-two
years more." Regarding his candidacies, see *Daily News*, April 10, 1926, and April 5,
1930. He was elected alternate to Republican National Convention in 1932.

independent church, Berean Baptist, he was very influential on primary and election days. However, in the larger sphere of city politics he was associated with the Deneen faction of the Republican party which was not generally popular with the colored voters and failed to win many of the local offices which were of primary interest to the group. Like Bishop Carey, he was busy with his church work and he did not have the necessary time to devote to large-scale political organization. Extremely able as a pulpiteer, his style of oratory lost little of its effectiveness on the political platform.[24] However, an independent within the Baptist church, he preferred to act as an independent in politics. Of such material political machines are not ordinarily made.

The political activities of many other colored ministers show similar tendencies. While the colored church-goers are used to hearing political speeches, they do not ordinarily look to their ministers for the leadership which unites all the elements of a party organization. The political importance of the Negro clergy is not as great in Chicago today as it was in the South during the reconstruction period. However, the Negro churches are more important in politics than the Protestant churches in other sections of the city.

THE NEGRO PRESS

Because of the indifference of the white press to the real aims and interests of the Negro group, there have been established in the city of Chicago a number of Negro weekly newspapers which endeavor to build up the morale of the group and to correct impressions created by other agencies of mass opinion. Like the foreign-language newspapers,[25] the Negro weeklies have been useful to the politicians because they reach a special group of voters. These papers lack adequate financial backing because their circulations are frequently small and the important advertisers do not care to appeal to a market made up for the most part of persons in the lower economic levels. Consequent-

[24] It was said that he acquired something of the pungency of language that is generally supposed to be the result of army associations.

[25] R. E. Park, *The Immigrant Press and Its Control* gives some examples of the manipulation of the foreign-language press by the politicians.

ly, the colored weeklies are peculiarly susceptible to the advances made by the politicians and by business men who have an interest in controlling the government. According to Ayer's *Newspaper Annual* the Negro newspapers in Chicago have had a high mortality rate. Of the four weeklies which were in existence in 1905, only one, the *Chicago Defender*, survives today.[26] Of the seven which were listed in 1919, only two, the *Defender* and the *Bee*, have survived the vicissitudes of time.[27] Many more Negro papers which have been published at various times have not even been listed in the volumes compiled by Ayer & Sons.[28]

If it is difficult to make a complete list of these newspapers, it is clear that it is very hazardous to make any statements regarding their circulation and influence. According to its own figures, the *Defender*, "The World's Greatest Weekly," has the largest circulation and its estimates in recent years run from 100,000 to 200,000.[29] The greater part of this circulation is outside of Chicago and competent observers have estimated that the city circulation of the paper is from 15,000 to 35,000. Its nearest rival in the last ten years was the *Chicago Whip*, which estimated its circulation at about 16,500, a figure large in view of the fact that the paper ceased publication in 1932. While small in circulation, the *Broad Ax* carried considerable political news during the thirty-two years of its existence.

Since the *Defender* is the largest and the most firmly established of the race papers, its rôle in Chicago politics will be considered first.[30] Although it was founded by its present pro-

---

[26] The *Conservator*, founded in 1878, was not listed after 1912. The *Appeal*, established in 1885, was not listed after 1925. The *Broad Ax*, established in 1895, was not listed after 1921 and it stopped publication in 1927, and the *Illinois Idea*, established in 1903, was not listed after 1922.

[27] In addition to those mentioned in the preceding footnote, the *Whip*, established in 1919, ceased publication in 1932. The *Enterprise*, founded in 1919, changed its name to the *Chicago World* in 1926, a paper which is not listed in *Ayer's*.

[28] The *Searchlight* is mentioned in the *Negro in Chicago* p. 557. Copies of the *Chicago Review* and of the *Chicago World* have been examined by the writer.

[29] N. W. Ayer & Sons, *Directory of Newspapers and Periodicals, 1933*, p. 209, gives the figure 110,000. The higher figure was given by *Los Angeles Express*, biographical sketch, April, 1920, in the files of the *Chicago Daily News*.

[30] The following paragraphs are based upon first-hand observation of the files of the *Defender* since 1914.

prietor, Robert S. Abbott, in 1905 on twenty-five cents, a lead pencil, a scratch pad, and training acquired at Hampton Institute, it was not listed by Ayer until 1919. The World War, with the subsequent demands for news about the colored troops, and the northward migration, with the market for news about Chicago, were two factors which greatly aided in building up the paper. Besides, Editor Abbott had a model near at hand which demonstrated how journalism could be made a success from a business standpoint. The *Chicago Tribune* was criticized by Abbott for discriminating against Negroes, but its features, its treatment of the news, and its makeup did not escape his attention. During a primary or an election campaign, the political advertisements and the political news items that appear in the *Defender* are conspicuous. Local and judicial candidates run their pictures with brief comments and sometimes a city-wide candidate will purchase an entire page.

The news items and the editorials are the main contributions which the Negro press has to make to the political organizations. What have been the political policies of the *Defender?* Acting on the rule that bad publicity is better than none, some candidates are not mentioned at all. Other candidates who have no friends on the editorial staff can only secure space in the advertising columns. Still other candidates are praised or denounced in news items, special signed articles, or editorials. Generally speaking, the Mayor Thompson faction of the Republican party and the Negro organization leaders associated with this faction have been supported by the columns of the *Defender*.[31] The paper classes itself as independent in politics and, like other journals of this type, it tries to reflect the feelings of its readers and to avoid offending any large block of them. While its ever present bias is one of race, it did not advocate the election of a Negro congressman until after Madden died. Congressman Madden was an important member of the Republican organization and in times past he had been a friend of Editor Abbott.[32]

[31] Mayor Thompson was defended in the following issues: April 15, 1916; April 13, 1918; April 5, 1919; February 5, 1927; April 11, 1931; and many other issues.

[32] *Defender*, May 31, 1930.

During the period from 1925 to 1934, when N. K. McGill, Abbott's brother-in-law, was the business manager of the paper, its policies appeared to be more dependent upon certain personal considerations. As assistant state's attorney, McGill supported the renomination of Crowe, and when his superior was defeated in the primary he was luke-warm toward the election of Swanson. In the 1932 primary McGill, as an assistant attorney-general under Carlstrom, took an active part in the campaign of his superior for the Republican nomination for governor as against ex-Governor Small, who had Thompson's support. On both occasions the paper espoused a losing cause.[33]

Sometimes when rival factions within the Negro group are contending for power, the *Defender* has taken sides. This was the case in 1932 when both DePriest and Anderson sought the Republican nomination for Congress in the First District. While the claims of both candidates were presented in special signed articles, the leanings of the paper toward Anderson were unmistakable. The articles regarding Anderson appeared first, an editorial for Anderson was run, and the paper permitted its columns to be used to perpetrate a campaign trick. Alderman Anderson was running for the office of Second Ward committeeman as well as for Congress. From a political standpoint, the two offices were closely linked together. His opponent for the ward post was William E. King, a member of the DePriest organization. Anderson put up a man by the name of William H. King for ward committeeman and then withdrew him on the eve of the primary. The *Defender* headline read: "King Concedes Ward Office to Alderman Louis B. Anderson."[34] The unsuspecting reader might not know that William E. King and William H. King were two different persons. The trick failed, as Anderson went down to an overwhelming defeat. This would tend to indicate that the political views of the paper were discounted by its readers.

As a matter of historical interest the party policies of the *Whip* might be considered briefly. Founded in 1919 as a militant race paper, the *Whip* for several years did not hesitate to

---

[33] McGill is no longer the manager of the *Defender*.   [34] Issue of April 9, 1932.

criticize the Mayor Thompson administration and the Negro leaders connected with it for shortcomings along various lines. About 1925 it reversed its critical attitude toward the organization politicians and began to praise them. Mayor Thompson was attacked on September 11, 1920, but on January 17, 1925, his re-entry into the political affairs of the city was welcomed. Oscar DePriest was praised in the issue of April 14, 1923, called "Devil DePriest" in the issue of January 29, 1927,[35] and his past record of achievement was lauded in the issue of April 7, 1928. These reversals of position probably detracted from the weight of the opinions given and the paper was not regarded as a factor of prime political importance. In addition, the impression was current that the *Whip* supported the candidates and measures which were favored by the Insull utility interests.[36]

What has been the relationship between Negro journalism and candidacy for public office? Of the successful candidates who were journalists at some time or other, Alderman Anderson and State Representative Sheadrick B. Turner stand out. Anderson regarded the law as his main profession, but he had done some work in journalism. When a young man in Washington, D.C., Anderson had been commissioned by Mr. Dew of the *New York World* to interview Frederick Douglass regarding the pending Lodge force bill which was designed to carry out the Fourteenth Amendment. This gave him a start in newspaper work as a reporter, a calling which he followed in New York and Philadelphia before he came to Chicago as a publicity man in connection with the World's Fair of 1893. In Chicago he studied law and was admitted to the bar in 1897, but from time to time

[35] "Oscar DePriest who brought disgrace on himself when he was indicted on graft charges a few years ago and who was saved from a term in jail only after his friends and supporters had worked desperately day and night in his behalf, is attempting to reinstate himself in the good graces of the people. He is now frantically clutching onto the coat tails of ex-Mayor Thompson in the hope that he may ride into political prominence on the wave of Mr. Thompson's popularity among the black people of Chicago."

[36] See issues of March 21, April 11, May 16, and June 13, 1931, for advertisements of the Elevated Lines, the People's Gas Light and Coke Company, and the Commonwealth Edison Company.

he helped Editor Abbott of the *Defender*.[37] Representative
Turner was the editor of the *Illinois Idea*, a paper which classed
itself as Republican and which claimed a circulation of some
2,800 at the time of his election to the state legislature in 1914.[38]
This paper was founded in 1905 and no record of it appears after
1922, although Turner was elected to the legislature twice after
this date. Turner was also known as a lawyer and bondsman,
and his paper was not a decisive factor in his political career.
There were several other journalists who were candidates for
elective office but they did not meet with success at the polls.[39]

While only a few of the Negro journalists ran successfully for
elective offices, many of them found their way into appointive
positions. Thus, the editor of the *Whip* was appointed as a
member of the Library Board, the former manager of the *Defender* held several appointive legal positions, the publisher of
the *Appeal* was appointed as a United States Customs inspector,
and the editor of the *Conservator* was an assistant state's attorney. It is evident that the white politicians prized the good-
will of the Negro newspaper men.

The Negro press did not play the same rôle in politics in the
Negro community that the metropolitan dailies did in the larger
community. Financially, the Negro newspapers were too weak
to take strong and independent positions. Appearing only once
a week, they could not keep hammering away at certain objectives as the dailies could, and they frequently could not strike

---

[37] *Defender*, May 31, 1930.

[38] Ayer, *op. cit.*, 1913, p. 177. An account of Turner's journalistic career in Springfield, Illinois, may be found in I. G. Penn, *The Afro-American Press and Its Editors*
(Springfield, 1891), p. 256.

[39] F. L. Barnett, the lawyer who came so near to being elected a judge of the municipal court in 1906, was the editor of the *Conservator*, a paper which set its circulation at
1,000 in 1903. See Ayer, *op. cit.*, 1903, p. 146. Joseph Bibb, the editor of the *Whip*, was
an unsuccessful candidate for state representative from the Fifth District in 1932 primary. Roscoe Conkling Simmons, who was known as a public speaker as well as a
journalist, ran unsuccessfully against DePriest for the congressional nomination in the
Republican primary of 1930. J. Tipper, the editor of the *Enterprise*, and later of the
Chicago World, failed to win the nomination for state representative from the Third District in 1930 and ran a poor fourth in the race for Republican committeeman of the Second Ward in 1932.

until it was too late. Only in the case of Abbott did journalism appear to be a main and all-consuming occupation. The editors of the other journals that came and went were usually lawyers or business men as well as journalists. The inhabitants of the South Side looked to the weeklies for news and gossip of the Negro world but they did not rely heavily upon them for political guidance. Nevertheless, in an exciting campaign they are part of the machinery of the Negro political organization and they were relatively more important than local community papers in other parts of the city.

ECONOMIC AND PROFESSIONAL GROUPS

The close relationship between business and politics in American cities has been commented upon in many places. While the masters of industry and finance do not as a rule run openly for elective offices, they exercise great influence upon the course of municipal affairs. In Chicago the dethroned monarch of the utility industries, Samuel Insull, was able to pull wires that were attached to important personages in both of the major political parties. When the local governments in the Chicago region fell into straitened financial conditions following the depression which started in 1929, the leading bankers of the city practically dictated the municipal budget policies. Through such devices as campaign contributions, inside tips to favored politicians, and the withholding of credit facilities, the industrial and financial magnates have kept a firm hold on the party organizations. This hold has been strengthened by the political activities of lawyers and publicity men whose allegiance to the community at large is sometimes subordinated to their loyalty to their business employers.

In the Negro community there were no great industrial and financial leaders who were concerned with exercising influence upon local politics. There were no utility companies, no great contracting concerns, and no banks in the financial center of the city that were run by Negroes. Relatively speaking, the Negro group was weak in economic power.[40]

[40] It is very difficult to estimate the relative economic position of the Negroes in Chicago. In 1930 only 0.28 per cent of the homes paying a monthly rental of $200 or

Two Negro banking institutions arose on the South Side during the early twenties but neither of them could withstand the
depression which began in 1929. The first of these banks was
established by Jesse Binga, who in his early days was successively a barber, a Pullman porter, a huckster, and a real estate
agent.[41] In 1908 Binga established a private bank in connection
with his real estate business, and in 1920 he obtained a state
charter for the Binga State Bank. His bank closed its doors in
1930 and Binga, a broken old man, was tried and convicted of
embezzlement. At the height of his power Binga never cared to
mix in politics and his contributions were to private charities
rather than to political campaign chests.[42] The other Negro
bank was the Douglass National Bank which was chartered in
1923. Its president, Anthony Overton, made a fortune in the
manufacture of cosmetics in Kansas and brought his business to
the city in 1911. Shortly after the bank was established he
launched the Victory Life Insurance Company, which was the
first colored company to do insurance business under the rigid
requirements of the state of New York. The bank and the insurance company both failed in 1932 but the Overton Hygienic
Company is still in operation. Like Binga, Overton had neither
the time nor the resources, nor the inclination to mingle in
politics.[43]

The political indifference of the Negro bankers did not mean
that all Negro business men kept aloof from politics. Negro
real estate operators, undertakers, and insurance officials have

more were Negro homes. In other words, although 85 out of every 1,000 rented homes
were Negro, only about 3 out of every 1,000 rented homes of the most expensive variety
were Negro. *Census Data of Chicago, 1930*, p. xv.

[41] On Binga's career, see *Broad Ax*, December 25, 1909; *Daily News*, December 14,
1916, and July 12, 1932.

[42] In an interview reported in the *Chicago Tribune*, May 8, 1927, he said with reference to politics: "The double crossing, the knife in the back one day and the handshake
the next—I never took to that. I vote but I don't know today what ward I live in. I am
no politician, but a recent political event made me very happy. I mean the way our
group held itself in when attempts were made in the mayoralty campaign to inflame
them."

[43] On Overton, see *Chicago Tribune*, November 11, 1922; *Daily News*, June 4, 1927.

from time to time taken an active part in political affairs.[44] Congressman DePriest's real estate business, in which he has been engaged since 1906, has furnished him with contacts and with the financial resources with which to stay in politics. State Representative Kersey and Ward Committeeman Dan Jackson ran two of the leading undertaking establishments which catered to Negro trade.[45] H. H. Pace, an insurance official, was named executive vice-chairman of the advisory commission to Secretary of Commerce Roper.[46]

Of the professional groups in the city at large, the lawyers have been the most active in politics, both individually and as a group. Because of the objections of white lawyers to their participation in the Chicago Bar Association, the Negro lawyers, under the leadership of men like Edward H. Wright, formed an association of their own in 1915 called the Cook County Bar Association. This association has ranged from 50 to 150 members, and it takes an active part in judicial elections. Its members appear in churches in order to urge the voters to support the candidates which it has endorsed, and large numbers of marked ballots are distributed.[47] As an organization it is independent in politics but its members are found in important positions in every one of the political factions. Of twenty-nine Negroes who were successful candidates for elective office, fourteen were lawyers by profession. Since 1914 the proportion of law-

[44] According to the *Fifteenth Census: Occupation Statistics, 1930*, IV, Table 12 for Illinois, the number and percentage of Negroes in these occupations in Chicago were as follows:

OCCUPATION	TOTAL	NEGRO	
		Number	Per Cent
Real estate agents..................	11,253	270	2.4
Undertakers.......................	981	116	11.8
Insurance agents and officials.......	10,867	535	4.9

[45] Colored undertakers were among the first colored business men because white undertakers commonly refused to handle colored business.

[46] *Defender*, September 16, 1933.

[47] *Ibid.*, May 31, 1930.

yers elected has been higher than before that date.[48] The younger lawyers who have won elective offices have invariably held
appointive legal positions before they became candidates. Their
initial training in political office came as assistant county attorneys, assistant corporation counsels, assistant state's attorneys,
or as employees of the Secretary of State. The typical course of
advancement of an able young colored lawyer is shown in the
case of William E. King, who was successively assistant corporation counsel, assistant state's attorney, state representative,
ward committeeman, and state senator.[49] Senator King has
been unusually successful because of his facility at personal contacts, his fine stage presence, and his excellent reputation. Other colored lawyers, like Representative Gaines or Alderman
Dawson, have had similar careers.

The other colored economic and professional groups have not
attempted to exert direct influence in politics. However, the
associations organized for Negro physicians, dentists, druggists,
and engineers have increased the social contacts of the professional men involved. A doctor with a large clientèle, who is active in his association and who can influence the views of some
of his colleagues, is a factor in politics.[50] Dr. Alexander Lane
was appointed assistant county physician in 1905, and in the
following year he was elected to the state legislature. One of
the most prominent colored physicians, Dr. George Cleveland
Hall, was an unsuccessful candidate for the county board in
1914, and in 1925 he was appointed a member of the Chicago
Library Board.[51] In the following year he was made a member

---

[48] Nine out of the 15 elective office-holders were lawyers. Some of the young Negro
lawyers find politics a profitable source of income. According to the thirteenth and
fifteenth censuses, the number of Negro lawyers in Chicago increased from 44 in 1910 to
170 in 1930.

[49] His election as state senator is being contested by Bryant A. Hammond at the
time of this writing.

[50] According to the *Fifteenth Census, loc. cit.*, there were 264 Negro physicians and
surgeons in Chicago in 1930.

[51] Dr. Hall was also a member of Governor Lowden's Commission on Race Relations.
For further details see *Daily News*, October 3, 1914, June 18, 1930; *Defender*, June 21,
1930 (obituary).

of the Municipal Voters' League, a civic organization which reports upon the qualifications of candidates for the city council.[52]
In the labor world the Negroes in Chicago are largely unorganized.[53] There were some members of the Pullman Porters' Union, a few Negroes belong to the mixed unions of the American Federation of Labor, and some are independent unionists, but the aggregate number of labor-union members is small and there are no outstanding Negro labor leaders in the city who can make a bid for political power.[54]

In the Negro community the political power exercised by Negroes was not ordinarily derived directly from economic power. Most of the funds for financing the political organizations in the Second and Third wards came from the white leaders, and the colored leaders who failed to recognize this sooner or later came into difficulties. In the early days some of the Negro leaders came from the lower economic levels; two of the early state legislators were waiters before they became active in politics. As the Negro community grew in size and in wealth after 1914 the political leaders came more largely from the rising business and professional classes.

FRATERNAL, MILITARY, AND RACIAL ORGANIZATIONS

A large proportion of the colored men of means belong to one or more fraternal organizations. In Chicago the membership in these organizations has been large and the interest strong until recently, when financial difficulties came upon many of them.

[52] *Whip*, January 2, 1926.

[53] The great bulk of the 85,046 Negro men who were gainfully employed in 1930 were unskilled laborers, porters, and semi-skilled operatives. Almost 29 per cent were in domestic and personal service. The Negroes were not numerous in the trades which are highly organized. Thus, only some 5,000 were employed as carpenters, iron molders, mechanics, painters, and tailors. *Fifteenth Census, loc. cit.*

[54] For a discussion of the Negro postal workers organizations, see below, p. 313. The Chicago Commission on Race Relations, *op. cit.*, pp. 411–12, collected some figures on Negro membership in Chicago local trade unions. They found that out of the total of 294,437 trade-union members in the city at that time, 12,106 were Negro. They pointed out that the proportion of Negro union members to the Negro population in Chicago was almost exactly the same as the proportion of white members to white population in Chicago. Since a larger proportion of Negroes were gainfully employed, this meant that the Negroes were relatively less organized.

One of the masonic chapters is nearly sixty years old.[55] The group solidarity of these organizations has been of importance in politics. White and colored candidates sometimes appear before the members of the lodges during primary and election campaigns.

According to the available information, it appears that the Negroes who have been elected to public office are almost invariably members of one or more of these societies. The Elks, the Odd Fellows, the Masons, the Knights of Pythias, and the Foresters are the orders which the successful candidates most commonly list in their biographies. Some of the colored politicians have been high officials in the friendly societies. County Commissioner John Jones founded one of the masonic lodges, State Representative Morris was the Grand Master of the Grand United Order of Odd Fellows, State Representative Kersey was Grand Chancellor of the Knights of Pythias, State Representative Lucas was the State Grand Secretary of the United Brotherhood of Friendship, and Alderman Jackson was a Major General in the Uniform Rank of the Knights of Pythias. Alderman Jackson was especially noted for his activity in the fraternal orders. He belonged to practically all of the secret societies and he was also the president of the Appomattox Club, an exclusive social organization founded by County Commissioner E. H. Wright in 1900.[56] The fraternal and social organizations sometimes had affiliated or auxiliary women's societies which were of some political importance after the coming of woman suffrage.

Closely connected with the fraternal groups were colored military organizations. Those in active service and those who belonged to one of the veterans' associations were looked upon as leaders in the community. While sporadic attempts were made in the seventies to organize colored troops as part of the Illinois militia, it was not until 1895 that the Ninth Battalion, a Negro military unit which was started in 1890, was definitely recognized by the state. One of the first majors of the battalion was State Representative John C. Buckner, who held the position

[55] *Chicago Bee*, October 19, 1930. [56] *Whip*, May 10, 1929.

until he got into difficulties with Governor Tanner in 1897. His position was taken by Captain John R. Marshall, who was promoted to a colonelcy in 1898 to take command of the Eighth Regiment of Illinois Volunteers during the Spanish-American War. In 1900 the regiment was reorganized as the Eighth Illinois Infantry, with Colonel Marshall as the commanding officer. Colonel Marshall was nominated by the Republican County Convention for the county board in 1902 but he lost in the election by a narrow margin. His influence in political affairs was recognized by the many appointive positions which he has held. At different times he occupied such posts as deputy collector, deputy sheriff, deputy in the county clerk's office, deputy state game warden, and state parole officer.[57]

Upon Colonel Marshall's retirement from active military duty in 1915, his place was taken by Colonel Franklin A. Dennison, who led the regiment in the Mexican expedition of 1916 and also in France during the World War. In the governmental service Colonel Dennison held such important positions as assistant city prosecutor, assistant corporation counsel, and assistant attorney-general. As a candidate on different occasions for such offices as county commissioner, municipal judge, and delegate to the Illinois constitutional convention, he did not achieve success, but the Republican party honored him at several national conventions.[58] Among the other officers of the Eighth Regiment, who were also active in politics, the names of Colonel William Warfield, Adjutant Bish, Major Robert R. Jackson, and Major William S. Braddan stand out.[59] The frequent intertwining of civil and military careers was part of the development of Negro political leadership.

In all parts of the city the American Legion has been an important factor in politics since the World War. In 1919 the George Giles post was organized by Negro veterans under Colo-

[57] Interviews. See also *Chicago Defender*, November 5, 12, and 19, 1932.

[58] *Chicago Defender*, April 15, 1916; *Chicago Daily News*, October 31, 1914; January 11, 1916; September 9, 1916; April 15, 1932.

[59] Bish was elected to the state legislature in 1892. On Major Jackson, see pp. 67–68, above. Major Braddan was the chaplain. For his rôle as a minister, see pp. 99–100, above.

nel Dennison as commander. In the following year Attorney Earl B. Dickerson became the commander. The post has had several other commanders and it has fluctuated in membership from under 100 to 250 members during the past ten years.[60] Among the members who have been active in politics are State Representatives Blackwell, Warfield, and Jenkins, Assistant Attorney-General Dickerson, and Alderman Dawson. In his campaign speeches Dawson frequently referred to his experiences in the army, and his "buddies" helped him in the aldermanic contest of 1933.[61]

The racial and interracial organizations have not as a rule been directly concerned with politics. The local branch of the National Association for the Advancement of Colored People (N.A.A.C.P.) is a "pressure group" which seeks to protect racial interests. Its principal efforts have been in the direction of securing justice in the courts and preventing discrimination in public accommodations. The Urban League is an interracial organization which has served as a clearing house for information and co-operation regarding the social and economic problems of race relations. It has also served as a research organization and as an employment agency for Negroes. On the other hand, the Universal Negro Improvement Association (U.N.I.A.), also called the Garvey movement after its founder Marcus Garvey, a West Indian Negro, has from time to time taken an active part in politics. In Chicago, this movement, with its "Back to Africa" slogans and its appeals to race pride, was able to turn over a considerable number of votes to certain Negro candidates.[62]

[60] *Chicago Defender*, March 1 and 8, 1930.

[61] Report of political meetings of February 20, 1931, and April 1, 1932.

[62] In the 1924 primary in the First Congressional District the movement was active for the Negro candidate, who later said: "But the U.N.I.A. did help me. One of their leaders heard me speak. He was impressed with what I had to say and so he made it possible for me to speak before them. They liked my talk and they voted to support me. Some people say that I bought them off. But I didn't give them a cent and they didn't ask for a cent either. They worked like Trojans for me. They were bold and fearless. They were a material factor in my campaign. I don't know how many were in the organization but it was very powerful and I got every one of their votes. Five thousand is a very conservative estimate of their strength."

The parts of the Negro political organization which have been so far discussed appear to be somewhat disjointed. However, there is a central thread of race consciousness which holds them all together. In comparison with other ethnic groups the Negroes may lack wealth and social prestige, but in politics they make up for these deficiencies by utilizing to the full their own community life. The churches, the press, and the economic and social groups of the Negro community have a stronger hold upon the rank and file than corresponding institutions have in other local communities. Some of the Negro political leaders may neglect a few of the community groupings, but the most successful try to win over as many as possible. The Negro leader who offends the churches, the local press, the lodges, or the veterans may find himself in difficulties. As the Negro community has expanded the political leaders have been drawn more and more from the growing group of lawyers and business men who took an active part in the religious and social life of the group.

CHAPTER VI
THE UNDERWORLD AND POLITICS

In a city like Chicago, where the wet sentiment predominates and where there are many persons with liberal views on prostitution, gambling, and other human failings, the existence of a powerful underworld, with its alliances with business men and politicians, can be taken for granted. The combination of agencies which is able to give immunity from the law because of its political power is sometimes called the "Big Fix."[1] Under several administrations bootleggers, racketeers, gambling-house keepers, panders, thieves, and other hoodlums have enjoyed extraordinary immunities from interference on the part of the law-enforcing agencies. The gangsters and other criminals realize that this freedom from restraint depends upon how useful they can make themselves to the politicians. When asked to make campaign contributions or to produce results upon election day, the leaders of the underworld cannot very well refuse. When word is passed down from the gangster chiefs, all the beer runners, the proprietors of speakeasies, the book-makers, the burglars, the pickpockets, the pimps, the prostitutes, the fences, and their like are whipped into line. In themselves they constitute a large block of voters and they can augment their power at times by corrupt election practices. Personators, repeaters, chain voters, and crooked election boards are recruited from the ranks of organized crime.[2] In the badlands of the city those engaged in border-line activities often control the election of important public officials. One of the notorious Al Capone's lieutenants was elected as ward committeeman and state senator. At political meetings, in the City Hall, in the State Capitol, and at party conventions, this representative of the gangster world might be seen with his faithful bodyguard.

[1] C. E. Merriam, *Chicago* (New York, 1929), p. 26.

[2] J. Landesco, "Organized Crime in Chicago, " Part III of the *Illinois Crime Survey* (Chicago, 1929), pp. 837 ff.

Into this atmosphere of lawlessness, grafting, and easy-gained riches have been introduced in a short period of time tens of thousands of colored migrants. While the criminal statistics for the city of Chicago show that the Negroes furnish more than their share of the total number of persons accused and convicted of crime, it cannot be said that the Negro community is among the worst crime centers of the city. There are no organized gangs of Negro criminals who prey upon the public in all parts of the city. In the districts inhabited largely by colored citizens there are petty thieves, stick-up men, pimps, street-walkers, window-tappers, crap-shooters, lottery policy operators, small-scale bootleggers, and persons who have been accused by the police of disorderly conduct, but the official figures regarding the numbers of these law violators are misleading for several reasons.[3] Negro criminals are conspicuous because of their color, they are more liable to arrest than whites because many of their activities are on the street, and when arrested they are less able to protect themselves because they are frequently unable to hire lawyers. Considering the rapid growth of the Negro community, the social disorganization in some of the areas where the Negroes are forced to live, the lurid example furnished by the white criminals, and the severe struggle for existence in an unfavorable environment, the wonder is that there are not more law-breakers among Negroes.

In fact, it is in such areas as are open to Negroes that the white underworld leaders frequently locate their activities. Here they are more secure from molestation since the Negroes cannot protect themselves as well as some other groups.

BOOTLEGGING

All of the wet and dry referenda held in the city of Chicago have shown the territory inhabited largely by Negroes to be dripping wet. In 1930 the voters of the Second Ward were 10 per cent wetter on the question, "Should the Illinois Prohibition Act be Repealed?" than the voters of the rest of the city.[4] In the

[3] Chicago Commission on Race Relations, *The Negro in Chicago*, pp. 328 ff.

[4] Percentage of vote in favor of measure to total vote on measure, in city 80 per cent, in Second Ward 90 per cent. Only the depreciated areas of the First Ward, inhabited

days before the Eighteenth Amendment was passed the business streets used by the colored population were lined with saloons.[5] One view of the situation during the prohibition era is given below:

> Bootlegging once was the important South Side racket and held sway until the bottom dropped out of the price, which followed the expansion of the industry. Shortly after prohibition went into effect a few far visioned Southsiders, perhaps at the suggestion of neighbors from the West Side, jumped into the bootlegging business wholeheartedly. That was when you had to walk long and carefully to find a speakeasy and then you had difficulty getting a drink, because the houseman required positive identification.

> But as more people learn the science of boozemaking, regardless of how mediocre the knowledge, the racket as a financial venture becomes less significant. Those who had made money in the better days branched out into other fields.[6]

According to another view the trade in illicit liquor became a greater source of wealth for law-breaking Negroes than gambling.[7] On the South Side Negroes were close competitors with the Italians for the control of the bootlegging industry. Many colored venders of alcoholic beverages had select lists of white clients and some boasted monthly sales of several hundred gallons to drug stores. A map showing the distribution of the federal padlock cases for 1929 and the first half of 1930 indicates that the Negro community had its full share of cases.[8] Negroes were also in demand as runners for Italian bootleggers. From time to time colored men were seized in connection with raids on Capone breweries.[9] While exact figures are difficult to obtain, it is clear that the Negro bootleggers were an important element in the colored electorate both from the standpoint of numbers and

---

by homeless men and underworld characters, were as wet. In Morgan Park, where the Negroes were only one-third of the population, the voters were drier than in the city as a whole.

[5] *The Negro in Chicago*, map facing p. 346.   [6] *Defender*, September 24, 1932.

[7] Negro physician cited by C. Binder, *Chicago and the New Negro* (Chicago, 1927), p. 15.

[8] W. C. Reckless, *Vice in Chicago* (Chicago, 1933), p. 202. The area of greatest concentration is the central business section of the city. In 1929 the rate in census community 35 was second highest rate in the city outside the central business area.

[9] *Whip*, April 18, 1931.

wealth. That the party organizations could not ignore the bootleggers is shown by the following record of a conversation at a
party headquarters which hits variations of a theme that was
common during the dry era.

> *Precinct worker:* I ain't in this thing for no job. Why I can count the jobs
> I have held in my life on this one hand. Work was made for fools and slaves.
> I got along before I joined up with this crew and I can get along afterwards.
> I ain't never seen inside of the Bridewell and I have that first time yet to pay
> a fine.
>
> *District leader:* What kind of business are you in?
>
> *Precinct worker:* It's legit'.
>
> *District leader:* Whaddye mean your business is legitimate? I've heard
> differently. If it is what do you want? You must want something or you
> wouldn't work so damn hard.
>
> *Precinct worker:* I said legit'. I've got the cops with me. All I do is sell
> moonshine.
>
> *District leader:* Sell moonshine, why .... haven't you ever heard
> of the law?
>
> *Precinct worker:* You'r' so .... smart that you oughtta be a lawyer. I
> don't rob nobody. I don't make the stuff. All I do is sell it. I got cops coming
> into my saloon all the time. 'Course I suppose you could get to me. That's
> why I come in here.[10]

After the repeal of the Eighteenth Amendment, the Negro
Community was again lined with "taverns," as the saloons were
euphemistically called, and many of the bootleggers became
liquor dealers. The license requirements and the closing laws
kept the liquor business in politics.

VICE

The manager of a colored weekly once said that "vice on the
South Side is 75 per cent human and 25 per cent black. The fact
of color makes the offense more conspicuous." The Negroes
who migrated to Chicago from the South during the last twenty
years cannot be held responsible for prostitution in the areas
where they settled. In the districts where color was not a bar to
their penetration and where rents were low enough to suit many
of their incomes, vice was already prevalent.[11] The so-called

---

[10] Manuscript document, March 1, 1933.

[11] The Chicago Vice Commission report, *The Social Evil in Chicago* (Chicago, 1911),
p. 37; *The Negro in Chicago* (Chicago, 1922), p. 341; E. F. Frazier, *The Negro Family
in Chicago*, pp. 194 ff.; W. C. Reckless, *op. cit.* (Chicago, 1933), p. 25.

transitional or blighted areas nearest the business center of the city where many of the migrants first settled contained the old "red-light" district, which was closed in 1912. As the Negro community expanded outward there was a tendency for the vice areas to expand with it. The reports of the Committee of Fifteen, the records of the law-enforcing agencies, and other sources which are confidential all show the attempts of the vicious elements to invade the regions newly inhabited by colored people. This situation has been commented on by the *Bee* as follows: "Everywhere the self-respecting colored citizens, singly or in groups, have fled to new neighborhoods free of vice as a haven for their children and families. Fast on their heels vice has followed in their wake, a menace to society at large and colored groups in particular."[12]

According to the analysis of the available statistics made by Reckless there has been a considerable growth of Negro prostitution since 1910, when it was almost negligible.[13] In recent years a disproportionate number of the vice resorts that have been investigated have been colored houses of prostitution. Of the women in the Morals Court reported on as to color, about 6,000 or 70 per cent were colored women in 1930.[14] The rapidity of the migration, the attendant maladjustments in the new environment, the demoralization and lack of privacy found in some of the poorest neighborhoods, the lack of economic opportunities for colored women, the weakness of the reform elements in the Negro community, and the unreliability of the official statistics, particularly in matters relating to color, have been among the explanations offered for the disproportion of Negro prostitutes.

Vice in the colored districts is largely the result of economic causes. Girls have only limited opportunities for work. They can teach school, do domestic work or train to do clerical and office work. The opportunities for teachers and stenographers are limited. Some girls of good families come to Chicago and find themselves out of funds. Some of them turn to walking the streets. Because they are green and do not have bondsmen to protect them they may be arrested by the police.[15]

[12] Quoted by Binder, *op. cit.*, p. 17.

[13] *Op. cit.*, pp. 25–30.

[14] *Ibid.*, p. 27.

[15] Interview.

It occasionally happens that colored girls who have graduated from high school look about them for work in keeping with their training and find the doors of opportunity closed to them on all sides because of prejudice. These doors are shut all the tighter in a period of economic depression.[16] On the other hand, they may read in a colored weekly about the popular entertainer Miss G.: "Her smart fur coats, diamonds and automobiles made her the envy of many of the girls who attended high school and Sunday school with her a few years ago, but most of them turned thumbs down on the manner in which she is alleged to have obtained her clothes and jewels."[17]

So severe has been the competition for jobs that some Negroes have been willing to accept positions as maids or porters in houses of ill fame. According to several accounts, most of the male and female servants connected with houses of prostitution have been colored.[18] The entertainers in some of the notorious black-and-tan cabarets have been practically all colored. The Negro's flair for music and dancing have been capitalized by the white vice overlords. Bootleggers, white slavers, panders, prostitutes, and other underworld characters have been known to frequent the black-and-tan cabarets. The Negroes employed by sporting elements have many temptations to face. Sensual pleasure, power, and wealth are flaunted before their eyes.

Black people have made their easy money for many years in servile capacities around the so-called sporting elements. They have seen the white world unclothed as it hearkened back to primitive and brutish passions. The white man has set a terrible example for the black man to follow, as morals go. . . . . For some unexplainable reason a cloak of immunity has been draped around notorious vicious institutions operated by white people for white people in black districts.[19]

Since it is easier to observe immoral conditions among a poor and unprotected people, colored prostitutes are much more liable to arrest than white prostitutes. White women may use the big hotels or private apartments for their illicit trade, but the colored women are more commonly forced to walk the streets.

[16] *Whip*, February 28, 1931.   [17] *Defender*, January 7, 1933.

[18] Reckless, *op. cit.*, p. 29; *The Negro in Chicago*, p. 343.

[19] *Whip*, August 4, 1928.

Another factor, according to a person familiar with the situation, was the method sometimes employed by the police officers, which led to mistakes and racial misunderstandings.

Officers will arrest white and colored persons on almost any pretext and charge them with prostitution. That is, when they find a mixed couple they immediately believe that the woman is a prostitute. As soon as an officer sees a Negro woman talking to a white man, he may arrest her for soliciting, while in white districts a white prostitute may approach men without being conspicuous.[20]

Because of their great liability of arrest, Negro prostitutes have been willing to grasp any apparent means of protection. In the most demoralized communities, where some Negroes are found, commercialized vice is undoubtedly under the control of the white vice overlords. In the First Ward the name of a white Democratic precinct captain and real estate operator has been mentioned in connection with organized vice.[21] In other parts of the South Side prostitution has not been so highly syndicated and the pimp system has arisen.

Pimping is a rather new thing, at least in its modern form. When vice was allowed to run openly there was not much need for a pimp. The madame took care of everything. However, when the "line" was closed, the prostitute found it necessary to have a protector, and the pimp went into politics.

In order to be a pimp, then, one had to acquire power. Then you saw them going into politics to influence the police. To properly look after his girls' interests he had to have an "in" at court. Out of this situation you have crime and gambling also.

Much of the fixing power of these men was more apparent than real. And many of the fixers do not and cannot fix. The fixing business is a great racket and there are no more gullible fools than prostitutes and pimps who themselves live on the "illegit."[22]

One of the reasons why Negro pimps and prostitutes rarely received any real protection was the wariness with which politicians handled such matters. No politician could afford to be linked up in any direct fashion with the protection of vice. On the other hand, the political machine had to be careful not to antagonize openly this body of voters. Untrustworthy as the official court statistics may be, they indicate that an important fraction of the colored electorate was involved in vice activities.

[20] Interview, April 30, 1932.
[21] Various interviews.   [22] Interview with Dr. Benjamin Reitman.

GAMBLING

Another underworld group of some numerical importance in the Negro community is the one connected with gambling. In the United States, which had its frontier communities until recently and which still has its stock market and race tracks, gambling has been generally prevalent. The desire to acquire property without sustained toil, the seeking after feelings of faith in self-safety in the face of danger, and the interest of mortals in the future are powerful motives to human action. When the environment is uncertain, the incentives to gambling are even greater. In parts of the Negro communities in Chicago conditions have been favorable to the development of gambling. When people whose existence is precarious, whose employment is erratic, and whose faith in magic and luck is great, are presented with apparent chances to make great gains with small risks, is it amazing that some take these risks? A field examination showed that in Census Communities 35 and 38 there is a concentration of unemployed,[23] relief cases,[24] spiritualists, mediums, stores selling lucky curios, incenses, oils, candles and other luck products, and gambling houses.[25] In the entire South Side district there were at least some 81 spiritualists, 42 lucky products stores, and 26 alleged gambling shops.

All the well-known gambling devices have been used by colored gamblers in Chicago. Dice, cards, roulette, faro, fan tan, horse racing, prize fighting, and other games and events have been used for betting purposes. The gambling game which has been popular among the Negro masses in Chicago is called "policy." The game did not originate in Chicago and it was not invented by colored people. In a New York law suit decided in 1878 there is a reference to a Kentucky lottery which resembles the modern policy game found in northern cities.[26] In a Michigan case, which was decided twelve years later, the following description of the game was given:

[23] See Table III above, p. 34.   [24] Frazier, *op. cit.*, p. 266.

[25] The author is indebted to some of the students in the Department of Sociology at the University of Chicago for these figures.

[26] Wilkinson *v.* Gill, 74 N.Y. 63.

Persons who wish to play "policy" as he calls it, pay the respondent a sum of money, usually from 5 to 50 cents, and at the same time select 2, 3 or 4 numbers, from one to 78. If the player selects 2 numbers, it is called a "saddle"; if he selects 3 it is called a "gig." If he selects 4 it is called a "horse." If all the numbers selected by the player came out in the drawing, he won a certain amount from the policy dealer. In the case of a "gig" or 3 numbers, if the player won, he received 10 dollars for 5 cents; in case of a "saddle," the odds were proportionately less; in case of a "horse," proportionately greater.[27]

At this time thirteen numbers were drawn by lot in Kentucky and the results were telegraphed to various centers. According to the recollections of old residents in Chicago, policy also bears some relationship to the Louisiana lottery where drawings were made once a month.[28] Later drawings were made locally at more frequent intervals, and when the newspapers took lottery advertisements the game assumed large proportions. In New York City the policy shops were run by whites, and the policy kings were reputed to be millionaires.[29] A drive against the game in New York was made about 1901, and the gambling propensities of many New Yorkers were routed in other channels.[30] In Illinois a bill, which was modeled after the New York anti-policy law, was passed in 1905.[31] A conviction under the Illinois act, which was carried to the state Supreme Court in 1908, showed that policy as played in Chicago twenty-six years ago was essentially the game that is played today, and it closely resembles the Kentucky lottery.[32] The player selects the numbers he wants to play and puts up the amount of money which he wishes to wager on those numbers. One original and two carbon copies of these numbers and the amount paid are recorded on slips of paper. The player gets one copy, the policy-writer keeps one, and the third is sent to the main office that employs

[27] People v. Elliott, 74 Mich. 264.   [28] Manuscript documents.

[29] New York Herald, December 13, 1901.

[30] The conviction of the policy king, Albert J. Adams, was confirmed in People v. Adams, 176 N.Y. 351.

[31] Illinois Laws, 1905, p. 192. Compare with New York Laws, 1901, chap. 190. On the passage of the Illinois law, see Chicago Record Herald, April 21, 1905.

[32] People v. Krueger, 237 Ill. 357. The lawyer for the plaintiff in error was Edward H. Morris, former state representative and one of the counsels for the state was F. L. Barnett.

the policy-writer. At the present time the Negro policy-operators use 78 numbers, which are put in a wheel or barrel. At a
drawing 24 of these numbers are chosen by lot and reported in
two columns of twelve numbers each. After each drawing copies
of the numbers drawn are given to the persons who have wagered on that special drawing. If a player's slip contains three
numbers that later appear in one column of the drawing, he
wins one hundred times the amount of his bet. According to
mathematical analysis the chances of a player making a "catch"
with a particular "gig" are about 1 in 174.[33]

Although the odds against the player are great, the chances
for trickery on the part of the operators are many, and the
dangers of raids or "shut out" plays are ever present, the game
has persisted under cover. Some players have faith in mediums,[34] others trust in their dreams.[35] Among some who have not
become adjusted to the urban mechanical environment the
animistic apprehension of things still persists. It is a game for
the masses which can be played in small amounts, as low as five
cents. As one retired business man put it, "Not bad, for twenty
cents a day to always have something on your mind." Since
the sums involved are not large, it is necessary for the operators
to organize surreptitiously on a large scale if their business is to
pay. The average number of writers for a successful wheel is
about 300, and some wheels have over twice this number. "Policy-writers flood the streets, and invade barber shops and pool
rooms, collecting hundreds of dollars daily."[36] It has been esti-

[33] At a drawing, 12 numbers are drawn first. These are put back and another 12
drawn. The author is indebted to Dr. Henry Schultz for checking the analysis.

[34] "I went to a medium and got a good gig to play. I walked all the way down from
41st Street to 31st Street figuring to myself whether to play it or not, like the medium
said, and I decided to play it that way. But when I got to the Place I changed my mind
and played it differently than the way I was instructed. Then, the numbers came out
all right, but because I played it the way I did I only hit for a few dollars. But according
to the way the medium had it I could have made $907." Manuscript document.

[35] "I plays pretty heavy when I does get a good dream. . . . . Most of the numbers
I gets from my dreams. I dream something and then look it up in my dream book. . . . .
I had a dream last night and I'll play it for three days and it's bound to come out."
Interview.

[36] *Whip*, July 26, 1924.

mated that there are at least 6,000 of these writers who are making daily canvasses for prospects. The total sum wagered in the game during a year is at least six million dollars.[37] The law against policy is extremely difficult to enforce because of the ease of carrying the game on under cover and because of the very spasmodic interest of the public in its enforcement. Consequently, the policy king is ready to protect his position by political manipulation.

Large as the amount of money involved in policy and other outlawed activities appears to be, it is extremely difficult to estimate the importance of underworld in the emergence of a Negro political organization. The opinions expressed on this subject have been highly conflicting. One local editor said regarding the men involved in policy: "They constitute a powerful political organization. It is a prize to the political party to be able to dictate to them and form a syndicate which will support them politically. They also derive a tariff which supports the political organization."[38] A municipal judge made the following comment about the same group:

> The policy kings are the most powerful men in the Black Belt. A policy king is more powerful than any ward committeeman because he holds the extreme confidence of many people. Each policy king has two or three hundred people as his clientèle. He gives them something which is abstract—a ticket which they have paid for. They trust him with that money. Whereas the ward committeeman gives them things in the concrete. Thus, in reality the Negro has more faith in his policy king.[39]

On the other hand, a man in close touch with the situation made the comment: "Of all the no good people in politics, the pimps, the prostitutes, and the policy writers are the worst. They are not fit to do political work." In explaining why, he said: "They are with one party today and with another tomorrow. They are lazy and naturally treacherous."[40]

A brief review of the careers of the principal Negro gambling leaders will throw some light on the political rôle of the group. A little over twenty-five years ago death ended the activities of

[37] *Defender*, August 18, 1928; *Daily News*, June 15, 1927; *Whip*, August 29, 1931.

[38] Interview.   [39] Interview.   [40] Interview.

one of the picturesque figures in the Chicago gambling world, John "Mushmouth" Johnson. For seventeen years "Mushmouth" Johnson ran a saloon and a gambling house at 464 South State Street, which was a meeting-place for railroad men, waiters, porters, and professional gamblers—Chinese, Negro, and white.[41] In an interview shortly before his death, Johnson said, "I am fifty-three years of age and have lived in Chicago for fifty years. I guess I know the city pretty well and it knows me. I was born in St. Louis. While my family went in for religion and all that, I didn't exactly fancy so much book learning and went out to see where the money grew. Some of those who know me say that I found it."[42] As a porter in a white gambling house in 1880 he studied the system from the gamekeeper's side and selected the productive end.

His resort was unique in the fact that the gamblers did not stake their money against the money of the house but bet with each other. His rule was: "Any two men with money and a gambling disposition can fight it out at 464 and there'll be a gamekeeper on the spot to collect the rake-off."[43] He also discerned possibilities that his white tutors had overlooked and went after the nickels, dimes, and quarters that were sometimes referred to as "chicken feed." "Craps" and draw poker almost eliminated the more aristocratic games of faro and roulette. He was also said to have had an interest in policy. In fact, one of the motives given by one of the legislators who sponsored the anti-policy act of 1905 was that he wished to see the activities of "Mushmouth" Johnson in this field curtailed. When Johnson died his wealth was estimated at $250,000.[44]

In his way "Mushmouth" Johnson was known as a philanthropist. He was one of the many professional gamekeepers who did not gamble himself. "A man that gambles had better be without money anyway," he declared to losers who appealed

[41] *Daily News*, September 14, 1907.

[42] *New York World*, July 25, 1907. This is part of "Mushmouth" Johnson's interview denying the report that his sister, Cecilia Johnson, passed for white while at the University of Chicago.

[43] *Chicago Record Herald*, August 24, 1907.

[44] *Chicago Daily News*, September 14, 1907.

to him. "I may put it to some good use; you wouldn't know
how." Through his mother, Johnson contributed to the Baptist
Church; through his family he founded an old folk's home; and
he was a liberal donor to various other causes. When a boy from
a prominent Negro family came into his place, he would look
into the matter. If the boy insisted that he was going to gamble, and if not allowed to gamble here he would go somewhere
else, he advised him to go elsewhere. Whether this action was
motivated by race pride, a desire to avoid personal embarrassment, class consciousness, or a carry-over of early religious
training cannot be ascertained. Like other gamekeepers, Johnson was a hard-headed business man and at the same time something of a sentimentalist.[45]

In politics "Mushmouth" Johnson was primarily interested in
protecting his business. As one of his friends put it, "When a
mayoralty campaign came around he would give $10,000 to the
Democrats and $10,000 to the Republicans so that no matter
who won, he'd be protected."[46] The law-enforcing officials rarely raided his place, and when they did he was usually tipped off
in advance so that he could make all the necessary preparations.
Although he was fined many thousands of dollars and was indicted once as a gambling-house keeper, he was never in serious
difficulties with the law. When "Hinky Dink" Kenna and
"Bathhouse John" Coughlin became the ruling political powers
in the First Ward, Johnson made his arrangements with them
and they protected him against raids. While not directly concerned with other aspects of the political game, he urged Negroes to register and vote in the First Ward, he attended party
conventions, and he was known as a political power.[47]

When Johnson died in 1907 there was no one who took his
place immediately. Prominent among the gambling kings of the
time was Robert T. Motts, who started as a porter at Johnson's
place. When he saw what there was in the business, "Bob"

[45] For evidences of this, see the *New York World* interview, July 25, 1907.

[46] Several persons interviewed made statements similar to this. The amounts mentioned were sometimes smaller.

[47] *Broad Ax*, May 17, and September 20, 1902, claimed that he was influential in
nominating a county commissioner.

Motts started in for himself some three miles south of the Johnson establishment. A native of Washington, Iowa, Motts came to Chicago when he was about twenty. He was rewarded for his insight in establishing his saloon, cabaret, and gambling joint in the Second Ward, as the Negro population was moving into this area. In connection with his saloon and restaurant Motts also ran a theater called the "Pekin," which was a center of community life. Many of the theatrical performers of the race today got their start in his stock company.[48] While he lacked the force of Johnson, Motts was very successful because of his geniality. Like his former employer he made donations to the churches and was interested in Negro advancement.

"Bob" Motts was particularly concerned with the bettering of the Negro's position in politics. He was not only a good "pay off" for the police and the politicians, but he was also active in organizing the Negro voters. He would pay political workers five dollars to register people and to get them out to vote. Even before woman suffrage, wives were also enlisted in the process of "ringing door-bells and seeing faces." In return for his political activities he demanded jobs for Negroes. Through his efforts some forty women were placed in the Recorder's office. He was also instrumental in securing the election of Edward Green to the state legislature in 1904.[49]

About the time that Motts died in 1911 another colored leader in the saloon and gambling business was forced by pressure from a white organization to move his operations from Hyde Park to the Second Ward. Henry "Teenan" Jones was a contemporary of both Johnson and Motts, and at times he had had dealings with each.[50] He was among the Negro saloon keepers who profited from the great influx of migrants that began about 1914. Born a slave in Alabama in 1860, he was brought to a small town in Illinois when he was eighteen months old. Here he went to a

---

[48] *Broad Ax*, December 28, 1907, May 16, 1908. J. B. Wood, *The Negro in Chicago* (Chicago Daily News pamphlet, 1916), p. 15.

[49] *Chicago Defender*, February 4, 1933.

[50] When Jones was a young man he followed a gambler by the name of Tierann who would bet everything he had on Faro. The nickname was corrupted to "Teenan."

mixed school through the fifth grade and then started to work. At the age of sixteen he left home with another boy to try his fortune in Chicago. In looking back over his early experiences Jones now says, in a philosophical way, that he made many mistakes in learning the game of making a living in the big city against the great odds of inexperience and racial prejudice.[51]

His early life clearly illustrates how the newly emancipated Negroes suffered in the North because of a lack of traditions of workmanship and a lack of training in business methods. He lost one job after another in his process of training. As a pantry boy the pastries were too much for him en route; as a bell-boy in one hotel he was too obliging to his fellow-workers; as a bell-boy in another hotel where he watched a gambling game for a guest he made too much money; as a waiter in another hotel he rolled too many dice in the basement; as a porter for a gambling house he gave the address of a customer to the wrong kind of ladies and made some unfortunate remarks to another customer; and as the proprietor of his first saloon he failed to appreciate the value of location and the question of overhead. "Teenan" Jones learned quickly, and in 1895 he was well established with a saloon and gambling place in Hyde Park, where he ran games of dice, roulette, draw and stud poker.[52] Everything went well until he was driven out by the Hyde Park Protective Association in 1910. He then opened two saloons in the Second Ward that were called Elite No. 1 and Elite No. 2. Until prohibition went into effect in 1919 his saloons were flourishing, and prior to the famous DePriest trial of 1917 he was known as the head of the Second Ward gambling syndicate.[53] Like "Bob" Motts,

---

[51] He ran a column in the *Chicago Defender* each week entitled: "Reminiscences from an Old-Timer's Scrap Book." In commenting on a draft of this chapter he said, "The real foundation of my business was whites. I had contacts with Vernon Castle, Leon Errol, and others. The leading lawyer in the hotel used to say to white visitors and gay slummers, 'Go to Teenan.' I enjoyed my experience in learning the ways of the big city. Needless to say, I had my ups and downs."

[52] Located at Lake Park Avenue and Fifty-sixth Street. His outside show was a saloon and garden for Negro waiters in the Windermere, Chicago Beach, and other hotels, but his real business came from white people.

[53] Elite No. 1 and Elite No. 2 were at Thirty-third and State streets and at Thirty-fifth and State streets. See *Chicago Defender*, January 17, 1931, and *Broad Ax*, January 15, 1915.

"Teenan" Jones was a patron of Negro theatricals and Negro athletic contests.[54]

While he was still in Hyde Park "Teenan" Jones was looked upon as a political power. He was on friendly terms with the Republican Committeeman. During the time that Carter Harrison II was mayor an order was issued to have all the gambling houses closed up, but the mayor decided that the Negroes would be allowed to shoot a few craps. It was under these circumstances that white men began increasingly to drop into colored places, including Jones's saloon in Hyde Park. During the period from 1910 to 1918, when he was located in the Second Ward, Jones made contributions to all of the politicians. He opened headquarters for State Representative Turner, he hired halls for meetings for B. Mosley, and he helped Aldermen DePriest and Anderson at different times. He did not expect them to do things for him as his main hook-up was with the police.[55] In those days the politicians did not have the control over the police which they acquired later. During the Mayor Thompson administration the police were shifted about for political considerations. Jones had also supported Maclay Hoyne as a candidate for state's attorney from 1912 to 1920, but he could not prevent Hoyne from indicting him for conspiracy in 1917, along with Alderman DePriest and Captain Stephen K. Healy.[56] When Jones turned state's witness at the DePriest trial and confessed that he had been the head of a gambling syndicate, his political influence was greatly diminished.[57]

Most noted of all the gambling kings was Daniel M. Jackson, also well known as an undertaker, who reached the height of his power in the underworld during the second and third Thompson administrations. "Dan" Jackson first came to Chicago with his father in 1892 from Pittsburgh, Pennsylvania, where he was born in 1870. Unlike Johnson, Motts, and Jones,

[54] He started one of the first motion-picture companies. In the eighties he owned a baseball team. His theatrical adventures were launched in 1921–22. See *Broad Ax*, November 1, 1913.

[55] Testimony in the DePriest trial, *Chicago Tribune*, June 5, 1917.

[56] *Ibid.*, January 19, 1917.   [57] Interview, February 26, 1933.

Jackson was a college graduate, having attended Lincoln University, Pennsylvania. With his father and brother, Charles, he went into the undertaking business and opened an establishment at Twenty-sixth and State streets. This was near the neighborhood where William Hale Thompson and George F. Harding lived in the nineties, and Jackson knew them both.[58]

In 1900 he was nominated for county commissioner by the Republican convention, but he was defeated in the election.[59] During the first twenty years of his stay in Chicago, Jackson was a bachelor, and went around with men like Edward Green and "Bob" Motts. After Motts's death he married Lucy Motts, the sister of his friend, who inherited her brother's estate. Ostensibly an undertaker, "Dan" Jackson ran several gambling joints, including one that was located in his undertaking parlors and another that was located in the Pekin Theater building.[60] However, he was chiefly known as the head of a great syndicate that controlled vice, bootlegging, cabarets, and such gambling games as craps, poker, and policy.[61] When he died in 1929 his estate was probated at $75,000, but well-informed persons have said that its actual value was at least three times this figure.[62]

In the Negro community "Dan" Jackson was noted for his generosity. He furnished coal and paid the rent for endless numbers of persons, and it was said that he never turned anybody away. He was also a good business man, one of the first colored men to introduce modern undertaking methods on the

[58] Testimony of DePriest in the 1917 trial; see *Chicago Tribune*, June 6, 1917.

[59] *Broad Ax*, February 9, 1901.

[60] The Appellate Court handed down a decision in 1933 that the estate of the late Daniel M. Jackson was not liable for rent due for the old Dunbar Club, 3441 Michigan Avenue, because the lessors knew the place was being used for gambling purposes. The lessors contended that it was rented for the purpose of operating an undertaking establishment. *Chicago Defender*, February 25, 1933.

[61] The *Chicago Daily News* carried many articles about his activities. See issues of March 24, August 6, October 12, 13 and 21, 1921, June 5, December 29, 1922, January 9, February 27, April 30, June 13, 1923, March 8 and 10, September 29, 1928, May 17, June 18, 1929. See also *Chicago Whip*, October 6, 1928; *Chicago Herald and Examiner*, September 9, December 1, 1928; *Chicago Journal*, September 9, 1928; *Chicago Tribune*, September 24, 1928; *New York Times*, September 30, 1928.

[62] Interview, dated February 12, 1933.

South Side. One Negro journalist made the following comment about Jackson's position:

> I don't like to admit it but an open town is far better for the Negroes than a closed town. An underworld boss with a little public spirit can do a lot of good too. The money that now goes to the police under Dan Jackson often went for charities and good movements. Of course these bosses make a lot of money, but while Jackson was in control he donated thousands to charities, the N.A.A.C.P., working girls' homes and the like. While Jackson was in power the colored people always had a friend to go to. If some old fellow got in jail and his son came down Jackson would sign his bond and send a note to the judge.[63]

The evidence as to "Dan" Jackson's political power is far from complete, but it is nevertheless impressive. He was rated as the head of the strongest syndicate ever organized in the "Black Belt," the czar of the colored underworld. Canny and close-mouthed, he could be trusted by the police and by the politicians. His agents made regular collections from the privileged establishments on a percentage basis. Those places which did not belong to the syndicate were raided by the police and put out of business or whipped into line.[64] The famous Tia Juana policy wheel ran openly and made public drawings in the presence of large crowds. When the Democratic administration came into power, under Mayor Dever, some of the operations of the syndicate were driven under cover.[65] The re-election of Mayor Thompson in 1927 was a signal for a grand reopening of South Side resorts, and there followed "an epidemic of policy gambling."[66] Jackson had recently replaced Edward H. Wright as committeeman of the Second Ward by appointment of Mayor Thompson and State's Attorney Robert E. Crowe, so he was in a position to look after the interests of the syndicate. In the famous "Pineapple Primary" of 1928 Jackson was elected ward committeeman by the Republican voters of the Second Ward. During one of these affluent days he was held up by gunmen on

[63] Interview, December 5, 1931.   [64] *Chicago Daily News*, August 6, 1921.

[65] *Ibid.*, June 13, 1923; *Chicago Whip*, July 26, 1924.

[66] *Chicago Daily News*, March 8, 1928. The difference between the two administrations was probably not as great as the *News* pictured it. Policy gambling was more openly carried on under Thompson.

the steps of the City Hall and robbed of $25,000 in cash that he
had on his person.[67] While his rule was evidently profitable to
the inside group, he was also able to protect the ordinary Negro
against police brutality[68] and against interference in his petty
vices. Governor Small recognized his position of power and influence in the Second Ward by appointing him as a member of
the Illinois Commerce Commission. Shortly after this, in September, 1928, he and some of his associates ran into difficulties
when they were indicted by a special grand jury for conspiracy
to protect gambling.[69] The election of John A. Swanson as
state's attorney added to the troubles of the syndicate. When
"Dan" Jackson died in 1929 his trial was still pending on the
criminal court docket.

Since the passing of "Dan" Jackson no one man has arisen as
the leader of the colored underworld. There are several "big
shots" but there is no czar. Among the alleged operators of
policy wheels are the nephew of a late gambling king, who
also has a real estate office,[70] the brother of another late gambling magnate,[71] and the son-in-law of a former alderman.[72] The
defeat of Mayor Thompson in 1931 by Anton J. Cermak, the
Democratic candidate for mayor, made it necessary for the policy kings to make new arrangements. The process by which
these arrangements were made is very well illustrated in the
case of the Jones boys. Like "Dan" Jackson, the three Jones
brothers are men who have had educational opportunities.
After a number of raids and arrests by the police, Mayor Cermak declared that the policy kings were on the run. "Many
people like a game of chance," said the mayor, "but all the
decent people of the Negro community, including some who
play policy, are asking that the policy resorts be cleaned out be-

[67] *Chicago Tribune*, July 10, 1928.   [68] *Chicago Whip*, April 9, 1927.

[69] Records of the Clerk of the Criminal Court, September 29, 1928. See also *Chicago
Daily News*, September 29, 1928.

[70] *Chicago Defender*, April 19, 1930; October 1, 1932, December 31, 1932.

[71] *Chicago Whip*, August 27, 1921; *Chicago Daily News*, August 16, 1927.

[72] *Chicago Daily News*, March 6, 1928; *Chicago Defender*, May 23, 1931; November
26, 1932; and manuscript documents.

cause the colored people are near starvation and these thieves under the pretense of operating games are taking their nickels and dimes and giving them one chance in 20,000 to win." "I am told," the mayor proceeded, "that George Jones of Jones & Jones, Julian Black and a man named Brodie, the biggest policy operators on the South Side, will agree to quit the business if all the little fellows will quit."[73] Some time later the Jones brothers were found in the ranks of the Democratic party. In the aldermanic contest of 1933 in the Third Ward they came out openly for the candidate backed by the Democratic organization.[74]

The political importance of the colored underworld in Chicago politics does not depend merely upon the campaign contributions made by the underworld leaders and the votes cast by the prostitutes, policy-writers, bootleggers, and the other persons directly involved in outlawed activities. It is true that these services alone are important.[75] In commenting on this situation one prominent Negro said: "The highly respectable business and professional Negro does not take very much concern or interest in politics. While, on the other hand, the vice lords and petty vice indulgents cater very largely to the support of the politicians by votes and money." He went on to say, "Now, if I were to run for a political office, I would have to raise campaign expenses. If I went to every professional man in the town, I would not be able to raise two hundred dollars. But if I went to the vice lords and policy kings, I would get two or three thousand from a couple of them."[76] In addition to these direct services, the underworld has many indirect contributions to

[73] *Chicago Daily News*, August 11, 1931.

[74] Julius Benvenuti, an Italian who has been referred to as a policy operator, has been with the Democratic party in the Second Ward for some time. *Chicago Defender*, July 25, 1931; *Chicago Review*, January 9, 1933; and manuscript documents.

[75] "Contrary to Dr. DuBois no colored alderman here heads up any gambling syndicate nor is the underworld most effective in getting out the vote. The organizations composed of hard working precinct captains and workers get out the vote and not a third of the whole outfit is tied up with subterranean activities." *Chicago Whip*, May 4, 1929.

[76] Manuscript document, February 13, 1932.

make to the political organizations. The vice interests are woven into the fabric of the community and affect it at many points. In relation to other enterprises run or partly controlled by Negroes the total amount of money involved in the under-cover activities is large. The drug stores, the taxi cab compa-nies, the beauty parlors, the bonding houses, the small shops, the criminal lawyers, the real estate companies, and even the bankers in the communities where the "racketeers" are numer-ous and well supplied with cash may depend in part for their own prosperity upon the patronage of those engaged in illegal activities.[77] Thus, a policy king was on the board of directors of a bank which is now defunct, real estate operators did not al-ways examine too closely the activities of their tenants, and several prominent gamblers were also professional bondsmen. The result of the liaison between legitimate business and the underworld was that in the bright-light areas the general com-munity was more or less tolerant toward certain types of law breaking. Particularly around election time, the leaders of these districts could not afford to antagonize the vicious and criminal elements. As one politician put it, "Politics is a dirty game as it has to be played. If we did not go along with these fellows, they would beat us."[78]

[77] The case of United States *v.* Jackie Reynolds *et al.*, also known as the Britton and Howland case, illustrates how the owner of a taxi cab company, a drug store, the pro-prietor of a haberdashery store, a daily newspaper, police officers, thieves, and others may be mixed up together, some with and some without any direct connection with criminal acts.

[78] Interview.

CHAPTER VII

THE MACHINE AT WORK

The Negro political organizations with leaders of their own in control first emerged in 1920 and have had many difficult tasks to perform. The rapid migration from the South and the high mobility of the Negro population within the city meant that the political organizations had to be constantly on the alert to keep track of the voters and to marshal their full strength. Many of the voters were without experience in casting a ballot, and they had to be carefully instructed as to the details of election procedure. In some cases the migrants had had so few educational opportunities in the South that the instruction of new voters had to be done orally. The widespread distrust of the daily newspapers made it all the more necessary for the political organizations to establish and maintain face-to-face contacts with the voters in the areas of Negro settlement.[1] Such contacts are dependent upon careful canvassing and upon political mass meetings which are entertaining, informing, and emotionally satisfying. The election returns indicate that the work of the Negro party organization has been thoroughly and well performed.

Long before a Negro was placed in charge of a ward organization Negroes had risen to important party positions. As the colored population expanded, the white political leaders came more and more to recognize the advantages of having colored precinct captains, supervisors, and speakers to work with the colored voters. The Democrats in Chicago have been the slowest to see these advantages, although they have long followed this procedure with reference to various foreign-born groups. An able Negro precinct captain understands his constituents, knows the peculiar meanings which they give to certain words,

[1] According to the *Chicago Daily News* Home Coverage survey, only 8 per cent of the Negro families interviewed had the *Daily News* in the homes.

has an appreciation for their resentments and ambitions, avoids stepping on their toes, and he is bound to them by the tie of race. The Negro political worker who has been recognized by the party organization and who has a definite political function enjoys a status in his own group which a white worker in a white area does not ordinarily have. His prestige may be enhanced by a governmental job, but without this it is still considerable.

If a voting area inhabited largely by Negroes is under the domination of white political workers, many of the Negro voters in it will be found to be restive and dissatisfied. In some of the West Side wards of Chicago this condition is found at the present time. An assistant colored precinct captain complained of his status in the following words: "I tell you it's a shame over here. We have a 'dago' alderman, a 'dago' precinct committeeman, a 'dago' legislator, 'dagoes' on the senatorial committee. In fact 'dagoes' in everything, and the colored men ain't got nothing. And we are in a majority. It sure ain't right."[2]

The history of the Second and Third wards, where there are now powerful Republican organizations manned almost entirely by Negroes, shows how the obstacles of color, lack of experience, and lack of economic power have gradually been overcome. The rise of a small but active professional and business group among the Negroes living on the South Side forecast the taking-over of the Republican organization soon after the population ratios warranted the transfer. Many of the colored migrants who came to Chicago learned with great rapidity the rules of the game of politics. They saw that the ward committeemen elected directly or indirectly by the party voters in a primary or caucus exercised great powers over the affairs of

[2] Interview April 12, 1932. Another Negro in the same district said: "The precinct captains are appointed. Therefore we have had Jews. Now the Italians are coming into power and they are being appointed precinct captains. They will not have a colored precinct captain even when the precinct is 90 per cent colored. Some of the white precinct captains do not live in the precinct at all. Just before election they will get a colored man who knows the district. They call him the assistant precinct captain. But really he's nothing. They will give him five or ten dollars a day to go around and line up the votes. . . . . But they never give a Negro a job like they are supposed to." Manuscript document, May 12, 1932.

government. They saw that these ward committeemen were willing to appoint as precinct captains those who could control a block of voters on primary and election days. They saw that the successful precinct captain, the man who continued to deliver votes or the man who made himself useful in some other way to the politician whose star was in the ascendancy, was rewarded by receiving some political job or favor. They watched the methods that were employed to win votes and they added a few of their own that were adapted to the customs of their people.

One of the peculiarities of American politics is the smallness of the units reporting election returns.[3] The state of Illinois is no exception in this matter, as the election precincts are required by law to contain 400 and not more than 600 voters. Thus, a precinct might contain two city blocks or many more, depending upon the density of the population. Since the Negro population at any given time was largely located in certain voting precincts it was possible to ascertain the Negro vote. The colored precinct captains took advantage of this and concentrated their efforts on making the best showing possible. In a well-organized ward each precinct captain would be given a diagram showing the boundaries of his precinct[4] and he would be held responsible for creating a skeleton organization in the precinct made up of a president, a vice-president, a secretary, a treasurer, and block workers.[5] While the functions of these subprecinct officers were slight, an attempt was made by the colored leaders to give as many party workers formal recognition as possible.

The roster of precinct captains for typical Republican organization in the Second of Third wards would be made up of persons who in some way had shown their superiority over their fellow party-members. In some cases the precinct leaders were men who enjoyed the advantages of a professional education in law or medicine. An ambitious young lawyer, trained in an-

---

[3] In Great Britain the Parliamentary election returns are compiled by constituencies.

[4] Report of political meeting held November 20, 1931.

[5] Report of political meeting.

other part of the country, found it to his advantage in starting his practice in Chicago to make some political connections. Among the precinct committeemen would likewise be found men who had been porters, tailors, chauffeurs, and common laborers. These men had risen above the masses of the party followers because of their greater aggressiveness, their longer residence in the city, and their superior political experience. The average man could not hope to win a precinct captaincy until he had lived at least fifteen years in the city. There would be, in addition, some representatives of the underworld—gambling kings and bootleggers—who were concerned in protecting their interests. As compared with wards of similar economic composition there would also be a large number of women precinct captains, perhaps a fourth. These women leaders usually came from families with political backgrounds. They were thoroughly familiar with their local neighborhoods, and they had demonstrated their abilities as canvassers and organizers. During the days of the Republican ascendancy in city and state practically all the precinct captains of the dominant faction in these wards would be political office-holders.[6] Their zeal for their party cause would thus be closely tied up with their bread and butter.

Since the winning of votes among the Negroes depended largely upon the establishment of primary relationships, it was necessary for the precinct captains to get acquainted with the prospective voters in their bailiwicks. As a municipal judge expressed it:

The Negro votes for the man who is his friend and he tries to find out who that man is. Thus, he has a standard for casting his vote. You or I haven't. We read newspaper editorials, use sample ballots, and decide our votes on petty prejudices, usually resulting from hearsay. We have no real standards for voting.[7]

The precinct captains canvass the districts in order to tell the voters who are their friends. It is probable that in no part

[6] A pamphlet issued in the 1934 primary on behalf of Third Ward Democratic committeeman, "Mike" Sneed, listed each job of the Democratic precinct captains. The jobs were distributed as follows: County, 15; City, 12; Municipal Court, 5; Board of Education, 5; State of Illinois, 4; Municipal Tuberculosis Sanitarium, 2; Circuit and Superior courts, 2; Sanitary District, 2; Public Library, 1; no job listed, 21; total, 69.

[7] Interview, June 3, 1932.

of the city was the canvassing by the Republican party workers more thoroughly and frequently done. In the Second Ward one Republican precinct captain reported that he was in very close and accurate touch with the voters of his precinct, since he employed four assistants to make house-to-house canvasses and to issue reports of their investigations to him. He in turn maintained a card index system to keep track of these investigations, and he knew exactly when anyone moved in or out of the precinct. He was proud of the fact that he knew everyone in the area.[8] Other precinct captains in this organization did most of the canvassing themselves. Colored women were found to make excellent house-to-house workers, and in one ward campaign over 1,100 women block canvassers were organized.[9] At a ward meeting the workers were addressed as follows: "Go into homes again and again. Let them know the facts of the case. If sister is washing go down into the laundry and help her wash. If cleaning, get yourself a feather duster and talk."[10]

The canvassers learned by experience to adapt their appeals to their listeners. One precinct official boasted that he could talk with any of his constituents. He could pray with an old woman, talk craps with a gambler, and talk with men about their women or anything they wanted to talk about. He could also talk "highbrow."[11]

In every way that is not too costly the party workers try to perform actual services for the voters which will be remembered on election day. Where the precinct captain is unable by himself to perform the task, he gets in touch with someone in the organization who can. In other words, the precinct committee-

---

[8] Interview, March 15, 1928.   [9] Report of political meeting, April 1, 1932.

[10] Report of political meeting, January 24, 1932.

[11] Interview, January 26, 1932. Another precinct captain claimed that he was very successful in campaigning in the underworld: "Tell me the vice and liquor joints in any precinct and I can carry the precinct. I go in and say, 'I want you folks to help me get a job.' They'll say, 'We're for X.' I'll say, 'He isn't doing anything for you and what I want you to do is to help me get a job.' The man I'm with will get me a job. 'Come on men, let's have a little drink.' Then we set up a couple of times. I leave. I return later and say, 'Set the house up' and they are with me." Interview, January 27, 1932.

man is an agent or broker for a great variety of services which are used to cement voters to the party machine.

The party organizations in the Second and Third wards recognize that there are many Negroes who are in need of legal advice. One precinct official, a lawyer with an office elsewhere, hung out a shingle in his precinct because of the constant demand for his services on the part of some of the inhabitants who were getting into stabbing and cutting scrapes. Another party official engaged in the practice of law was continually being called upon to intercede for policy-writers, bootleggers, and others who had been arrested by the police. He said: "I spend my mornings in the police courts fighting as hard as I can like I was getting some money, but I'm not. I just like to help the poor devils."[12] He was also called upon to make tax adjustments, to fix traffic slips, to obtain sixty-day free licenses for lunch rooms, lunch wagons, and flower stands, and to raise bail. Since relatively few Negroes owned their own homes, the tax-fixing activities of the precinct captains were less widespread than in some of the predominantly white wards.[13] Altogether, however, a heavy demand was made upon the party workers who were skilled in interpreting the complicated laws of the city, state, and nation, and who understood how to mitigate the rigors of these laws as they applied to individuals.

Because the occupational opportunities for Negroes are limited, the function of the party workers as employment brokers was an important one. The government offices, the utility concerns, and various private companies were approached for jobs. A John Brown Political Club was organized, which went so far as to stop white men from working on a street car track in a neighborhood inhabited by colored people. In this instance the picket method proved successful and the ward leaders jumped in to claim the credit. In describing the political appointments that had been obtained by the Second Ward organization during the height of Thompson's power one speaker said:

[12] Interview.

[13] Tax-fixing by party agents in Chicago has been reduced to a low ebb by the events of 1932–33.

I wonder sometimes if you realize what wonderful things have been accomplished by this organization. Forty years ago when I came here there were just a handful of Negroes in this organization, eighteen hundred dollars was the largest job any Negro held, and there were scarcely a half dozen jobs. From there we have come to the place where we have controlled 350 jobs with a payroll up into the hundreds of thousands.[14]

The jobs were never plentiful enough to go around and the party organization has been frequently called upon to act as a relief agency. In times of prosperity the number seeking aid has not been so great that the organization itself could not supply some of the wants. Precinct captains would be called upon to furnish coal, rent, food, and clothing. At one meeting it was said: "Contact your precinct captains—let them know about all needy cases that come under your observation in your precincts. We promise you earnestly that they will really be taken care of."[15] One precinct official handled his cases as follows: "I go out among white friends and gather up old clothes, hats, coats and like that and give them out to the people here."[16] A prominent white politician with large real estate holdings in the district would be lenient toward his tenants around election time. Another white politician who was in the coal business had a working arrangement with the organization regarding the distribution of coal. Around Christmas time the whole organization would be asked to co-operate in the raising of a fund to be used to distribute Christmas baskets. Tickets would be sold for a general benefit, grocers would be asked to make voluntary contributions of food, and raffles would be held to augment the fund. Single organizations have distributed as many as six thousand Christmas baskets.

During a period of general unemployment and economic distress the party organizations fall far short of meeting even the most needy cases. The best that they can do is to refer their constituents to the proper relief authorities and try to secure as much credit for themselves as possible. Some party workers have developed a special technique for approaching the relief agencies. As one of them put it:

[14] Report of political meeting, November 20, 1931.
[15] Report of political meeting, November 27, 1931.   [16] Interview, May 13, 1933.

Yes, lots of people come to me about charity. Some of them want charity, some food, some coal. I tell them how they must do to get charity. First they got to apply for it themselves. They got to go over and register for it. Then if they get turned down they are to come back to me and I see what I can do for them. Then I send in a letter or get the ward committeeman to send in a letter. I tell them that a lady will come to see them, an inspector. And when that lady comes it is best to not have their house very clean and to look sorta ragged. If that lady comes in and see them looking hungry and with just one shoe on she may do something for them. Best not to have the house warm either when she comes.[17]

In 1931 and 1932 special semi-political organizations sprang up which endeavored to secure favors from the relief agencies. The regular organizations also had their social work secretaries. One of them said: "I was a social worker and I've just butted in on the organized charities. We have over six hundred charity cases in our files at the ward office."[18] While the actual influence of the party workers with the relief agencies was slight, it seemed important to some of the persons served.

As a result of the many favors which the precinct captains have performed or promised to perform for their constituents, they are able to get a hearing when they come around and ask for votes. The first step in securing votes is to see that all those who are favorably disposed are registered. This is not an easy task in a district where the citizens are constantly moving "from pillar to post" to find lower rents, better homes, or places where they can escape paying rent for a while. There are also some who are too "ornery" to register. A watch must also be kept that hostile factions or parties do not try to pad the lists of registered voters. On the eve of a recent registration one of the organization leaders said to the party workers: "We have to be mighty careful about this registration business. Even if a man has moved in the same building have him record this. Know the location of every vacant house. They will try to play tricks. We'll nip that. I know the Democrats from the Republicans in my precinct."[19] At one election it was claimed that the Democrats attempted to enter false names on the registration books

---

[17] Interview, May 13, 1933.

[18] Interview, May 22, 1933.   [19] Report of political meeting, February 19, 1932.

in an attempt to defeat Congressman DePriest. This plot was "nipped in the bud by the alert and decisive action of the precinct captains in the First and Second wards."[20] Care was also taken to counteract the possible use of "suspect notices" to harass qualified voters. These notices made it troublesome for the voters in question to establish their right to vote and it was claimed that they were used to disfranchise the voters. The South Side citizens were peculiarly sensitive to the use of these notices.[21]

A second task in the conducting of a campaign which required the attention of the organization was the circulation of nominating petitions. Because of the technical requirements of the law and because many of the party workers were without clerical or legal training, this was a job which required careful instruction. Particularly in an aldermanic election a careless slip might throw the candidate's name off the ballot. The regular Republican organizations were usually careful about tending to all the legal details, but a veteran like ex-Representative Kersey filed a petition for alderman of the Second Ward in 1933 which was held defective.[22]

Another function of the precinct captain, which is based partly upon custom and partly upon law, is the recommendation of two or three persons in his precinct to serve as judges and clerks of election. A given political party is entitled to three of the five members of the board of election in every other precinct. Even when a party is out of power in the county and city it still retains the privilege of naming judges and clerks of election. In some parts of the Second Ward, where illiteracy is high and underworld influences are strong, difficulties have been encountered in getting properly qualified persons to serve on election boards.[23] The overwhelming Republican character of many

[20] *Chicago Defender*, October 25, 1930. On fraudulent registration in the Second Ward see also *Chicago Daily News*, September 25, 28, October 7, 1920; April 6, 1928.

[21] *Chicago Defender*, April 2, 1926; February 19, 1927; *Chicago Whip*, April 2, 1927; and report of political meeting, April 1, 1932.

[22] *Chicago Defender*, February 25, 1933. In 1931 Edgar G. Brown's name was kept off the ballot in the Fourth Ward. See *Chicago Daily News*, February 13, 1931.

[23] *Chicago Whip*, July 30, 1927. See also, *In re* Maguire, County Court of Cook County, pp. 1604, 2088, 2171 (June–July, 1930).

of the precincts meant that it was also hard to find genuine
Democrats to serve as judges and clerks. One woman Democratic organizer met the situation in the following fashion: "We
made contacts with the Election Commission and got reliable
judges and workers. I told the judges and precinct workers that
if they came up with only one vote in a precinct it would mean
their jobs. And further that we were going to hold them not
only for their vote but for their family and a few friends."[24] It
was not uncommon in Republican organizations for the leaders
to insist that the judges and clerks attend the organization
meetings.

On the eve of a primary or an election final instructions are
given to the precinct captains by the ward chieftains. In a primary election, where there is no party column to guide the voter,
instructions were very explicit as to how the same ballots were
to be used. In the words of one of the leaders, "When these
sample ballots come out, instruct the people how to select their
candidates. Count down four places on the list of committeemen and vote for X as your ward committeeman."[25] The mention of the counting procedure was a recognition of the fact that
some of the voters could not read. The instructions went on to
cover such matters as to how to keep a check-list of those who
had voted, how to round up the laggard voters, how to guard
against the chain fraud, short penciling, and other election
frauds, and how to select political workers.

The impression is current that bribery and election corruption
are prevalent in the sections inhabited largely by Negroes.[26] It
is common for candidates to say that they lost in the "Black
Belt" because they did not spend money there. However, re-
counts, special investigations, and the records of prosecutions
show that corruption and ballot thievery are as common in
white as in colored neighborhoods. It is true that money is used
on election day in the near South Side wards, but most of this

---

[24] Interview, February 7, 1933. The situation which she described no longer exists
in 1935. In fact, in some Negro precincts it is hard to find loyal Republican judges
and clerks.

[25] Report of political meeting, April 1, 1932.

[26] *Chicago Daily News*, July 30, 31, September 20, 1928.

money is spent to pay election workers. In primary elections as much as fifty dollars would be allotted to each precinct.[27] This practice extends over the entire city, and the money used for such purposes is usually furnished by the central headquarters of the party. The hiring of workers may be an indirect method for buying the votes of the person so hired, but it is not contrary to the customs and laws of Illinois. As to the actual buying of votes and the paying of precinct election boards to falsify the returns, the evidence is meager and inconclusive.[28] When popular racial candidates are at stake, there is no need for the colored Republican political workers to take great risks.

Violence and intimidation as political devices have been more commonly used against Negro voters than for them. In the West Side and in the near North Side wards where the Negroes have been looked upon by the foreign-born white politicians as unwanted voters, some outstanding examples of the use of strong-arm methods have occurred. In the 1928 primary the colored candidate for ward committeeman in the Twentieth Ward was shot down in cold blood by a gang of white political henchmen who wished to intimidate the colored voters generally in the district.[29] Two years later a Negro political worker in the Forty-second Ward was killed by a white precinct captain.[30] In the Second Ward the workers of the minority Republican factions have sometimes been harassed, but there are no records of political murders.[31] The situation in the precincts which the colored party workers controlled has not been such as to demand such strenuous tactics.

[27] United States Congress, Senate, *Select Committee on Senatorial Campaign Expenditures*, 71st Congress, 2d Session, Part 2, Illinois (Nye Committee), pp. 310, 313.

[28] Manuscript documents. Fraudulent returns were discovered during the Heller-Hasten recount in a number of precincts inhabited by colored people. See Women's Civic Council, *Dishonest Elections* (Chicago, 1934). Election steals would be managed by underworld figures who looked to the politicians for protection.

[29] *Chicago Daily News*, April 12, 13, 14, 16, 17, 25, 27, 1928; *Chicago Tribune*, April 11, 12, 14, 18, 1928; *Chicago Whip*, April 14, 21, 28, 1928.

[30] *Chicago Defender*, March 15, 1930.

[31] For examples of violence see *Chicago Defender*, April 17, 1926, and *Chicago Daily News*, March 22, 1928. On January 29, 1933, a protest meeting was held regarding violent methods of campaigning.

The Negro political leaders have assembled organizations which have, as a rule, functioned smoothly. The new voters from the South, who have lacked political experience and urban sophistication, have been rapidly assimilated. The organization workers have quickly learned the current political methods and adroitly adapted them to the habits of their constituents.

POLITICAL MEETINGS

While organization is important it tells only part of the story of the participation of Negroes in Chicago politics. Political meetings are the great means employed to develop and main-tain party morale. The Republican rallies in the Second and Third wards are unique affairs, not to be duplicated in other parts of the city. Most of the large political meetings have taken over some of the patterns of religious revivals or camp meet-ings. A party gathering which was not packed and which did not stir up an emotional response was looked upon as very un-usual. A Negro audience is attentive, enthusiastic, patient, good natured, and content to sit for many hours on uncom-fortable seats. When a speaker says something which strikes a popular chord, they shout, clap, or wave programs, hats, or hands in the air. Politics is evidently something which is very close to their daily life and their racial aspirations. They feel that their jobs, their freedom, their right to vote, their happi-ness, their very lives almost are at stake unless their candi-dates win. At least that is what the speakers say, and the audi-ence responds as if it sincerely accepted it as true.

An appraisal of the Negro political meetings is difficult to make because, as one tries to examine the parts, the vital, ex-citing whole is lost sight of. Not all the meetings are held in large halls; there are precinct meetings in homes, regional meet-ings for a group of precincts, and organization meetings in the party headquarters or some convenient hall. These meetings are usually well staged and provide for entertainment, instruc-tion, and incentives to political action.

The entertainment features of a mass meeting are sometimes used to attract a crowd. Home talent is used extensively for these purposes. In the intervals between speeches, bands, tap-dancers, jazz orchestras, male quartets, comedians, buglers, chorus girls, community choirs, and soloists may be brought in to vary the program. When a given faction is weak or on the downgrade, professional entertainers may be employed to stem the tide. When the faction sponsoring the meeting is full of vigor, a few campaign ditties executed by school children are regarded as more in keeping with the meeting. The Democrats, and less frequently the Republicans, sometimes draw a crowd by issuing free coupons for a meeting. These coupons are collected at the door and during the meeting drawings are made from them by lot. The persons holding the lucky numbers receive money, hams, or some other valuable consideration.[32]

A skilful master of ceremonies at one of the Negro political meetings arranges the order of the speakers so that the tempo is varied. One speaker is crude in his language, unpolished in his style of delivery, but obviously sincere and forceful. Another is gifted with words, skilled in voice inflection, but lacking in drive and human understanding. A third is learned in history, entertaining, a master of phrases, humorous, adroit at touching upon race foibles, but too obviously an actor. A fourth is able to work himself into an emotional frenzy, to stir his audience profoundly, to recall vividly examples of race persecution. Still a fifth exhibits an extraordinary smoothness, a pleasing quality of voice, a wonderful flow of language, a mastery of Bible history, law, and politics, and an ability to arouse his listeners as well. The chairman of a political meeting in the Second or Third wards has a great variety of oratorical talent to call upon and he has himself to blame if the meeting is not a success.

The language used by the colored orators reflects the interests and habits of their listeners. Biblical and religious references are common even in the mouths of speakers who are known to be non-church goers. Ministers of the gospel are also frequently included in the program of meetings and they are expected to introduce some of the atmosphere of a revival. In starting a political denunciation one speaker gave as his text the

[32] Report of political meetings, April 1, 1930, February 27, 1933.

first verse from Isaiah, fifty-third chapter: "Cry aloud and spare not." Another modified a biblical phrase in the following manner: "Father forgive them for they are all messed up."[33]

The Negro's love of songs has been cleverly played upon by their speakers. At a large meeting the opposition was ridiculed in the words of song titles. The speaker began by quoting, "You'll Understand It Better, Bye and Bye" and he ended with the titles "I'll Be Glad When You're Dead, You Rascal You" and "That Was the Human Thing To Do."[34] References would also be made to the gambling propensities of some of the voters. As one speaker put it, "I don't care if you play policy or not. If you think you can pick a gig or saddle, it is O.K. with me. You can spend your dimes and walk around broke while the boys ride around in their high powered cars if you want to."[35] The responses of the audience in each of the cases given indicated that the speakers were treading upon familiar ground.

The appeals made at the political meetings were fitted to the needs and aspirations of the group. A great deal of emphasis was placed upon the importance of political action with reference to jobs, public and private. The achievements of a given Republican organization in the past in winning jobs for Negroes was pointed to with great pride. The job-holders were warned that failure at the polls would mean the loss of their positions. In the case of a new and rising organization appeals would be made to the disappointed office-seekers. Those who were candidates for legislative positions promised to protect the group against discriminatory measures, and those who sought to influence administrative officials through the party hierarchy promised to work for fair treatment in the schools, the courts, and police stations.

Appeals to rational self-interest were not regarded as sufficient to stir the voters to action. A successful meeting introduced appeals to race consciousness, party loyalty, and civic pride. A masterful exhibition of this style of oratory was given

[33] Report of political meetings held November 27, 1931, and April 3, 1932.

[34] Report of political meeting held April 9, 1932.

[35] Report of political meeting held February 17, 1933.

in the campaign of November, 1930. So effective was the appeal that voting appeared to be lifted out of the realm of personal choice into the area of impersonal service for others. In part the orator said:

You have done marvelous things in Illinois. Negroes who have been fighting these fetters against discrimination for fifty years can rise in a crisis like this and register interest in what is going on. This great advance is evidence that Negroes, though beaten down, will not stay beaten. The Negro has that everlasting spirit that rises. There has been an effort to break the spirit of the Negro. I can tell you that the Negro spirit is far from being broken. The Negro with indomitable courage is still facing the rising sun. . . . . You aren't going to vote against us. You aren't going to run from Negroes.[36]

The applause that greeted these words was deafening. While few colored orators are able to make so dramatic an appeal as this one, race pride is an ever recurring theme at political rallies.

Much more difficult to dramatize is an appeal to civic pride. Judge Albert B. George, in the primary of 1930, pitched his campaign arguments at a high level. He said in effect that there were 150 colored lawyers in Chicago and as their representative on the bench it was up to him to make good in every way. He was often stopped on the street by people he did not know and was told that he had been very fair in some case before him, even though the speaker lost the case. He knew that a colored man on the bench in Chicago would have a hard time. His supporters knew that too, and he was glad to say that the leaders had come to him before he took up his judicial duties and told him they would not ask political favors of him and thus embarrass him.[37]

Treatment of abstract issues was only a part of the task of the Negro orator. The voters pass upon personalities as well as issues and it was necessary for the organization to "sell" its candidates. The speakers must build up favorable pictures or stereotypes of their own organization candidates and unfavorable pictures of those of the opposition. Some of the spell-binders

[36] Report of political meeting, October 31, 1930.

[37] Political meeting, March 30, 1930.

took their cue from Mayor Thompson and tried their skill at extravagant praise, sweeping claims, wild and preposterous charges, and reckless buffoonery. This style could not be carried to an extreme as the audience became critical, but within limits it could be used to reinforce characterizations that had a fair degree of probability.

The creation of favorable stereotypes was not always easy as Negroes have shown a tendency to distrust their own leaders. To counteract this, one candidate would be pictured as a "fearless fighter," "a pioneer, rough but pure gold within," "a man of understanding, self-made and successful," "a loyal race man who was unpurchasable," a man who "admits no inferiority" and who "has broken down social and economic barriers." Another candidate would be painted as a "man of intelligence," a "man who had known poverty and who had a large, generous heart," a statesman, and an experienced public servant who knew the value of tact. Still a third candidate might be pictured as the "popular churchman," the "well-known fraternal leader," the "man with a smiling face and a steel backbone." The qualities that seemed to be appreciated by the voters were fearlessness in race matters, adroitness in coping with situations of importance to Negroes, and friendliness toward the masses.

The evolving of a Negro political organization made necessary the unification of various elements in the Negro group. Bitter factional quarrels resulted during which unfavorable symbols were employed by rival leaders in a ruthless fashion. At political meetings the opposition candidates would be called "ignorant and inefficient," "despisers of religion," "dummy numbskulls," "oxen in parlors," "grinning jackasses," "cowards," "traitors to the race," "double-crossers," "job sellers," "licentious, crooked, lying hypocrites," "dirty Negroes with aversions to blacks," "white folks' niggers," "pussy footing, hat-in-hand Uncle Toms," "handkerchief headed Negroes," "back-steppers and backbiters," "low belly-creepers," "lousy rats," "teeth skinned back like Cheshire cats," and "tools of the lily whites." These loaded epithets would not all apply to the same candidate, and some of them would be deemed so inappropriate that they would not be taken seriously. However, when a candidate's past record had some weak points the opposition was not slow to take advantage of them, provided, of course, that the opposition itself was not too vulnerable.

The vocabularies of encomium and vituperation of the Negro orators were particularly rich. To the language habits of the peasants was added the vernacular of city streets. Money was by no means the sole incentive which moved the colored voters to action. When the colored orators hit the proper chords they could move their listeners to support given candidates at the polls even though the campaign funds were against them. This is clear proof that some of the Negro leaders were masters in the manipulation of slogans and symbols.

CHAPTER VIII

EDWARD H. WRIGHT, THE IRON MASTER

The Negroes were not really admitted into the inner councils of the Republican party in Chicago until one of their group became a ward committeeman. According to custom the party councils were made up of the ward committeemen. While the legal position of these party officials has been confused during the past twenty years, their *de facto* functions have gone on. Each party or faction needed a representative in each ward and when a given faction controlled several offices it used its ward representatives to distribute the patronage whether he was the duly elected ward committeeman or not. The elected ward committeemen had, in addition, the power to nominate certain judges and to send representatives to party conventions. The power of a given ward committeeman depended upon the success of his faction in winning office, upon the share that he contributed to that success, and upon his ability to get along with the other party leaders.

EDWARD H. WRIGHT

The first colored ward committeeman, Edward H. Wright, was elected to the post by the Republican voters of the Second Ward in the primary of 1920. The rise of this six-foot, heavy, dark-skinned, and deliberate, slow-spoken Negro to a position of power and influence in the Republican councils of the city of Chicago is closely connected with the struggles of the Negroes for recognition in the state. Characterized by his friends as "pop-eyed with a face like a bull frog," "a bull dog in temperament," he mastered the handicaps of color and poverty to achieve a position of prominence in the political life of the city.

153

Committeeman Wright was born in New York City in 1864. He attended the public schools of that city and graduated from the College of the City of New York when he was seventeen. After teaching school in New Jersey for three years he came to Chicago "penniless and unknown," earning his transportation by assisting one of the porters on a Pullman car.[1] He worked in a real estate office and in the registry department of the post-office until 1887, when his energy and forcefulness attracted the attention of the Republican politicians and he was given a position in the county clerk's office. Two years later, as a reward for his activities in the Republican state convention of 1888, he was given the position of bookkeeper and railroad incorporation clerk in the Secretary of State's office in Springfield.[2] This was the first clerical position in the state government to be held by a colored man. At the end of the term of the man who appointed him, Wright entered the city clerk's office in Chicago and two years later was elected South Town Clerk, a local office with a one-year term. In the Cook County Republican Convention of 1894 he was instrumental in securing the nomination of Theodore W. Jones for county commissioner.[3] Two years later Wright himself was nominated for county commissioner and in the same year he was admitted to the bar. These were the days of the caucus, the convention,[4] rough-and-tumble politics, "boodle" aldermen, and public utility scandals. Out of the strife and turmoil he emerged as the third colored man to be elected county commissioner from the city of Chicago.

Commissioner Wright's activities on the county board showed him to be shrewd, forceful, and highly race conscious. Shortly after his election he deliberately held up the appropriation for the office of State's Attorney Charles S. Deneen in order to se-

[1] *Broad Ax*, February 10, 1900.

[2] Washington Intercollegiate Club, *The Negro in Chicago*, I, 135.

[3] See above, p. 82.

[4] The 1896 Cook County convention has been used as an example of evils of the convention system. Many of the delegates had criminal records, over one-third were saloon-keepers, and one-fifth were political employees. See *Review of Reviews* XVI (1897), 332. This passage is cited in P. O. Ray, *An Introduction to Political Parties and Practical Politics* (New York, 1922), p. 128.

cure the appointment of a colored man as assistant state's attorney. When Deneen was informed as to why his appropriation was delayed, he is alleged to have said: "I want you to understand, Mr. Wright, that I am all powerful in this office." To this Wright replied: "Yes, and I am county commissioner."[5] A few days later Ferdinand L. Barnett became the first colored assistant state's attorney for Cook County and Deneen's appropriation was passed. During his second term as county commissioner Wright was elected president pro tem of the county board by the thirteen remaining white members when the president was away for a short time in 1900.[6] This election was secured by going around to all the members of the board individually and telling them that he did not hope to be elected president pro tem but he would appreciate one or two votes as a sign of recognition among his own people. There were two prominent contenders and when the votes of the county board were counted Wright received every vote except two. During the entire period of his service on the board he attended the sessions regularly and took an active part in the proceedings. Some years later one of the daily white newspapers made critical references to his vote on a street car franchise ordinance and his vote on a tax levy for township purposes, but no evidence was presented which raised any doubts as to his honesty.[7]

After his second term as county commissioner Wright failed to secure a renomination and for fifteen years he wandered

[5] A. N. Fields' version of this in the *Defender*, October 8, 1932, states: "Wright went over and Deneen said to him: 'Ed, what's the idea of you holding up the appropriation for my office?' Wright replied: 'You had an understanding with me that in the event of your election you would appoint F. L. Barnett assistant state's attorney and you have failed to keep your word: until that is done I shall continue to prevent the passage of your appropriation.' Deneen replied: 'I am state's attorney of Cook county and you can't dictate to me.' "

[6] Board of Cook County Commissioners, *Official Record of Proceedings*, September 10, 1900, p. 793.

[7] *Daily News*, April 2, 1910: "He supported a measure granting a blanket franchise without compensation which would have given the Metropolitan Traction Company a monopoly in building street railways over the principal highways in Cook County lying outside the limits of Chicago and not already occupied by street car tracks. One of his last official acts was to fight for the passage of a resolution authorizing the old town boards of malodorous memory to levy a tax of $152,500 for township expenses."

about the political wilderness without finding any satisfactory haven. For a period he moved out of the district where he had been a political power. When he moved back he was unable to make satisfactory arrangements with Martin B. Madden and George F. Harding, the political powers of the South Side, so for the time being he was relegated to the background. In 1906 he worked with Second Ward Committeeman Chauncey Dewey, and he was chosen as state central committeeman for the First Congressional District, but this position did not bring him much power.

> Col. Ed. H. Wright, who has worked harder for the success of the G.O.P. than any other colored Republican in the State of Illinois, and who has so far been left out in the cold by the powers that be, has an itching desire to become the new city sealer of Chicago, but it appears that there are too many German-Americans after that job for Col. Wright to land it.[8]

In 1910 Wright made an unsuccessful attempt to win a seat in the city council. The white organization candidate had the backing of the Republican committeeman and George F. Harding, the other alderman, but the idea of Negro representation helped Wright and he polled nearly one-sixth of the vote cast. In certain precincts it was reported that Harding spent money liberally and that attempts were made to intimidate the Wright forces, but the votes went largely to Wright.[9] This campaign demonstrated the fact that a militant Negro leader could attract votes in spite of great obstacles in the areas where the colored voters had become race conscious. In the five years that followed this campaign Wright continued as an independent Republican, agitating for race representation and stirring up trouble in the regular Republican ward meetings. During these days his prestige and his economic resources were at a low ebb.

Ex-Commissioner Wright's opportunity to stage a comeback in politics came in 1915 when William Hale Thompson was elected mayor of Chicago. He was very active in pre-primary campaign helping Fred Lundin collect pledge cards for Thompson. After the election Mayor Thompson recognized the serv-

---

[8] *Broad Ax*, May 4, 1907.

[9] See above, p. 74, and *Broad Ax*, March 26, April 9, 1910.

ices that Wright had rendered during his campaign by appointing him as an assistant corporation counsel with a salary that was higher than that of any other colored appointee. Wright was again part of the dominant Republican faction in the city. The temporary eclipse of Alderman DePriest, following his indictment and trial in 1917, eliminated a dangerous rival and Wright became the outstanding colored organization leader of Thompson's campaigns for United States senator in 1918 and for mayor in 1919. In December, 1919, Mayor Thompson conferred a new honor upon Wright by making him one of the attorneys for the traction commission at $100 a day. Some time before the 1920 primary Congressman Madden decided not to run again for Republican committeeman of the Second Ward. The Thompson leaders on the South Side agreed to support Wright for this position. The *Defender* made the following editorial comment on the choice:

> The almost certain election of Edward H. Wright as Republican ward committeeman of the Second Ward will be a distinct gain politically for our racial group. Mr. Wright belongs to that progressive element which has done and is doing so much to advance our cause along right lines. No member of our group has ever been elected ward committeeman in Chicago since the law provided for such elections by popular vote.
>
> We need a man in the managing committee of our party who has brains and the courage to use them for our interests. At the same time our representative should have those qualities that command the respect and co-operation of his associates. He should have experience as well as ability and his past record should demonstrate that he knows how to do things. Mr. Wright has all of these qualifications.[10]

Wright easily defeated Warren B. Douglas, the Deneen candidate for the position, and he was established as the titular and actual head of the Thompson forces in the Second Ward. While the law under which he was elected was later declared unconstitutional and there was some doubt as to his legal status as committeeman, he remained the recognized spokesman of the dominant Republican faction for a period of six years.

---

[10] *Chicago Defender*, April 10, 1920. By this time the *Broad Ax* was more favorably inclined toward Wright. In 1917 and 1918 it made a good deal of the fact that Wright was caught in a gambling game. See issues of September 22, 1917, December 28, 1918. The *Whip* criticized him for the same reason in its issue of February 7, 1920.

As ward committeeman Wright was aggressive in race matters, strict in discipline, indifferent to personal publicity, and
loyal to his word at all costs. It was said that he was feared by
the men that he controlled and had made. He kept a card index
of all of his followers, and on the eve of an election he would
call in his precinct captains and say, "I'm keeping a record of
each man at this election. When the time comes to pay off, I'm
paying on the basis of the way you produce. See that you deliver."[11] In the primary of 1926, for instance, he had $2,900 from
the city headquarters to distribute among his fifty-eight precinct captains or $50 a precinct, and according to his testimony,
"They all act in harmony or else they do not stay."[12] He was a
realist in politics and recognized the necessity of having the
rougher elements represented in his organization. He was criticized for this by one of the colored weeklies, but he lived to see
the day when this paper came around more to his point of
view.[13]

In wresting jobs and favors from the white politicians for
himself and the organization Committeeman Wright was unusually successful. While he was the leader of the organization,
the Negroes of Chicago secured their first state senator, their
first municipal judge, and their fourth state representative.
After Mayor Thompson's retirement in 1923 he became associated with the Republican faction led by State's Attorney Robert E. Crowe. The election of Albert George as municipal judge
in 1924 was looked upon as one of his greatest political feats.
He demanded a pledge from every Republican ward committeeman that in return for the support of the regular ticket in
the "Black Belt" they would support George. He made them
promise individually that they would deal with George fairly.[14]

[11] Manuscript document, information furnished by a close friend of Wright's.

[12] U.S. Congress, Senate, *Hearings before a Special Committee Investigating Campaign Expenditures in Senatorial Primary and General Elections*, 1926, 69th Congress, 1st session, Part II, p. 1681. These hearings were commonly referred to as the "Reed Hear-
ings."

[13] The *Whip*, April 17, 1920; July 7, December 1, 1923; February 16, 1924; January
31, 1925, was critical of Wright because of vice conditions in the Second Ward, but its
attitude was changed later as shown by the issue of April 24, 1926.

[14] Interview, March 14, 1933.

Important appointive positions were also secured for the organization. After the Democrats gained control of the city administration in 1923 he was appointed a member of the Illinois Commerce Commission by Governor Len Small, whom he had helped to nominate in the primary of 1920. His chief lieutenants were located in such positions as assistant state's attorneys, attorneys for the sanitary district, deputy sheriffs, deputy coroners, deputy bailiffs, and many other responsible positions. As he later put it, "Every conspicuous political appointment of a colored man or woman in Chicago and Illinois from industrial commissioner and Illinois commerce commissioner down, has been brought about by the Second Ward Republican organization under my leadership."[15]

The power of the organization was used to secure legislative favors as well. When the South Park Board refused to permit the placing of a statue in honor of the Eighth Regiment on Grand Boulevard, Wright threatened to work for the defeat of the park bond issues at a coming referendum. The consent of the park board was then granted.[16] He had a very important share in the nomination of a white man for an important county office in 1926.[17] So well disciplined were his troops that it appeared he was in an impregnable position. His power and personality are illustrated by his testimony at the hearings of the senate committee investigating campaign expenditures in 1926. In answer to Senator James Reed's question, "And that same group, the Crowe-Barrett group, in your ward at least, were supporting Mr. Smith?" he replied, "Well, there is not any Crowe-Barrett group in my ward . . . . I am the group."[18]

Committeeman Wright little realized how soon his boast before the Reed committee would be shown to be an empty one. In 1924 he had reached out into the Third Ward and was instrumental in naming ex-Representative Kersey as ward committeeman in that district. The aldermen of both the Second and Third wards were indebted to him for aid in several cam-

[15] *Chicago Daily News*, March 12, 1927. See also *Chicago Defender*, February 28, 1925.

[16] *Chicago Defender*, March 20, 1926.

[17] *Ibid.*, December 31, 1932.

[18] *Reed Committee Hearings*, II, 1678.

paigns. The first break came in a quarrel with Thompson and Crowe in 1926 over the designation of a Republican committee-man from the First Ward to succeed the late Francis P. Brady. Thompson was trying to prepare the way for his re-election as mayor and proposed the name of Daniel Scanlon, while Wright urged the selection of his friend, State Senator Adolph Marks. Bitter words were exchanged and Thompson charged Wright with attempting to set himself up as a dictator in the South Side, while Wright threatened to bolt the ticket in the coming election if his choice were not selected. Wright left the meeting and the designation of Scanlon followed.[19] The Second Ward committeeman failed to see that this was the beginning of the end. White politicians were becoming jealous of his power and a false step would be fatal to his political fortunes.

A more difficult dilemma was presented to Wright in the first part of the year 1927. Thompson was an avowed candidate for the Republican nomination for mayor but his former associate, Governor Len Small, was not backing him in the campaign. Fred Lundin, the governor's political adviser, was grooming a former health commissioner, Dr. John Dill Robertson, for the mayoralty race. What should Committeeman Wright do? He owed his position as commerce commissioner to the governor, but the signs of the times were pointing to a rise in the political fortunes of the former mayor. His friends urged him to go along with Thompson, and Thompson himself pleaded with him, but all to no avail. When it was clear that he could not be moved the Crowe-Thompson group warned him that his patron-age would be taken away from him and that Dan M. Jackson would be named as their committeeman. He called his precinct captains into council and is alleged to have said, "I have chosen my own course. I am not asking any of you to quit your jobs. I am able to take care of myself. You go over to Dan Jackson— he is your new leader."[20] One of his captains later said, "That was one of the most moving things I have ever seen in my whole life. Wright knew that he was sealing his political doom. When

[19] *Chicago Daily News*, October 7, 1926.
[20] *Chicago Defender*, December 24, 1932.

a man comes big enough to do a thing like that, they don't come any bigger."[21]

The deposed chieftain issued some brave statements but he was unable to stem the tide. "I told them," Mr. Wright said, "that I'm no political slave, that I was chosen committeeman by my people in a regularly held election in 1920 and that I didn't propose to sell them out to satisfy the whims of the downtown bosses."[22] More than fifty jobs were allotted to the new Second Ward organization led by Daniel Jackson and the public sentiment for Thompson grew stronger and stronger. One by one Wright's erstwhile lieutenants deserted him, some before the primary and others before the election. In the final election his candidate running on an independent ticket polled only 526 votes in territory that had delivered nearly a 10,000 plurality for the Republican ticket six months before.

Divergent views have been held regarding the causes of Committeeman Wright's downfall. Some of his friends who naturally put a high estimate on the man himself, his services to the Republican party and to the members of his race in Chicago, felt that Wright had committed political hara-kiri out of loyalty to Governor Small and the regular Republican organization. Others view his political suicide as the result of a political mistake. As Mayor Thompson put it, "He had to choose and he made the wrong choice. This was his big mistake. All politicians make mistakes at times."[23] After spending years in building up a stereotype of Mayor Thompson as a second Lincoln, Wright found that he could not efface it in a few months. He failed to foresee that Governor Small and Mayor Thompson were only temporarily apart and would soon come together again. He failed to see that no political leader, no matter how powerful, can withstand an overwhelming tide of public sentiment among his people. He failed to see that he could not carry with him even his close associates on a path that led to political destruction. Without money, without patronage, without a

[21] Interview.

[22] *Broad Ax*, January 22, 1917. See also *Chicago Daily News*, March 12, 1927.

[23] Interview.

cause that stirred the imagination of his constituents, his political experience and acumen were of no avail. His harsher critics accused him of having delusions of grandeur, of needlessly arousing the jealousy of white politicians, and of displaying overweening arrogance among his own people.[24]

In retrospect, Wright became a race hero. The Negro estimate of the man is based on his services to the race rather than to the party. This is clearly indicated in the editorial of the *Chicago Whip:*

> He was a strong man, an astute politician, who knew all of the angles and squares. He did not truckle and bow, he had no inferiority complex and in consequence he won the respect of both his white conferees and his brothers in blood.
>
> Men like Wright are not born every day. He typified and characterized the rugged, unbending type. He gave no quarter and asked for none and we frankly believe that we will wait a long time before another like him comes on the scene. In the study of his life much inspiration can be found, ambitions fired, and new found respect will be generated, for he was a great strong man who led his people into the enviable position they now have in holding the "balance of power" in Illinois politics.[25]

Both white and colored politicians in Chicago agreed that Wright was an aggressive ward boss and a man of his word.[26] During the period of his control of the Republican organization in the Negro community many new elective and new appointive positions were filled by Negroes, many white politicians were put under obligation to the colored voters, and the Negroes became more conscious of their political power. During his lifetime Wright was accused of neglecting the unsanitary conditions, the growth of vice, the lack of police protection, and the lack of recreational facilities in the colored neighborhoods.[27] Whatever his responsibility was for these deficiencies in the governmental services, he now stands out as a fighter for the Negro race who obtained his share of the jobs and privileges.

[24] Interviews.   [25] August 16, 1930.

[26] Former Senator Deneen said: "Wright was a very forceful man and an able lawyer. He was powerful in one of the wards." Interview, June 1, 1931. The late Dr. John Dill Robertson said: "Ed Wright was a very clever politician. He knew the game from A to Z. He was always a man of his word." Interview, January 9, 1931.

[27] See below, pp. 178–79.

CHAPTER IX
OSCAR DE PRIEST, MILITANT ORGANIZER

Of the various Negro political leaders who struggled to secure political position in Chicago, Congressman Oscar DePriest emerged as a national leader. His name has appeared in prac-

OSCAR DE PRIEST

tically every newspaper in the country, and he has been a figure admired and hated by black and white leaders alike. His career is of special importance in understanding the rôle of the Negro in Chicago politics because it touches so many phases of Negro life. As a migrant from the South, as a laborer seeking to earn a living in the North, as a business man in the growing Chicago community, as a precinct captain in the Republican party when it was consolidating its power, as an important office-holder, as a political propagandist, as a party organizer, DePriest participated in the political hopes, triumphs, disappointments, setbacks, and advances of his people. His relations with fellow-members of his race and his relations with white people typify many of the experiences of the Negroes who migrated North in the last forty years. Even when he was temporarily out of power he was the best-known, the most publicized, and the most striking personality in the Negro political world in Chicago.

Many conflicting views have been expressed regarding De-Priest's political career. In some of the daily newspapers run by whites he has been denounced as a cheap politician who was wholly unreliable. At times the colored weeklies have been highly critical of his official record. However, there was no period during his entire public life when he was without many ar-

dent admirers. He did not address himself to the daily newspapers because he knew that his followers got their political
opinions from other sources. He turned his attention to the
great mass of Negroes who were coming into the South Side of
Chicago. They saw in him a great political leader.

Congressman DePriest is a man you would notice in any
crowd. His height of over six feet, his great shock of white hair,
his firmly built frame and erect carriage, and his rugged appearance command attention anywhere. His color is such that he is
not conspicuous in a crowd of white people. In fact, he has been
taken for white on a number of occasions.[1]

FAMILY AND EARLY LIFE

As in the case of many other colored leaders in Chicago, De-
Priest was born in the South, of freedman stock, and experiences
which he had in early life left a deep impression upon his mind.
Although his family moved from Alabama to Kansas when he
was only seven years old, the hardships which his relatives suffered in the South during the first fifteen years of their freedom,
and the disappointments which came to them following the collapse of the reconstruction governments, cast a shadow over his
childhood and youth. His older sisters and brother carried
away vivid pictures of what life was like for Negroes in the
South in the troublesome years that followed the Civil War.

Oscar DePriest was born in a cabin on March 9, 1871 in
Florence, Alabama, where his father was a teamster and farmer,
his mother was a part-time laundress, and his uncles were deco-
rators. Although a small man physically, his father was of an
independent nature, and in the days of slavery defied his over-
seers. When this action was reported, his master said "You'll
have to kill him if you whip him and I don't want him killed."[2]
Following the emancipation the elder DePriest earned his living
by hauling material in drays from the river and from the trains,

[1] When he ran away from home at the age of seventeen, he was taken for white in
Dayton, Ohio. About the time of the World's Fair in 1893 he obtained employment
from a man who thought he was white. After he became congressman, a white passenger
on a train mistook him for white.

[2] Interview with member of family.

as well as doing a little farming. His new occupation freed him to a certain extent from the soil and this increased mobility was to the freed man one of the real changes incident to his new status. It was from his mother that Congressman DePriest inherited his huge size, and her influence upon his personal development was also considerable, as she participated in every important family decision.

While his father was without the educational opportunities, he was intensely interested in politics and took a lively part in all campaigns. He was once approached by a white man who asked him to vote the Democratic ticket. When the elder DePriest refused, a threat was made to deprive him of his hauling business. His answer was, "Take it."[3]

Florence was a town which was buzzing with political activity because it was the birthplace and home of James T. Rapier, United States Representative from Alabama to the Forty-third Congress. DePriest's father knew Rapier well and one evening on the way home he overheard some men say that they were going to capture Rapier. He hurried home to tell the news and found Rapier in his own house. The lights were put out and the men sat out under the trees in the dark, watching the crowd as it moved up and down the Negro section looking for Rapier. When the crowd came to the DePriest home, it got no help. DePriest's mother was greatly frightened by this episode and began to long for an environment which promised greater personal security for her family.

Shortly after the attempt to kidnap Rapier, three white men were lynched on a nearby corner. One of the men broke loose and was shot very near the DePriest home. The next day the children, including Oscar, discovered the blood stains where the man had fallen. This was the last straw and the family decided to move North.

While the family was still in Florence, Oscar DePriest attended a Congregational church school. This church school established a religious contact which persisted in later years.[4]

The entire DePriest family migrated to Salina, Kansas, in

[3] Interview with member of family.   [4] *Chicago Defender*, April 20, 1929.

1878. Kansas had been admitted as a free state in 1861 and the DePriests were in the vanguard of an exodus of many Negroes to this new haven. There was only one other colored family in the town when they arrived and here the boy, Oscar, entered the second grade of a school attended by white children who had never seen any Negro children before. Because of their strangeness, the six DePriest children were picked upon, and constant fighting was the order of the day. Oscar himself was so provocative that he earned the nickname "Meddlesome Bunk." As one writer described him, "He was sandy haired, long legged, barefoot and rolled pantaloons, light complexion and blue eyes. An opprobrious reference to his race was a sure signal for a fight— a real fist fight."[5] His sisters as well as his brother sometimes came to his assistance in these school-day fights. In later life DePriest directed part of his combativeness toward the racial struggle for patronage, fair treatment, and recognition.

The younger members of the DePriest family found it necessary to augment the family income in any way possible. Oscar DePriest was early noted for his energy and shrewdness.[6]

After finishing the grade school, DePriest went to the Salina Normal School, where he took a business and bookkeeping course for two years. This completed his formal education. As compared with some of the younger colored leaders in Chicago, DePriest's educational opportunities were limited. The future congressman was not a man who relied heavily upon book knowledge. In his speeches he sometimes made grammatical mistakes and his pronunciation was never distinct, but he proceeded directly to his point and he was rarely misunderstood. His formal education was sufficient for his immediate needs, he was very quick and accurate at figures, he was a good judge of character, and he learned rapidly from experience.

Like many of the more adventuresome members of his race, DePriest at an early age took to the road. One of the essentials

[5] *Ibid.*

[6] One account runs as follows: "Being a hustling lad he was often hired for chores and odd jobs. One job he obtained under a contract price of $1. Resorting to his sense of business, he hired five boys at 5 cents a piece, successfully bossed the job, and collected 75 cents for his brainwork." *Ibid.*

of freedom was liberty to move about. At the age of seventeen he ran away with two white boys to Dayton, Ohio. After about a year he became tired of his white companions and left them abruptly to come to Chicago in 1889.

BEGINNINGS IN CHICAGO POLITICS

When DePriest arrived in Chicago there were only fourteen thousand Negroes in the city and just a handful of these were found in business and professional occupations. E. H. Morris and E. H. Wright were just starting on their legal and political careers. John Buckner, who later became the political sponsor of DePriest and of several other leaders, was a head waiter for private parties. While Buckner was not as highly educated as Wright, he had the manners of polished gentlemen and like Wright he was actively interested in increasing the economic opportunities for Negroes. At the time, so limited were the openings for colored people, that in the Negro community head waiters, porters, and barbers stood near the top of the occupational scale.

In Chicago DePriest followed the footsteps of his uncles and became a painter and decorator. Some of the old residents of the city can remember when he carried a ladder up and down State Street. There were times when he found it difficult to obtain work. Employers would keep him until they found out that he was colored and then they would fire him. Finally, he obtained work with a white man by the name of Peters, who valued his ability to see a job through and helped him get started in business for himself. As an independent decorator he made business by going into places that appeared to be run down and offering his services. An early press mention of DePriest refers to a judgment which he obtained against a church for decorating.[7]

Regarding his start in politics DePriest himself relates the following:

A friend of mine came by one evening and said, "Come go to a meeting with me." I had nothing to do so I went. It was a precinct meeting and they were electing precinct captains. The vote was 20–20 for rival candidates and I saw right away that a deal could be made. So I went to one of the candidates

[7] *Broad Ax*, April 18, 1903.

and said, "Now you're the man who ought to be captain, I'll give you two additional votes if you'll make me secretary." The man refused. I went to his rival and made the same proposition; he accepted. I was made secretary. I kept at it because it was recreation to me. I always like a good fight, the chance, the suspense interests me. I never gambled nor played cards so it was fun to me.[8]

The new precinct secretary was not noted as a public speaker. There were many colored men who excelled him in the field of oratory. However, he was a good organizer and he made himself so useful to John Buckner that he attracted the attention of Martin B. Madden. DePriest's nomination for the county board by the Republican Cook County convention in 1904 was a surprise to many. There were a number of colored leaders whose legislative experience far excelled his. Edward H. Wright had served two terms on the county board and E. H. Morris, John Buckner, and E. L. Martin had had experience in the House of Representatives at Springfield. The white dailies commented unkindly upon the nomination.[9] The following account has been given as to how it was accomplished.

These were the days of conventions. Madden wanted the support of the Negro elective precinct captains that Oscar controlled. The deal was that in return for their support of Madden, Oscar was to be elected county commissioner. The state convention was to come first. Oscar knowing that if Madden was elected he would have no hesitancy in forgetting his promise to see Oscar county commissioner at the county convention that came later, manipulated it so that the date of the county convention was set before that of the state convention. Madden in a tight place saw Oscar's election through.[10]

DePriest was elected at the age of thirty-three against the opposition of older and more experienced contenders to a county-wide post. His campaign manager was a lawyer named Edward Wilson, who in later years played quite a different rôle.[11] As county commissioner, DePriest's record was such that he

[8] Interview. November 4, 1931. A contemporary account of his start in politics runs as follows: "Like most successful politicians, he started working among his neighbors, always in the interest of the regular organization. His energetic efforts in behalf of the Third Ward organization without price or place soon attracted the attention of Congressman Martin B. Madden." *Broad Ax*, December 30, 1905.

[9] *Chicago Tribune*, November 10, 1904; cited in *Broad Ax*, November 12, 1904.

[10] Interview, November 13, 1931.   [11] *Broad Ax*, July 30, 1904, and below, p. 83.

was able to secure a renomination in 1906. Although he was re-elected, his popular vote was less than that of his first election. While on the county board he helped educate the Negro poor to avail themselves of the relief resources of the county, and as a member of the Building Committee he secured some important contracts.[12]

Following his second term as county commissioner, DePriest failed to secure a renomination in the county convention. His defeat was attributed to the fact that he joined hands with State Senator Samuel Ettelson in a factional fight against Congressman Madden and Major Buckner. DePriest was accused of disloyalty to the men who were primarily responsible for his rise to public office.[13] While he was elected as an alternate delegate to the Republican National Convention of 1908, the Madden and Buckner forces crushed his ambitions to return to the county board or to make a race for the state legislature.

Temporarily out of power in political circles, DePriest turned his attention to business. In addition to his work as a contractor and decorator, he began to act as a real estate agent. He opened an office on State Street and persuaded a number of property owners to allow him to handle their real estate. On the fringes of the advancing Negro community he would take a long lease on a building that had been occupied exclusively by whites and then fill it with colored people. Since Negroes were charged higher rents than the whites, this business was profitable.[14] In this way DePriest built up a private fortune which enabled him to become an investor in real estate, stocks and bonds.

The period of seven years from 1908 to 1915 was one in which

[12] *Broad Ax*, December 30, 1905.

[13] *Ibid.*, August 15, 1908. It said in part: "In order to reward Congressman Madden and Major Buckner for extending to him a helping hand in politics at the time he sadly needed it, shortly after his re-election as County Commissioner in 1906 the honorable Oscar DePriest seemingly turned his cold back on them and joined hands with State Senator Sam Ettelson."

[14] As one commentator put it, "When the migration began he would lease whole buildings in sections where white people had lived and were paying $20 a unit rent and rent them to colored for $40, while his obligation for the same unit ran about $10, thus leaving a $30 profit. Negroes weren't aware of being overcharged anyway. Times were good and they didn't mind. And if DePriest hadn't gotten it, someone else would have."

the political fortunes of the Negroes in Chicago advanced slowly. Republican factional quarrels, the Progressive split of 1912,
Democratic victories in national, state, and local elections, and
personal jealousies in the colored community retarded the development of Negro politics. It was said that DePriest during
this period was opportunistic rather than faithful. He returned
to the Madden fold and remained loyal to Madden personally,
but it was stated that he supported a Democratic candidate for
alderman in 1911 and a Democratic candidate for state's attorney in 1912. During the campaigns of E. H. Wright, Charles A.
Griffin, and William Cowan for alderman, DePriest took the
side of the white organization candidate.[15] He was evidently
waiting for the time that would be auspicious for a racial candidate for the city council.

THE FIRST ALDERMAN

Mention has already been made of the election of DePriest as
the first colored alderman in 1915. In the present connection we
are interested in why he, rather than some other colored man,
was selected for this honor. Many months before the primary
he was busy securing endorsements and holding meetings. By
the end of November, 1914, an appeal was presented to Congressman Madden, Second Ward Committeeman, which contained the endorsements of thirty-eight precinct captains, the
Hotel Waiters' Association, the Chicago Colored Barbers Association, ministers of the Chicago Baptist Churches, ministers of
the Chicago Methodist Churches, women's church clubs, the
Physicians, Dentists and Pharmaceutical Club, and many individual party workers.[16] In December he secured the backing of
the Second Ward Republican Organization and from that time
on his election was practically assured. As a candidate for elective office, he was much stronger than he had been in 1904. He
had back of him four years' experience as county commissioner,
he had money of his own, and conditions were favorable. Former Commissioner Wright was on the outskirts of the organization and he lacked personal funds to put into the campaign.

---

[15] *Chicago Defender*, January 16, 1915.   [16] *Broad Ax*, November 28, 1914.

William Cowan was disheartened by his narrow defeat the previous year, and Louis B. Anderson was waging his first campaign for elective office. At a mass meeting in January, at which an attempt was made to limit the field to a single colored candidate, Anderson was conciliatory, but DePriest flatly refused to make any compromise and stated that he was the choice of the Republican organization and that it was the duty of all voters to abide by the organization's choice.[17] DePriest was nominated by a safe margin and carried the election easily in a three-cornered race against two white candidates, one a Democrat and the other a Progressive.[18]

While the white press did not welcome DePriest's entrance into the city council,[19] it was hailed as a great event by the colored community. The *Chicago Defender*, which had been lukewarm toward DePriest in the early stages of the campaign, wrote after his election:

In the Second Ward, where the voters of the Afro-American race in large numbers reside, the excitement was at fever heat. The race had one of its own on the ticket for Alderman. . . . . They came to the front 11,000 strong for Oscar DePriest, and for the first time in the history of the city of Chicago a member of this race will sit in that august body. . . . .[20]

It was said that when Alderman DePriest appeared on State Street crowds of people followed him. The Thompson administration brought other colored leaders to the front but none of them were more conspicuous than DePriest. As an alderman he defended Mayor Thompson, introduced a civil rights ordinance, and looked after the interests of his constituents as he saw them. His record did not commend itself to the reform organization known as the Municipal Voters' League,[21] but his followers were

---

[17] *Chicago Defender*, January 2, 1915.

[18] The final vote was Al Russell, Democrat, 6,893; Oscar DePriest, Republican, 10,599; Samuel Block, Socialist, 433; Simon P. Gary, Progressive, 3,697. *Chicago Daily News Almanac for 1916*, p. 567.

[19] Scarcely mentioned in the *Chicago Tribune*.   [20] April 10, 1915.

[21] *Twenty-second Annual Preliminary Report* said: "OSCAR DEPRIEST—Finishing first term with bad record; no alderman in Chicago's history piled up a more notorious record in so short a time. . . . . Alderman DePriest's voting record is important only as showing how such aldermen vote; he voted against giving Finance Committee an ex-

not guided by this organization. The Municipal Voters' League was a non-partisan organization which made recommendations on the candidates for aldermen. It was interested in efficiency and economy and was not concerned with questions of racial representation. Alderman DePriest, on the other hand, was interested in finding jobs for Negroes.

Alderman DePriest probably did not realize toward the end of 1916 that he was approaching a crisis in his political career. There were murmurs that the man who came into office with the backing of many ministers was dealing with the underworld. It was known that he had attended banquets for Robert Motts[22] and that, while not a gambler or drinker himself, his views were liberal on questions affecting the regulation of public morals.[23] In the middle of 1916 he made a public denial of the report that money was paid him to use his influence to open the Panama Cafe, a notorious saloon and cabaret that was constantly getting into difficulties with the police.[24] In view of the general political situation which the new alderman found at the city hall and in his own ward, it was inevitable that his name would be associated with activities which were criticized in the daily press. He could either denounce or go along with the leaders of the colored underworld. For reasons which have already been discussed it was exceedingly difficult for an organization candidate to do the former.

State's Attorney Maclay Hoyne was a Democrat and he was anxious to discredit the new Republican administration in the city of Chicago. DePriest had supported Hoyne in 1912 but in 1916 he worked for the Thompson candidate for state's attorney. On January 18, 1917, Hoyne announced that the Grand Jury had indicted Alderman DePriest along with several others

---

pert staff, against keeping city expenditures within income, against business methods of hauling ashes and garbage, against publicity on "60-day" jobholders, against prohibiting aldermen soliciting jobs from public service corporations, against compelling school board to disclose facts about its finances and against non-partisan organization of council; one of the 'budget aviators'; not a candidate."

[22] *Broad Ax*, February 3, 1906.   [23] *Ibid.*, January 15, 1916.

[24] *Chicago Defender*, August 26, 1916. For a description of the Panama Cafe, see J. B. Wood, *The Negro in Chicago*, p. 25.

for conspiracy to allow gambling houses and houses of prostitution to operate and for bribery of police officers in connection with the protection of these houses.[25] It was later disclosed that the indictment was the result of written confessions made by Captain Stephen K. Healy of the Stanton Avenue Police Station and Henry "Teenan" Jones, owner of the Elite, both of whom turned state's evidence.[26] One of DePriest's bondsmen was Elijah H. Johnson, the brother of the late John "Mushmouth" Johnson, whose gambling activities have been described above. At the trial several Negro gambling-house keepers testified that their places had been raided by the police until they paid Jones, the head of the syndicate, for protection. Several policemen testified that they had been demoted for raiding places which were under the wing of the syndicate. One of DePriest's agents told of collecting graft money from gambling clubs and paying it to the alderman himself. When "Teenan" Jones took the stand he said that he paid $2,500 to DePriest during a period of four months and that he gave additional sums of money to Captain Healy. The latter testified that DePriest had caused the removal of his predecessor at the station and told him that he was a "friend of the city administration and expected favors."[27] Captain Healy further stated that he had received money from Jones for the protection of gambling clubs and that he had talked with DePriest about gambling.

DePriest, himself, on the witness stand admitted that he had received $1,000 from Jones, that he had reduced detectives to "harness" because their actions displeased him, and that he had spoken to Captain Healy in behalf of Jones, in whose place he frequently dined. The defense lawyers, Clarence Darrow and E. H. Morris, based their case on the ground that the money which DePriest received was not given for police protection but merely as a campaign contribution, part of which was turned over to the Thompson candidate for state's attorney. In his closing argument Darrow warned the jury against race prejudice. When the jury brought in a verdict of "not guilty," State's

---

[25] *Chicago Daily News*, January 19, 1917.

[26] *Chicago Tribune*, June 12, 1917.   [27] *Ibid.*, June 5, 1917.

Attorney Hoyne called the action disgraceful and declared that DePriest must stand trial again on one of the other pending indictments.[28]

The immediate effect of the trial on DePriest's political fortunes was disastrous in spite of the favorable verdict. The primary election for alderman came before the trial was called and he was prevailed upon by the organization not to seek a renomination.[29] At the trial he offended a very prominent state senator by accusing him of being interested in a gambling club. Although he was acquitted of the conspiracy and bribery charges made against him there were many colored people who did not like the idea of their representative acting as a collector of party campaign funds from confessed gambling kings.[30] The trial did not reflect favorably upon the tone of politics in the Second Ward and there were many Negroes, including some editors, who thought that it was best to forget the whole sorry mess. On the other hand, the long-run effects of the trial did not interfere greatly with DePriest's political career. Part of his following felt that he had been persecuted because of his color and his political connections. His defeat of his persecutors in the trial marked him as a man who could stand up under fire. As time went on the details of the trial faded from popular memory and the stereotype of DePriest as the man who had beaten back his detractors loomed larger.

REBUILDING

Immediately following the trial, DePriest began to rebuild his political fortunes. In the face of repeated defeats and many discouragements he kept doggedly at the game for ten years before he reached his goal. During this time he stepped nimbly on the shifting and ever changing sands of Chicago politics. The story of the many factional alignments which he made is an intricate one and can only be related here in broad outline. As he was frequently thrown upon his own resources, he was compelled to make up for a lack of patronage by developing methods for mass

[28] *Ibid.*, June 10, 1917.

[29] *Ibid.*, January 27, 1919.   [30] *Chicago Defender*, February 16, 1918.

appeals. He apparently worked on the theory that if he could make himself troublesome enough, the organization would be compelled to take him in.

DePriest's friends claim that at the time of his withdrawal from the aldermanic race in 1917 the organization gave him assurances that if he cleared himself he would be backed in a campaign for vindication the following year. While he was acquitted of the charges of conspiracy and bribery in the June trial, there were six other indictments which hung over him for several years. These indictments did not deter him from entering a number of political contests, now on one side and now on another. The first struggle was for the aldermanic nomination in February, 1918. He waged a desperate battle against Robert R. Jackson, who was backed by the Second Ward Republican organization for the position and who therefore had the support of men like Edward H. Wright, Alderman Anderson, State Senator George F. Harding, and Congressman Madden.[31] Defeated by a narrow margin in the primary, he refused to drop out of the race and organized a group called the People's Movement to sponsor his candidacy as an independent in the election. A second time the DePriest forces were turned back for a loss but they did not disband.[32] They flirted with the McCormick and Deneen factions of the Republican party and replenished their ranks for aldermanic struggle of 1919.[33] DePriest's indictments, his alleged deception of both sides in the mayoralty campaign, his failure to secure jobs for Negroes while he was alderman, and his attacks upon the regular Republican organization were some of the points raised against him.[34] His third attempt to re-enter the City Council failed by a narrow margin.[35]

[31] *Ibid.*, March 2, 1918; *Broad Ax*, March 2, 1918.

[32] The results of the final election on April 2, 1918 were: Kuehne, Democrat, 3,187; Jackson, Republican, 6,669; A. E. Halm, Socialist, 312; DePriest, Independent, 6,021.

[33] *Broad Ax*, September 21, 1918. *Chicago Defender*, February 15, 1919.

[34] *Chicago Defender*, February 8, 1919.

[35] The final returns were: Louis B. Anderson, 6,735; William A. Wallace, 726; Oscar DePriest, 6,216.

Following the primary of 1919, at which Thompson was renominated as the Republican candidate for mayor and Louis B. Anderson as the Republican candidate for alderman in the Second Ward, DePriest changed his tactics. The Thompson faction of the Republican party in the colored community, led by Edward H. Wright and his associates, was too strong for him, so he declared a truce and joined forces with the Wright organization. It is possible that the race riots in the summer hastened the coalition of the two factions. DePriest's conduct was such during the riot that he gained the reputation for fearlessness in the presence of physical danger.[36] At a private conference in the fall Wright agreed to support DePriest for the position of delegate to the Republican National Convention. At a harmony meeting of all the factional leaders who had lately engaged in bitter denunciation of each other, this arrangement and the renomination of Alderman Jackson was agreed upon.[37] For a while the troublesome DePriest was back within the fold of the regular organization. This political somersault was criticized by a local weekly which failed to see that such acrobatics were common in Chicago politics.[38]

Although a delegate to the Republican National Convention which met in Chicago and nominated Warren G. Harding for president, DePriest remained in the background during the years from 1920 to 1922. After the new ward lines went into effect in 1921, the headquarters of the People's Movement was transferred into the new Third Ward. Eventually this move proved to be a great advantage to DePriest, as it coincided with

[36] Report of political meeting, January 24, 1932.

[37] *Chicago Defender*, November 15, 1919. In an interview, the following account was given of this conference: "When the group arrived, DePriest said, 'Well, I'll be chairman.' Nobody objected and he turned to Bob Jackson saying, 'Well, I guess you want to be committeeman.' Bob said, 'No.' They quarreled a bit. The question of Bob's council job aroused DePriest but DePriest consented to support him. Wright spoke up, 'Well, I want to be committeeman.' Harding here said, 'DePriest should have the job.' Thereupon Ettelson said, 'Why don't you two fellows go outside and fix it up between yourselves?' They went out. Once outside, Wright said, 'What can we talk about?' DePriest said, 'Let's talk about those fools in there.' After a little, they returned and announced Wright would be the man."

[38] *Chicago Whip*, January 31, 1920.

a general movement of the colored population in the city. While some of his property was bombed[39] and many years elapsed before he could make headway against the white leaders in the ward,[40] he laid the foundation for subsequent victories.

Mayor Thompson decided not to be a candidate to succeed himself in 1923. The Republican faction headed by Senator McCormick was successful in putting over the nomination of Arthur Lueder as the Republican candidate for mayor. During the election DePriest, along with Alderman Anderson and some of the other colored leaders, supported William E. Dever, the Democratic candidate for mayor. Considering the strength of the Republican tradition among the colored voters and the fact that DePriest was just coming to be recognized as the Republican leader of the Third Ward, this was a bold move. It was prompted, apparently, by a number of considerations, among which was the feeling that the Democrats were going to win and that it was desirable to be on the winning side; the fear that if Lueder won, he would use his power to destroy the Thompson faction; and the desire to pave the way for a return of Thompson to power at a later date. It was alleged that the Insull utility interests furnished large sums of money in order to turn the trick.[41] DePriest brought into play all his skill as an organizer and as a propagandist. Lueder was pictured as the candidate of the Ku Klux Klan, as a public official who discriminated against Negroes, as an avowed enemy of the Thompson faction, and as the puppet of the hated *Chicago Tribune*. In the words of a contemporary account, "Ghosts defeat Lueder."[42] As a reward for their efforts the colored leaders who supported Dever were given some patronage under the new administration.

The first mention of DePriest as a possible candidate for Congress to succeed Madden appeared in 1923. At a mass

[39] *Broad Ax*, April 9, 1921.

[40] He supported E. Marshall for the state legislature in 1922 primary in the Third District. *Chicago Whip*, February 18, 1922, The final vote was: Warren B. Douglas, 7,653½; A. H. Roberts, 9,058½; George T. Kersey, 10,717; E. J. Marshall, 5,818; Morris Lewis, 1,346; Oliver A. Clark, 1,254½; A. L. Williams, 2,752½.

[41] *Broad Ax*, March 17, 1923.

[42] *Chicago Defender*, April 7, 1923. See also *Chicago Tribune*, March 17, 1923.

meeting called to pay tribute to DePriest as a political leader, a resolution was adopted to the effect that he should be supported as a candidate for Congress in the event that Madden ran for governor.[43] From this time on the combinations and maneuvers of the former alderman may be interpreted in the light of this resolution.

The very next year after contributing to the defeat of Senator McCormick's candidate for mayor, DePriest urged the colored voters to support the Senator for a renomination. This remarkable shift in his factional alignment required an entirely new set of slogans to counteract some of the old ones. DePriest was severely criticized by Committeeman Wright[44] but he persisted in organizing a meeting for Senator McCormick in his own ward and even carried the battle into Wright's ward. The primary election returns, showing that McCormick lost the Third Ward by a mere 600 votes, whereas Lueder had lost the ward to Dever by 2,000 votes were a testimonial to DePriest's organizing abilities.

The coolness between Wright and DePriest during the senatorial primary of 1924 developed into an open break in the beginning of the following year. DePriest fired the first gun in the campaign when he announced that his independent organization was backing A. L. Williams against Anderson for alderman in the Second Ward and Dr. R. A. Williams against Jackson for alderman in the Third Ward. Committeeman Wright answered this blast by persuading the Republican leaders in power to deprive the DePriest organization of all the patronage which it enjoyed.[45] Since DePriest announced the return of Thompson as mayor as the avowed aim of his campaign, he lost his Democratic patronage as well. However, the DePriest forces were well supplied with funds and waged a strenuous campaign which rivaled the 1918 and 1919 aldermanic struggles in bitterness and vilification.

Leading the attacking forces of the "Outs," DePriest charged the "Ins" with responsibility for the dirty streets and alleys, the

[43] *Chicago Defender*, May 26, 1923.

[44] *Chicago Whip*, February 16, 1924.   [45] *Chicago Daily News*, January 17, 1925.

growth of vice, the misery brought upon the families of the discharged office-holders, the lack of adequate police protection,
the lack of bathing beaches and recreational facilities, and the
commercializing of residential neighborhoods.[46] The Wright
forces responded that DePriest's record was not that of a con-
sistent Thompson supporter, that his attacks on the organization were prompted by selfish and revolting ambitions, that his
candidates were tarred with the Democratic brush, and that he
was trying to wreck the leaders who had advanced the cause of
the Negroes.[47] The DePriest forces made an excellent showing
but again they were defeated.[48] After the election charges and
countercharges filled the air. Alderman Jackson charged that
Samuel Insull, the utility magnate, had spent large sums to defeat him; one of the ousted office-holders charged that DePriest
had withheld part of the campaign funds, one of the election
commissioners produced a letter alleged to have been written by
DePriest to a tenant, promising a reduction in rent if he would
help elect DePriest's candidate, and A. L. Williams charged that
he had been defeated by corrupt election practices.[49] The On-
looker in the *Defender* commented on the exceedingly low plane
of the campaign.[50]

These defeats might have discouraged a person with less determination and stamina than DePriest. Disgruntled members
of his own organization were holding outside conferences,[51] the
Wright forces in the Third Ward were consolidated under the
leadership of the genial George T. Kersey,[52] the Thompson fac-

[46] *Chicago Whip*, January 3, 10, 17, 24, 31, and February 7, 21, 1925.

[47] *Chicago Defender*, December 13, 1924; January 10, 17, 24, 31, and February 14, 21,
1925.

[48] In the Second Ward the vote stood: L. B. Anderson, 6,421; R. E. Parker, 138;
A. L. Williams, 4,549. In the Third Ward, R. R. Jackson, 9,551; R. A. Williams, 7,247.

[49] *Chicago Defender*, February 28, 1925; *Chicago Daily News*, March 2, July 10, 1925;
and *Chicago Whip*, March 7, 1925. The Insull charges were substantiated many years
later. *Chicago Daily News*, May 28, 1934.

[50] March 7, 1925.   [51] *Ibid.*, May 9, 1925.

[52] George Kersey was designated as the Third Ward Committeeman by the Wright
faction of the Republican party in the ward in November, 1924. This was not a legal
selection as the law providing for ward committeemen had been declared unconstitutional. In fact, Kersey was recognized by the dominant Republican faction in the city.
See *Broad Ax*, November 29, 1924.

tion of the Republican party was not in a position to help as the
mayoralty election was two years off, and a coolness had arisen
between DePriest and Daniel Shuyler, the attorney for Samuel
Insull. In spite of these setbacks, DePriest inspired his workers
to continue their quiet collection of Thompson pledge cards and
wait patiently for developments. Herein lies one of the secrets
of DePriest's success. He never knew defeat. If he had allowed
his organization to disintegrate, if he had kept his name out of
the papers by inactivity, or if he had ceased to become a challenge to the other leaders, he would not have been in a position
to take advantage of the quick turn in events which started in
1926.

THE FIRST NORTHERN NEGRO CONGRESSMAN

The Thompson and the Crowe-Barrett factions of the Republican party which had been at swords' points with each other
buried their differences in the primary of 1926 and agreed upon
the nomination of George F. Harding for county treasurer.
Wright was firmly intrenched with the Crowe-Barrett group
and the Governor Small wing of the Republican party and he
did not appear fully to appreciate the significance of this change
in the factional alignments. When Wright broke with Thompson, DePriest was ready to step into the gap as an independent
Thompson supporter. There were some who resented DePriest's
intrusion as the following excerpt from the *Whip* clearly shows:

"DEVIL DePRIEST"

Political philosophers and prophets feel that DePriest is a heavy liability to
the Thompson forces and that any recognition given to this blundering, blus-
tering schemer will mitigate against the best interests of all concerned.[53]

The article went on to accuse DePriest of lack of gentility, of
unscrupulousness, of selfishness, of coldness, of treacherousness,
of incapacity for sustained allegiance, of miserliness, and of
brow-beating characteristics. A few years later, except in a
Communist paper, such an article would have been impossible.
The *Whip* itself soon reversed its position. A complete change

[53] January 29, 1927. The occasion of this bitter article is difficult to determine. The
Whip supported the DePriest forces in 1925. For fuller citation see above, p. 104n.

of popular sentiment regarding DePriest was brought about within a little over two years.

After Thompson's re-election, DePriest began a struggle with Kersey for the mastery of the Third Ward Republican organization. Because of his great activity in getting Thompson pledge cards and because of his large personal contribution to the party's campaign fund, DePriest stood in the good graces of the new administration. He finally persuaded Mayor Thompson to name him as the dispenser of city patronage in the Third Ward. It was said that Alderman Jackson went to see the Mayor about Third Ward patronage. The Mayor said, "Have you seen Oscar?"[54] This action on the part of the Mayor meant that Kersey was to be displaced as ward committeeman. Kersey was appeased with a job under the Board of Local Improvements and DePriest was appointed as an Assistant Commerce Commissioner by Governor Small. However, the real prize was the committeemanship since, in the crucial year that followed, it proved to be a stepping-stone to Congress.

In the famous "pineapple" primary of 1928 DePriest was a candidate for two offices, Republican committeeman for the Third Ward and delegate to the Republican National Convention. As a cog in the Thompson-Crowe organization, he supported Madden for renomination to Congress from the First District. It has already been indicated that Madden was opposed by a young attorney, William L. Dawson, who made a vigorous campaign on ground that a Negro should represent the district.[55] State's Attorney Crowe and Governor Small were defeated for renomination but DePriest and Madden were successful in their contests. When the news of Madden's death flashed over the wires shortly after the primary, DePriest and Anderson were both out of the city at a summer resort. DePriest acted first. He telegraphed to the other ward committeemen who, with himself, made up the committee which had the legal power to fill the vacancy. He notified them that he would like their support for the nomination to succeed Congressman Madden. He also telegraphed Mayor Thompson. When De-

[54] Interview.   [55] See above, p. 79.

Priest returned to the city and saw the Mayor the latter was reported to have said: "You know, Oscar, I'm for you."[56] DePriest then asked whether Committeeman Dan Jackson would want Anderson or Roberts from the Second Ward to have the nomination. When the Mayor asked Jackson regarding his choice, the latter said, "I'm with you, Mr. Mayor." The Mayor replied, "Well, I'm with Oscar."[57] Since DePriest and Jackson controlled the largest wards in the congressional district, this settled the question. DePriest had the nomination before the other aspirants woke up as to what was happening.

Although the First Congressional District of Illinois was ordinarily a safe Republican district, DePriest's difficulties, even after he secured the nomination, were by no means over. Hardly was his candidacy announced before Assistant Attorney-General William H. Harrison declared that he was willing to become an independent candidate for Congress against DePriest.[58] When Harrison entered the race a few days later he stated that he was "against disreputable leadership of the gangster, gambler, grafter type."[59] Another blow was dealt to the DePriest camp a few months later when the Special Grand Jury investigating election crimes indicted DePriest for "aiding, abetting and inducing" South Side racketeers to operate gambling houses and disorderly places and "to protect them from the Police."[60] The Harrison forces then asserted that if elected, DePriest could not be seated and they pointed to the recent exclusion of Senator-elect Frank L. Smith. Just before the election DePriest was also severely criticized for supporting some of the Democratic candidates. DePriest declared that he was innocent of all the charges made, that he was being persecuted by his political enemies, and that the indictments were part of a plot to keep a Negro out of Congress. He asserted that the indictment was "a nefarious scheme, hatched through the erstwhile oligarchy of

[56] Interview.

[57] Interviews. A number of different accounts agree on the main features of this story.

[58] *Chicago Daily News*, May 2, 1928.

[59] *Chicago Tribune*, May 6, 1928.   [60] Records of Chicago Crime Commission.

pseudo-Republicans which waged the battle in the spring of
1927 against William Hale Thompson when hundreds of men
and women were promiscuously thrown in jail, all of which was
aimed at our leadership."[61] DePriest won, but his margin was
not a large one. In a district which had given Madden a 14,000
plurality in 1926, DePriest's plurality was only 3,800.[62]

The Congressman-elect next turned his eyes toward Washington. Would he be seated? Already he was experiencing the
change in his status which had been brought about by the election and he was all the more anxious to taste the fruits of victory that seemed so near at hand. The ward politician, the
scarred veteran of many factional fights, was no longer a local
figure. He was becoming a national symbol, admired by Negroes and feared by many whites. In fighting for his seat his
plan was to present his credentials at the extraordinary session
of Congress in April, 1929. He anticipated that his right to his
seat might be challenged either upon his indictment on charges
of graft or his moral fitness to be a member of the House. At
the inaugural of President Hoover, DePriest was described as
follows: "A conspicuous and withal a lonely figure in all the glit-
tering array of fashion and pomp in the senate chamber was
Oscar DePriest, the newly elected colored member of Congress
from Chicago. He sat in the rear row of the chamber, an interested spectator."[63] In the meantime DePriest's attorneys in
Chicago were pressing his case for trial. A few days before Congress convened the prosecution announced that the evidence
against DePriest was insufficient to warrant the defendant's
being brought to trial and the case was dismissed by the court.[64]
At the national capitol Mrs. McCormick, Representative-at-
large for Illinois and widow of the late Senator McCormick, was
skilfully maneuvering to remove the last obstacle in the way of

[61] *Chicago Defender*, October 6, 1928.

[62] An article in the *Defender*, November 10, 1928, also stated: "A letter signed by a
'Kenwood resident' and distributed to white people throughout the district urged the
solid support of white people for Baker."

[63] *Chicago Whip*, March 9, 1929, citing a white daily.

[64] *Chicago Defender*, April 13, 1929.

DePriest's taking his seat. It was still feared that some Southern representative, acting on the right of the House to judge the
qualifications of its members, might offer objections to the
swearing-in of DePriest and this would send his credentials to a
House Committee for action. According to the usual practice
the oath was administered to members by groups of states, and
those already sworn in could offer objections to the swearing-in
of any member in a subsequent group. On the basis of the current stories that the real objections to DePriest were racial, Mrs.
McCormick interceded on his behalf with the Republican powers at Washington.[65] When Speaker Longworth arose to swear
in the members he stated that owing to the complete disorder
that was apt to accompany the general practice of administering
the oath he thought that it would be more "comport with the
dignity and solemnity of this ceremony" if he administered the
oath to all members at once.[66] This move caught the dissenters
unawares and DePriest was sworn in along with all the rest before anyone had an opportunity to raise objections.

The new congressman was compelled by circumstances to
look upon himself not merely as the representative of the First
Congressional District of Illinois but as the representative of the
eleven million Negroes in the United States. The eyes of all the
colored citizens were focused upon their single spokesman in
the national law-making body. He was in constant demand as a
public speaker in all parts of the country, and his actions were
followed closely by the colored newspapers. In a little over two
months a colored weekly in Washington, D.C., wrote:

In this short time he has risen to eminence and power and has been the
leading source of news among Negroes. He is the most representative man on

[65] Mrs. McCormick was a close friend of Mrs. Alice Roosevelt Longworth, the wife
of the late Speaker Nicholas Longworth.

[66] *Congressional Record*, 71st Congress, 1st Session, Part 1, p. 21. Mrs. McLemore,
The Rôle of the Negroes in Chicago in the Senatorial Election, 1930, p. 15, made the following comment on this incident: "To those who have never known the experience of in-
sult because of the mere fact of race and who do not know what it is like to be without
rights as a means of protection, this may seem a trivial service, but it was not so judged
by Mr. DePriest, the Negroes of Chicago or the Negroes of America, for if Mr. DePriest
had been insulted every Negro in America would have felt the blow."

Capitol Hill. He has been quite active and sought after as a speaker. His first act of appointing young men to West Point and Annapolis made a favorable impression all over the country. His sending out 10,000 copies of the Declaration of Independence and Constitution and following this up in his speeches has had an excellent effect upon the populace.

DePriest is courageous, independent and resourceful, and therefore easily the outstanding man of the race. The papers of the race have rallied to him with a zeal that is commendable. He is one Negro that the papers have unitedly supported.

To the race, Congressman DePriest has become the National idol, inspiring, and to some extent uniting the race. He is in the position to render a great service. His months in Washington have given the Negro new hope, new courage, new inspiration.[67]

While many Negroes were encouraged by DePriest's election, some of the whites in the South were alarmed. The first incident which caused a burst of indignation from the South was the attendance of Mrs. DePriest, the wife of the congressman, at a tea given by Mrs. Hoover in the White House to all the wives and families of Congressmen. Many of the southern daily papers played the incident up with big headlines.[68] Within a few days some of the southern state legislatures began to pass resolutions "condemning certain social policies of the administration in entertaining Negroes in the White House on a parity with white ladies." Senator Blease of South Carolina offered a resolution in the Senate which contained some poetry which Senator Bingham termed "indecent, obscene doggerel." Senator Blease's resolution which requested President and Mrs. Hoover "to remember that the house in which they are temporarily residing is the 'White House' and that Virginia, Texas, Florida, Tennessee, and North Carolina contributed to their becoming its custodians" was finally withdrawn and the verse expunged from the *Congressional Record*. This was only one of the incidents concerning DePriest that has alarmed the southerners. DePriest's speaking tours in the South were very unpopular with portions of the white population, and in Birmingham, Alabama, where he was scheduled to make a speech in June, 1930, he was burned in

[67] *Washington Tribune* cited in the *Chicago Whip*, July 6, 1929.

[68] *Tri-State Tribune*, June 22, 1929; *Afro-American*, June 22, 1929.

effigy by members of the Ku Klux Klan.[69] In election campaigns in the South, DePriest's name was frequently used to stir racial antagonisms against independents.[70]

In Congress Representative DePriest was a very busy man, but his work was not like that of the ordinary congressman. His speeches on the floor of the House were few in number and he scarcely introduced any bills or amendments. His chief interest in the formal business of the House was to look out for matters that might be of interest to Negroes. In the proceedings of the House he is first mentioned in connection with a bill for the Turtle Mountain Indian School. He started to object to the consideration of the bill because it contained the words "white children" but he was persuaded to withdraw his objection on the assurance that there were no colored children in the territory.[71] His first formal speech was a plea for the passage of the bill providing for a Haitian survey. He took advantage of the occasion to say, "I am very glad to see the gentlemen on the minority side of this House so very solicitous about the condition of the black people in Haiti. I wish to God they were equally solicitous about the black people in America."[72] Whenever the appropriations for Howard University came up he was very active on the floor and in the lobbies.[73] At first he was opposed to federal grants to the states for relief purposes, but the conditions in his own district during the winter of 1932 compelled him to reverse himself on this subject.[74] Usually he voted as a regular Republican, but he looked upon his vote as a weapon which he could use for bargaining purposes. He hoped to get more important committee assignments than those to which he was first assigned.[75] While not constantly engaged in legislative matters,

[69] *Chicago Defender*, June 28, 1930.

[70] P. Lewinson, *Race, Class and Party* (London and New York, 1932), pp. 180, 275.

[71] *Congressional Record*, 71st Congress, 1st Session, Vol. LXXI (June 7, 1929), Part 3, p. 2536.

[72] *Ibid.*, 2d Session, Vol. 72 (December 18, 1929) Part 1, pp. 912.

[73] *Ibid.*, 3d Session, Vol. 74 (December 12, 1930), Part 1, p. 656.

[74] *Ibid.*, January 30, 1931, Part 4, p. 3648, and 72d Congress, 1st Session, Vol. 75 (March 3, 1932) Part 5, p. 5213.

[75] Enrolled Bills, Indian Affairs, Invalid Pensions.

his routine in Washington was a very strenuous one. He and his secretary, Morris Lewis,[76] handled an enormous amount of daily correspondence. There was a constant file of visitors into his office, and his evenings were filled with speaking engagements, conferences with fellow-politicians and delegations, and entertainments.

Like other congressmen, Representative DePriest was compelled to watch his local political fences while he was away in Washington, D.C. His first test in a Republican primary came in April, 1930, when he was opposed for renomination by Roscoe Conkling Simmons, nationally known colored orator, who had been active in the Republican presidential campaigns of 1920, 1924, and 1928.[77] Simmons based his campaign on the grounds that DePriest had not submitted his candidacy to the people, that it was the wish of Madden that he, Simmons, should go to Washington, and that he would "represent the spirit of his country, the patience, the intelligence and the progress of his people."[78] While the Deneen faction gave a little support to Simmons, the dominant Republican organizations in the district did not take his candidacy very seriously. DePriest won the nomination by a 12,000 plurality.

In the 1932 primary DePriest faced more determined opposition. His opponent was none other than Alderman Anderson, Second Ward Committeeman, who had come through eight aldermanic contests unscathed. Under the 1931 ward lines Alder-

[76] Mr. Lewis served as a private secretary on the staff of United States Commission to the Paris Exposition, under Commissioner General Ferdinand Peck, appointed by President McKinley. For further details about DePriest's routine in Washington, see *Pittsburgh Courier*, June 22, 1929.

[77] According to a Second Ward Republican Club pamphlet, Simmons had been president of the organization under Dan Jackson. Committeeman Jackson died May 17, 1929. Alderman Anderson was appointed committeeman in his place. Anderson backed DePriest in 1930.

[78] *Chicago Daily News*, October 16, 1929; February 27, April 5 and 7, 1930. At a Deneen meeting Simmons said: "The word 'congress' means a 'meeting of minds.' Now that is the kind of meeting where Roscoe Simmons belongs. No one has a right to try to keep him out of that body. I am you, when I go there, you go there. . . . . If I had one word to the Negro in Chicago it would be 'patience.' I deal with white people in the charming language of undefeated patience. I was raised in the home of Booker T. Washington, whose motto for the colored was 'Labor and Humility.' "

man Anderson's ward was extended south so as to include a large portion of the old Third Ward. A congressional reapportionment was passed by the Illinois Assembly, which extended the boundaries of the First District southward. Congressman DePriest moved into what he supposed was his new territory. However, the Illinois Supreme Court declared the new congressional lines unconstitutional and the old lines went into effect.[79] This meant that the new Second Ward contained the major portion of the First Congressional District. If Alderman Anderson wished to maintain his control over his local organization it was necessary for him to organize the new precincts which had formerly been in Committeeman DePriest's bailiwick, and if Congressman DePriest wished to continue to represent the First District, it was necessary for him to have the support of the Second Ward voters. Here was a political situation which made a bitter struggle inevitable.

Almost ten months before the primary Alderman Anderson began to fire into the DePriest camp. The following points were stressed. On the basis of the *Congressional Record* DePriest was charged with "negligence, incompetency, ignorance and failure to perform the duty for which he was elected."[80] DePriest neglected his duty in that he was absent when the Tinkham amendment to the reapportionment act was lost by one vote.[81] It was pointed out that this proposal would have put "teeth" into the Fourteenth Amendment in that it would have reduced the representation of the southern states which disfranchised Negroes. He was called unfit because of his failure to have the objectionable words, "white children" stricken out of the Turtle Mountain Indian School bill. He was charged with being the laughing-stock of Washington, D.C., because he made himself ridiculous in a tilt with Congressman Blanton of Texas. In the words of Alderman Anderson, "I said it is better to be silent and con-

---

[79] Moran *v*. Bowley, 347 Ill. 148 (January 13, 1932).

[80] Report of political meeting, April 3, 1932.

[81] *Congressional Record*, 71st Congress, 1st Session, Vol. LXXII (June 6, 1929), p. 2457.

sidered a fool than to speak out and remove all doubts."[82] De-
Priest was further charged with giving aid to the Democratic
party in his various speeches throughout the country. "Here a
Negro Republican Congressman advised Negroes to go into the
Democratic party. He evidently doesn't know about the traditions of the Democratic party. He doesn't know the Jim Crow
laws in the Democratic states. If the law down there prohibits
Negroes from taking part in primaries, how could they vote
Democratic?" The final blast was that DePriest was ineligible
because he was not a resident of the First Congressional District. These arguments were presented in political meetings, in
a pamphlet entitled "The Blunders of DePriest" and in the
first-hand contacts of the precinct captains.

In meeting the attacks made upon him DePriest had several
advantages. The loss of patronage following the Democratic
victories in 1931 left many disgruntled elements in the Anderson
organization. Starting with a fresh organization, which was
sustained largely by sentiment and hopes, DePriest was able to
build up a good morale among his followers. His associates
called him the "fearless, staunch defender of the race."[83] In accordance with the tactics which he had seen Mayor Thompson
use, DePriest put his foes on the defensive: "They say I have
done nothing in Congress. I've only been there one and a half
years. They have done nothing in the City Council in fifteen
years. Only thing he's done is to keep colored people from getting jobs."[84] At another meeting he said, "My opponent has
scored me for going about the country speaking when I should
be in Washington. I'm doing far more good for the race travel-
ling through the country teaching down-trodden, oppressed
Negroes race pride and how to fight for themselves." Anderson
was ridiculed because of his claim to be diplomat. "Diplomacy

[82] Report of political meeting, April 3, 1932. The remarks referred to are found in
Congressional Record, 72d Congress, 1st Session, Vol. LXXV (January 12, 1932), Part 2,
p. 1840.

[83] Report of political meeting, October 2, 1931.

[84] Report of political meeting, October 18, 1931.

is just another name for fear and cowardice."[85] In answering the
criticisms made of him because of his tilt with Congressman
Blanton of Texas, he said: "Everyone was afraid of Tom Blanton, but I wasn't afraid of him. I'm ready to rise at any time,
anywhere, with anybody and speak out in defense of my people."[86] The stereotype of DePriest as courageous leader of his
people was reinforced by his lieutenants at every opportunity.
His political meetings had all the aspects of a religious revival—
enthusiasm, zeal, and high spirits. The opposition was pictured as being in league with the kings of the nether regions.

DePriest was renominated by a large majority and the control of the Second Ward organization changed hands.[87] This
made DePriest the undisputed leader of the two wards that had
the largest colored population. The following year Alderman
Anderson retired from the City Council and William L. Dawson,
one of DePriest's lieutenants, was elected to his place.

The Congressman's path was soon beset with new difficulties,
which led to his defeat for re-election in the Democratic landslide of 1934. There first broke out a factional quarrel in his
own organization between King and Dawson, the two young
men who had contributed greatly to Anderson's downfall. In
the battle for position of Second Ward committeeman DePriest
backed Dawson, but King won by a narrow margin. With divided and disgruntled forces, DePriest then had to face for the
first time a colored Democratic opponent in the fall elections,
Arthur W. Mitchell. Although Mitchell had been in the city
for only six years, and was not known by many of his fellow-
citizens, he received the solid support of the white Democrats
and sufficient help from the Negro Democrats to defeat the
veteran DePriest.

ANALYSIS OF DE PRIEST'S LEADERSHIP

As in the case of Mayor Thompson, widely divergent views
have been expressed about the character of DePriest's leader-

[85] Report of political meeting, November 6, 1931.

[86] Report of political meeting, January 24, 1932.

[87] The final vote was: DePriest, 21,252; Anderson, 5,457; James L. Scott, 979. The
vote for second ward committeeman was: Louis B. Anderson, 4,518; William E. King,
13,467; W. H. King, 874; scattering, 126.

ship. In the eyes of some of the white anti-Thompson politicians, DePriest was a demagogue who exploited and misled his
people. However, the great mass of the colored people held a
different view. To them he was the "old Roman," "the old
sycamore," the great leader who fought for the race and blazed
new trails.

DePriest appealed to the great mass of the colored voters because he came from humble origins. He was never ashamed of
his slave parentage. In fact, he frequently referred to himself as
a man of the people, and he constantly reiterated the sentiment,
"I come from the common herd."[88] After a trip through the
southern states he referred to what he saw as follows: "When
I was in New Orleans I saw a slave block where they, the Democrats, bought and sold us like cattle. My mother used to tell
me that her own mother in Florida was put on the auction block
and sold." He continued, "Now these same Democrats are doing the same thing to Negroes here in Chicago. The only difference is that in the South they bought and sold while here they
buy and kick you out."[89]

His critics said that he was bombastic, in a great hurry,
coarse, crude, and talked as though his mouth were full of hot
pancakes. Congressman DePriest never pretended to be a great
orator, but when he talked the people listened. Like Mayor
Thompson, he had startling things to say. One never knew when
he would burst forth with blunt remarks like the following:

I spoke in Nashville, Tennessee. Someone said I should talk on social
equality of the races. But the whites of the south are not an appropriate audience for talk of social equality. The federal census shows an increase by thousands and thousands in the birth of mulattoes, mostly in the south. They have
Jim Crow theatre laws and Jim Crow street car laws, but what they need
is Jim Crow bedroom laws.[90]

His manner was democratic as well as his speech. The man
on the street could say, "Now you take DePriest. If you see
him on the street and say 'Hello, Congressman' he will stop and
shake hands with you."[91] In Washington, D.C., it was written
of him: "About 5:00 o'clock, and sometimes as late as 6:00, the

[88] *Nashville Globe*, June 7, 1929.   [90] *Chicago Tribune*, July 15, 1929.

[89] Report of political meeting, April 3, 1931.   [91] Interview.

chauffeur makes his appearance. . . . . All of the office force
pile into the Congressman's car. You know he is very democratic. He couldn't be a snob if he wanted to."[92]

DePriest's appearance was a great asset. "He doesn't need
to say anything," said an admirer. "All he needs to do is stand
up in front so the people can see him. He looks like a fighter."
He not only had a large and impressive frame but he was a man
of tremendous energy. His working day was a long one and he
played politics 365 days in a year.

Shortly after his election as representative it was announced
that he had joined a Congregational Church in Chicago.[93] He
was also a frequent visitor at other churches, and usually he
was asked to make a few remarks. He was conservative on economic questions and a vigorous opponent of communism. At a
recent meeting he said, "The communists are spreading propaganda among the Negroes of the North and South for the over-
throwing of the government of our country. I want to state that
I am irrevocably opposed to their doctrines and any other doctrine that has such aims. While we are not satisfied with conditions faced by our people in this country, the communist doctrine is not the way out. The right use of the ballot is the way."[94]
While not a drinker or a gambler, he was politically "wet" and a
liberal in his views on the regulation of gambling.

While some white politicians thought that DePriest was
troublesome, his constituents looked upon him as resourceful,
particularly in working around the limitations that are imposed
upon colored people. He built up a flourishing real estate business[95] because he was one of the first to see the opportunities in
the field brought by the migrants from the South, and he won
the nomination as alderman in 1915 and the nomination as congressman in 1928 because he was more active in forging ahead

[92] *Pittsburgh Courier*, June 22, 1929.

[93] *Chicago Tribune*, December 17, 1928.   [94] *Chicago Defender*, January 9, 1932.

[95] The *Chicago Defender*, May 21, 1932, made a reference to his income tax return for
1929. A petition filed with the board of tax appeals showed that in 1929 he had a gross
income of $94,041.21 and a taxable net income of $75,718.53. The petition further
stated that the sum of $44,279.72 of his taxable net income represents capital net gain,
while $31,438.81 was ordinary net income.

than the other contestants. He refused to recognize defeat and took many a blow that would have overcome a less rugged character. The indictment in 1928 was a shock but he refused to give up the fight. "Indictment or no indictment, I am going on with the campaign and I am going to win."[96] He turned the accusations into a cry of persecution and was able to carry most of the colored voters with him.

DePriest possessed a quality which his critics called "impudence," but his followers named it courage. Those Negroes who had suppressed desires to assert themselves in the presence of whites welcomed this quality in their leader. In meeting racial violence and in social contacts with whites DePriest had a reputation for fearlessness. It was said that he called on a prominent white politician one morning on behalf of an ousted job-holder and without preliminaries announced: "You blankety blank blank, you put my man back on that payroll or I'll ——— you." The white politician angrily replied, "You can't talk to me like that." DePriest persisted and his man was put back on the payroll.[97] On another occasion he sent some Negro truck drivers with their trucks to one of the city departments. There was trouble with the white drivers and one of the Negro drivers was struck. DePriest sent his men back the next day and caused a great uproar. He said that the trucks were going to be driven if if he had to mount machine guns on them and drive them himself. At a meeting of both white and colored persons, during the period that new Negro homes were being bombed, DePriest was reported as saying: "Negroes are going to move anywhere they can pay rent and if the white people don't like it, we'll run them into the damn lake."[98] Such daring is what Negroes like to see in their leaders.

As compared with some of the other colored leaders of his time DePriest was less bound by tradition and party loyalty. He was a supreme opportunist and calculated each step coolly and shrewdly. He did not regard himself as bound by party loyalty, by personal loyalty to any white man, or by loyalty to any ab-

[96] Interview.

[97] Interview with employee of department concerned.   [98] Interview.

stract cause. In local politics he shifted from Republican to
Democratic candidates when he thought that such a move
would serve his purposes best. In national politics he advised
Negroes to vote Democratic in sections where the Democrats
had the most to offer them. A week later in his own bailiwick
where he was a candidate on the Republican ticket he would denounce the Democrats in violent language. No white politician
could ever claim his steadfast loyalty. He made successive alliances, breaks, and realignments with Congressman Madden,
State Senator Ettelson, Senator Deneen, Senator McCormick,
County-Treasurer Harding, and Mayor Thompson. While still
enjoying the city hall patronage under Thompson in 1931, he
was luke-warm toward Thompson's candidacy for renomination. Thompson's political day appeared to be waning and De-
Priest did not want to be caught upon a sinking ship. Only a
direct appeal from the Mayor was able to bring DePriest back
from Washington to take part in the campaign.[99] In his political
views, also, DePriest was an opportunist. He did not insist upon
any abstract principles of race representation. While Madden
was alive, he opposed the Negro candidates for Congress. In a
factional quarrel he might even sacrifice a Negro candidate for
the state legislature,[100] but on other occasions he was the great
advocate of race representation.

DePriest could make the many shifts in politics that his op-
portunism directed because of his great skill in making mass appeals. He was a master in the art of arousing sentiment among
the colored voters. He took advantage of every weakness in the
armor of his opponents, and when he felt that the issues were insufficient to arouse the prejudices of the masses he manufac-
tured some issues of his own. Thus, in his campaign against
Lueder in 1923 he said that Lueder was a klansman and the
candidate of the *Chicago Tribune*. These charges were flatly de-

[99] *Chicago Defender*, January 31, 1931; *Chicago Whip*, February 14, 1931; and reports
of political meetings.

[100] In the 1932 primary the DePriest organization in the First Senatorial District
supported a white man as against a colored man for the second Republican representative.

nied but they were effective in rallying the colored voters to Lueder's opponent. Because he kept in close touch with the common man, because he knew what the colored people were thinking about and what they wanted, and because he knew how to manipulate the symbols that brought quick responses, he was a political propagandist who was admired by his associates and feared by his opponents.

Above all, DePriest was regarded as a "race man." A white politician said: "Oscar DePriest is a race man. I have never definitely found out what they mean by race men, but that is what counts. If you can get that characterization you are sure of getting the Negro support." When DePriest received word that President Hoover was displeased with his action in working against the confirmation of Judge J. J. Parker, he defied the President's spokesman. When some of the representatives grumbled that he used the House Restaurant, he brought in the blackest man he could find. When Mayor Thompson urged him to support a man who had been quoted as saying: "This is a white man's country," he opposed the Mayor openly. These actions were interpreted as those of a race man.

That DePriest felt his obligations to his race cannot be denied. His seat in Congress represented a symbol of Negro achievement. It stood for the recapturing of a banished hope. It meant that the Negro was part of the national government.

CHAPTER X

NEGROES IN APPOINTIVE POSITIONS

One of the forms of recognition sought by Negro political leaders, Negro party workers, and Negro voters generally has been appointment to governmental office. In the dark days of Negro political advancement following the collapse of reconstruction and the erection of barriers to Negro participation in government in the South, some appointments, mostly federal, were still available as a sign that all was not lost. A few diplomatic posts and such positions as Recorder of Deeds of the District of Columbia and Register of the Treasury were accepted by Negroes as a symbol of their new status. So firmly fixed was the idea that these positions were a sign of Negro advancement that when recent administrations failed to appoint a Negro to one of them, bitter resentment was expressed in the colored newspapers.

The enterprising Negroes who migrated to the North and built political organizations of their own soon struggled for local and state political appointments in competition with the native white and naturalized citizens. When the Negroes had developed a small professional and business class, when their importance to a given faction or party was strategic, when they found white politicians who were courageous enough to back them under the fire of hostile sections of the white public, they secured some local and state positions. At first Negroes were appointed to minor posts, but gradually, as their political power grew, the number and importance of the appointive positions held increased. However, it is likely that the rate of increase of these positions was slower than for some of the foreign-born groups. In these northern cities many white politicians, citizens, and visitors were not used to seeing colored persons in political jobs. Hostility to the appointment of Negroes might come from white factional leaders, appointing officers, employees, or citizens using the government services.

The Negroes have generally taken a realistic view toward political patronage. The spoils system was well entrenched before they became an important factor as voters, and the Republican party to which they generally belonged applied the system rigorously. The Negro politicians accepted the system as they found it. John R. Lynch, Negro Congressman from Mississippi, wrote to President Grant in 1875: "In my opinion, there ought to be a man in that office who will not only discharge his duty in a creditable manner, but who will also be of some value to the party and to the administration under which he served. We lost the county that (this postmaster) is in by a small majority. If an active and aggressive man . . . . had been postmaster . . . . the result in that county might have been different."[1]

The Negro political leaders have always been ready to supply active and aggressive men to come to the aid of their party and their country. They have developed some ingenious techniques to make sure that some of their recommendations are accepted. Whenever the Negro vote increased they were ready at hand to press their claims for more jobs. Since the larger jobs were yet to be won, they could bargain all the more effectively for the lesser positions. They studied the situation in a more or less objective manner and showed great skill in the art of political trading.

The political patronage in the metropolitan region of Chicago has for many decades been enormous. The many conflicting and overlapping authorities all have important appointive positions to be filled. Since 1895 civil service laws have reduced the proportion of jobs that can be used for patronage purposes, but the number remaining is still impressive. The Negroes in Chicago were particularly interested in the appointments made by such main governmental agencies as the United States government, the state of Illinois, the County of Cook, the Sanitary District, the city corporate, the Board of Education, and the South Park District. In the city corporate alone about one thousand positions are exempt from the Civil Service Law. Appointments to these positions are made by the following agencies: the mayor, the Board of Election Commissioners, the chief justice, clerk and bailiff of the Municipal Court, and the Board of Education.

[1] *Facts of Reconstruction*, p. 147.

CITY PATRONAGE

Negroes had found their way into some branches of the government of the city of Chicago as long ago as 1872. Shortly after the first Chicago fire, Mayor Joseph Medill, a Republican, appointed a Negro fire company composed of nine men. This was said to be the first company of its kind in a northern city.[2] A Negro police officer was also appointed in the same year.[3] Mayor Medill had broken the ice and gradually it became accepted by Democrats and Republicans alike that a few Negroes should be found in the city service.[4]

Before and after the Civil Service Law was passed in 1895 the positions in the legal departments of the city government were wholly within the control of the mayor and were looked upon as more or less political. The first colored man to receive recognition in the city law department was Franklin A. Denison, who was appointed assistant city prosecuting attorney by the Republican mayor, Hempstead Washburne, in 1891. Denison was singled out because of his brilliant academic record. Born in Texas in 1862 he moved North at an early age and graduated from Lincoln University, Pennsylvania, with high honors. He then moved to Chicago and graduated from the Union College of Law in 1890 as the valedictorian of his class.[5] He was continued in office by the Democratic administration which followed Washburne's, and when a Republican mayor was elected again in 1895 he was chief assistant prosecuting attorney in charge of all extraordinary writs in which the city of Chicago was involved.[6]

Denison's six years' service as a member of the city law department set a precedent which has been followed by all subsequent city administrations whether Democratic or Republi-

[2] Interview.　　　　[3] Negro police officers are discussed in chapter xii.

[4] *Chicago Daily News*, March 29, 1883, cited by C. O. Johnson, *Carter Henry Harrison I* (Chicago, 1928), p. 252, gives the following comment by a Democratic mayor in 1883: "I went to John Ender at the last election, a first-class detective and a colored man. 'John, don't you think you could vote for me now? You have been here two years.' 'Well, Mr. Mayor, I can't go back on my party.' 'All right, John, vote as you please, but be a good policeman.' "

[5] *Broad Ax*, December 31, 1910.　　　　[6] *Chicago Defender*, April 23, 1932.

can. In 1898 when Carter H. Harrison II, a Democrat like his father, started his first term as mayor, S. A. T. Watkins, a law partner of Denison, was appointed assistant city prosecuting attorney, "in recognition of the valuable services rendered the mayoral ticket."[7] Watkins was born in Tennessee and he graduated from the Le Moyne Institute of that state. He studied law with T. F. Cassells, ex-assistant attorney general of Tennessee, and came to Chicago in 1892. He served as assistant city prosecutor for eight consecutive years under Harrison and Dunne. When a Republican administration returned to power in 1907 in the city hall, Denison was brought back to the law department as assistant corporation counsel. Four years later Watkins was appointed to the same position by Mayor Harrison at the beginning of his fifth term. Thus for twenty-four years these two law partners shifted back and forth between the city law department and their private practice.

When Mayor Thompson started his first administration in 1915 it was a foregone conclusion that some colored leader would be appointed to a position in the city law department. The questions were whether more than one would be appointed and how important would the positions be. Mayor Thompson answered these questions by appointing both Edward H. Wright and Louis B. Anderson as assistant corporation counsels and Bishop Carey as an investigator in the law department.[8] Years later Bishop Carey claimed that he presented the wishes of the colored people for the $5,000 a year job which was finally given to Wright.[9] When protests were made to Mayor Thompson regarding the appointments which he had made, the Mayor answered his assailants as follows:

[7] *Broad Ax*, December 27, 1902.   [8] *Chicago Defender*, July 17, August 7, 1915.

[9] *Ibid.*, February 5, 1927; he was quoted as saying in a speech: "I asked the Mayor for a high salaried job for a representative of our Race. He told me that he had three civil service jobs paying $3,500 a year. I refused to accept them and demanded a job at a salary of $5,000 a year. Lundin jumped to the floor and flatly said he would not give Edward H. Wright or any other Negro such a job. When it appeared that there would be a break 'Big Bill' arose and told Lundin that he would give Edward H. Wright the job; that the South Side citizens desired it as Americans and he wanted to show his appreciation."

I know that in some quarters I have been criticized severely for appointing Negro citizens to positions of honor, trust and dignity. I am glad to take the full responsibility and the honor for making every one of those appointments, and I want to ask my critics to be as manly and to come out in the open light of day with such un-American sentiments.

My reason for making such appointments were three fold: First, because the person appointed was qualified for the position. Second, because in the name of humanity it is my duty to do what I can to elevate rather than degrade any class of American citizens. Third, because I am under obligations to this people for their continued friendship and confidence while I have been in this community.[10]

Considering the appointments of colored men to the city law department that had already been made by other mayors and those that were made in later Thompson administrations, this was a modest beginning. When Wright was elevated to the position of attorney for the traction commission in 1919, William E. King was appointed as assistant corporation counsel. Corporation Counsel Ettelson as well as Mayor Thompson was willing to recognize the rapidly growing group of energetic young colored lawyers. The peak of this recognition came during Thompson's third administration when six assistant corporation counsels, five assistant city prosecutors, and one assistant city attorney were appointed.[11] In addition there were law department investigators, making the total number of colored appointees about 14 per cent of all the employees of the department. The men holding these positions were recommended for the most part by the Second and Third Ward Republican organizations, and many of them held key political positions in their wards, such as regional director or member of the executive committee.

No matter how well the colored attorneys in the city law department under Mayor Thompson performed their tasks, they were destined to be replaced following the Democratic mayoralty victory of 1931. They played too important rôles in the Republican organizations of their respective wards to hope to carry

[10] *Ibid.*, September 25, 1915.

[11] This does not agree with the figure given by G. F. Robinson, "The Negro in Politics in Chicago," *Journal of Negro History*, XVII (April, 1932), 214, but it has been checked by men who were in the office.

over under a Democratic administration. Mayor Cermak received his lowest relative vote in the Second and Third wards, and he was therefore not under obligations to give heavy rewards to the colored voters. The number of Negroes on the legal staff of the city returned to the proportions of the Dever and Harrison administrations.[12] The Negroes paid the price for supporting a given party in block fashion, but they were not deprived of all recognition.

Outside of the law department the Negroes have been given comparatively few appointive city positions, even under the Thompson administrations. It was Mayor Dever who made the first appointment of a colored man to the Library Board, a body of nine unpaid members which had supervision over some one thousand employees. Dr. George Cleveland Hall, a Republican, a classmate of Colonel Denison, a well-known surgeon and civic leader, was selected by a Democratic mayor to serve on the Library Board. In 1929 Mayor Thompson named J. D. Bibb, the editor of the *Whip*, a graduate of the Yale Law School and a practicing attorney, to succeed Dr. Hall. Bibb's appointment was recommended by Congressman DePriest and Assistant Corporation Counsel Prescott.

One of the most outstanding appointive positions held by a colored man in Chicago was that of civil service commissioner. It has already been pointed out that Bishop Carey was named to this position by Mayor Thompson in 1927.[13] While a friendly colored weekly looked upon this appointment as a stepping-stone to greater recognition,[14] Bishop Carey went down to his grave under an indictment for malfeasance in office, and no Negro was appointed to the commission under Mayors Cermak and Kelly.

The Negroes in Chicago have achieved some recognition in the appointive positions of the city corporate during the last forty years. However, they have not yet won the headship of a city department and at no time have they received in the

[12] One assistant corporation counsel and two assistant city prosecutors. See *Chicago Defender*, May 16, 23, 1931.

[13] See above, pp. 56, 98.   [14] *Chicago Whip*, April 23, 1927.

patronage positions as a whole rewards which were commensurate with their voting strength. Even Mayor Thompson failed to name a colored man to the Board of Education, the Board of Local Improvements, or a city cabinet position. As far as the relative number of positions held by colored citizens is concerned, it is difficult to see why the city hall was referred to as "Uncle Tom's Cabin" during the Thompson administrations. It was the fact that there were more Negroes in conspicuous city offices than there had ever been before that brought forth this comment. Jealous factional leaders, unfriendly newspaper editors, and white migrants from the South combined to create an unfavorable impression regarding the recognition given to Negroes by Mayor Thompson.

MUNICIPAL COURT

There are between seven and eight hundred employees of the Municipal Court of Chicago, and all of them are exempt from civil service law. Curiously enough, the appointment of these employees is not centered in any one individual or in any body. Three popularly elected officials, the chief justice, the clerk, and the bailiff of the Municipal Court, each have a share in the selection of the persons who assist the judges in the performance of their duties. Ever since the establishment of the court in 1906 many of the court positions have been used to pay political debts. In looking for jobs which would help to establish their political status, the Negroes in Chicago, as soon as it was established, turned to the Municipal Court.

The first man to be elected clerk of the Municipal Court was a Republican and he naturally kept the Republican wards in mind when he was selecting deputy clerks. One of the clerks he appointed was Adelbert H. Roberts, later a state representative and a state senator.[15] While Roberts had a legal education, he went into politics rather than into the practice of law and his appointment as a deputy clerk in the Municipal Court was in recognition of his services as an orator and as an organizer. One of the judges under whom he served in the early days of the

[15] See above, p. 69.

court said that he was industrious, bright, and very much interested in his work.

Robert's career as an employee of the Municipal Court lasted from 1906 until the present time. For twenty-eight years, during the terms of Democratic clerks as well as Republican, while the court organization was controlled by anti-Thompson leaders as well as by Thompson, and during the period that he himself was serving as state representative or senator, he kept his position as deputy clerk. In the press, in the courts, and on the platform, he was attacked from time to time for holding two positions but he managed to turn back his critics. To the press he issued a statement that he was not drawing pay from two sources.[16] He also won his case in the courts.[17] As a deputy clerk he made himself the outstanding expert on a specialized phase of court administration, namely, replevin and garnishee. No patronage office which serves a critical public like the legal profession can afford to dismiss all the employees who have knowledge and experience. Roberts was careful to see that he came within the group of deputy clerks who were needed for the smooth running of the office. Then, he used his position as a state legislator to strengthen his standing with the court. He sponsored bills which concerned the Municipal Court, and when the Democrats elected the clerk of the court he went along with the Democratic program of legislation.

The clerk of the Municipal Court has social workers and other employees to appoint as well as deputy clerks. The first Negro worker in the social service department of the Municipal Court was Mrs. Georgia Jones Ellis, who was appointed in 1925 by the clerk in office who belonged to the Deneen faction of the Republican party. Previously, Mrs. Ellis had been employed in the county recorder's office and in the office of the clerk of the Circuit Court. While in the recorder's office she had completed her legal education and passed the bar examination. During the five years that she worked in the social service office of the

[16] *Chicago Tribune*, June 25, 1921. He secured a leave of absence from his position in the Municipal Court while he was at Springfield.

[17] *Chicago Daily News*, March 31, 1926.

Municipal Court only one of her decisions was reversed by a judge. All this time she was active in the Deneen organization of the Fourth Ward. When a Democrat was elected as clerk she was not reappointed and a semi-civil service examination system was instituted for the selection of social workers. Under this new system three Negroes have entered the service.

The probation officers of the Municipal Court are appointed by the chief justice. During the first twenty-four years of the life of the court the chief justice was Harry Olson, a Deneen Republican. The first woman adult probation officer whom he appointed was Mrs. Ida Wells Barnett, who held the position for three years.[18] There have been other colored probation officers, but none have been as aggressive in race matters as Mrs. Barnett.

The popularly elected bailiff is the third officer of the Municipal Court who has appointing powers. The deputy bailiffs are more purely political than any of the other employees of the court. For example, during the period that Bernard W. Snow, a Harding-Crowe-Thompson Republican, was bailiff (1924–30) there were 28 Negroes out of a total number of the some 375 employees in this branch of the court. After the election of a Democratic bailiff in 1930 all of the 28 Negro employees were discharged and about half a dozen Negro Democrats were put on the force. One of the deputy bailiffs under the Snow régime was the secretary of a Pullman porters' union. He was appointed because of his political activities in the west end of the Sixth Ward where he was a section chief. Like the others, he was discharged when there was a change of administration.

The Thompson organization obtained only partial control of the patronage in the Municipal Court of Chicago, but it was very liberal toward the Negroes with the share that it had. The Deneen officials of the court were more restrained in making appointments of colored citizens, and even more so were the Democrats. In spite of this a colored deputy clerk with superior experience was able to survive alternate Republican and Democratic administrations.

[18] See above, p. 25, for a discussion of her rôle in politics.

COOK COUNTY PATRONAGE

The dispersion of responsibility for the selection of official personnel is even greater in Cook County than in the city of Chicago. The popularly elected county judge, probate judge, clerk, treasurer, sheriff, state's attorney, probate clerk, superintendent of schools, clerk of the criminal court, recorder of deeds, clerk of the Superior Court, clerk of the Circuit Court, surveyor, coroner, and president of the county board, all have some patronage to dispose of outside of the county civil service.

Curiously enough, the county judge has important appointing powers. Among the key officers whom he selects are the three election commissioners who have charge over the election machinery of the city at all elections. The some 200 permanent employees of the board and the 15,000 precinct judges and clerks of election are all exempt from civil service. A writer in the *Whip* wrote the following description of the career of Robert L. Taylor in the office of the election commissioners:

This was my first glimpse of Robert L. Taylor, officially, Assistant Attorney for the Board of Election Commissioners, but unofficially the leading authority upon the Illinois election law. Taylor, for the past thirty-six years has been a trusted and valuable employee in the election commission, serving without change under both Democratic and Republican administrations. A native of Springfield, Ill., first appointed to the election commission offices under Judge Carter, a Republican county judge in 1894. As the only colored man in the department, Taylor early set about to make secure his tenure in office by making himself the most efficient and competent clerk in the office. . . . .

Rising steadily from the position of clerk to positions of greater responsibility and trust in the election commission, Taylor was soon recognized by his superiors as a talented and able student and commentator upon the election laws. His care of detail and painstaking exactness made him invaluable in drawing up legal documents pertaining to the work of the department. . . . . For his valuable services in revising the state election laws, Taylor was admitted to the bar. . . . .

His contribution toward the education of the official at the polls is of great value toward the improvement of the system of conducting elections, and is an important step forward toward clean politics. Taylor's efficient services have made him invaluable to the election commission, securing his position regardless of political changes. He has received recognition and commendation from the City Council, the State Legislature, the Chicago Bar Association, and various other groups who have benefited by his information and advice. He has built up a reputation for reliability, efficiency and authority in his work which has justified the watchword of the election commission—"See Taylor."[19]

Taylor is noted for great tact in handling people of all races and nationalities.

The state's attorney has the largest legal staff of any public official in the city of Chicago, and because of the powerful and dramatic character of his work he is besieged by young and ambitious lawyers who desire to make their mark. The first colored man to be appointed as assistant state's attorney was Ferdinand L. Barnett, the husband of Ida Wells Barnett. Born in Tennessee in 1859 of a father who had purchased his freedom, Barnett was brought to Chicago at an early age, where he was educated in the city schools and the Northwestern University Law School. After editing a weekly newspaper for a few years he entered the practice of law in 1892.[20] He took an active part in the Republican presidential campaign of 1896 and immediately following the election was appointed assistant state's attorney by Charles S. Deneen. County Commissioner E. H. Wright was active in securing the appointment,[21] but Barnett soon established himself in his own right. He was put in charge of extradition and habeas corpus proceedings, and became an expert in these branches of law. During the fourteen years that he remained on the staff of the state's attorney's office he achieved a reputation for his judicial temperament.[22]

Another assistant state's attorney, whose term of service was even longer than Barnett's, was Edward E. Wilson, a native Texan of freedman stock. He came to Chicago in the nineties and has described his subsequent career in the following words:

If ever a man's career could be said to be based on luck, you could say that of mine. I left my home in Texas and went to Oberlin. From Oberlin I went east to Williams College. While there I met a fellow by the name of Maclay

[19] Article by John J. McKinley in *Chicago Whip*, December 13, 1931.

[20] *Broad Ax*, November 10, 1906.   [21] See above, p. 155.

[22] Report of Chicago Bar Association on candidates, 1906.

Hoyne. Hoyne and I became pretty close friends. After I graduated from Howard Law School, I came here to Chicago where I soon became connected with Mr. Ed Morris.

Hoyne decided he would run for the office of state's attorney. He called me up and asked me if I wouldn't give him a little help here on the South Side. I answered that I would be glad to help him. He promised that if he got in, he would give me a place. I certainly had no thought of holding office but I worked in a precinct and got a fairly good vote for Hoyne. After the election, he called me up one day and asked me to come over to see him. I've been in the office ever since.[23]

Assistant State's Attorney Wilson went on to say that during the twenty years that he had been in office the politicians had been on his trail. While he was serving under Hoyne they could not get to him although they tried to persuade the Democrats to let him go. Wilson's activity as a prosecutor in the DePriest trial of 1917 was very displeasing to some of the colored leaders on the South Side.[24] When Crowe, a Thompson man, came in, the politicians renewed their efforts. They went to Committeeman Wright to see about getting him out and Wright told them that he had a list of things to ask Crowe and if Crowe wanted to keep Wilson and give the organization the things which it wanted, he was very sorry but he would not insist on Wilson's removal. They then heard that Judge Barrett was responsible for Wilson's retention. Judge Barrett told them that the organization had great things in store for Crowe and that Crowe had to make a record in the office of state's attorney in order to realize these things. Wilson was a man who could help Crowe, and if they did not want to embarrass the party there was only one thing to do. When Swanson was elected as state's attorney on the Deneen ticket another judge wrote a letter on Wilson's behalf and again Wilson was retained. Wilson specialized in the writing of briefs for cases taken up to higher courts on appeal, and so efficient did he become in this work that he outlasted the vicissitudes of Chicago factional politics.[25]

It was under State's Attorney Crowe that the Negro lawyers in Chicago received their greatest recognition in the prosecuting

[23] Interview, December 13, 1932.

[24] *Chicago Defender*, June 16, 1917.   [25] His salary was raised to $9,000 a year.

office. At one time during Crowe's administration there were at least ten colored assistant state's attorneys, and in addition to these some six clerks and law investigators.[26] Of the assistant state's attorneys, one was prominent in the field of journalism, one became a ward committeeman, two were later elected to the state legislature, and three were subsequently unsuccessful candidates for judicial office.[27] When Crowe came up for renomination in the primary of 1928, he received strong support from the Second and Third Wards in spite of the fact that he went down to defeat elsewhere in the city. After the inauguration of Swanson as state's attorney, the number of colored assistant state's attorneys was reduced to five. There was a still further reduction following the Democratic victory of 1932.

The county sheriff has the largest number of employees under him of any single elective county officer, and consequently his post was carefully watched by the colored leaders. The first colored deputy sheriff was Colonel John R. Marshall, who was appointed to the position the day after he was mustered out of active military service following the Spanish-American War. Colonel Marshall was born a slave in Virginia in 1859 and his schooling extended to a year's work at Hampton Institute, where he knew Booker T. Washington. While selling newspapers in Washington, D.C., he became acquainted with a congressman who helped him get a position in the government service as an apprenticed bricklayer. In 1880 he came to Chicago to practice his trade and soon after he began to take an active part in politics as a Republican precinct captain.[28] Some ten years later he was appointed deputy assessor and deputy collector of South Town by one of the justices of the peace. He was one of the founders of the military group that later became the Eighth Regiment of the Illinois Infantry. The fact that he was made

[26] *Chicago Defender*, April 10, 1926, and interviews. The *Defender* article gives the names of those who had served at any time under Crowe up to the date given.

[27] Two others were candidates for judicial office. One was an assistant state's attorney under Wayman and the other was a candidate for judge before he was appointed as one of Crowe's assistants.

[28] As he expressed it, "I ran around ringing doorbells and soliciting votes. I would sit down and talk politics and try to show the best traits of our candidates."

the colonel of this regiment marked him as a man who would be useful in politics. He has described his appointment in the sheriff's office as follows:

I got the job through the Governor of Illinois who fixed it up while I was still in the service. In those days the justice of the peace was appointed by the Governor and on a visit to Springfield, the sheriff asked the Governor to appoint a friend of his as justice of peace. The Governor asked what position this man held at the present time. The sheriff told him that he was a deputy. The Governor then said, "I will appoint your man if you will give Colonel Marshall the position as deputy as soon as he is mustered out." The next day I went to be sworn in as deputy sheriff.

The sheriff said to me: "Colonel, you will have no trouble and I will have no trouble. If I sent you out and some one asks, 'Is this a colored deputy?' some one else would say, 'Yes, but it is Colonel Marshall.' And then you wouldn't have any trouble."[29]

Colonel Marshall's duties were to serve writs and make levies on property to cover bonds. While he had police powers to carry out his orders, he exercised these powers only when it was absolutely necessary. He resigned his position in the office when a Democratic sheriff was elected in 1902.

The control of the sheriff's office has oscillated between the Republicans and the Democrats during the past thirty years. Under recent Republican administrations there have been at least two colored deputy sheriffs and many other colored employees. Even under the Democratic régime which began in 1928 the group secured a deputy sheriff, a deputy bailiff, three guards, a matron, and in addition some twenty janitors, cooks, and window washers.[30] The precedent is well established that Negroes are to be recognized in this office.

The coroner's office force is much smaller than that of the sheriff and consequently it was harder for the Negro leaders to gain recognition in it. It was not until 1922 that a deputy coroner was finally appointed in the person of E. M. Cleaves, a member of Committeeman Wright's organization in the Second Ward. Cleaves was a native of Ohio and he graduated from the

[29] Interview, February 5, 1933.

[30] Interviews. This is about 4 per cent of the total number of employees of the office.

Cleveland high-school system. In Chicago he worked in a bank, and after he became active in politics, he obtained a job in the corporation counsel's office as an investigator.[31] He became interested in the work of the coroner's office and told Wright that he wanted to be a deputy coroner. At every organization meeting someone from his section of the ward would rise and say that he thought the organization should be represented in the coroner's office. One night there was a banquet at which the coroner, Wright, and Cleaves were present. Wright again asked for one of the positions as deputy coroner. The Coroner said that there were only fourteen such jobs, that all of the townships of Cook County must be represented and that they could not give one to a Negro. A clerkship was offered and refused, and finally the coroner gave in. Cleaves found that there was a lot of sentiment in the office against having a Negro on the staff, and when he reported for duty nobody would talk to him. He asked what he should do and was told to stay in the office and do whatever he saw needed doing. He replied that he would not know what to do and was told to read a newspaper. He refused to do this and was assigned to the Department of Estates and Effects. After a while he became acquainted with a Jewish clerk in the office who told him what was happening, and he finally got adjusted.

In contrast to some of the other county offices, the Negroes have secured more positions in the coroner's office under the Democrats than under the Republicans. Under the administration of Coroner Bundesen there were six colored employees out of a total of thirty-seven.[32] Two were deputy coroners, two were coroner's physicians, and two were court reporters. All of them were college men and they were assigned to the regular tasks of the office. One of the physicians said that his first appointment was non-political, as it was based on the recommendations of an advisory committee of prominent physicians in the city. He claimed that his experiences in the office were unusual in that he had been assigned to an exclusive white district and

[31] *Broad Ax*, December 27, 1924.

[32] Elected in 1928 on a Democratic ticket, running far ahead of all others on the ticket.

the representatives of the big insurance companies had to come to the South Side to get his verdicts. Dr. Bundesen's policy in the office was a personal one and not that of the Democratic party.[33]

In addition to the offices discussed, there are many other county offices which gave appointive positions to Negroes at one time or other. The county treasurer, the assessors, the recorder, the clerks of the various courts, and the county board which had charge of a number of institutions, all recognized the importance of distributing the jobs at their disposal among the various racial and neighborhood groups in the county. Usually when a Republican controlled a given county office the recognition given to the Negroes was greater than when the Democrats were in, but this was not always the case. In some offices there was a tendency to place Negroes where they would not meet the general public; in other offices they were given full responsibility for conspicuous work.

SANITARY DISTRICT

Another one of the local governments which has far-reaching powers is the Sanitary District of Chicago. The nine elective sanitary trustees have charge of matters relating to drainage, sanitation, sewage treatment, and water navigation in the region of Chicago. Because of trials concerning the so-called "whoopee era" from 1926 to 1928, the Sanitary District does not enjoy a savory reputation. No Negroes were in a position where they could be held responsible for any of the scandals, but a few were caught in the net which had been woven by others.

Before and after the days of the Sanitary District scandals there were colored appointees of the district who performed faithful and valuable services. One of the early assistant attorneys for the district was Willis V. Jefferson, a graduate of the University of Michigan Law School. His appointment was brought about by Committeeman Wright and he was considered

[33] *Chicago Defender*, December 19, 1931. When Dr. Bundesen resigned, Frank Walsh, another Democrat, became the coroner. Walsh let one of the deputy coroners go.

an authority on certain subjects.[34] Another assistant attorney whose work was above reproach was Warren B. Douglas, former state representative. He was appointed by the board in 1930 and held a position in the legal department for three years. His appointment was sponsored by the Deneen faction of the Republican party.

The class of appointees of the Sanitary District who were severely criticized were the so-called pay-rollers who did no work except draw their salary checks. In this group was a colored attorney who was on the pay-roll for fourteen months but admitted that during all that time he was never given any work to do nor called upon to act in his official capacity. He secured his appointment through the late George E. Brennan, who was then known as the boss of the Democratic party. The attorney explained his position as follows: "I reported daily for the first five or six weeks. After that I reported three or four times a week. Each time I insisted that I be given something to do. After four or five months I began to believe that I was being discriminated against because I was colored."[35] The term of his appointment was ended before he had an opportunity to earn the salary he received and he found himself classed with the pay-rollers.[36] There were some other colored pay-rollers of the district who had less to say for themselves,[37] but their conduct was in keeping with the rules of the game of politics as they were played by many white politicians.

[34] *Chicago Defender*, February 28, 1925, and *Chicago Whip*, May 3, 1930.

[35] Court proceedings reported in the *Chicago Whip*, January 31, 1931.

[36] He was suspended for a few months by the Illinois Supreme Court, See *Chicago Tribune*, February 24, 1933.

[37] *Chicago Daily News*, December 11, 1931 reported the following: "——— ———, a Negro, testified that while he was drawing sanitary district pay checks he did no work for the district but managed the ——— cafe, black and tan whoopee spot."

In the sanitary district case testimony, pp. 131–36, an example is given of a colored minister who was on the pay-roll for nearly a year. His job was to survey the water from Thirty-ninth Street to Randolph Street. All he did was to walk up and down along the water front. He had no instruments and he made several reports to the clerk of the Water Department. As he put it: "I reported that the mark, the lake level mark, was about 6 or 8 inches different as the case appeared day after day."

Because the city of Chicago contains over half of the population of the State of Illinois, and because many of the important
state offices are located in the city, Illinois officials have found it
necessary to be generous in their treatment of the residents of
the city when they are distributing the state patronage. The
fact that the candidates for governor, lieutenant-governor, secretary of state, auditor of public accounts, state treasurer, and
attorney-general are nominated in a state-wide primary, means
that the party leaders must cultivate the votes where they are
found.[38] As the colored population increased there was a tendency to appoint more and more colored men to state positions.

One of the earliest appointments of a Negro to a position in
the state government was the selection of E. H. Wright as a
bookkeeper and railroad incorporation clerk in the office of the
Secretary of State in 1889.[39] After the presidential and state
elections of 1896 the Illinois Secretary of State appointed Edward Green to a clerical position. Green had helped to organize
the Pullman porters for the Republican campaign and he had
agreed with the other colored leaders to look to the state government for his reward.

The most important legal positions in the state government
are under the attorney-general. James G. Cotter was one of the
first Negroes to be appointed as assistant attorney-general. A
native of Kentucky, a graduate of Fisk University and the
Illinois College of Law, an active party worker in the bailiwick
of Congressman Madden, an orator of considerable ability, an
attorney who had handled a number of celebrated cases, Cotter
was appointed to the state prosecuting staff by Attorney-General Brundage in 1917.[40] It was later said of him that he served
the state with honor and distinction until 1919, when he resigned to follow his private practice.[41] Other attorney-generals
have appointed colored assistants since Cotter's time, but no

[38] Direct primaries for state offices since 1907.

[39] See above, p. 154.

[40] *Broad Ax*, October 5, 1918.   [41] *Chicago Daily News*, November 20, 1920.

attorney-general has been as liberal toward Negroes as some of
the city and county legal officers in Chicago.

It remained for a governor, nominated and elected with the
support of the Thompson faction of the Republican party, to
give to the Negroes in Chicago the same kind of recognition in
the state government that they had been receiving in some of
the city departments. Governor Len Small surprised many of
the citizens of Illinois when he announced the appointment of
John B. French as a member of the Illinois Industrial Commission in 1922. One of the daily newspapers made the following
comment: "The rôle of spokesman for the captains of industry
was given to John B. French, a Negro known in the Wilson
Avenue neighborhood, for several years as the owner of French's
Pantry, a small restaurant on Broadway."[42] French was born
in Kentucky and brought to Chicago as a small child. After
completing grammar school, he was successively a traveling
Jubilee singer, a bell-boy, a shipping clerk, a caterer, the manager of buildings and grounds at Tuskegee Institute, the steward
at a country club, and the owner of a restaurant.[43] North Side
politicians used to patronize his café and they persuaded him to
organize the colored group which was found there. After Small
had been elected governor, one of the prominent Chicago advisers of the Governor told French to get Committeeman
Wright's endorsement for the position as industrial commissioner. Wright refused to do this at first on the ground that the
position was needed in his ward,[44] but when the "higher ups"
told him that the job was for French, he complied. The chief
functions of the Industrial Commission were to adjudicate
claims for injuries by employees against employers. On the
Commission, French made many friends because of his tact and
skill at bringing about understanding between the contending
parties.

The second major position to which Governor Small appointed a colored man was that of Illinois commerce commissioner.

[42] *Chicago Tribune*, November 12, 1922.

[43] *Chicago Whip*, February 16, 1924; *Chicago Defender*, September 26, 1931.

[44] A $5,000 a year salary was attached.

When Edward H. Wright was made a member of the commission which regulates public utilities in the state, it was said that Governor Small was making a bid for the colored vote[45] and was trying to checkmate the gubernatorial ambitions of Frank L. Smith, the chairman of the commission. If Smith had resigned to enter the race against Small, his actions would have been branded as proof of race prejudice against Wright.[46] While the position carried a salary of seven thousand dollars a year, it also obligated Wright to the Small faction of the Republican party and the temporary split between Small and Thompson in the spring of 1927 forced Wright to make decisions which led to his political undoing. When Wright resigned as commissioner in 1928 on account of ill health, Dan Jackson, who had just displaced him as committeeman, was appointed for the four remaining months of his term. That Governor Small set a precedent that a colored man should be appointed as one of the seven Illinois commerce commissioners is shown by the appointment of Herman E. Moore to this position by Governor Horner in 1934.[47]

The Honorable Louis L. Emmerson owed his nomination for governor in 1928 to the anti-Thompson faction of the Republican party, and his vote in the Second and Third Wards was comparatively light. Consequently, it could not be expected that he would be as generous in his recognition of the colored leaders as Governor Small had been. However, Governor Emmerson appointed William H. Harrison, colored attorney, as a member of the Board of Pardons and Paroles. Harrison was the son of parents who had been slaves, and he lived on a farm in Mississippi until he was sixteen years of age. After graduating from a denominational college in Tennessee, he taught school, studied law, and was admitted into the bar in Oklahoma. When he came to Chicago in 1918 he was known as one of the Liberty Loan orators. Seven years after his arrival in the city he was selected as an assistant attorney-general by Oscar Carlstrom.[48] He was appointed by Governor Emmerson to the Board of Par-

[45] *Chicago Whip*, December 1, 1923.   [47] *Chicago Defender*, December 15, 1934.
[46] *Chicago Tribune*, November 21, 1923.   [48] *Chicago Whip*, October 3, 1925.

dons and Paroles in 1929 and two years later he resigned under charges of conspiracy and bribery. He was acquitted of the charges made against him,[49] but in the meantime Judge Albert George had been appointed to his position on the board.

Many other colored citizens in Chicago have been appointed to state positions under recent administrations. In the state Department of Public Welfare, in the state grain inspection office, in the state parole office, and in the Department of Registration and Education Negroes have been selected for both civil service and appointive positions. The advancement of Negroes has been slower in the state government than in some of the city governments because the obstacles have been greater. The prejudice of some of the whites in outlying parts of the state, the strength of the rural areas in the state legislature, and the relatively small amount of patronage available have all helped to prevent governors and other state officers from giving the colored leaders the same consideration that other sectional and group leaders receive.

FEDERAL PATRONAGE

In the distribution of the federal patronage the colored citizens of Chicago were recognized somewhat later than those in other northern cities, partly because of the recency of the migration. However, even in the eighties and nineties, there were some colored citizens in the federal service. Before the passage of the Civil Service Act of 1883 there were a few colored employees in the Chicago post-office who took an active part in political campaigns.[50] In the nineties an appointment was made by President Cleveland which disregarded party lines. Dr. Daniel H. Williams, the noted colored physician, was appointed as surgeon-in-chief of the Freedman's Hospital in Washington, D.C. In so far as he took an active part in politics, Dr. Williams was known as a Republican.[51] Recognition in other branches of the federal government followed slowly.

The United States district attorney's staff in Chicago has al-

[49] *Chicago Tribune*, December 5, 1931.

[50] *Broad Ax*, September 9, 1905. On the post-office, see below, p. 302.

[51] *Chicago Defender*, August 8, 1931; J. W. Gibson and W. H. Crogman, *The Colored American* (Atlanta, 1903), p. 588.

ways been considerably smaller than the legal staffs of the city and county governments. In 1909 President Taft appointed the first colored assistant district attorney in Chicago, S. Laing Williams. Williams graduated from the University of Michigan in 1881 and taught school for a short time in Alabama. He was then appointed to a position in the Pension Office at Washington, D.C. After studying law at Columbia University, he resigned from the Pension Office and came to Chicago to practice law.[52] In the office of the United States district attorney for Northern Illinois, where he served for about four years, he was one of eleven assistant attorneys. A number of other colored attorneys have been appointed as assistant district attorneys under subsequent administrations, but there has never been more than one at a time.[53]

The federal government maintains many other offices in Chicago which contain altogether more than nine hundred employees who are not under the civil service rules and regulations.[54] Negroes have been appointed in some of these offices, such as the office of the collector of internal revenue and the marshal's office, but they have made little headway in many of them. In recent years there has been no United States senator who received the overwhelming support of the voters of the Second and Third wards.[55] Consequently, the colored leaders have had no senator to whom they could make a special appeal for greater recognition.

In spite of the obstacles which stood in their way, many Negroes have been appointed to important governmental posts in the Chicago region. The advances which have been made have sometimes been due to the merits of particular individuals and sometimes political power of the Negro voters. Colored men have been selected for appointive positions because of their scholastic records, professional achievements, oratorical abil-

[52] Gibson and Crogman, *op. cit.*, p. 573.

[53] James G. Cotter, 1926–28; Nathan S. Taylor, 1928–29; Heber T. Dotson, 1929—.

[54] United States Senate, Document No. 173, 72d Congress, 2d Session, *Positions Not Under the Civil Service*, pp. 101–5.

[55] Charles S. Deneen received a large vote in the primary of 1924 but this was largely the result of the fact that Thompson disliked McCormick more than Deneen. Frank L. Smith received a large vote in 1926 but he was not seated.

ities, organizing powers, or their friendships with white political leaders. On the other hand, some have been selected because of the weight of the political organization behind them. In general, personal contacts with whites are less important and professional training and organization support more important than twenty years ago. Mulattoes have been favored as political appointees largely because a light skin is not as conspicuous as a dark one. However, when a dark-skinned man has a superior education, a long acquaintanceship with urban problems, and undoubted organizing abilities, he may achieve the highest post won by the group. Negro appointees have a difficult rôle to play. They must live in the white world, which controls most of the appointing agencies, and they must live in the Negro world which supports their claims for the positions they hold. The successful job-holder must be able to find his way about in both worlds.

At best it is difficult for a racial minority to maintain its hold on certain political positions in a great metropolitan community. Changes in factional politics and in the attitudes of the appointing officers frequently sweep away gains that have been made. An office-holder may get into trouble and cause a setback for the entire group. When one of their office-holders gets into difficulties, they present another candidate for the position whose record is untarnished. Some Negro appointees work so hard at their jobs and become so efficient that their services are retained by administration after administration regardless of political considerations. In order to get ahead the colored man tries to be a little better than his white competitors. These appointees usually do not rely upon political pressure of any sort but fall back upon their records. With reference to other positions, the group tries to establish a tradition that they are to be filled by Negroes. One administration and its colored appointees may be swept out of power but the incoming administration will put some of its colored adherents in the positions which have been vacated by Negroes. An endeavor has been made to establish such traditions in the legal departments of the city, county, and state governments, and a measure of success has been achieved.

CHAPTER XI

CIVIL SERVICE POSITIONS[1]

Besides the fundamental requirement that appointments and promotions be based upon competitive examinations, the Illinois Municipal Civil Service Act of 1895 included a number of new ideas in public personnel management, such as the elimination of discretion in the making of appointments, the requirement of hearings for removals, and the granting of investigating powers to the commission. According to the act, the appointing officer was required to offer appointment to the eligible standing highest on the list and no person in the classified service could be discharged without a hearing before the commission. Theoretically, these provisions should have made the municipal service very attractive to Negroes. If a Negro stood the highest in a given entrance examination, then the law stated that he should have the appointment. If a change in administration should bring in a department head who was prejudiced against Negroes, then the Negroes already in the classified service would be protected against arbitrary removal. If a colored man stood the highest in a promotional examination, then he should be one of the three persons certified for the position. The law said nothing about the race of applicants and it endeavored to open the service to all citizens regardless of political considerations. The law promised treatment on the basis of merit and security for all faithful employees. One colored candidate for state senator referred to the law as "our greatest opportunity of getting decent employment."[2]

The Negroes in the United States have had many bitter disappointments in the way in which certain laws have been carried out in practice. The Fourteenth Amendment to the Federal

[1] This chapter will be confined to a discussion of the civil service positions in the city corporate. There are also civil service commissions for Cook County, the state of Illinois, and the South Park Board. For figures on the Negroes in the county and South Park civil service systems, see Appendix I.

[2] *Defender*, April 1, 1922.

Constitution has never given the protection which it seemed to provide. The Municipal Civil Service Act was another measure which promised more than it gave. The Civil Service Commission, a body of three members appointed by the mayor, has sometimes been made up of politicians who were frequently more anxious to evade the law than to enforce it. Under various administrations, examinations were not held when they were needed, vacancies were filled with sixty-day appointments which were renewed time after time, favoritism was sometimes shown in the examining process, and the removal trials were not seriously conducted. Furthermore, the Commission shared the responsibility for the personnel system of the city with the finance committee of the city council, the mayor, and the department heads. The Negroes in Chicago who sought employment in the classified service were willing to accept whatever benefits the law held out to them, but they also looked to the men who were charged with enforcing the law. As one veteran Negro employee put it: "When Civil Service came in 1895, things were a bit better. But you know Civil Service is run by friendship— that is, even if it isn't run by money—and under that sort of arrangement, Negroes won't come out on top."[3] During the Thompson administrations the Commission took a peculiar view of its duties. According to one authority, "instead of regarding themselves as an independent agency provided by law to bring about the employment of a competent personnel, they assumed the position of patronage dispensers for the mayor."[4]

---

[3] Interview with retired civil servant, October 23, 1931. He also said: "If there could be a system devised where appointments and advancements were made on merit, we would be a lot better off. But I guess that will never be as long as men run things for men. After all, people are just people. It is natural for a white man to love another white man more than he does a black man. Just the same way, a black man loves his people best."

[4] J. B. Kingsbury, "The Merit System in Chicago from 1915 to 1923," *Public Personnel Studies* (November, 1926), pp. 312–13. On page 318, Prof. Kingsbury says: "Coming into office when the municipal service was at a high point of efficiency, Mayor Thompson left it eight years later in the worst state it has been since 1895. Key positions were occupied by spoils appointees under 60-day authority, but practically permanent; the practice of political assessments continued in spite of the civil service law and a grand jury investigation; employees who wished to get ahead were obliged to do politi-

There are many positions under the jurisdiction of the Civil Service Commission of Chicago that have been of interest to Negroes. The classified service includes some twenty-two to twenty-five thousand employees of the city corporate, the Library Board, and the business department of the Board of Education. The positions are grouped under four main headings: administration, operation and construction, health and welfare, and public safety. Such services as the clerical, engineering, library, medical, and nursing services are of special interest to colored citizens because their opportunities in these fields are limited.[5] The fire and police services are so peculiarly governmental that participation in them is taken as a symbol of participation in government.[6] In the South opportunities of this sort are denied to Negroes, and when a Negro in the North wears the uniform of a fireman or policeman it is taken as a recognition of equality of citizenship. While the building maintenance, public works, and labor services are similar to services in private industry that are open to Negroes, the government cannot be neglected as an employer by a group which is in need of work.

ENTRANCE INTO THE CIVIL SERVICE

The colored citizen who decides that he wants to enter the municipal service has a number of obstacles to overcome before he can realize his ambition. First he has to pass the physical and mental examinations. During a Thompson administration these examinations may have furnished no serious hurdle, but

---

cal work at election time, to lobby for salary increases, or to resort to union tactics and even to strike; the carefully worked out classification and compensation plans were thoroughly demoralized; and the personnel agency was a joke and a byword."

[5] L. D. White, in his *Prestige Value of Public Employment* (Chicago, 1929), p. 94, gives a table which shows the distribution of opinion on twenty paired occupations favorable to city employment by racial groups. The Negroes (average number 222) who answered the questionnaire were most favorable to the following city occupations: accountant, chauffeur, draftsman, nurse, assistant engineer, detective, statistician, machinist, library assistant, and chemist. The largest taxi cab companies do not hire colored drivers. The Negroes have done very well in the Public Library. The general index for Negroes was high.

[6] See chapter xii, below.

in some other administrations they were carefully administered and the competition was keen. In pointing out that the new Democratic city administration had no special favors to bestow, one of the colored aldermen said at a political meeting in 1932:

Civil service was created by the legislature. The local boards are set up by the Mayor. We used to have a Civil Service Board. You know what I mean. That was one where we could go and talk a little. Cermak has appointed a board that has two reformers and a politician on it. One, Collins, is a millionaire who has so much money that he is free from entanglements. Another is Professor White, one of the master minds from the University of Chicago. You could touch Professor White about as easily as I could fly. The third member of the commission is the politician. You can approach him. There is absolutely no chance to get past Collins and White. They have it fixed so you have to take exams on merits.[7]

This alderman clearly indicated that abstract considerations have not always ruled the commission. The physical examination may prove to be a stumbling-block. An official in one of the public safety services was asked why there were not more Negroes in the service. He replied that he thought they were counted out on the medical examination. This was also a common belief on the part of many Negroes who had applied for positions.[8] On the other hand, a civil service commissioner insists that the physical examinations were fairly conducted in 1931–32, and that many of the colored applicants were ruled out because of flat feet or other defects.

In facing the written examinations for positions like those in the clerical, engineering, and library services, the colored applicants usually have superior educational backing. Practically all of the colored clerks are high-school graduates, and many of them have had business college or legal training besides. One of the junior engineers was a graduate of Armour Institute of Technology. Over three-fourths of a group of colored library assistants interviewed said that they had had some college training and a large proportion were college graduates. Many

[7] February 15, 1932.

[8] An article in the *Chicago Defender*, July 10, 1926, stated that this method was used by the Boston Civil Service Commission.

of the women library assistants had also had a number of years' experience in library work or teaching before they took the city examinations. There is no question that the colored clerks, engineers, and library assistants passed the entrance examinations on the basis of merits. The following case illustrates how highly this group of employees prizes education and how willing they are to try a number of different examinations:

I come from a professional family. My father was a very well educated man. Father always told all of us children to study hard and get an education. That was impressed on all of us and we all tried to go through school.

I was born in New Orleans. I was educated there until I was old enough to go to high school. Then I was sent to Spellman College in Atlanta, Georgia. When I finished college I began to teach school. The first year I taught in the rural districts of Louisiana.

I didn't like teaching school so my father told me that I would have to go back to school and learn something else as I would have to have some sort of a profession. So then I came up north and went to Decatur, Illinois, where I graduated from Brown's Business College.

After I graduated from Brown's I went for a visit to Washington, D.C. to see one of my brothers. There I saw all of the colored people in civil service work and I thought that I would like the work. The pay was good, much better than what I had been getting and the work seemed pleasant. I took the examination for a federal position but they found out that I was colored and I didn't get the job.

Then I came back to Illinois and took the state civil service examination. I passed and was put on the list. They first sent me to Elgin as a stenographer. I liked it very much down there, but in a few days they told me I would have to leave. I did everything I knew to stay. I even telephoned the Governor, a Democrat, and he said that I should stay and that if the others didn't want to work with me he could replace them. But that was just a lot of words because I had to leave anyway. They have the right to let you go within six months. There were some write-ups in the papers about it at the time.

When I came back to Chicago I took the examination for library typist and was appointed. I also took the junior stenographer's examination and after a bit I was called for that too.[9]

In many cases there is no such inner drive to take civil service examinations. In fact, many colored citizens have to be urged to try an examination. The impression is current among some of them that political influence is still more influential than

[9] Manuscript document, dated December 17, 1932.

merit alone. In 1927, when the Board of Education gained a temporary control over the school clerks by removing them from the classification of teachers and placing them under the civil service rules, the way was opened for the free play of political influences. The school clerks had been teachers assigned to that duty by their principals, but under the new regulations the board could fill these positions as they saw fit until the examinations were held. The president of the board wrote a letter to some of the June graduates of the Chicago Normal College explaining to them that in order to get assigned as a teacher clerk under the new arrangement it was necessary to get a letter from the precinct captain and to bring it down to the office of the president of the board.[10] In this fashion some 350 positions were temporarily filled. In the meantime a training course for prospective clerks was offered downtown in order to prepare the appointees for the examination which actually did not come until two years later. Colored normal-school graduates who went through this procedure could not be expected to hold political influences lightly in connection with the municipal civil service.

The school clerks were not the only ones who had their entrance into the civil service made smooth for them by the help of the politicians. An important official in one of the bureaus of the Department of Public Works gives the following account of his appointment and examination:

When I was the secretary to the ward committeeman, a white man came and asked the committeeman to do what he could to get him appointed in an important public works position. The committeeman and I went down to see George Harding (then County Treasurer). Neither of us thought that we had a Chinaman's chance to swing it. I stopped in the outer office while the committeeman went in to see Harding.

Pretty soon the committeeman came running out and said, "Would you rather have the position or go to the legislature?" I said that I'd rather have the position. He said that he'd gone in and told Harding what he wanted. Harding had said that he thought a Negro could be placed if the committeeman had a person. The committeeman mentioned me. Harding said that I would be a good man and that I should get a letter in to him that day. I dictated a letter and the committeeman signed it. I telephoned to the alderman

[10] M. J. Herrick, *Negro Employees of the Chicago Board of Education* (University of Chicago M.A. Thesis, 1931), pp. 47–58.

to come and sign it. The chairman of the central committee on patronage had no other choice but to sign it. I got a temporary appointment. Then I took the civil service exam. I was seventh on a list of 200. There were 15 vacancies to be filled. Every small man in politics wants to get a good civil service job.[11]

A slightly different procedure was followed in the case of the semi-skilled and unskilled workers in the operation and maintenance services. When one of the aldermen was asked how many such workers had been appointed from his ward, he said that he didn't know the exact number as he didn't know how many had paid the union fees. The applicants found it necessary to see both the ward boss and the trade-union officials before they took the civil service examinations. The asphalt workers, street cleaners, janitors, and janitresses all found it necessary to join the union in view of the closed-shop policy of the Civil Service Commission and the appointing authorities. No persons could get work of this sort unless they paid the union fees; the initiation fee was sometimes fifty dollars. The party organization sent the approved lists to the unions and the unions exacted their tribute. The particular unions concerned had very unsavory reputations because of their flagrant racketeering activities.

Even after the examination has been successfully passed the applicant is not sure of an appointment, particularly if the position sought after is of a clerical or technical nature. The law seems to be explicit on the point that the highest person on the list should be certified for the first position which is open, but in practice this is not always done. When a Negro gets on a list, his troubles may be just beginning. When he is reached and certified to a department for work, the department head, if he is prejudiced against Negroes, may refuse to take him. The department head may decide not to fill the position and there is nothing in the civil service law to compel him to make the appointment. A Negro who has been turned down for one job will go back on the list and he may try several other jobs. Then

[11] Interview. This same appointment was described in the *Chicago Defender*, January 21, 1928. It said that the appointee merited the city plum because he had been the campaign manager for nearly every man of the race who had run for office in the ward and he was a faithful Republican worker.

some person will come to him and ask him to waive his right to a certification. The Negro may be so discouraged by this time that he waives his right and loses out altogether. This process is called the "run around." As a colored senior clerk recently put it, "Many heads of departments are prejudiced and when they see a Negro is to be appointed, they refuse to declare a position open. Just recently a Negro girl was certified as a clerk to this office and the head of one department refused to take her. And the job is still to be filled."[12] The chief clerk who refused to make the appointment explained his position as follows: "We have a division of stenographers of about twenty women. They are all white women and all working in one room. You can see how I can't set a Negro woman down there with all those white women. It would just raise hell."[13]

Attitudes such as those which have just been given explain in part why more colored clerks and stenographers have not been appointed. However, many Negroes have passed the hurdle of certification and appointment. Some of those who have received appointments are light-colored Negroes. As one official put it: "A Negro with a light skin will fit better into an office. He won't be so different. The department heads lean toward this type of person."[14] Others have shown persistence, tact, and courage in standing up for their rights. One of the older colored clerks relates the following account of his early experiences in the service:

I was first certified from the civil service list in 1906. The individual who was head clerk then is still here. When I presented the certification he had me sit down and disappeared for two hours. When he came back he said that the job was not open just then. I answered that I had a certification and therefore the job must be open. Then he asked me to go back home and think it over, saying that perhaps some other job would be more satisfactory. He then showed me what I would have to do. He took me to a back room and showed me a large stack of books and told me that every mistake would be charged against me and the job might be very expensive.

I went home and told my parents about it. It was very embarrassing to

[12] Interview, October 21, 1932.

[13] Interview, November 15, 1932.   [14] Interview.

stand around with everybody looking at me and knowing that they didn't want me there. But my folks encouraged me to go back and try to stick it out.

When I went back the chief clerk asked me if I had decided not to take the job. I answered that I had decided to take it. He seemed very put out about this but finally certified me to a branch office. There was a store yard out there. They sent the white clerk from there in to fill the job to which I had been certified.[15]

Even after certification and appointment the applicant is by no means sure of a regular civil service position. According to the law any new appointee may be dismissed without a trial during a probation period of six months. In a number of departments colored appointees are permitted to stay only a short time before they are dismissed. However, one of the former colored fire captains said that he never discharged a colored man attached to his company, although the department often called and told him that he need not keep a new man if he was in any way lacking in efficiency. He said also that the department did this because they did not want so many Negroes in the service. As a result of this policy his company became abnormally large and the odd men would fall off the truck from time to time. One of the white officials in the department said that they looked like a picnic party when they went to a fire.[16] The company was finally divided into two companies and in this way more places were provided for Negro applicants.

Colored appointees sometimes discover that it is very difficult for them to learn the duties of their job during the probation period. The head of the department may deliberately fail to instruct them so that he can turn in a low efficiency mark and recommend their dismissal. This happened in the case of a newly appointed library assistant. She complained that the librarian in charge of the branch to which she was assigned wouldn't show her how to do the work and consequently she was given a low efficiency mark which resulted in her being summoned to the office of the manager of employees.[17] Cases of this sort might be multiplied.

[15] Interview.

[16] Interview with official in the city hall office.

[17] Interview with library assistant.

The most unfair treatment of probationers is found in some of the labor services where the racketeering trade unions maintain a closed-shop policy. The initiation fee to join the Municipal Janitors' Union is fifty dollars and this fee is forfeited if the new member loses his job after two months' work. Among the colored school janitors appointed during the third Thompson administration there was an unduly large number of dismissals of those who had served slightly more than two months. The union was then free to go after some new victims who had to pay the initiation fee. It appeared that there was some collusion between the union heads and persons in the political hierarchy. A janitor's job did not prove very remunerative considering the fact that the union initiative fee, the union dues of seven dollars for every three months, and the pension charges of three dollars every two weeks all had to come out of three or four months' wages at one hundred and thirty-three dollars a month. As one janitor expressed it, "Civil service really doesn't mean much. You can be fired any time. Somebody is makin' thousands off us poor working class."[18] Since about one-third of the school janitors were Negroes, it is clear that the Negro workers suffered considerably under this vicious system. The colored political leaders were unable or unwilling to protect the workers from their wards against the racketeering unions.

Some of the unions which included city employees had a definite policy or practice of excluding all Negroes. Among these were the Technical Engineers, the Draftsmen and Architects' Union, and all the building trades' craft unions except the plasterers' union. There were some building trades' unions, like the electricians' and carpenters' unions, which organized separate locals for Negroes but these locals did not secure much of the public business. There were other unions, like the bricklayers, which ignored the clause in their international constitutions against discrimination. The school engineers had a powerful union which included no Negroes. This was not due to the policy of the international union as there were Negro members in the general body, but it was the result of the keen competition

18 Herrick, *op. cit.*, p. 66.

for the positions. Such attitudes were not peculiar to the public service. Negroes who seek public employment in the skilled trades have had to face the general hostile attitude of craft unions.

CONDITIONS OF WORK

The colored municipal employee who has passed the civil service examination and who has served the six months' probation period has other problems to face. He may find the conditions of work unpleasant because of assignment to uncongenial work, segregation, social ostracism, or uncertain tenure. Mayor Thompson could not control the racial attitudes of the white municipal employees, many of whom entered the service long before he was elected. In some offices the presence of Negroes was disturbing to the morale of the white employees and the department head took steps to reduce the friction. Some of the Democratic mayors have come into power with comparatively little support from the Negro voters and have therefore had no great incentive to try to change racial attitudes. The colored community through its press, its churches, and its political leaders has tried to improve the conditions of employment.

It has already been indicated that Negroes who passed the examination for the fire department were assigned to companies in which the rank and file were all Negroes. One colored fireman said that Negroes were not assigned to white companies because there would be social problems in eating and sleeping together and any Negroes so appointed would be given so much drudgery that they would quit.[19] He went on to say that the segregated companies were discriminated against in a number of ways. The buildings in which they were housed were permitted to remain in a dilapidated state as compared with the quarters of nearby white companies, the districts to which they were assigned were too large to be covered adequately, and when on duty they were given very dangerous posts. The colored politicians were appealed to constantly to remedy some of these conditions. Week after week the *Chicago Defender* ran a bitter article on the Jim Crow fire department. The headings of

[19] Interview.

these articles might change slightly but the contents were essentially the same. "Blot Out Jim Crow" and "Jim Crow Flag
Still Waves in Fire Department" were among the favorite headlines.[20] Constant agitation was kept up for more colored men in
the fire department and against the discriminatory practices of
the department. When a fire department bond issue was presented to the voters, the *Defender* urged its readers to vote
"no."[21] During election campaigns the voters were urged to
support candidates who would fight against the segregation policies of the department. The kind of propaganda which this
paper circulated is illustrated by the following:

It's important that citizens continue petitioning public officials to take
steps to end segregation in the city fire department. The Chicago Defender
has for years fought for a distribution of firemen of all races in the various fire
stations.[22]

While it is not the Defender's plan to contend that the two stations our
men now control should be wiped out, it is this paper's fight to see that others
who join the department be assigned to stations throughout the city. . . . .

The city of Chicago isn't running the department to suit the social whims
of any fireman. When a man or woman turns in an alarm, he or she wants the
firemen to put out the fire in question and they don't stop to ask the operator
whether a white or black fireman is coming. Any man, regardless of race or
creed, should be eligible to secure a job. The placing should be according to
the grade on the civil service list. If any man of color's name appears and he
is subject to call his name is passed over for no other reason than the hook and
ladder company and the engine company crew, manned exclusively by race
men, are all filled up. This violates the letter of the law in the civil service.

The citizens demand that these Jim Crow practices end in the fire department. It is taxation without representation.[23]

No other city department employs openly the segregation
policy which is found in the fire department, but complaints
have been made that some of the departments try to isolate the
Negro employees. One expert on municipal employment in the
city said that Negroes seem to be segregated into a few offices
because of the attitudes of the various department heads. He

[20] December 13, 27, 1930; March 14, 1931; and many other issues beginning at least
with the issue of April 22, 1916.

[21] March 24, 1928.   [22] April 23, 1932.   [23] June 18, 1932.

knew of three department heads who were particularly antagonistic. In the smaller offices it was harder to certify Negroes because there were fewer divisions where the Negroes could be put off by themselves. He further stated that in the larger offices there were many little corners and small divisions where they can put a Negro and he will be out of sight and out of the way.[24] This policy is resented by the colored clerical employees in the city hall. One employee in one of the smaller offices said: "It is only when you get ten or more Negroes in an office that you get that competition and undercurrent of bad feeling. I would rather not have had a promotion than to have gone into the ——— Department or the ——— Bureau."[25] Under the recent Democratic administration the colored nurses of the Municipal Tuberculosis Sanitarium have complained that they have been concentrated in the South Side whereas they used to be in all parts of the city.

The colored community feels in general that it has received very fair treatment at the hands of the library authorities. The proportion of colored assistant librarians is higher (7 per cent) than that in any other professional or clerical group in the entire city service. Colored assistant librarians have been assigned in all parts of the city. The library authorities have not, however, been able to combat the prejudices of all white employees.

Miss ——— (the librarian in charge) flatters herself that she is impartial and unprejudiced but she is easily influenced by those around her. The other girls on the staff were very prejudiced against colored people. They would not speak to me except on library business and did everything they could to make me leave. It was very depressing to me and at times I dreaded the thought of going to work the next day. I may sound unladylike, but those girls at that branch put me through one year of hell.

When the staff gave a joint dinner and they couldn't very well leave me out of it they tried to get me to eat alone with the boy page of the branch. The patrons were very nice to me. The superintendent of branches told me that I had been given the lowest efficiency mark he had ever seen. If I hadn't had high efficiency marks before, I guess I would have been fired.[26]

Permanency of tenure during good behavior was theoretically guaranteed by the civil service law until the retirement age was

[24] Interview, November 15, 1932.   [25] Interview, November 7, 1932.   [26] Interview.

reached, but there were still some ways in which a given individual might be separated from the service through no fault of his own. The position itself might be abolished by being left out of the budget made up by the finance committee of the city council. This is the case of a colored woman senior stenographer:

The first of this year I was laid off. I still have the letter from the council. It said that they didn't have any place for me. But that was just a lie. I was just recently talking to some people who are on the finance committee and they said that that very department has asked for the position which I held.

Now after sixteen years of service I am right back where I started, at the bottom. There were plenty of people who were working temporarily and here I had been working for the city sixteen years and couldn't get on. They told me down there that they would put me to work as soon as they found a job for me and that they would protect my civil service rights. They told me that none of the department heads would have a senior stenographer who was colored. Well, I think that is pure discrimination. Why should any head of a department say that he would not have a citizen or a taxpayer just because he happened to be colored?[27]

The most uncertain tenure of all is held by the temporary civil service employees. The politicians have used the sixty-day appointment powers in order to reward the faithful party workers without regard to the merit system in the civil service. When Mayor Thompson first came into office there were complaints that he was abusing this power in order to build up a political machine. Sixty-day appointees were reappointed time after time and no qualifying examinations were held. When Mayor Cermak came into office in 1931 he said that he was going to reduce the number of temporary employees but this promise was never carried out. During a favorable administration the colored citizens have received a share of the temporary appointments. However, a shift in political fortunes sweeps all the temporary employees out of the city hall. "Republicans Fired by New Mayor; South Side Is Affected," ran the headline of the *Defender* following Cermak's inaugural. "The Democrats, now in power, let out 2,260 city employees who had been on temporary payrolls during the Thompson administration. The

[27] Interview, December 17, 1932.

Race was hard hit. That was the first day's work of Chicago's new Mayor."[28] The total number of temporary employees in the city service varies from four to six thousand depending upon the closeness of elections. The turnover is such that it would be very difficult to estimate the number belonging to a given racial group at any one time.

Regular civil service employees enjoy considerable security. During the third Thompson administration, however, some complaints were heard about the trial board and its failure to protect the Negro employees.[29] The Civil Service Commission which was appointed by the following Democratic administration was at first welcomed because of its fairness and impartiality in trial matters. However, the attorney for one colored employee who was brought before the board raised the issue of race discrimination. This trial was greatly prolonged and cost the city a large sum of money in stenographer's fees and other expenses. While the employee was discharged, it cannot be said that he did not have a hearing. The proceedings fail to show that the employee was unfairly treated.[30]

PROMOTIONS

One feature of the civil service law which has appealed to Negroes is the provision that promotions shall be made on the basis of merit. As in the case of other provisions of the law, this provision has not always been strictly applied. A practice which is sometimes used to evade the spirit of the law is the system of waivers. According to the Civil Service Commission's rules an eligible may "waive" his right to a certification. This means that under certain circumstances a person who is eligible to be considered for higher rank and higher pay may be persuaded to waive his chance for a given appointment. If an employee who

[28] April 11, 1931.

[29] *Defender*, October 26, 1929; *Chicago Daily News*, October 24, 1929; Robinson, "The Negro in Politics in Chicago," *loc. cit.*, p. 204; interview material in our files.

[30] Records of Civil Service Commission. In the next chapter, page 275, a case is given in which a colored man boasted about his ability to obtain lenient treatment from the Civil Service Commission because of his skill in appealing to the fact that he was a Negro.

is not one of the top three has the favor of his bureau chief he may receive the appointment just the same if he can persuade all but two of those ahead of him to waive certification. Political, racial, and personal considerations may influence a bureau chief to desire to promote someone who is not at the top of the list.

In the fire department where for many years there was a single company to which colored men were assigned it is obvious that a Negro could be promoted only when there was a vacancy among the higher positions in that company. One of the former Negro fire captains stated that after he had been in the department for a few years he took a lieutenant's examination. He was eleventh on the list. When it was time to appoint him, the fire marshal asked him to waive his right to appointment as there was no place for him in the Negro company. Twelve years passed and he was still waiting for his appointment. Finally under a Republican administration, one of the colored assistant corporation counsels who was a friend of his wife's sister-in-law "went to the front" for him and he was appointed as a lieutenant. When he took the examination for the captaincy one of the colored aldermen, a friend of the fire marshal, supported his candidacy and there was no trouble.

Colored women in municipal positions constantly run into the waiver system. One woman who was in a given division for ten years said that she took two senior stenographer examinations. "I did a lot of waiving on the first examination," she said. "People told me that I had to do it. In fact, I just waived myself right out of the first examination."[31]

Promotions in the civil service of the city may be brought about in either of two ways. Persons who have passed the promotional examinations may be given work which involves greater responsibility or the position which they hold may be regraded. The grading of positions is done by the finance committee of the city council, and if a given employee can bring enough pressure to bear upon this committee he may secure an advancement in pay and rank with no change of duties. Since the department

[31] Interview, December 17, 1932.

heads were reluctant to put Negro civil servants in responsible positions where they would be supervising the work of white people, many of the colored employees who have received promotions in the city service have used the method of regrading. One of them, now a principal clerk, said: "I had no difficulty being certified to this department. The only difficulty was in getting the appropriation and the regrading. You have to get this any way you can, by hook or crook. You have to see your local politicians and get them to bring their influence to bear on the finance committee and on your department head. I have always been very friendly with our Negro politicians and didn't have much difficulty."[32] An efficiency survey was made of the city employment in 1931 which unearthed some of the anomalies of the classification scheme. Some of the colored clerks who had been promoted by the system of regrading were in fear of being demoted, but no action has been taken on the basis of the report.

At every hand the colored municipal employees discover that the spirit of the merit system may be violated. This being the condition, they appeal to the law when the law appears to offer some protection and look to their political friends when political influence appears to be stronger than the law. Negro employees say that when they have sought promotions they have been asked, "Have you any political influence?" or "Who are your backers?" One principal clerk said: "The superintendent told me to get all of the political pressure I could and to get what waivers I could from those ahead of me and that he would appoint me. I did and was certified."[33] One of the assistant librarians who had been promoted several times stated that she always let it be known that she had a good political pull. Her last promotion was secured partly because of political connections. She had passed the examinations but before they appointed her she heard that the list was to be thrown out. She went to see her ward committeeman and the corporation counsel and was appointed before the list was discarded.

Up to the present time, merit, the civil service regulations, and political influences have not been able to carry the colored

[32] Interview, October 29, 1932.   [33] Interview, October 21, 1932.

employees of the city beyond a certain point. In 1933 there were among the Negro civil servants two sixth-grade librarians (the highest grade), a fire captain, a ward superintendent of streets, two police lieutenants, six police sergeants, some six principal clerks, two bacteriologists, three chemists, an operating engineer (water bureau), a junior efficiency engineer, and a few others in positions equally as high in rank and pay who may have escaped attention.[34] The highest basic salary of any of these is $4,000 a year. As far as we have been able to ascertain, there have been no Negro fire marshals, no Negro police captains, no Negro school engineers, and no Negro head clerks in the city hall. Regarding his future in the service, one principal clerk said: "I don't know how far I can go in civil service. I may be able to get one more grade. Chief clerk will be absolutely as far as I can get, if indeed I can get that far. I can't imagine getting any higher."[35] A former fire captain never heard from the examination which he took for fire marshal. In the higher ranks of the municipal service the Negroes in Chicago have as yet much to achieve. Some have given up hope for the present of being able to reach the highest positions in the classified service, but others are still struggling on.

PROPORTION OF COLORED EMPLOYEES

The colored leaders were not only interested in getting as high positions as possible but in getting as many positions as possible. A very rough measure of the fairness of the appointing officers would be a comparison of the population ratio with the ratio of colored employees. Such a measure would be based on the assumption that the occupational distribution of the Negroes in the city was approximately the same as for the total population. This is obviously not the case, so the recruiting of

---

[34] G. F. Robinson, *op. cit.*, p. 196, gives slightly different figures. He fails to state the period during which his statistics were gathered. From the context it appears that they were collected in 1927–28. According to the clerk of the police department there were never three colored lieutenants at one time. Robinson evidently did not investigate the library situation at all. The ward superintendent of streets was classified under appointive officers (p. 214), but in fact he is a civil service employee.

[35] Interview, October 29, 1932.

Negro employees in certain branches of the municipal service would proceed much more rapidly than in others. It is extremely hazardous to estimate the proportion of Negroes employed by the city of Chicago at any one time. The total number of city employees is changing constantly and no records are kept which show the color or race of the employees.[36] The investigator has to make personal inquiries and by the time he has covered the hundreds of offices in the city hall and those in the school system, the libraries and the other public buildings as well, the materials which he first collected are out of date. Furthermore, it is not possible to get full co-operation in all of the offices. Some department heads are very sensitive on the subject of race relations and say in answer to questions about the number of Negroes in their offices that they do not note differences in color, race, or creed. The figures given in Table VIII are highly tentative, but they are the best obtainable with the resources at hand.

It has already been pointed out that the Negroes in Chicago were about 7 per cent of the total population in 1930. According to the estimates given in the table the proportion of Negro employees in the classified service in 1932 (6.4 per cent) was not greatly below this ratio. As compared with the situation as it was said to be twenty years before, this is a decided improvement. The Juvenile Protective Association published a study in 1913 which stated that the Negro employees of the city at that time were only 1.9 per cent of the total.[37] According to the United States census figures for Negroes in public service in Chicago (not elsewhere classified) the progress has not been quite as great (1.3 per cent in 1920 and 4.0 per cent in 1930) but the census figures are not comparable to those which have been presented here and are less useful for our purposes.[38] In gross

[36] The police department is an exception, see below, p. 251.

[37] L. de K. Bowen, *The Colored People of Chicago: An Investigation Made for the Juvenile Protective Association* by A. P. Drucker, Sophia Boaz, A. L. Miram Schaffner. Text by L. Bowen (Chicago, 1913).

[38] The census does not give figures for the total number of persons in public service. Thus, clerks in the municipal service would be classified under clerical occupations and not under public service, and janitors working for the city would be classified under

proportions, then, the Negroes in the city have not fared so badly in the city hall.

It is only when the kinds of positions held by Negroes are examined that the real situation comes to light. The proportion of Negroes in such jobs as janitors, janitresses, and laborers has exceeded the population ratio, but the proportion in clerical and professional occupations is far below that ratio. Only in the Department of Health, the Bureau of Parks and Recreation, the Bureau of Water, and the library service have the Negroes in Chicago come near to their population ratio in positions which are largely clerical and professional. In the uniformed forces, particularly in the fire department (0.8 per cent), the Negroes have fallen far behind their population ratio. The reasons why the Negroes have done better in the police department than in the fire department will be discussed in the next chapter. The situation in the Health Department is undoubtedly the result in part of the personal attitude of Dr. Herman N. Bundesen, who has been commissioner for over eight years. Although he has sometimes been criticized in the colored weeklies, as a rule his work and attitude have been praised by the Negro journalists and public men.[39] In the library service the Negroes have been successful because of such factors as their long record of efficiency,[40] the presence of one of their group on the Library Board for a period, and the work of a very fair-minded manager of personnel. It is apparent that to Mayor Thompson directly

---

domestic service. Furthermore, the census does not give the number of employees in public service by the particular governments which employ them. In other words, the census figure for the number of policemen includes all the policemen in public service, whether hired by the city of Chicago or one of the park boards. Another drawback to the census data is that the title "guards, watchmen, and doorkeepers," includes persons who are not in public service. In reaching the proportions given above I have therefore omitted the guards, watchmen, and doorkeepers. The Director of the Census informed me that he could not make a more detailed classification than the one used in the printed volumes. He could not subdivide the employees in public service by the governments which employed them. For the census figures, see Appendix I.

[39] *Chicago Defender*, December 27, 1927; March 1, 1930; May 24, 1930; January 24, 1931; *Chicago Whip*, May 3, 1930.

[40] Washington Intercollegiate Club, *Negro in Chicago, 1779–1929*, II, 95, "Negro Goes Ahead with Library," by Blanche V. Shaw.

the Negroes in the classified service do not owe a great deal. Dr. Bundesen has served under both Democratic and Repub-

TABLE VIII

NEGROES IN THE CLASSIFIED SERVICE OF THE CITY OF CHICAGO, 1932

	TOTAL NUMBER ON PAYROLL MARCH, 1932† (1)	NEGRO EMPLOYEES, 1932*			
		Clerical, Professional; Commissioned (2)	Janitors, Laborers, and Estimated Temporaries (3)	Total (4)	Per Cent of Total (Column 4 of Column 1) (5)
Comptroller's Office...............	143	3	....	3	2.1
City Collector	158	2	....	2	1.3
Police...........................	6,551	143	32	175	2.7
Fire.............................	2,713	22	....	22	0.8
Gas and Electricity, Department of .	872	4	1	5	0.6
Public Service...................	51	....	1	1	2.0
Building, Department of..........	112	1	....	1	0.9
Weights and Measures, Department of.............................	31	....	2	2	6.5
Health, Department of............	891	70	50	120	13.5
Board of Local Improvements......	429	9	....	9	2.1
Public Works, Commissioner's Office...........	13	1	....	1	7.7
City Hall, Bureau of............	180	1	26	27	15.0
Bridges, Division of.............	409	1	....	1	0.2
Streets, Bureau of..............	4,435	6	500	506	11.4
Sewers, Bureau of...............	67	....	11	11	16.4
Parks, Recreation, Aviation, Bureau of......................	328	23	....	23	7.0
Water Works, Engineer..........	172	1	....	1	0.6
Pumping Stations.............	1,512	6	6	12	0.8
Construction & Water Pipe Ext..	1,172	4	185	189	16.1
Bureau of Water..............	462	29	....	29	6.3
Board of Education, Business Department	5,291	69	637	706‡	13.4
Library Board...................	949	42	17	59	6.2
Municipal Tuberculosis Sanitarium..	903	3	....	3	0.3
Offices in which no Negroes were found........................	1,858	....	....	....	0.0
Total......................	29,702	440	1,468	1,908	6.4

* As of 1932 as far as possible.
† Figures from the office of the Civil Service Commission. ‡ Figure for 1931.

lican administrations and he was dismissed during the third Thompson administration. A Negro was in charge of a library branch as long ago as 1903, the first Negro member of the Library Board was appointed under a Democratic administration, and the manager of personnel is a civil service employee. In exempt and temporary civil service positions, Negroes have done better under Thompson than under Democratic mayors, but in the permanent service other factors have been more important than the political. Under any administration the Negroes must face unfriendly racial attitudes on the part of some department heads and some of the users of governmental services.

TYPES OF ADJUSTMENT

The table shows that there are around 440 Negroes in the clerical, professional, and uniformed services of the city of Chicago, exclusive of the teachers in the public schools. For all practical purposes, these employees enjoy the same permanency of tenure, pension rights, and other privileges possessed by the civil service employees in general. Some colored employees are bitter because their opportunities for promotion seem to be limited, or because they are concentrated in certain bureaus or departments, or because their conditions of work are not always pleasant.

How the handicaps under which the colored people suffered in the city service affected their personality adjustments to their jobs may be shown by some illustrations. A few Negroes apparently accepted the view of the Negro's position that was held by some of the department heads. In one of the bureaus of the Public Works Department there was a single Negro employee, a dark-brown-skinned young man, who appeared to have made an adjustment by taking for granted some of the common attitudes toward Negroes found among the white civil service employees. He was very jealous of his position in his bureau and he did not welcome the thought of having to share it with other Negroes. He endeavored to protect his position by trying to win the favor of his immediate superior.

I started work as a messenger in the civil service about eight years ago. Through the goodness of the men in this office three years ago I was certified as a junior clerk. The procedure is when a Negro is certified to try to put him either in the Water Bureau or the Health Department. It was only through friends in this office that I was kept here. My boss asked that I be returned to this office.

I was certified under a Democratic administration. But there are good and bad people among all groups and I happened to hit in with some good people. One advantage I had when I was promoted to junior clerk was the fact that in the office there are a lot of college trained men. A man with an education, as a rule, isn't so prejudiced.

I have a very good boss who appreciates a man who works hard whether he is white or black. Why just last week-end he took me home with him to do some work for him and we all, his wife and family and myself, sat down and had lunch together. I used to drive his car. I would take his kids to school and often drive them around Lincoln Park. He looked awfully tough but he was good to me. They used to call me the "pet" around here and they were all very friendly to me because of the boss. If the boss shows that he likes you, the rest will perhaps go along.

I haven't thought much about my possibilities for advancement. There is a possible chance that I will be a principal clerk. The boss is a fine man and he may see that I get advancement.

I don't believe all the things people tell me about prejudice down here. Of course I know there is some, there's no getting around that fact. When I took the promotional examination I heard a lot of the people saying that they were marking all of the colored peoples' papers with a "c." But they didn't mark my paper because I passed. You can't tell what to believe.[41]

In the library service there was a colored woman, a person who reached one of the highest grades, who had a mixed personality. She was a marginal type that tried to live in both the colored and white worlds. Her divided interests gave rise to conflicting reports about the nature of her work. She was described as very fair, nice looking with sharp features and "good" hair. In other words, she was not highly visible in a crowd of white persons. She was a native of Chicago and lived in a white neighborhood with her mother and father, the latter being a tradesman. She was a member of the American Library Association and the Chicago Library Club, both predominantly white organizations. On the other hand, she was well known in Negro society and belonged to a number of Negro clubs. Some persons

[41] Interview, November 7, 1932. Robinson, *op. cit.*, p. 202, gives a similar example: "An employee in the Bridge Division of the Department of Public Works had carried this cultivation to its logical extreme. Classified as a draftsman, he has done personal and domestic service for his present division head. He mentioned scrubbing floors in the north side apartment of the head of the Department, and acting as chauffeur for his wife. He refused pay for all of this personal service, and when asked what return he expected he said that he wanted to be taken care of."

who came in contact with her work regarded her as very efficient and conscientious, while others thought that she was inefficient, a poor disciplinarian, and played favorites. The fact that she received steady advancements must mean that her superiors generally took a favorable view of her work. This librarian disclaimed having any political connections and said about her work:

I have never been troubled with race prejudice in the library. I have worked in white neighborhoods and in Negro neighborhoods, under white librarians and under colored librarians. The people who patronize the libraries are only interested in service. I have white girls working under me now and I never have any trouble with race prejudice. Many girls magnify little incidents and call them acts of race prejudice. If I put a little boy out of the library for acting rude and he yells through the window that I am a "Nigger," I never think that this is an act of prejudice because I know that if any Jewish girl on the staff put him out he would yell "dirty Jew" at her or if an Irish girl did it he would yell "Shanty Irish."

Negro girls who have worked under me say that certain white librarians were prejudiced and gave them low efficiency marks. They said that they were always being "bawled out" about their work just because they were colored. I had to "bawl out" those girls and give them low efficiency marks too, because their work was so poor. Many girls try to cover up reprimands that they get for poor service by saying it was because the librarian was prejudiced.[42]

There are many Negroes in civil service positions in other local governments in the Chicago region. Lack of space prevents the discussion of the colored employees of such units as Cook County, the South Park Board, and the other park boards. However, mention should be made of the recognition which has been given to the trained Negro social workers. During the depression which started in 1929 there was a great increase in the number of social workers. At the beginning of 1933 there were 102 colored social workers under the Cook County Bureau of Public Welfare, or 5.7 per cent of the total of 1,797. Two of the assistant supervisors were colored.

The civil service rules in the city of Chicago have helped Negroes to some extent in their struggle to get ahead. The great bulk of the colored employees in the classified service enjoy a

[42] Interview, November 29, 1929.

security which is not possessed by the purely political appointees who may at a given time receive higher salaries and greater distinction. Incoming administrations, both Democratic and Republican, have assailed the merit rules but they have not been able to disturb more than 10 or 12 per cent of those already in the service on a regular basis. While the colored employees may meet with partial segregation, resistance to advancement and unpleasant treatment, they can turn some of these very disadvantages into advantages. In the fire department captaincies have been open to colored firemen in the companies to which colored men have been assigned. When some of the higher positions have closed the colored leaders have been more insistent in their demands for jobs in the lower grades of the civil service.

CHAPTER XII

NEGRO POLICE OFFICERS[1]

The police officers of the city of Chicago are regular civil service employees, but there are a number of reasons why in a study of race relations they should be considered apart from the rest

OFFICER X

of the public employees. The police department is the only department in the city of Chicago which keeps a record of the color of its employees. When Negroes have sought to become policemen, a number of questions have been raised. What would be the attitude of the white and the colored communities? Would the prejudice of some of the whites make it difficult to use Negroes for police duty? Would the Negroes themselves respect officers of their own race as well as white officers?

An expert on the subject of American police systems has recently said: "Police administration has become almost synonymous with partisan control and political corruption."[2] In an earlier chapter it has been pointed out that the Negro underworld is a part of the Negro political organization. All underworld leaders, regardless of color, are vitally interested in that immunity from the enforcement of the ever increasing number of criminal laws called police protection. Would colored officers arrest policy-operators as readily as white officers would? Would colored officers tend to become a part of the local political machine and divide their allegiance between it and the department? Would Negro policemen take on the brutal and ex-

[1] The author is largely indebted to Mr. Horace R. Cayton for the materials on which this chapter is based.

[2] Bruce Smith, "Politics and Law Enforcement," *Annals of the American Academy of Political and Social Science*, CLXIX (September, 1933), 67.

ploitive patterns of behavior that were exemplified by some white officers?

The criminal and judicial statistics for the city of Chicago show that a disproportionate number of Negroes are arrested and convicted of violations of the law.[3] What effect did this have on the demand of the colored community for police officers and the effectiveness of Negro officers in their own community?

DEMAND FOR COLORED OFFICERS

The distrust which the American public has in general of police officers has been greatly intensified in the colored community in Chicago. The journalists, the politicians, and the ministers in the "Black Belt" were constantly complaining bitterly against the stupidity, prejudice, and brutality of the white police officers. In connection with the race riot of 1919 it was said by the Commission on Race Relations, "Lack of proper action by the police may have made the riot possible."[4] Many Negroes were conscious of this situation because their grievances had been made articulate by the Negro press.

Among the caustic critics of the police department was the *Chicago Defender*, which long before the race riot printed criticisms of the white police officers.[5] Some years later the *Defender* was still waging the same campaign:

There is no law, municipal or otherwise, which calls for the insulting of respectable Race people by these big, rawboned sapheads, who are maintained by tax-paying citizens of which class thousands of our people form a part. It is hard to understand on what basis these "hounds" of the law are accorded encouragement in their dastardly practices by station house superiors by word of mouth, and by their chief himself, by his ignoring of protests made by their victims. Something will and must be done. Bulldozers should have no place in Chicago's police department and birds of the stripe of ———— and ———— should be kicked off the force before something serious happens to them at the hands of some outraged citizen.[6]

[3] Chicago Commission on Race Relations, *Negro in Chicago*, chap. vii; Reckless, *Vice in Chicago;* Edward E. Wilson, "The Responsibility for Crime," *Opportunity*, VII (March, 1929), 95–97; United States National Commission on Law Observance and Enforcement (Wickersham Commission), *Report* No. 10.

[4] *Op. cit.*, p. 405.

[5] August 5, 1916.   [6] September 13, 1924.

One of the results of this campaign against the police was a growing demand for Negro officers. As a woman leader in one of the West Side settlements put it, "The police were bothering our people so badly that we got together and asked to have some colored police sent out. Then we got four police to guard our interests."[7] A year before the race riot the *Defender* reported that a committee of "Race" people appealed to Mayor Thompson for better police protection, an efficient detective system operating in the immediate vicinity of the lawlessness, and more patrolmen of the Race assigned to the district.[8] The *Chicago Whip* called attention to the issue in the following words: "A determined stand should be taken by the voters of the South Side upon the demand for colored officers on the South Park police force."[9] When the board failed to act on this demand the *Whip* urged the colored voters to vote "no" on the South Park bonds.[10] The constant agitation of these agencies kept the subject before the attention of the Negro voters and the city-wide leaders who were trying to attract that vote. Because it was made an issue, the colored community was in a position to act in a united fashion on election day.

The Negro community was not only interested in the services which officers of their own race might be able to render but it was also concerned with the prestige which colored officers would bring to the race. In many parts of the United States, particularly in the South, there were no Negro policemen. In the eyes of many persons, whose economic status is similar to that of the great mass of Negroes, the police officers are the local government. The appointment of Negro policemen was regarded as a sure sign that the race was recognized as a participant in government. Although the Negro community was greatly disappointed in the character of some of the colored officers, the newcomer from the South could say, "What colored man's heart

[7] Interview, May 29, 1932. These colored officers proved to be a disappointment.

[8] July 6, 1918.

[9] January 31, 1931.   [10] February 2, 1931.

does not beat a little faster when he sees a Negro officer go by in his neat uniform of blue?"[11]

HOW NEGROES PENETRATED THE
POLICE DEPARTMENT

It has been noted that the first Negro policeman was appointed in 1872 by a Republican mayor some 23 years before the civil service law was passed. This officer served only three years and was replaced in 1875 by a colored appointee of a People's party mayor. The next mayor of Chicago was a Republican who appointed a Civil War veteran as the third Negro officer but during the last two years of his administration this mayor had no colored policemen on the force. Then came Mayor Carter H. Harrison's four consecutive terms of two years each. Although a Democrat, Mayor Harrison appointed four colored policemen and reinstated another. At first the colored officers were put in plain clothes, but in 1884 when the Democratic National Convention was held in Chicago and John Kelly came to the city with a New York delegation, Mayor Harrison put two of the Negro officers in uniform for the occasion.[12]

---

[11] Interview with unidentified Negro. The following extract from Rudolph Fisher's "The City of Refuge," cited in Allain Locke, *The New Negro*, p. 58, illustrates this same attitude:

"The Southern Negro's eyes opened wide; his mouth opened wider. If the inside of New York had mystified him, the outside was amazing him. For there stood a handsome, brass-buttoned giant directing the heaviest traffic Gillis had ever seen; halting unnumbered tons of automobiles, and trucks and wagons and pushcarts and street-cars; holding them at bay with one hand while he swept similar tons peremptorily on with the other; ruling the wide crossing with supreme self-assurance; and he, too, was a Negro:

"Yet most of the vehicles that leaped or crouched at his command carried white passengers. One of these overdrove bounds a few feet and Gillis heard the officer's shrill whistle and gruff reproof, saw the driver's face turn red and his car draw back like a threatened pup. It was beyond belief—impossible. Black might be white, but it couldn't be that white!

" 'Done died an' woke up in Heaven,' thought King Solomon, watching, fascinated; and after awhile, as if the wonder of it were too great, he said, half aloud; then repeated over and over, with greater and greater conviction, 'Even got collud policemans—even got collud. . . . .' "

[12] Interview, February 27, 1933. See above, p. 198, regarding Mayor Harrison's attitude toward the early appointees. He did not look upon them as purely political appointees.

Following the elder Harrison's fourth term as mayor, the control of the city hall oscillated back and forth between Republican and Democratic mayors for a period of ten years. While the number of Negro policemen increased much more rapidly under the Republican than under the Democratic mayors, there was a steady increase from 4 in 1886 to 23 in 1894. Political and personal considerations were important in securing the appointment of colored officers during this period. Most of the applicants relied upon powerful white friends to assist them in making the proper connections. A police officer who was appointed in 1888 under a Republican mayor gave the following account of his entrance into the service:

> When I came to Chicago I got a job working for the flour company of Swanson and Eckhart. I worked very hard and made a good reputation for myself. But I saw that I wasn't getting any place working for them so I decided to try to get into the Police Department. There had been a few Negroes appointed and I thought that may be through the influence of my white friends I could get an appointment.
>
> So I spoke to Mr. Eckhart about it. He referred me to his brother, Barney Eckhart who was in politics. Barney Eckhart spoke to several others until I finally reached a man who gave me a letter to Chief Hubbard and I was appointed.[13]

There are many similar cases which could be cited. In a few instances the initiative came from the white friends. The oldest living Negro policeman in the city stated that he was working for a private family which decided to go to Europe. "They didn't know what to do with me and started looking around for a job for me," was his comment. "Then the son of the chief of police who was a friend of the family suggested that I be given a job as policeman. I was very pleased as I thought I would like that sort of work."[14] The first police matron who was appointed in the early nineties had similar experiences.[15]

During this period there were also indications of the beginnings of political pressure from the colored community itself. One officer who was appointed under a Democratic administration was kept on during a Republican administration because he

[13] Interview, October 15, 1931.

[14] Interview, October 14, 1931.   [15] Interview, October 23, 1931.

got the endorsement of a colored group called the John Brown Political Club.[16]

These early policemen were very uncertain as to their positions. Mayoralty elections came every two years and every new mayor made wholesale changes. Of all the administrations during this period, that of Mayor Washburne's from 1891 to 1893 was the most liberal toward the Negroes. This Republican mayor appointed eleven new colored officers and reinstated two others. An officer who was appointed in this administration tells how he was able to stay on through succeeding administrations:

> An officer had to keep himself out of politics in those days, too. I remember Mayor Harrison who came in (1893) fired a list of men that would reach from here to the corner. I got past that because I wasn't playing politics. Another mayor, a Democrat, fired even more than that and I got past that. It was so bad that if they heard you were at a political meeting of some candidate for mayor and he was not elected, the other fellow would fire you without any recourse. This was all before civil service. When civil service came in, I passed that too. It was pretty hard to keep a job on the police force in those days. Just one wrong move and you were through.[17]

This officer went on to say that when civil service came in 1895, "things were a bit better." Things may have been better for this particular officer but for a period of ten years following the inauguration of the merit system the recruitment of Negro officers progressed slowly. In fact, only six new officers were added to the force during this time and five of these came under Mayor Swift, a Republican. The actual number of Negro policemen decreased from 23 in 1894 to 16 in 1905. This decline in the number of Negro officers was probably due to the scarcity of colored applicants, the smaller number of vacancies open, the lack of educational qualifications on the part of many Negroes who applied, and the use of the merit system to eliminate the colored candidates. One of the officers who was appointed during this period said that he and another were the only colored persons out of four thousand who took the examination.[18]

[16] Interview, February 1, 1932.

[17] Interview, October 23, 1931.   [18] Interview, May 7, 1932.

About 1905 conditions began to change and the number of Negro policemen again began to increase. The police force was increased so there were many vacancies,[19] a new chief examiner for the Civil Service Commission proved to be very active in holding examinations,[20] and the Negro applicants were more energetic in preparing themselves for the tests. The result was that the number of colored officers rose from 16 in 1905 to about 50 in 1914. While the net increase during the Republican administration of Mayor Busse was large, the recruitment of Negro policemen went on about as rapidly during this time under Democratic as under Republican administrations. In this respect, the fifth term of Mayor Harrison II (1911–15) was quite different from his earlier terms. The wife of one of the officers appointed during this period gives the following description of her husband's preparation for the examination:

Then he went to the stockyards for two years. But in 1903 he wanted to better his condition so he started to look around for a civil service job. We started reading the civil service paper together. But one day he says to me, "I haven't got enough education to pass these examinations. What am I going to do?" So I told him I would carry him through the eighth grade and that's all you were supposed to have for those kind of jobs. So we got to work. Sometimes we would study all night long. Then he got so he used to love to write. Well, finally we got through the eighth reader.

Then he went down to take the tests. He said, "I will take all of the tests I can and if I don't pass one I may pass another." So he took a test for janitor at the City Hall, driver of a hospital wagon and policeman. Well you will be surprised to know that he was called on all three.[21]

The beginning of the big migration of Negroes from the South to Chicago coincided with the first Thompson administration. The number of colored policemen rose from about 50 when Thompson first took office in 1915 to a new level of 116 in 1922. Among the reasons for this increase were a general increase in the total number of all police officers, the publicity campaign of the *Chicago Defender*,[22] and the insistent pressure

[19] *Chicago Daily News Almanac for 1924*, p. 876.

[20] J. B. Kingsbury, "The Administration of the Civil Service Law under the various Mayors," *Public Personnel Studies*, IV (May, 1926), 161.

[21] Interview, November 1, 1931.   [22] March 1, 1930.

brought by the Negro political organization. One officer said regarding the situation: "(My appointment) was in the early days and there was not as much prejudice against colored people then as there is now since the migration. But, on the other hand, the colored people had less political power . . . . and that's what counts."[23]

Negro officers reached the peak in numbers in 1930 during the third Thompson administration when there were 137 on the force. Considering the increase in the Negro population in the preceding decade, one might have expected to find an even larger number. The presence of Bishop Carey on the Civil Service Commission did not mean any great change as no more Negro officers were added to the force than under the preceding commission. Since Mayor Thompson went out of power the number of colored policemen has declined slightly. In 1933 there were 124 Negro patrolmen, 4 sergeants, 2 lieutenants, 1 police operator, and 2 police women, a total of 133.[24] A summary of the influx of colored officers is presented in Table IX, which shows the number of appointments and reinstatements by two-year periods.

During the three Thompson administrations an aggregate of 122 Negroes were appointed on the force and 86 were reinstated. In other words, about one-half of all the 267 appointments of Negroes since 1872,[25] and about the same proportion of the reinstatements, were made under Thompson. This high ratio was partly the result of the coincidence of the Negro migration with the Thompson régime.

It is apparent that this number is related to the total number of Negroes in the city and to the size of the police force at any given time. One retired officer stated that in the late eighties "there was an unwritten law that there were to be only four Negroes on the force at one time as there were only three thousand Negroes in the city at that time."[26] As we have seen this

[23] Interview.

[24] Figures furnished by the Office of the Secretary of Police, as of April 5, 1933.

[25] Forty-six per cent of the appointments and 51 per cent of the reinstatements.

[26] Interview, October 14, 1931.

"law" held for only a short period (four years). It was simply one of the rules for distributing patronage among the different racial and religious groups in the city. After the adoption of the

TABLE IX

APPOINTMENT, REINSTATEMENT, AND TOTAL NUMBER OF NEGRO
POLICEMEN IN CHICAGO BY TWO-YEAR INTERVALS, 1871–1932*

Two-Year Period Beginning	Name of Mayor	Party of Mayor	Negro Police Officers		
			Appointed	Reinstated	Total Number At End of Each Period
1871......	Jos. Medill	Republican	1	0	1
1873......	H. D. Colvin	Peoples	1	0	1
1875......	(continued one year) (Monroe Heath)	Republican	1	0	1
1877......	Monroe Heath	Republican	0	0	0
1879......	C. H. Harrison I	Democrat	0	1	1
1881......	C. H. Harrison I	Democrat	3	0	1
1883......	C. H. Harrison I	Democrat	0	0	3
1885......	C. H. Harrison I	Democrat	1	0	4
1887......	John A. Roche	Republican	4	0	6
1889......	DeWitt Cregier	Democrat	4	0	9
1891......	Hempsted Washburne	Republican	11	2	18
1893......	{ C. H. Harrison I†	Democrat	0	1	18
	{ John P. Hopkins	Democrat	2	2	23
1895......	Geo. B. Swift	Republican	5	3	24
1897......	C. H. Harrison II	Democrat	0	1	19
1899......	C. H. Harrison II	Democrat	1	0	21
1901......	C. H. Harrison II	Democrat	0	1	19
1903......	C. H. Harrison II	Democrat	0	0	17
1905......	Edw. F. Dunne	Democrat	20	1	28
1907......	Fred Busse	Republican	13	5	51
1909......	(continued)		3	0	48
1911......	C. H. Harrison II	Democrat	9	3	52
1913......	(continued)		23	3	47
1915......	W. H. Thompson	Republican	6	4	66
1917......	(continued)		11	7	80
1919......	W. H. Thompson	Republican	29	15	89
1921......	(continued)		40	11	116
1923......	Wm. E. Dever	Democrat	25	9	121
1925......	(continued)		10	6	120
1927......	W. H. Thompson	Republican	13	7	116
1929......	(continued)		25	3	137
1931......	A. J. Cermak	Democrat	8	0	126

* Figures from the Secretary of Police Office. Due to some omissions the figures do not check.
† Assassinated.

merit system for the recruitment of municipal employees this patronage rule did not apply to the police, at least not in theory. Table X shows the number and percentage of Negro officers in the last four census years.

A comparison of Table X with Table I shows that the percentage of Negro police officers has fallen behind the population ratio, particularly in the decade following 1920.[27] While the proportion of Negroes in the total population increased from 4

TABLE X

NUMBER AND PERCENTAGE OF NEGRO POLICEMEN IN CHICAGO
BY RANKS, 1900–1930*

YEAR	PATROLMEN			SERGEANTS			LIEUTENANTS			TOTAL		
	Total	Negro		Total	Negro		Total	Negro		Total	Negro	
		Number	Per Cent		Number	Per Cent		Number	Per Cent		Number	Per Cent
1900	2,505	20	0.8	257	1	0.4	63	0	0.0	2,825	21	0.7
1910	3,785	45	1.2	370	3	0.8	71	0	0.0	4,226	48	1.1
1920	3,683	79	2.1	864	9	1.0	84	1	1.2	4,631	89	1.9
1930	5,443	129	2.4	570	6	1.3	150	2	1.3	6,163	137	2.2

* Information furnished by the Secretary of the Police Department.

to nearly 7 per cent in the period 1920–30, the ratio of Negro policemen remained almost stationary at about 2 per cent. The lag in the police ratio was greater for sergeants and lieutenants than for patrolmen, and in the highest ranks of the force there were no Negroes at all. What were some of the factors which kept colored men from becoming policemen? A strict physical examination, a mental examination, a probationary period of six months, and an unfriendly attitude on the part of some of the highest police officers were among the obstacles to be overcome by the colored applicants. In addition, the impression was current in the Negro community that appointments on the police force had to be paid for.

[27] Table I is given on p. 16.

CONDITIONS OF WORK IN THE POLICE DEPARTMENT

Once a Negro was given an appointment on the police force he soon discovered that he had new problems to face. His assignment to a given district, his allotment of duties, his treatment on disciplinary matters, and his efficiency ratings were subject to manipulation. The staff officers, try as they may, sometimes find themselves using special methods with the colored men under them. Police administrators seem to be very sensitive as to the attitude which the white public takes toward the Negro officers. The following is the comment of a student of Chicago police problems:

> The appointment of Negroes to the police force has been the source of considerable embarrassment to the department. Their presence in the white districts is resented and, if present, they must be assigned to the most obscure posts. Such posts are difficult to find in a police department where contacts with the public are extremely frequent. They may be sent to areas of Negro concentration but here they get into trouble through abuse of authority. However, this is the disposition made of the greatest number of Negro officers.[28]

The first Negro officers were put in plain clothes probably because the police chiefs have wished to make the colored policemen as inconspicuous as possible. However, some of the early Negro patrolmen were placed in uniform and assigned to districts inhabited by white people where they found comparatively little trouble. One such officer, who was put on the force in 1888, said: "I was detailed to the North Side and, by the way, was the first colored man to work there. I stayed there for four or five years. At no time was I bothered or did I have any unpleasant experiences in the neighborhood."[29]

The success of a Negro patrolman in a district which was inhabited by whites depended upon the economic status of the district, the personality of the patrolman himself, and the attitude of the officers commanding the district. In middle-class areas with sympathetic captains, colored policemen had no special difficulties. One officer who worked in such a neighborhood thirty-five years ago said:

[28] Manuscript document dated June 11, 1931.   [29] Interview, October 15, 1931.

I liked this station much better (Woodlawn Station). The people were of the better class, wealthy people, and working was much easier. I travelled every beat in the district and met little or no prejudice. In fact, when I was made desk sergeant, the word got around that if a person wanted something done they would be treated better by me than by anyone else. I handled the public with more consideration and politeness than the Irish policemen.[30]

In some of the poorer districts the Negro officer actually had to defend himself against attacks. One of them said about his work in a near West Side district: "I would take my night stick and whale the living daylights out of those toughs. They seldom hurt me as I was a big strapping fellow." He continued, "There were times, too, when walking my beat that someone would take a pot shot at me from the cover of some building. But I never backed up. I would pull my gun and go for the place where I thought the bullet came from. If I saw anybody run I would fire at them. They thought they could get my nerve by shooting at me."[31] The people in this neighborhood finally found out that this officer was not going to bother about anything which was not his business and they began to like him. At least, he stated that he got along well after the people came to know him.

In other districts colored officers were so unpopular with their white fellow-officers that attempts were made to "frame" them. One of the methods employed is shown in the following:

I was working under a hard-boiled sergeant. He and the sergeant at the station wanted to get me. And when they wanted to get you in those days they didn't just want to get you transferred, but they wanted to get your job. They wanted to get me for two reasons, first, I was a Negro and they didn't like Negroes, and second, I didn't stand for any foolishness. I believe that the law was made to enforce, not to make money out of.

Once they framed me. The sergeant came to the corner where four beats adjoined one another. He rapped on the pavement with his night stick which was the call for the four officers. I was there within four minutes and was the only officer that showed up. He bawled me out for awhile for nothing and then told me to go back to my beat. Just after I left him a fellow called to me and asked me to come to his house. I told him I couldn't go into any house while on duty. But he answered that this was police duty that he wanted to see me on.

So I went up to the house and stood in the doorway but didn't go in. I even

[30] Interview, November 6, 1931.   [31] Interview, October 23, 1931.

held my hand on the door knob so that the door couldn't swing shut. The man wanted to get some information about swearing out a warrant. I told him what to do and turned around and started out. Just then the sergeant stepped up and said that he had caught me. He said that I had been in there for two hours. I told him that I couldn't have been as I was just talking to him less than fifteen minutes ago. But he called me a liar and walked away. The next evening when I reported for work I was told that I was to go before the trial board the following morning.[32]

After the heavy migration of Negroes to the city from the South there was a definite tendency to concentrate Negro policemen in the police districts inhabited largely by colored people. One officer who had been on the force for twenty-five years remarked: "I've noticed one difference in the treatment of Negro policemen, that is, they will not send colored officers into white districts. It didn't use to be that way."[33] Although there is no hard-and-fast rule as in the fire department, Table XI indicates most of the colored officers have been assigned to districts which are largely inhabited by Negroes.

Two-thirds of the Negro policemen were in districts whose population was 80 per cent or more colored. When Negro officers were assigned to a police district which had a Negro minority, they were usually placed on the beats which had the largest number of colored inhabitants. Thus, in the Twenty-second Police District the four colored patrolmen were sent to the near West Side Negro settlement.

The tendency to concentrate the colored officers in certain districts is the result of a number of influences. On the one hand, there is the prejudice of the public. On this topic, one police captain said: "Negro officers meet a little prejudice when they work in the loop, but not so much in the residential districts as one would suppose. It's not the Chicago resident who is prejudiced against the Negro officers. They are accustomed to seeing them around. It's the visitors from the South."[34] Then there is

---

[32] *Ibid.*   [33] Interview, May 3, 1932.

[34] Interview, October 8, 1931. This is confirmed by a retired Negro patrolman who said: "The only time that any friction arose was when some southern white man objected. I have had southerners tell me that I couldn't arrest them. Once I arrested a young white boy and he resisted me. I slapped him and a southern white woman came running up and wanted to hit me with her umbrella." Interview, October 14, 1931.

the prejudice of the higher officers in the department. In the words of one of the colored lieutenants, "Prejudice in the department lies with the command rather than with the general public."[35] Finally, there is the preference of many of the officers themselves to work in districts which were inhabited largely by their own people. As one officer said:

TABLE XI

ASSIGNMENT OF NEGRO POLICEMEN AND
NEGRO POPULATION IN SELECTED
POLICE DISTRICTS

Police District Number	Percentage of Population Negro in 1930[*]	Number of Negro Officers 1933[†]
2	19.0	2
3	47.2	25[‡]
4	80.2	33[§]
5	95.2	44[‖]
6	10.3	0
7	14.2	1
15	1.9	2
22	14.4	4
23	1.7	1
26	4.0	4
27	21.6	2
39	0.4	1

[*] Census data of Chicago used for getting ratios.
[†] Material furnished by the Secretary of Police.
[‡] Includes three sergeants.
[§] Includes one lieutenant.
[‖] Includes one lieutenant.

A ranking colored officer should be in a colored district. There he can do much good. Hundreds of colored people are arrested who have committed no crime. A Negro officer can do much to protect his own people in this way. If there was a fair minded Negro to appeal to, much harm could be done away with in handling our people. And this, too, without lowering the standards of efficiency or the morale of the department."[36]

This view is not universal among Negro policemen, as some have expressed a preference to work in districts which are mainly white. While Negro officers have done well in all parts of the city, the needs and demands of the South Side community and a

[35] Interview, May 13, 1933.   [36] Interview, February 15, 1932.

lack of appreciation elsewhere are drawing them to a few selected districts.

In the assignment of duties within a given station the Negro
officers may be singled out for special treatment. Positions of
honor, such as bodyguards at parades and large public gather-
ings, are usually given to white officers. "When officers are
needed at the ball park," one officer said, "white officers are
usually sent out and if there are Negro officers they are often
kept outside to direct the cars."[37] The colored weeklies have
made the Negro community conscious of this form of discrimination. During the Republican Convention of 1932 the *Chicago
Defender* bitterly complained that the "six detectives detailed
for duty at the Republican National Convention by the commanding officer were turned down by the higher-ups in the department."[38] When this policy was reversed at the Democratic
Convention which followed shortly afterward and the Negro
officers were assigned to various positions, it was regarded as a
triumph for the race.[39]

The appointment of Negroes as detectives has proceeded very
slowly in Chicago. While the first colored men appointed on the
force were made detectives, later Negro officers found it difficult to achieve the favored rank of detective. The colored detectives were found for the most part in the districts of Negro
concentration, and even here they were not found in large numbers. "In that district," said one officer, "the people are 96 per
cent colored, but the detectives are 98 per cent white."[40] The
South Side community was made keenly aware of this situation
by their weekly papers, which carried on a campaign to increase
the number of Negroes assigned to detective duty.[41] The attitude displayed by the following comment of a station commander shows in part why more colored detectives have not been appointed:

Some Negro detectives are very bad. They are full of ego and simply want
to walk down the street and have everybody point them out as a plain clothes

[37] Interview.

[38] June 11, 1932.

[39] *Chicago Defender*, July 9, 1932.

[40] Interview, February 15, 1932.

[41] *Chicago Defender*, April 9, 1932.

man. In the Negro districts they are sometimes overbearing and hard on the other Negroes and in white districts they are sometimes too timid. But again we have some plain clothes men who plug along and are very hard workers and aren't bothered by an inflation of the ego. After all, they run just about the same as other officers, but these tendencies are found more often in the Negro officer than in the white officer.[42]

Another desirable position on the police force is that of squad-car member. The selection of Negroes for this post has not gone forward very rapidly. When the Democrats recently replaced the Republicans in the city hall, some of the colored squad-cars were broken up. Regarding one police station, the comment was made: "There used to be a colored squad-car under the last administration. Recently they put on about seven new cars and he (the captain) made just one colored squad-car and that of uniformed men. He will not have a squad-car of colored detectives."[43] The Negro press kept agitating this matter and when one police captain formed a new Negro squad he was praised very highly for his fairness.[44]

As a general rule, colored and white officers are neither teamed together as detectives, nor placed together in the same squad-car. One captain stated that he would not put a Negro on the vice squad even in a district that was inhabited largely by Negroes. Contrary to the practice in New York City, none of the colored officers in Chicago have been assigned to the traffic department, either as traffic officers or as motorcycle policemen. The colored weeklies have carried on a vigorous campaign against this situation:

Citizens through their lack of interest have allowed the fire department, motorcycle division of the police department of Chicago and the police system of the South Park board to remain lily-white organizations. We must first urge our able young men to take every examination for these positions and make themselves eligible. Then we must work vigorously to force the civil service boards of Chicago and the park system to appoint them. We are taxed for the upkeep of these departments and there are no reasons why we cannot

[42] Interview, October 8, 1931.   [43] Interview, February 15, 1932.

[44] *Chicago Defender*, March 19, 1932: "Captain ——— this week disbanded one of the white squads at his station and turned it over to three members of the Race. The fair stand of the captain has brought forth much praise and has served to bring into bolder relief the conditions at other stations."

have our just share of representation in them. Our rights must triumph over racial hatred and discrimination.[45]

The nature of police duties is such that it is necessary for the department to maintain semi-military discipline. The morale of the force is maintained by a system of creditable mentions, fines, suspensions, and discharges. The awarding of creditable mentions is wholly within the power of the department, but the imposition of penalties for the breaches of the police rules is a function of the Civil Service Commission. The service records of the Negro officers show that some have received creditable mentions and that some have been brought before the trial board several times. It is useless to deny that political favoritism has prevented the dismissal of officers, white and black, who had powerful connections. When the Civil Service Commission has been very strict, such officers have been able to secure reinstatements by court action.[46] In a game of this sort the colored policemen have been at a disadvantage because they were not wholly within the system. It has not been practicable to compare the service records of the white and colored officers, but a partial examination of these records shows that no colored officer has ever had a record as bad as some white officers. Negro policemen have been reprimanded, fined, suspended, and discharged for a variety of reasons. The trial board proceedings show that the discharges have been for neglect of duty, sleeping while on duty, wilful maltreatment of citizens, unlawful use of weapons, intoxication while on duty, inefficiency in service, violation of criminal laws, insubordination, extortion, and conduct unbecoming an officer. When a Negro officer is discharged by the board it is doubly unfortunate. It is unfortunate for him personally and it is unfortunate for the other Negro officers and the future Negro applicants for police positions. Such a discharge tends to strengthen the conviction of some of the white commanding officers that Negroes do not make good policemen.

[45] *Ibid.*, March 1, 1930.

[46] J. B. Kingsbury, "The Merit System in Chicago from 1915 to 1923" *op. cit.*, p. 312. The failure of the Civil Service Commission to appear in court through the corporation counsel's office would mean a reinstatement.

As a rule, Negro officers through necessity try hard to keep their records clear.

Reliable standards for measuring police efficiency have yet to be devised. When the white commanding officers are asked to rate the colored men under them there is a tendency for them to reflect the views regarding the Negro that are common in the white world. However, some rating systems are better than others, and when the ranking officers are required to make a careful check on each man the results are more trustworthy. In 1932 the Civil Service Commission made a trial of the Probst Service rating system.[47] This system calls for the checking of selected items that fit or describe each employee.

In one of the districts which contains a number of colored policemen and a population which is 50 per cent colored a special examination was made of some of the Probst ratings. Thirty-one policemen, of whom ten were Negroes, were graded by six different officers, one of whom was a Negro sergeant. Each one of the thirty-one patrolmen was rated by each officer. On the basis of the score received each of the patrolmen was given a rank.

The rankings given in Table XII show that the white officers in this station had a high opinion of some of the Negro patrolmen under them and a low opinion of others. A composite rating of all of the superior officers places three of the colored patrolmen above or at the median and seven below. There is not much difference between the ranking of the Negro patrolmen made by the Negro sergeant and the composite ranking made by five white officers. It is true that the Negro sergeant placed one of the patrolmen third but a white superior officer placed one of them second. In both cases the mean for the colored patrolmen was about 20 and that for the white patrolmen about 12. The number of cases was so small that no definite conclusions can be drawn from these data.

Some of the statements checked opposite the names of the

---

[47] Instigated by Commissioner Leonard D. White. For a discussion of the Probst system, see J. B. Probst, "Substituting Precision Records for Guesswork in Personnel Efficiency Records," *National Municipal Review*, XX (1931), 143–48.

ten Negroes will give a little idea as to the attitude of the officers toward them. Among the favorable statements checked most frequently were: usually neat personal appearance, unusually courteous, cool headed, usually punctual, learns new work easily, usually reliable and dependable, and strong and active. Each of these items was checked forty times or more.[48] Among the unfavorable statements most commonly checked

TABLE XII

RANK AMONG 31 PATROLMEN HELD BY 10 NEGRO
PATROLMEN AS GRADED BY 6 RANKING
OFFICERS OF STATION X, 1932

NEGRO PATROLMEN	RANK BASED ON PROBST SCORES GIVEN BY		
	Five White Officers	Negro Sergeant	Six Rating Officers
A...........	10	10	10
D...........	13	28	17
C...........	14	18	16
H...........	17	9	19
B...........	18	3	15
F...........	19	16	23
J...........	24	30	27
E...........	25	25	25
G...........	29	20	29
I...........	30	29	30

were: slow moving, needs considerable supervision, and does not accept responsibility. However, these statements were only checked 17, 16, and 15 times, respectively.

The study of the efficiency ratings showed that opinions regarding Negro officers were scattered over a wide range. This agreed with the common-sense views expressed by the persons interviewed. Some Negro officers were regarded as excellent and others were looked upon as good, bad, or indifferent. However, there was a tendency for commanding officers to rate Negro policemen below white policemen.

[48] With 6 raters checking 10 persons, the maximum number of checks would be 60.

PROMOTION OF NEGRO POLICEMEN

While it is hard for a Negro in Chicago to become a patrolman, it is even harder for him to become a sergeant or lieutenant of police. As in the case of other civil service employees much depends upon the efficiency rating which is used as an important part of the promotional examination. "If you want to know about the Negro's chance for promotion," said a retired officer, "you had better see who gives him his efficiency rating. That's what holds him back."[49]

Even when a Negro policeman received an adequate efficiency rating and was placed high on the list, he was not sure of an appointment. Under the rule of three, he might be turned down for a given promotion and go back to the list time after time. Under the waiver rule, he might be asked to waive his chances to receive a given appointment. This is what happened in the case of the following officer:

I passed all three examinations and was among the highest in my rating for patrol sergeant. After the examinations were graded the chief of police called me in and asked me to waive my right for promotion to patrol sergeant. He told me that I didn't have to unless I wanted, but that if I did he would look after me when it came to appointments for detective sergeants. I hesitated. I didn't want to waive any right that was mine, but on the other hand, I knew that the chief would have the right to refuse me three times if I didn't waive this right. As he had promised to appoint me to a detective sergeant, I thought it better to get that job for sure than take a chance standing on my rights. So I agreed to waive my right for promotion to patrol sergeant.

For six months the chief held me off. I didn't hear anything and other men were appointed to detective sergeants over my head. I began to believe that he had lied to me and didn't intend to appoint me at all. I knew that there were eight or nine positions in the Bureau to be filled and was sure that he was going to keep me off altogether. I began to regret that I had waived my right to a place as patrol sergeant.[50]

In order to meet the obstacles that block their chances for promotion, the Negro policemen have worked out a number of techniques. Two months before the civil service law went into operation, Mayor Swift, a Republican, made many appoint-

[49] Interview.   [50] Interview, October 15, 1931.

ments and promotions among which was the elevation of the
first Negro to a sergeancy in the police department. These appointments and promotions were regarded as purely political
and many of them were undone when Carter H. Harrison II
became mayor in 1898. The first colored sergeant was demoted
in this year but shortly afterward another Negro was made a
detective sergeant on the basis of the promotional examinations.
The way in which political connections facilitate promotions is
illustrated in the following account of the appointment of one of
the later Negro sergeants:

In 19—, I took the promotional examination for desk sergeant. I passed
and was about eleventh on a list of forty, of whom all were to be promoted.
This caused a lot of discussion in the department as to whether to appoint me.
There was a lot of talk in the department about it and an effort was made to
get me to waive appointment. But I refused and to counteract this I went to a
friend of mine, a Negro who was a Democrat, and asked him to use his influence with the mayor (also a Democrat).

He got three influential white politicians together. They were the closest
friends of the mayor. These men wanted to see me and a meeting was arranged
in a Loop hotel. After we had talked for awhile, one of them said, "Rest assured, if you aren't appointed, no one else will be." (The appointment was
made.)[51]

Altogether thirteen Negroes have been made sergeants on the
Chicago police force at one time or another. Five were appointed in 1913 under a Democratic mayor by a process similar to
regrading, that is, all officers doing detective work were made
sergeants. No colored sergeants were appointed during Mayor
Thompson's first administration but two were named in his
second. There have been only three Negro lieutenants, and one
of these describes below how he overcame the difficulties in his
path:

While a sergeant I took two promotional examinations for lieutenant. But
I was never high enough to reach the number appointed. This was because of
the efficiency rating which was given me. When I joined the force I stood
eleventh out of a group of about 175 men. I know I had passed the examination for lieutenant with a proportionately high rating. Further, I knew that
my educational background was far above the average (one year at college).

[51] Interview, November 6, 1931.

I know that my efficiency rating was put low by the chief's office as my captain never hesitated to praise me.

In 19— I took another examination for lieutenant. The chief gave me an average rating and with this I was able to be placed fifth on the list. This was the first time I had ever been given a decent rating.

About two months after the list was posted, there were five positions which were to be filled. The chief said he couldn't see his way clear to appoint me. Then he asked me to waive the appointment. I told him that I didn't think it was right for him to ask me to waive any right that I had won by competitive examination. I would not walk out of his office and have it get to my people that I had waived my right to advancement.

For one year I was passed up. During the course of that year the list was called down to twelve below my name. Then I was appointed a lieutenant. But it was only a political trick. It was thought by the Democratic leaders that my appointment at that time would make it possible for them to carry a great many Negro votes for the Democratic candidate for president. The mayor was not unfavorably disposed toward me. Then too, a great many influential Negroes took an interest in the affair.[52]

After winning a promotion as sergeant or lieutenant the Negro officer soon finds that he has other difficulties to face. The white officers with whom he has to associate may resent his advancement. One colored officer who had just been made a sergeant met the following situation: "That evening not one person offered me a word of congratulation. Even the man with whom I walked my beat didn't mention the appointment. There seemed to be a common agreement among them not to mention the matter at all."[53] The Negro sergeants and lieutenants were usually given duties which did not involve active command. Of the thirteen sergeants, three were assigned to desk service, eight to detective work where they went out in pairs, and only two to patrol duty where they were in charge of a squad. One of the early lieutenants was put in plain clothes immediately after his promotion and sent to the Bureau of Identification, where he was practically buried. Bitter criticisms of this treatment appeared in the Negro press.[54] After a recent change in city administrations, the Negro lieutenants were relieved of their com-

[52] Ibid.　　　　　　[53] Ibid.

[54] Broad Ax, December 7, 1912; Chicago Defender, January 19, 1918.

mands and assigned temporarily to ordinary patrol duty, a course of action which they regarded as very humiliating.[55]

So far there have been no Negro police captains. All of the factors which make it difficult for a colored officer to become a lieutenant make it doubly hard for him to become a captain. Only the three lieutenants have been eligible to take the examinations for police captain. One of these encountered opposition from the colored political leaders, in addition to the coldness which he met in the police department itself. After taking the promotional examination for captain, he went to a prominent Negro politician and asked him "not to do anything crooked, but to use his influence to get the chief to give him a fair efficiency rating which would count for one-half of the examination." The politician refused and the lieutenant said: "It was simply that he didn't want me in the Black Belt as he couldn't make money out of me. . . . . He knew he couldn't handle me."[56] The lieutenant then had to face the expected opposition to Negro promotions without the support of the Negro political leaders.

There are no Negro captains because Negro officers are inferior in efficiency, mentality, personality, education, and general background. I say that as the truth, for I am far from prejudiced on the race question. In fact, I am very sympathetic toward the black race. To be a captain they have to compete with too many men who have superior mentality and education. Some of the Negroes are better than 40 per cent of the men eligible to be captains, but to be captain they have to be better than at least 90 per cent of their fellow officers.[57]

The above statement was made by a station captain who had held many positions in the police department. At another time this same captain, when he was not dealing with an abstract principle but with some concrete personalities, said: "We have had some very fine Negro officers, too. One lieutenant was as fine an officer as anyone could ask for, white or black. He was the first Negro lieutenant and should have had his captaincy."[58]

[55] Interview, February 15, 1932.   [56] Interview, November 6, 1931.

[57] Interview, June 8, 1932. It is a common saying that when a white man says he is not prejudiced, he is drawing a color line somewhere.

[58] Interview, October 8, 1931.

As a result of the attitude of the white commanding officers and a few of the Negro politicians, many of the colored policemen have given up hope of attaining the highest civil service ranks in the police department. So disheartened have some of them become that they no longer make attempts to secure promotions.

PRESTIGE OF NEGRO POLICEMEN

The prestige enjoyed by Negro police officers in their own community has varied from time to time and from group to group. The early policemen were part of a very small colony of Negroes which was not large enough to furnish the basis for any considerable business and professional class. Consequently, as compared with those in unskilled labor or domestic service, the colored policemen had distinctly superior social standing. A number of the early officers had important positions in the largest Negro churches, one was a superintendent of the Sunday School, and another was a deacon.[59] The names of these and of other officers appeared in the personal columns of the local press along with the names of the important professional, fraternal, and military leaders.[60] Some of the officers were very active in different fraternal organizations.[61]

As the Negro community grew larger and the number of lawyers, doctors, ministers, and business men increased, the status of the Negro policemen declined somewhat. The colored men in professional work did not look upon the position of a policeman as particularly desirable.

An examination of the former occupations of the Negro officers shows one of the reasons why the impression was common that these men had advanced their social position and that of the group. Records were available showing the occupation prior to entering the force of some 228 Negroes.[62] Of this number 35

[59] Interviews, October 15, 1931.

[60] *Broad Ax*, December 12, 1902; December 31, 1909.

[61] One officer said he belonged to the following organizations: Oriental Lodge, No. 68, A.F.&A.M.; Oriental Chapter, No. 21, R.A.M.; Hugh DePayne, Commandery No. 19, K.T.; Western Consistory, No. 28; A.A.S.R.F.M.; Arabic Temple No. 44, A.E.A.O.-N.M.S.; Masons, 33d degree, and Shriners.

[62] This refers to Negroes at some time on the police force.

per cent had been skilled or semi-skilled workers in manufacturing, transportation, or trade, 12 per cent had been unskilled laborers, 33 per cent had been in domestic service, 6 per cent had been in clerical occupations, 12 per cent had been in public service, and 1 per cent in professional service.[63] The most frequent occupations given were: porter, 30; unskilled laborer, 22; post-office employee, 19; chauffeur, 14; janitor, 13; clerks, 11; and butchers, 10. This situation was summarized by one of the police captains in a somewhat cynical fashion:

> You say you want to learn something of the Negro officers. I don't see why you have to question many officers to find out what that would be. You know that a Negro before he joins the force was either a porter or waiter on the railroad or a janitor or a laborer, and that he joined the force to get a better position. It shouldn't take a whole lot of work to see that. The same is true of white officers only that they are in more varied lines of work before they join the force than the Negro would be employed in.[64]

This police captain was a little hard on the Negro officers. Over half of them had been in skilled trades, clerical work, or public service. The individual cases analyzed showed that twenty-five or thirty years ago the colored policemen were more likely to be former porters or unskilled workers than now. However, positions on the police force are still highly prized by large numbers. As one officer expressed it: "Of course this is a good job. The average Negro without training for anything else is fortunate to have it. It is just about as good a job as the average Negro can get."[65]

Another rough indication of an individual's status in a community is the location of his home. In a city like Chicago the desirability of different sites for residential purposes varies enormously. Mr. Frazier has shown that this is just as true of the Negro community as of other communities in the city.[66] The least attractive dwelling-places were found in the so-called blighted sections nearest the business center of the city. Here

[63] The census classification is used except that a separate category is given for unskilled laborers in manufacturing, transportation, and trade.

[64] Interview, February 19, 1932.

[65] Interview. [66] *The Negro Family in Chicago*, pp. 97–116.

none of the Negro officers made their homes. The higher priced and more desirable housing accommodations were found at some distance out from the depreciated areas. It was in the better residential areas that the homes of the colored officers were concentrated.[67] Many of the officers owned their own homes and they had as their next-door neighbors people in professional, clerical, and business occupations.

NEGRO POLICEMEN AT WORK

The Negro police officer at best finds himself in a hot spot. Within the police department he discovered that he was a participant in a struggle between those who were trying to maintain discipline and those who were endeavoring to use the department for their own sinister and selfish purposes. Within the Negro community he found that he had to fight, exploit, or take no notice of the activities of the underworld. In the general contacts of the department with the colored public he had to decide whether to be arrogant and abusive like some of his white fellow-officers or polite and considerate in accordance with the demands of his people. Choose he must between these alternatives whether by action or inaction. To use a police expression, he was "in the middle" and whichever way he turned he was liable to offend someone. If he was a strict disciplinarian, he would run into trouble with some of his superior white officers, with some of the colored politicians, and with the leaders of the Negro underworld. If he was lax in noticing violations of the law, he would encounter difficulties with the strict white officers and with the colored churches and reformers. There might also come a time when loyalty to his race might conflict with loyalty to the police department.

The problems of the colored policemen can be illustrated by a number of cases. Imagine a young Negro who has just been sworn in and who takes his duties very seriously. To him an

---

[67] A tabulation made of the residences of 114 officers according to the seven zones which Frazier has defined gave the following results: Zone 1 (nearest to the business center), 0; Zone 2, 4; Zone 3, 11; Zone 4, 19; Zone 5, 32; Zone 6, 28; Zone 7, 20. Zone 7 is the farthest south, away from the center of the city.

order is an order and he wants to make a record by playing no favorites. He soon learns that impartiality makes matters very hard for himself.

I remember once that we got orders that all saloons had to be closed at 12 P.M. Two brothers on my beat had a saloon. One night I came past about a quarter to two and they were open. There were about fifteen customers in the place and the two brothers. So I arrested them and called the wagon. Next day in court the two brothers were fined fifteen dollars and costs and each customer was fined one dollar. But that night when I went back to work I found I was transferred. The next day I went back and looked up the records and found that all of the fines had been suspended. I learned my business right there. I learned a policeman cannot afford to do his duty.[68]

A few of the Negro policemen have taken over the worst patterns of behavior in the department. The articulate elements that had complained at the treatment received at the hands of the white officers were greatly disillusioned by the conduct of the colored officers who sometimes behaved in almost the same manner as the brutal and prejudiced white officers.[69] "Somehow the police department tends to spoil some people," was the comment of one observer in the community. "I knew a young fellow," he continued, "who had pretty good training, but after he got on the force he changed over night. He became arrogant and coarse and didn't have respect for anybody."[70] The following editorial shows how such officers were regarded by the community: "Complaints are being registered on Chicago's South Side against the brutality of the policemen. It is rumored that many of the policemen, both black and white, are "trigger loose" and "they will kill a suspect as quick as they look at him."[71]

[68] Interview, February 1, 1932.

[69] The *Broad Ax*, June 12, 1909, complains about two colored detectives who arrested a white woman who was talking to two colored men on a street corner late one evening, while waiting for a street car, She turned out to be the wife of a white policeman, and her conduct was beyond reproach. Her husband brought charges of false arrest against the two officers and they were discharged. The comment made by the *Broad Ax* was: "The experience . . . . should be a warning to all other police officers, white and black."

[70] Interview, November 20, 1931. Examples of officers of this sort may be found in the records of the Civil Service Commission. Some were crude in applying the techniques. Lack of space prevents the giving of examples here.

[71] *Chicago Whip*, August 8, 1925.

The resentment of the community against colored officers of the exploitive type was very deep. When it was announced in one of the local theaters that a certain officer had been discharged the entire audience burst into applause. The following letter was written to the commissioner of police regarding this officer and his associates. Two of the officers mentioned by name in the letter were later convicted of felonies and sent to a penitentiary.

There are four or five colored plain clothes men that are the dirtiest and biggest crooks, regardless of comparison, anywhere. . . . . These crooks are, instead of protecting citizens, using their guns and badges to rob people. These men should be put to work instead of joy riding all day, going around collecting graft money from buffet flats, pool rooms, bootleggers, policy wheel owners, as if they were on a pay roll. Riding from box to box outside their district.[72]

The number of officers of the predatory type was small but the activities of these officers were so conspicuous and the reactions of the community against them were so decided that they were given an importance out of proportion to their numbers.

In spite of the political corruption within the police department, most of the Negro officers have managed to carry out their police duties faithfully. One officer made a practice of reporting all violations of the law that came to his attention to his superiors and leaving the responsibility for action with them. Another officer, who had an excellent reputation for honesty and efficiency, said: "I like my work and tried to make a success of it. I covered more ground than any officer, white or black, at that time. I just worked on big stuff, holdups, burglaries, and murders. I wouldn't bother with little stuff. The officers trusted me because I was honest." He continued to the effect that he got "a kick out of trying to outwit people who were breaking the law" and that he went about his work scientifically, learning every phase of it, including the classification of finger prints.[73]

The colored sergeants and lieutenants had special problems of discipline, particularly when they were put in charge of white

[72] Records of Chicago Crime Commission.   [73] Interview.

and colored policemen. The difficulties were not insurmountable as is shown by the case of the following lieutenant:

After being made a lieutenant I was assigned to a station in command of one of the shifts. The morale of the station at that time was very low. I had always been a strict disciplinarian and determined to try and bring up this morale. The captain had requested that I try to do this. But I was also in a very ticklish position. I was the first colored officer who had been in command of a station. I didn't want the men to think that I was trying to be too big, but also I knew I would have to stand up like a man if I was to have the respect of the officers. So I decided that I would enforce the rules as they were regardless of the consequences.

I was transferred to the station on Christmas night and that very night I had to send a man up to the trial board. I had assigned him to watch a building, and because it was Christmas night, he went away and left his post. I hated to do it, especially as it was my first night at the station, but there was nothing else to do. The man was fired by the trial board.

That established my reputation in the station, but it also caused some resentment. It is hard on the police force to be strict and added to that was the fact that I was a Negro in charge of a shift. I had trouble for awhile; anyone who breaks the ice does. But soon the men got over their feeling of dislike and distrust. They found out that I was just as fair and favorable to them if they were in the right and would stick by them. However, during my command there, I never had a man refuse to obey a command. I have never had any trouble with citizens (white or with white officers).[74]

A number of creditable mentions have been awarded to colored officers for efficiency, alertness, and close attention to duty.[75] Many have shown great bravery in apprehending dangerous criminals. The occasions on which Negro officers have let race loyalty interfere with the performance of their duties have been rare.[76] While some of them have been of the exploitive type, the general stereotype in the white community to the effect that Negroes cannot make good officers is belied by the records of the Chicago Police Department.

LIFE-HISTORIES: TYPES OF ADJUSTMENT

The rôle of the Negro in the Chicago Police Department can be further elucidated by more detailed and typical personal his-

[74] Interview, February 15, 1932.

[75] Records of the Secretary of the Police Department.

[76] One police captain said: "Negroes will not arrest another Negro who is wanted for a capital crime in the South. They think he will not be treated right. But they will arrest one willingly for the same crime in the North."

tories. The life-histories that follow show how two individuals met the problems of recruitment, conditions of work, discipline, ordinary day-to-day police work, and promotion. One represents desirable sort of police material and the other does not.

The first document was furnished by the wife of a deceased officer. This document has been checked against the service record of the officer as given by the Secretary of the Police Department, against a news item appearing in the Negro press,[77] against the testimony of other officers who knew him, and against the records of the Civil Service Commission. All of these sources are in substantial agreement. It is clear from the story as here told that the officer failed to make a satisfactory adjustment to the complicated social situation in which he found himself. The work habits which he brought with him from the South, the notions of grandeur that he entertained about being a policeman, his loyalty to the Negro race, his disillusionment at being punished for doing his duty as a policeman, and his ideas about the money-making possibilities of his job influenced his behavior in conflicting ways on different occasions. Inconsistency and irrationality characterized many of his actions. He was alternately moved by race pride and by race humility. The document is not presented because it gives a picture of a typical Negro officer in Chicago but rather because it throws into relief some of the problems which are associated with the struggle of members of a racial minority to meet the demands which this peculiar situation imposes. Although the man described was on the force for twenty-two years, he was never fully adjusted to his job and he left the service under charges. The statements made by his estranged wife may be exaggerated but they are presented for what they are worth.

My husband was born in Mississippi in 1878. When he was just a young boy his father left his mother. And there she was, poor woman, with two kids on her hands—my husband and his sister. His mother died when he was ten. That just left him and his sister.

So then it was up to him to try and help his sister. So he got hold of a boot-black box and went out shining shoes. Later he got a job washing dishes twice a day for a white family. He was so small that he had to stand on a box

[77] *Chicago Defender*, July 11, 1931.

to reach up to the sink. And he could shine shoes after he was through with the dishes.

Of course he didn't have no learning. Never been to school a day in his life. But when he was about twelve years old the girls started to write love letters to him. He couldn't read none of them so he got the white boys to help him. Then he got them to answer them for him. But one day he said to himself, "My goodness, this will never do. Me twelve years old and can't read or write. I got to learn myself something." So then he got himself some books, a speller and an arithmetic. Of course, he couldn't go to school as he had to work. But he kept studying until he was seventeen years old and then he was in the third reader.

When my husband was seventeen years old he come to Chicago. He had been hearing for years what a wonderful place Chicago was and he had been wanting to go there for some time. When he was down south he had heard lots about Chicago and he believed everything he heard except that you could get white girls without being killed. He just couldn't believe that so when he come up he tried it and he wasn't killed. Then he believed that, too. But he didn't really want no white girl, he just wanted to find out about it. After that he never did go around any of them.

He went to work at one of the large restaurants as a waiter. Then he went to the stockyards for two years.

But in 1903 he wanted to better his condition so he started to look around for a civil service job. (How he prepared himself for the examinations is described above, page 250.)

Then he got a call to go to the police force (1906). No, he didn't have to pay any money or see any of the big fellows. Just took the examination and was called. He was always lucky. He did have to have some reliable people sign an application for him. The first one to sign was a real estate dealer.

He was first assigned to a station on Cottage Grove. I think most of the colored officers were at that station then. He stayed at that station for about ten years. In those years he had lots of trouble with his superior officers.

Well, my old man was working with a fellow named ———. They both got into a lot of trouble. One day the captain told them to come to work in civilian clothes. My old man was tickled to death at this; he was so proud he could hardly wait to go to work that night. They sent him and his partner out together. But the captain didn't tell them which place to go into.

Now there was a big parlor garden for white "sports." That night they walked by a couple of times and finally decided to go in there. The boss of the place met them and said to them, "I want you two men to get out of here and never to put your foot in here again. You are not to come into my place."

Next morning the captain called them both up and told them to come to work that night in uniform. Then he found out that he had also been transferred. The captain called him in and said, "You've got to learn to mind your own business."

Oh, yes, he was certainly in lots of trouble. He wanted to have his own way and have a good time so I just moved out and let him. We weren't living together for a long time.

The main trouble with him was that he got the swell head. After he got on the force it was terrible. He never called himself anything but Officer ————. And then he would say, "Here I am a poor ignorant country boy from Mississippi but I passed examinations high-school graduates couldn't pass. I'm a police officer in one of the largest cities in the world."

What kind of trouble did he get into? Mostly he was in trouble for being drunk, beating somebody up, or being asleep while on duty. He was awful mean when he was drunk.[78]

One time he was drunk and went into a Chinese restaurant. When he sat on a chair and it broke, he got awfully mad and said, "What's the idea of having such a chair for a gentleman and officer to sit in?" Then he jumped up and broke every chair in the restaurant. His sergeant come in to stop him but he didn't pay him no mind. So then the captain came. My husband said, "Stand back, I am a race man. The first white man that touches me dies." And they were afraid to bother him. So they got a colored fellow to go and get him home. I think he got fined sixty days pay for that. It beats all how he got away with that stuff. Bishop Carey, when he saw his record, the last trouble he was in, said, "I don't see how you have gotten away with this."

Then he used to get caught lots of times sleeping on duty. He used to get keys for people's basements and then go down there and sleep when he was on duty at night. He got me to make him a little cushion which fit into the seat of his pants and he would take that out and use it for a pillow. He said he had to have something soft to sleep on. I used to tell him that he looked foolish sticking out like that in behind but he said he would rather have comfort than style. Then he carried a little alarm clock with him, too. When he went into a basement to sleep, he would set the clock so he could wake up in time to make his ring. But sometimes he was so drunk that the clock didn't wake him up. Then the sergeant would come and find him and he was in trouble again.

But he always got out. People used to say that he must play politics to be able to stay on like that. But that wasn't it. He spent lots of money down there, made lots and spent lots, and everybody liked him.

When he used to be called up before the Civil Service Board, he would "Uncle Tom" something awful. He used to tell me about it when he got home and laugh. He was a good talker, too. You would think he was a college graduate to hear him. He would say, "Gentlemens, my skin is black but I can't help it. I am a Negro but I can't help it. Gentlemens, my heart is white,

---

[78] A fellow-officer said: "He wasn't a bad type of fellow. He started out all right. One thing, he wasn't like the average fellow of his type; he didn't abuse the public. But he was always walking into things and getting into trouble without intending to do any harm to anybody."

just as white, gentlemens, as anybody's in this room. Gentlemens, I am a Negro and I have made a mistake but don't take a job away from this poor old colored man. I needs it."

You know it was scandalous but he would get away with that time after time. One day one of the commissioners told him, "Well, never mind about starting that black skinned stuff today. That's got nothing to do with why you were asleep last night." But he went right on and got away with a fine.

You want to know about this last trouble he got into? Well, one day he was traveling his post and he noticed a colored fellow going into an old house. So he went in to see what was going on. And there he found a white fireman having bad relations with this colored fellow. So when the fireman saw him, he said, "Oh, my God! don't arrest me for this." And he turned around and gave my husband his full month's pay as it was pay day. So my husband took the money and turned him loose. The fireman ran right over and told the captain that he had been robbed with a gun. The captain didn't like him no how so he called him in and said for him to hand over the money. So my husband did. His lawyer thought that this was the best thing he could have done but the colored state's attorney thought that it was an awful mistake. Then he took a five thousand dollar mortgage on this place. You know he spent most of that beating that case and staying out of the penitentiary. But he finally got it fixed up. The case was called and dismissed because it was nol prossed.

Well, then he had to stand trial before the Civil Service Commission. His lawyer advised him to send in his resignation before he came to trial. He thought that would help. That cost him money too, but I don't know how much. But my old man got out of the trouble all right and then he went on the pension list.[79]

Well my old man was certainly a bad actor. But he had his good points. He made plenty of money and spent plenty, but he sent our two kids through high school and would have sent them further if they had wanted to go. He was certainly queer. He wrote down in a book all the things he did. He was a good lodge man, too. When he got out of the police force he was lost. After a man has worked at one thing for twenty-two years it's just like killing him to make him quit. And after he was off, he used to dress up in his uniform and go and sit around the station, just like it tells you in the paper. I don't guess no one but me will ever know how much it meant to him to be a policemen.[80]

The next document was furnished by a retired policeman who made a fine record in the police department. His superiors, his fellow-officers, and the Negro press had nothing but praise for his efficiency as a policeman. The Negro policy gambling kings did not like him and it is probable that some of the colored poli-

---

[79] By resigning before he was discharged he avoided court proceedings in case the opportunity opened for him to come back on the force.

[80] Interview, January 30, 1932.

ticians who came into prominence after 1915 would not have liked him had he been a member of the department then. He retired just before the emergence of the Negro political organization. In contrast with the officer described above, he was a strict disciplinarian and was never brought before the trial board. His deep religious convictions gave him a courage which was fanatical at times. His sense of duty was so ingrained that he enforced the law fearlessly and impartially.

I was born in a little town in Ohio about fifty miles from Cincinnati. My father was a minister and I was brought up in a strictly Christian home and atmosphere. The Bible was always read in my home at night and in the morning and prayers were said by the entire family group at least twice a day. This is a custom which I have kept up all of my life. We were also required to attend church, at least twice a day on Sundays.

When I was about four or five my parents went to Canada and we lived there until I was a young man. Then we returned and went to live in Pittsburgh. I then attended Avery College and completed my education.

Later my family moved to the State of Illinois and I worked for a number of years on a farm. But I soon got tired of living on the farm with no apparent future. So I came to Chicago when a relatively young man to try and get an opportunity to advance myself in the world. (His appointment is described above, page 248.)

While at the Harrison station I did a piece of work for which I was never given credit. There was a man around the neighborhood who cut up his common-law wife and almost killed her. When she got out of the hospital I met her and she told me where I could find the man. I finally found him and arrested him. He was tried, convicted, and sentenced to Joliet Penitentiary.

After a number of years the man was released and came back to Chicago. One day he killed three persons and ran into a building. The "Murder Squad" from headquarters arrived with high-powered repeating rifles and began shooting at the building. Then I began to think. This man had killed three people. He was a desperate and vicious killer but still he was a human being and should have a chance to make his peace with God. I knew the "Murder Squad" were going to kill him even if he surrendered.

Then the voice of God spoke to me and told me to go up and bring him down. I didn't hesitate because I knew God would protect me. I grabbed an axe and ran up the back stairs. The Inspector saw me going and ordered the men to stop shooting. I broke open the back door. It was dark inside—I fired four shots from my service revolver into the black room. I located my man near the door and dragged him out.

He was tried and sentenced to be hung. Just before he died I got a letter from him which I will keep always. In it he thanked me for making it possible to make amends with God before he died. I have always been thankful that

I was instrumental in giving that sinner a chance to repent before meeting God.

Shortly after this affair I was transferred to the Detective Bureau. While in that office I decided to take the examination for promotion. I remember while I was going over to the classrooms where the examination was held some of the white officers asked me where I was going. I told them that I was going right along with them to take the examination. They seemed very surprised and seemed to think either that I had no business taking the examination or that I wouldn't be able to pass. I took the three examinations which came up at that time. That is the examinations for: detective sergeant, desk sergeant, and patrol sergeant. I passed all three and was among the highest in my rating for patrol sergeant. (His promotion is described on page 264.)

At last I was promoted and sworn in as a full-fledged detective sergeant with a civil service rating. I remained in that department for a number of years. I was given eight or nine men to work under me. Some were white and some were colored. All of my men were loyal to me and I have never had any trouble with them.

At one time I broke up policy here in the city. The chief gave me a squad of men and told me to run the policy out of busines. I succeeded in stopping the policy game completely. But I won't say any more about that. You will think I am boasting and the Bible speaks against a braggard. Too, I don't want to criticize the department in any way now that I am retired.

I served as detective sergeant until 1913 when I retired from the force on a pension. In 1924 I started to work as floor man in a local bank.

In the twenty-six years that I served as a policeman I have never once been reprimanded for any infraction of the rules. I can still remember and quote the old rule book that I learned over twenty years ago. Once when I was testifying in court the judge said when the case was finished that he wished he had my personality. This was quite a compliment for a judge on the bench to give to an officer. I have never had my testimony turned down or questioned in court. My word has always been taken without question.

I have never let a white officer exceed me in anything, whether it was catching criminals, learning my duties and rules to be followed by officers, or earning promotions in rank. Criminals have always feared and respected me. I would arrest anyone who broke the law irregardless of consequences or possible unfriendly relations. An officer is a servant of the people and must at all times enforce the law.

I have met very little prejudice. I worked for years in the Loop district with a number of men, both white and colored under me.

One time down in that district a man was found dead in front of a saloon. He had been stabbed to death and thrown out into the gutter. I went down there and through a tip from the colored porter was able to arrest the murderer within twenty minutes after the killing. Later I went back and found the knife. That evening at roll call I was praised before the entire company.

I have always, even when working, tried to impress on people the fact that there is something in this life besides worldly pleasures. In that murder case, I was talking about a few minutes ago, I talked to that murderer who I took out of the building all the way down to the station and tried to get him to give up his soul to Christ. Thank God, I was successful. I have pointed out the light to every class of people I have come in contact with, even when I was working in the underworld district.

I remember there was once an old levee character who started to think about the hereafter. He saw me and told me he was going to California. I looked at him and saw that he had consumption and told him that he was not going to California but was going to Hell. Soon after that he became sick, and every night after roll call I went and prayed with him and read him the Bible. Finally, just before he died, he was converted and saw the light.

The day of his funeral the underworld had a big turnout for him and had him buried from one of the largest churches of the city. I went to the funeral and they asked me to say something. So I made a talk and tried to get them to accept Christ as their companion just as their friend had before he died. I am proud to say that one man did change his ways and I was thus instrumental in saving another soul for Christ.

As an officer I have never hurt anybody and have never been hurt myself. This is because I have always tried to live the life and have placed my life in Christ's hands. I didn't become really converted until 1911. I was in the detective bureau then and for the three days that God was working with me I didn't eat a bite. The fellows down there asked me what was the matter— was I crazy? But I told them that when God was working with you, one didn't need food. They tried to joke with me about it but when they found out how serious I was they stopped that altogether. I was converted in Quinn Chapel and when the power hit me I couldn't walk or stand up. Sister Bailey was on one side of me and Sister Ford on the other. If they had not held me up I would have fallen to the floor. I have had very little social life except through my church work.

I am proud of my record as a policeman. But more than that I am happy that I am a Christian and a saved man.

These men are extreme cases. But both illustrate the personal and subjective aspect of the problem which the Negro has to face in his struggles to live in a white man's world. They also show how the problems of police administration are complicated by minority elements. Some of the colored men who found their way into the department were poor police material. Instead of protecting the Negro community, they preyed upon it. On the other hand, other colored policemen were strong enough to resist the temptations which confronted them and became excellent guardians of the public safety.

CHAPTER XIII

NEGRO TEACHERS[1]

The schools are generally regarded by Negroes as a highly important part of local government. Many colored persons migrated to Chicago in order to obtain better school facilities for their children than were available in the South. Education is looked upon by many Negroes as the key to freedom. It can unlock the door to knowledge which frees men's minds from a narrowness imposed by harsh circumstances. Because of the high value which the group places upon education, it was hoped that participation in the educational process would yield large returns. Colored teachers, by reason of their interest in their work, could help raise the educational level of their group and they could help break down some of the racial prejudices which are formed in childhood.

It was not long after the adult Negro population in Chicago began to increase rapidly that the Negro school population went forward by leaps and bounds. In 1920, according to the Chicago Commission on Race Relations, there were ten elementary schools at least 70 per cent Negro and twelve more between 13 and 70 per cent.[2] According to a survey made for the present study at least twenty-six schools were 85 per cent or more Negro in 1931, including one senior high school and two junior high schools, and at least thirteen more elementary schools and three senior high schools were as much as 12 per cent colored. The census volumes show that the number of Negro children from 7 to 20 years of age, who were attending school in the city, increased from 11,140 in 1920 to 43,385 in 1930.[3]

With so many Negro children attending the public schools, it

[1] Mary J. Herrick, *Negro Employees of the Chicago Board of Education* (Chicago, University of Chicago A.M. Thesis, 1931).

[2] *Negro in Chicago*, p. 242.

[3] *Abstract of the Census, 1930*, p. 268; *Fourteenth Census, 1920*, Vol. II, p. 1083.

was natural that the colored community would be vitally interested in the policies of the school system. In Chicago there are
no separate schools for Negroes.[4] The Board of Education,
which has complete charge of all public schools, is composed of
eleven unpaid members, appointed by the mayor for overlapping terms of five years each, and not removable before the end
of their terms except by resignation or death. It has general
fiscal and administrative powers over the school system and it
employs a superintendent of schools who has very important
powers over the courses of study and the appointment, promotion, and transfer of teachers; a business manager who has
charge of maintenance and building; and an attorney. A demand for a Negro member of the Board of Education was made
articulate by the Negro press some time ago.[5] While Negroes
have secured representation on the New York Board of Education, they have had no success in this regard in Chicago, even
under Mayor Thompson.

Teaching positions in the Chicago school system were sought
after by many members of the Negro community. If Negroes
and whites are to live together satisfactorily in America, the
school system must be used to reduce race friction. Some colored persons thought that the presence of Negro teachers in
mixed schools would help promote race harmony. Negro women
took advantage of the fact that teaching was one of the few pro-
fessions which was open to them on a basis of equality in a city
like Chicago. The fact that some white women teachers were
sensitive on race matters complicated the situation but did not
present insurmountable obstacles. Colored women teachers felt
that they could understand some of the peculiar problems of
race relations and of the colored children who had migrated to
the city from regions where they had been denied equal educational opportunities with whites. Those Negroes who pene-

[4] This is not the situation in all parts of the state of Illinois. See M. C. Mason, *Policy
of Segregation of the Negro in the Public Schools of Ohio, Indiana, and Illinois* (Chicago,
University of Chicago Master's dissertation, 1917).

[5] *Broad Ax*, July 10, 1909; August 3, 1912; *Chicago Whip*, June 27, 1925; *Chicago
Defender*, February 11, 1933.

trated the school system were looked upon by the community as persons who were advancing the race.

APPOINTMENT OF NEGRO TEACHERS

There are no records in the office of the Board of Education like those in the Police Department which show the color of all employees over a period of time. Consequently, it is impossible to trace in detail the history of the entrance of Negro teachers into the Chicago school system. However, the process by which Negroes became teachers in recent years can be briefly described.

In order to become a regularly appointed public-school teacher in Chicago it is necessary to graduate from the Chicago Normal College or to pass a rigid examination which is open to teachers with accredited normal training who have had experience in other systems. In either case persons cannot enter the school system without demonstrating some capacity for teaching. The requirements for entrance into the Normal College, the requirements for graduation from this college, and the examinations which the Board of Education conducts eliminate persons who are clearly unfit to teach.

The proportion of Negroes enrolled in the Chicago Normal College is a rough index of the interest of colored people in becoming school teachers, since the Normal College furnishes the usual route followed to enter the system. Table XIII, which gives the enrolment figures for this college by color, shows that in 1934 the ratio of Negroes in Chicago Normal College was a little over half the population ratio, and that in recent years the absolute and the relative number of colored Normal College students has been declining.[6] This reflects general conditions in the Chicago school system. There have been relatively few positions to be filled due to the policy of increasing the number of pupils under each teacher, the low turnover in the teaching staff resulting from the economic depression, the discharge of 1,400 teachers as an economy move, and the uncertainty of the teach-

[6] In 1930 there were 1,090 Normal College students, of whom 72, or 6.7 per cent, were Negroes. From January, 1925, to January, 1934, there were 286 colored Normal College graduates. Figures were furnished by the Chicago Normal College.

ers' pay days during the tax crisis in the city. The growing competition for teaching positions with all their drawbacks may account for the greater relative decline in the number of Negro normal students. Not only are there fewer openings in the school system but the number of college graduates seeking teaching positions has increased. Four years ago, before the economic depression brought on the school crisis, the number of colored normal school students was increasing.

Normal College graduates may apply to be put on the substitute list. There are no stipulated requirements for temporary

TABLE XIII

STUDENTS AT CHICAGO NORMAL COLLEGE BY COLOR, 1934

Class Semester	Graduating	Total Number	Number of Colored	Per Cent Colored
Sixth.....	February, 1934	147	6	4.1
Fifth......	June, 1934	146	10	6.9
Fourth....	February, 1935	150	3	2.0
Third.....	June, 1935	56	1	1.8
Second....	February, 1936	74	3	4.1
First......	June, 1936	52	1	1.9
Total.	....	625	24	3.8

certification to this list and the oversupply of graduates from the college has been so great in recent years that more than a three-year wait is required before an assignment is in sight. Persons with college training, with or without teaching experience, may also obtain temporary certificates. The proportion of colored substitutes who are normal graduates as compared with the white substitutes is difficult to obtain because the authorities keep no such records. However, the head of the substitute bureau said that she had 150 colored substitutes on her list who were marked as such and who were sent only to schools which contained mostly Negro pupils. Since she estimated that the number on the substitute list was about 2,500 this would mean that the Negro group made up 6 per cent of the total.[7]

In spite of the practices of some of the assignment clerks, Ne-

[7] Herrick, *op. cit.*, p. 34. The number of elementary substitutes in April, 1934, was 2,631.

gro Normal College graduates have been appointed as substitutes to schools which were not predominantly colored. The following is the case of a teacher who had an A.B. degree from Atlanta University, Georgia, and who was also a graduate of the Chicago Normal College.

My first year's teaching was spent at a school on the West Side. When I first went there, most of the children were white but the neighborhood changed very rapidly. I had no trouble at all with either the white children or their parents. Nobody has every pulled any political wires for me. At the time I received my appointment I don't think there was any set policy about appointing. South Side girls went everywhere. I had no difficulty at all about color, that is, no trouble worth mentioning. Our chief trouble at that time lay in the fact that we Normal girls were supplanting the old political appointees, who naturally resent it. The principal did also for a time. I'm not saying that color didn't play any part at all then because some principals just wouldn't take colored girls.[8]

While length of time on the list seems to be the chief consideration in the appointment of substitutes, personal, social, and political influences may also be operative. Well-trained and qualified teachers waiting for assignment have at times been passed over, while a few less adequately trained persons on the substitute list have been given steady work.[9] Since prospective Negro teachers had many obstacles to overcome, it was natural for them to use all techniques available. Under the various Thompson administrations it appears that political pressures were exercised by a few colored applicants for school positions. The following is the case of a light-skinned, colored teacher who was appointed in the second Thompson administration. She graduated from a Chicago high school, the Chicago Normal College, and the University of Chicago. One of her relatives was prominent in the Thompson faction of the Republican party. She described how political influence might be used to reduce the operation of race prejudice.

[8] Interview, June 16, 1933.

[9] Herrick, *op. cit.*, p. 33. In Chicago the school system has been made a football of politics for many years. In two of his campaigns for mayor William Hale Thompson made the removal of the superintendent of schools a political issue. See George S. Counts, *School and Society in Chicago* (New York, 1928), chap. xii.

I, myself, haven't had many difficulties, though I am aware that Negro teachers do have them. It seems that the difficulty is increasing rather than diminishing. I recall the case of ――― ――― when she received her appointment. She had extreme difficulty when the various principals found out that she was colored. In none of my work have I run into any actual difficulties. I subbed at the ――― school (a near West Side school which had no colored pupils). The principal knew I was colored. I didn't have any trouble at all because the district superintendent had been "made" by ――― (her relative who was in politics.)[10]

During Thompson's third administration the appointment of substitutes was to some extent influenced by political considerations. This is illustrated by the case of a teacher who graduated from Howard University, and who had teaching experience in the schools of Richmond, Atlantic City, and New York City. It is evident that she was well qualified as a teacher but she thought it was necessary to seek the help of the Negro politicians in order to secure work. Whether the political influence used was of any importance in securing the work could not be determined.

When I was first on the substitute list, substitutes were assigned to districts. I was in the district whose headquarters were in Wendell Phillips High School. This plan gave more work to Negro teachers than the subsequent plan did. After this plan was abolished, there was much trouble in getting assigned. The assignment clerks just refused to send a Negro girl to an all-white neighborhood, or to any white principal, of whom there were many, who did not want a Negro teacher. I complained once to the clerk in charge of assignments. She called the assignment office at Wendell Phillips. The clerk asked over the telephone whether I was white or Negro. So you see, color is a factor in getting an assignment. Not only do they limit places where a colored girl can work, but they send white girls into these positions. This lowers the number of jobs even more.

I didn't know until about two months before I was appointed that one's alderman could help substitutes get work. An ordinance was passed which put married women off the substitutes' list. I went to see my alderman and told him that my husband's business was slow and that I needed work. He told me to write him a letter to that effect. I did and he sent it to the superintendent. I have a letter from the superintendent to the alderman saying that he would do what he could for me. I was put back on the substitutes' list. The alderman wouldn't take a cent for doing that for me. My husband had made some speeches for him in the campaign and he said that that was

[10] Interview, June 19, 1933.

enough pay for him. Mr. ——— is a fine man. He is a good alderman. He makes it a business.[11]

The demarcation between a substitute teacher and an assigned one is a very rigid one. Before being given a permanent assignment, all applicants, except normal graduates, must pass the examinations and have the necessary experience. In contrast to the civil service rules there is no absolute right of appointment for the first or first three persons at the top of the list. No proved instances of unfair examination grades have come to our attention and very few accusations of this sort have been made, but there have been many complaints about assignments. A qualified Negro applicant may remain on the list for years before being offered an assignment. The power to make such appointments rests with the principals of the various schools and the teachers so assigned must serve a three-year probationary period before they become part of the permanent staff of the school system under the provisions of the Otis law of 1917.[12] The chances of colored applicants obtaining regular appointments depend in varying degrees upon such factors as their qualifications for the positions concerned, the amount of political pressure that can be brought to bear upon the school authorities, the number of colored children in the schools concerned, the attitude of the principals involved, and the attitude of the public in the school districts under consideration.

It is probable that in the vast majority of cases political connections have had nothing to do with the appointment of Negro teachers in the Chicago public schools.[13] However, in a few instances there is evidence that political factors were at work. One colored teacher who used political influences to secure an appointment as a substitute stated first that she thought that

[11] Interview, August 27, 1931.   [12] Described in Counts, *op. cit.*, p. 42.

[13] One prominent Negro teacher said: "The politicians make me tired. One Negro politician, I recall, made a speech right after I had received my appointment and said that I had his 'approval,' whatever that meant. Another politician used to come up to me and say pompously, 'Your superintendent and I have been talking about you and he thinks highly of you.' This was always said around a crowd for the effect it would have on the politician's importance. I sincerely believe that all these gentlemen are only trying to take credit for something which would have happened anyway."

politics played no part in the school system but on reflection she admitted that "if politics enters at all, it only serves to step up appointments that would be made anyway."[14] This stepping-up process or the actual making of an assignment is crucial on many occasions. Regarding politics and the school system, one prominent colored attorney said:

Politics is a hard thing to prove in connection with the securing of school positions. You can yell either politics or you can say very charitably that the suspected appointment was the result of a lucky coincidence. I do know that a member of the state legislature had a niece come to Chicago in the summer and she was teaching the next fall in a high school.[15]

Of far greater importance than politics in the placement of Negro teachers has been the constant pressure of the Negro school population. If a given school is entirely or almost entirely made up of colored pupils because of the concentration of the colored population in certain areas, then it is practically inevitable that Negro teachers will be assigned to this school, given the general type of school system found in Chicago. Many white teachers seek transfers from schools in which the number of colored pupils is increasing rapidly. One of the recent presidents of the Board of Education said that the Board intended to appoint teachers to schools near their homes. If the Board looks for teachers in the areas of Negro concentration, they will find many Negro applicants. The situation works both ways. One prominent colored teacher said: "There are some teachers and principals who would prefer working in some district other than a Negro one. The school buildings in the Negro districts are, in general, old. The neighborhoods are poor."[16] All of these factors made the turn-over in the schools in Negro neighborhoods high and thus it made it easier to place Negro teachers in these schools.

The shift from white to colored teachers in schools which contained mostly Negro pupils was a slow process and rarely has there been a complete change. In only three branches of elementary schools were all the teachers found to be colored and

---

[14] Interview, June 19, 1933.

[15] Interview, June 20, 1933.   [16] Interview, August 25, 1931.

the principals for the main schools concerned were white. Table XIV shows that the neighborhoods which have been solidly colored for the longest period of time are most likely to have the largest proportion of Negro teachers.

TABLE XIV

NEGRO TEACHERS IN SELECTED CHICAGO SCHOOLS, 1934

School	ESTIMATED PERCENTAGE OF NEGRO CHILDREN		TEACHERS		
			1934		
	1920*	1934	Total Number Teachers	Negro Teachers	Per Cent Negro
Burke...............	....	95	40	0	00
Carter................		100	37	2	5
Drake...............	24.0	100	22	5	23
Felsenthal............	20.0	100	34	1	3
McCosh..............	15.0	95	43	3	7
Smyth...............	....	90	26	3	12
Willard..............	13.0	100	69	34	49
Forrestville...........	38.0	100	58	32	55
Oakland..............	26.0	98	17	2	12
Tennyson.............	28.0	95	16	6	38
Emerson..............	75.0	98	13	8	62
Mosely...............	70.0	100	16	6	38
Colman..............	92.0	100	33	28	85
Doolittle.............	85.0	100	44	20	45
Douglas..............	93.0	100	43	28	65
Farren...............	92.0	100	38	6	16
Fuller................	90.0	100	14	1	7
Hayes................	80.0	100	16	12	75
Keith................	90.0	100	14	10	71
Raymond.............	93.0	100	23	13	57

* *Negro in Chicago*, p. 242.

This table shows that in general it took many years before a school with an overwhelming Negro population secured a predominantly colored staff. There were a number of particular schools which had been almost solidly colored for more than ten years and yet the Negro teachers were still in a minority.[17] Altogether there were about 27,700 Negro children in the schools

[17] Doolittle, Farren, and Mosely schools.

located in the neighborhoods which were 95 per cent or more colored. The white teachers in these schools numbered 531 and the Negro 272 or 33.9 per cent of the total. These colored teachers comprised 88 per cent of all the colored teachers in the Chicago school system.[18] The South Side community is the oldest in the city and its ratio of Negro teachers in the type of schools under discussion was 37 per cent. In the newer West Side and near North Side communities the ratio was much lower.

The analysis of the schools in the areas of Negro concentration shows that influences other than those arising from population pressure have been at work. The racial attitudes of a white principal may retard considerably the recruitment of Negro teachers even in a neighborhood which has been colored for a long time. In the case of one South Side elementary school which was slow in accepting Negro teachers it was clear that the principal definitely disliked Negroes and would not take them if she could avoid it. She said that she had enough colored teachers. She was accused of finding some fault in the colored teachers sent to her from downtown and keeping them only a day.[19] The principal of another elementary school, which was similar in composition to the one just mentioned, openly declared that she would not take any more colored teachers.[20] The following case shows how a Negro teacher viewed the situation she met in seeking a regular assignment:

When it was my turn to be appointed, I was sent to a South Side school where there was a prejudiced principal. This principal was also full of nothing but theory. He used to teach over at the Normal College. About two o'clock of my first day's work, the assistant principal came to me and said that I had better waive my appointment, as my work was unsatisfactory. I said that they hadn't had time to see my work. I was entitled to five days' trial. She insisted and I went down to the Board of Education and asked them what to do. They said that since I hadn't been given five days' trial I should stay there and that they would look after me.

Two weeks later I got an appointment to Mrs. ———'s school as if I hadn't

[18] Figures in Herrick, *op. cit.*

[19] Herrick, *op. cit.*, pp. 24–25. Since 1930 a new principal was appointed and many colored teachers were added.

[20] Interview with teacher, June, 1933.

already been appointed. The reason they didn't want me at the other school was that I was on the first floor of the new building, and the white teachers wanted to keep Negroes off that floor, as they didn't want to use the same bathroom with them. Of course, the officials of the Board of Education wouldn't admit any of this. They say that they have no "colored schools" and that they appoint in order from the list of elementary-school teachers. On my own list that was not true.[21]

Another factor which conditions the number of Negro teachers found in a given school is the attitude of the general public in the immediate neighborhood. It was claimed by some of the principals who were slow in taking Negro teachers that Negro parents preferred white teachers. Such claims may have been rationalizations on the part of the principals, but it appears that there were a few colored parents who transferred their children from schools with a predominant Negro membership to schools with a Negro minority.[22]

In those schools where the Negro children are less than half but more than 15 per cent, the racial attitudes of the white public are important in controlling the number of Negro teachers. At the time that the present survey was made there were no colored teachers at all found in such schools. It happened that the schools which were in this class were located near places where there had been race friction in the past. Schools in the area where there was greatest violence during the race riot of 1919 had no Negro teachers, although the school population was 40 per cent colored. The principals of the schools in this territory said that it would be folly for them to add unnecessarily to the race friction by putting colored teachers over white children. When a colored substitute was sent to a school of this sort some years ago the children went on strike and their parents supported them.[23] In the areas farther south, where bombings were once common and where the white residents were still resisting the invasion of colored citizens, the same situation was found in the schools. As one observer has put it, "The whites who remain in a mixed or changing area are not likely to be the most sweetly reasonable of citizens."[24]

[21] Interview, August 27, 1931.   [22] The Negro in Chicago, pp. 251–52.
[23] Interview with white teacher who was at the school at the time.
[24] Herrick, op. cit., p. 19.

In some of the West Side schools, where the Negro children were less than 15 per cent, the white public was not antagonistic toward Negro teachers. Half a dozen schools in the old Italian district along Polk Street had few or no colored pupils and at least one colored teacher each. In the Italian and Polish neighborhoods near the Chicago Commons there were four schools with no colored children, and at least three Negro teachers. Altogether, some thirty-one Negro teachers were counted in some twenty schools which were nearly, or entirely, white.

In almost every case where the Negro teachers were given an opportunity to show their ability to handle immigrant white children, the principal volunteered favorable comment on their work. One assistant principal said that when students returned to visit, it was the first-grade colored teacher whom they all had to see and that she was one of the best-liked teachers in the school. At another school the principal said at first that he had no colored teacher, but on reflection he said that of course he had. She was a very good teacher and he had never thought of her particularly as colored, although she was quite dark. From this it is clear that an able Negro teacher could make her way in a school which was located in a neighborhood where the racial tensions were not strong.

How a colored teacher can become adjusted to working in a neighborhood which is largely white is shown by the following example of a teacher who was born in Virginia and educated in the public, high, and normal schools of Washington, D.C. As she admits, her light skin may have helped her somewhat.

I have been at a near West Side school for all the ten years that I have been a regular teacher. I have never been particularly race conscious. I have never had any trouble with the pupils or the parents. I have been told by substitutes that there is more of a discipline problem in schools where colored predominate.

I have had some very enjoyable contacts. One of the members of our P.T.A. is the wife of a prominent business man. I have gone to all of the luncheons in the house of this woman and have even gone to the downtown hotels.

There was just one colored substitute during the time that I have been there. I remember her because she proved something that I have been thinking a long time, namely, that the children don't think of a teacher as colored unless she has a black skin. I remember one of my children came in late and when I asked him the reason he said that he had been showing the "nigger" teacher her room.

The teachers at the school have for the most part been fine. They treated my daughter fine when she attended. She has been the only colored graduate of the school. I gave her a graduation party when she finished and all of her schoolmates came over and had a fine time.[25]

The exact number of colored teachers in the Chicago public schools is very difficult to ascertain because some of them are so light that attention has not been called to their racial origins. For instance, a colored music teacher in a North Side high school was considered white by her principal. A teacher at a South Side technical school, whose principal reported that he had no colored teachers, is quite aware that one of her fellow-teachers was "passing" for white.[26] One colored teacher at a South Side high school said: "I think it may be generally stated that a good many of the teachers got in as white and then made themselves so invaluable that they could not be dismissed."[27] These are isolated cases, but they show how difficult it is to obtain reliable information on the subject under discussion. In the more prosperous neighborhoods inhabited largely by native whites we did not find Negro teachers who were recognized as such.

The best estimates which could be made show that of the 8,337 elementary teachers in the Chicago system in 1934, some 285, or 3.4 per cent, were colored. The number is slightly higher than a few years ago because some of the principals recently assigned to South Side schools have been favorably inclined toward Negro teachers.

HIGH-SCHOOL TEACHERS AND PRINCIPALS

High-school teaching positions are more highly prized than elementary-school positions because of the larger salaries and the more specialized work. Until the 1933 economy measures adopted by the Board of Education there were 26 senior high schools and 30 junior high schools. The latter schools were abolished by the board action and the pupils sent back to the ele-

---

[25] Interview, June 19, 1933.

[26] Herrick, *op. cit.*, pp. 25–26.   [27] Interview, June 19, 1933.

mentary schools. In order to become a teacher in the senior high schools it is necessary to pass the examinations in at least three specialized subjects and to possess two years' experience in teaching either in the elementary schools in Chicago or in outside high schools.

The first-known Negro teacher in the Chicago public high schools was a teacher of manual training at Wendell Phillips, who was a graduate of the University of Illinois and had substituted around Chicago for several years. His early experiences have been described as follows:

Although they spoke very highly of him, none of the principals of the three high schools with small Negro percentages and in which there were vacancies could use him. The principal of Wendell Phillips, with a large proportion of Negroes, told, however, of a different experience when this teacher was at that school. "In answer to complaints by pupils I told them that this man was a graduate of the University of Illinois, a high-school graduate in the city, and a cultured man. 'Go in there and forget the color, and see if you can get the subject matter.' In the majority of cases it worked."[28]

The above statement describes a situation that was found some time before 1920. Since then Wendell Phillips has shifted from a high school which had a large proportion of Negroes to one which is almost solidly colored. In no other high school in the city at the time of the present survey was the proportion of Negro pupils higher than one-third. This obviously made it difficult for qualified colored teachers to find high-school positions. In Wendell Phillips there were 4 Negro teachers in 1920,[29] 23 in 1930, and 36 in 1934.[30] In the high schools with large colored minorities racial feelings have been very tense and consequently the principals have not appointed colored teachers. Thus, the Englewood High School had a Negro school population almost as large in absolute numbers as that of Phillips in 1930, but it had no Negro teachers.[31] Outside of Phillips, col-

[28] *Negro in Chicago*, pp. 252–53.

[29] Teachers at Phillips say there were four colored teachers there in 1920.

[30] In 1934 there were 103 teachers in Phillips High School. The colored teachers contituted 35 per cent.

[31] Englewood is a much larger school. The Negroes were 30 per cent of the school population.

ored high-school teachers were found in only two schools, one in a near West Side high school which contained a decreasing school population one-fifth Negro and four-fifths of immigrant origin, and another in a near North Side high school where the Negro pupils were only 2 per cent of the total. It is clear that the same factors were operating in the high schools that were found in the elementary schools, only with increased rigor because of the keener competition for positions and the greater sensitiveness of adolescents to race contacts.

The experiences of some of the Negro high-school teachers are described by one of them who has been in the system since 1921:

Principals of junior and senior high schools need not take teachers from the list in order. One of the most brilliant women in the entire system was refused at three high schools when the principals saw that she was a Negro. Finally, the principal of Phillips sent for her and accepted her.

It is very easy to lose sight of the fact that this sort of thing is the exception rather than the general rule. I remember how prejudiced everyone said the principal was. However, he took a colored teacher on at his school. She taught Spanish in a junior high school and was on the high-school list. The principal of the junior high went to the principal of the senior high and recommended the woman very highly. She was given a chance and the faculty welcomed her.

As to my career, I took the high-school examination in June. I stayed on the list for six months, receiving a regular appointment in 1922. At the time I took the examination, no other colored persons took it, although there were three Negroes teaching in the senior high schools at the time. I was assigned at Phillips, although I had my choice between Phillips and Crane, receiving a call to both places at once.[32]

The next position above that of high-school teacher in salary and rank was that of college instructor and after this came the principals of the elementary schools. There were no Negro instructors in the two colleges run by the city at the time that this survey was made.[33] However, there was one colored principal out of 302 elementary-school principals. Like all the other principals appointed in recent years, the colored principal, Mrs Bousfield, passed a difficult written examination and was given a succession of oral examinations and visits by committees o

[32] Interview, August 25, 1931.   [33] Interview, June 18, 1933.

principals and assistant superintendents. Regarding her appointment, she said:

During my last two years of teaching at Phillips I was a dean. At that time the dean was selected by the principal, or rather the candidates for the position were selected, for we all had to take an examination, the only one in fact that has been given for this position. I was assigned principal at the Keith school in 1928 and at the Douglas school in 1931. Most persons think that the Douglas assignment was a move up but it really wasn't for there was no increase in salary at all, only more work.

If there has been any politics in the school system, I haven't come into contact with it. I am not saying there isn't any. I just haven't come into contact with it. I know in my own case there hasn't been any. There was only one time when I was determined to bring very definite political influence to bear and that was when my turn for assignment as principal came. I was determined that if they skipped me I would make trouble. They didn't skip me so I didn't have to do anything.[34]

When the economy measures were passed in 1933, Mrs. Bousfield, like all the other principals who had been appointed recently, was sent back to her old position in a high school. However, in the following year she was restored to her position as principal. Other colored teachers have passed the principal's examination, but in view of the fact that the school board has been cutting down the openings because of lack of funds, it is not likely that new appointments will be made in the near future. The schools to which Mrs. Bousfield was assigned were schools which contained an almost solid Negro population. There are now a number of assistant colored principals in such schools. The appointment of Negroes to supervisory positions in the school system raises a number of issues. Mrs. Bousfield states that she had no difficulties in securing co-operation, either with white teachers or with colored. However, it is clear that some white teachers would not like to work under a colored principal no matter how well qualified that principal was. Consequently, a few Negro leaders expressed the feeling that it was unwise to put colored principals in charge of schools in which the pupils and teachers were almost entirely colored as it would be a step toward actual if not legal segregation. On the other

[34] Interview.

hand, the view was stated by other Negro leaders that the use of colored people as principals would not only increase the number of jobs available for Negroes but would produce better schools, as the tendency is to give poorer white teachers to schools with almost solid colored populations.[35]

As in other branches of the city service, the Negroes have not yet gone beyond a certain point. There have been no colored district superintendents, supervisors, or assistant superintendents. As there are only about one hundred such administrative posts, here is a field where the Negroes will meet the severest of competition.

CONDITIONS OF WORK

When a colored teacher is assigned to a school which has a minority of colored teachers she must face the possibility of meeting some unpleasant situations. While one might expect white school teachers to be somewhat more broad-minded on race issues than the ordinary employees of the government, unfortunately this is not always the case.

One of the best teachers in the system, a refined and cultured person, stated that when she went to get her first substitute's work at a West Side high school the principal would not even talk to her. He turned his back on her in his office, something for which she never forgave him.

In practically all of the schools where there was a large Negro population, colored and white teachers ate their lunches together, put on school functions together, and sometimes formed permanent friendships. However, in a few schools racial frictions developed from time to time. The remarks given below were made by a teacher who said that there was not much race prejudice.

There was a story out for a while that the principal of our school on the South Side had segregated us in the lunch room. There wasn't anything at all to this. We have always had a great many teachers at this school. Most of the old white teachers stay on the first floor and are very clannish, incidentally.

[35] Some of the parents of children in the Willard School petitioned for Mrs. Bousfield as the principal.

They hardly speak to us even now. There are two lunch rooms in the school and it seems that these women just naturally go to one while most everyone else goes to the other one. The principal has gone now, and strangely enough a whole lot of the clannishness of the first floor seemed to leave with her, although those women are still pretty bad.

I know there have been a lot of critics of our present principal. They say that she is a very prejudiced woman. What has happened is that small incidents have been magnified and called prejudice. A good example of this is what happened at our last graduation. One of the teachers had a son graduating and naturally she wanted to see the boy get his diploma. Instead of asking whether or not she could leave the room, she went on up to the assembly hall. The principal spotted her and wrote a little note reprimanding her. All of the colored girls got around and said how terrible this was of the principal.

I'm not saying there is no prejudice at all. I remember the first principal I worked under. She just didn't like Negroes. She would never praise me for anything I had done, but she always found some fault with something. She didn't even speak to us when she saw us in the halls. All of her prejudice was changed by an old teacher.

What prejudice there is around is caused, I think, by just such things as I have told you. The girls go around stirring it up themselves.[36]

Just what was the line between clannishness and ethnocentrism, this teacher did not say.

The granting of transfers is another matter of school administration which may be complicated by the factor of color. Negro teachers have no difficulty in obtaining transfers from schools which are nearly all white to those which are nearly all black. On the other hand, the transfer of a Negro teacher to a school which happened to have only white children might meet with the same obstacles as an original appointment in that school.

Another point of possible contact between the white and colored teachers is in the teachers' organizations. The most widely known of these is the Chicago Teachers' Federation, headed by Margaret Haley, which still claims about five thousand members. The members of this organization are recruited largely from the elementary-school teachers. No definite information could be obtained regarding the number of Negro members, but

[36] Interview, June 18, 1933.

the organizer for the Federation had met as many as sixty in three schools, and there were probably many more. There are many other organizations among the teachers besides the Federation. The Women High School Teachers' Federation had in its membership some ten Negro teachers out of two dozen in high schools, and the Men Teachers' Union had some fifteen Negro members out of an estimated fifty Negro men teachers in the whole system. Although they were small minorities in each organization, there was no evidence that they were segregated or discriminated against. There are other organizations in the school system which have no Negro members, [37] but the teacher groups in general were anxious to secure all the numerical and financial support that they could. Solidarity of the teaching force was the principal aim of the strongest organizations.

STATUS AND EFFICIENCY OF NEGRO TEACHERS

The colored school teachers in Chicago enjoy considerable prestige in their own communities. This status may be the result of such factors as family standing, cultural background, and education, and have little direct relation to the occupational position held. However, the fact remains that the teaching profession has attracted more persons of social standing in Negro groups than it has persons of similar position in the white world. One Negro writer in an article on Chicago's colored "Four Hundred" mentioned prominently a number of teachers.[38] Such would not be the case in an article on Chicago's "Four Hundred," taken from the city at large. The security that comes from great wealth has not as yet been made the basis of Negro "society." Consequently, teachers can be given a social rank on the basis of their accomplishments, personality, and sociability. Most of them keep up active membership in their college fraternities and sororities and some of them are leaders in fraternal organizations.

[37] Elementary Teachers' Union, International Union of Operating Engineers. For a fuller discussion of this subject, see Herrick, *op. cit.*, chapter iv.

[38] P. L. Prattis, "Chicago's '400,'" Washington Intercollegiate Club of Chicago, *The Negro in Chicago 1779 to 1929* (Chicago, 1929), p. 97.

The efficiency of the colored teachers was something which could not be determined in any satisfactory manner. Since there are no reliable methods for measuring teaching ability, any statement about a teacher's work must be taken with reservations. However, in a study of race relations it is important to know what kind of opinions school administrators hold regarding the colored teachers under them. These statements are not to be taken as decisive in regard to actual efficiency of the teachers concerned. They indicate rather the attitudes that Negro teachers must face in a school system like the one in Chicago. One assistant supervisor of a special service made the sweeping statement that none of the colored teachers were any good, none of them had enough background, and none of them should be allowed to try to teach. A few principals would say that the poor ones had such faults as irresponsibility, laziness, and an objectionable forwardness. Normal-school teachers said that some of their colored material was poor[39] and that some of it was excellent. An experienced assistant principal thought that the younger colored teachers should be judged leniently as under present conditions they had to substitute longer than whites, and four years of substituting was "enough to wreck anybody."[40]

There were many principals and supervisors who had high praise for the work of some colored teachers. Two Negro household arts teachers were rated as excellent by the supervisor. One administrator in the main school office rated the work of a colored vocational guidance counselor as excellent. One colored music teacher's work drew favorable comment at a music supervisors' convention, and another such teacher trained a glee club which won first place among small glee clubs at a city-wide contest. One colored weaving teacher's work was regarded so highly that she was made summer school instructor at the Normal

[39] Since all normal entrants must meet the same requirements, this statement is hard to understand. A comparison of the grades of white and colored normal students would be valuable here, but the figures were not available.

[40] Herrick, *op. cit.*, p. 24.

College. A printing teacher has been made an examiner and because of his excellence he has done much work for the downtown office. Negro teachers of the ordinary subjects have also received very favorable comments on their work.

The situation has been summed up by one of the prominent colored teachers.

It is often said that Negro teachers are not as capable as the white ones. I will certainly say that they are not any worse. Many of the Negroes came into the system with master's degrees. Most of them in the high schools have stood better than the whites. Many of the high-school teachers stood first on their lists when they took the examinations.[41]

Negro teachers, like white teachers, vary in ability and aptitude. Those who were interviewed in connection with this study showed a great fondness for their work. They were not mere time-servers but builders for the future.

GENERAL TRENDS

Has there been a real extension of vocational opportunity for Negroes in the school system of Chicago? In 1934 there were at least 321 regularly appointed Negro teachers in the public schools, or 2.6 per cent of the 12,199 assigned teachers in the system. The ratio of colored teachers in Chicago reported in the United States census for 1930 was 2.3 per cent. According to the 1920 census, the colored teachers in the city were 1.2 per cent of the total, and in 1910 0.5 per cent.[42] It is thus clear that in supplying teachers the Negroes in Chicago have lagged behind their population ratio, which was 6.9 per cent in 1930.

The colored teachers have also fallen behind the ratio achieved by the Negro librarians. A number of explanations may be offered for this. The appointing power in the school system has been scattered among some 340 principals, whereas in the library service it has been concentrated in a single personnel

---

[41] Interview, June 18, 1933.

[42] Compiled from the United States census volumes on occupations, 1910, 1920, and 1930. All school teachers, whether in public or private schools, are listed, and no distinction is made between regulars and substitutes. Our figure, including substitutes, is 458 for 1930. The census figure is 452. See Appendix I.

agency which has been very fair in making assignments. The Negroes have been represented on the library board but not on the school board.

The opportunities of Negro teachers in the Chicago school system in the future depend in part upon the kind of principals chosen. The agitation of the Negro press and of prominent Negro leaders for more harmonious relations in the schools seems to be having some effect. The recent principals assigned to South Side schools have in general been persons who were acceptable to the Negro communities. This will probably mean a gradual increase in the number of colored teachers.

CHAPTER XIV
NEGROES IN THE CHICAGO POST-OFFICE

Negroes have entered many of the different offices maintained by the federal government in the city of Chicago. However, their presence has been most conspicuous in the post-office and it is here that they have attracted national attention. In 1928 the colored employees of the Chicago post-office were made the subject of a heated discussion in the House of Representatives.[1] Congressman Stevenson from South Carolina quoted with approval a communication from a Chicago organization which criticized the administration of the Chicago post-office for having too many Negroes. The general efficiency of the Negro employees was also attacked. Representative Martin B. Madden made a spirited speech in which he came to the defense of the colored postal employees in the city.[2]

The exact situation in the Chicago post-office is difficult to ascertain because complete and official figures regarding the colored employees were not obtainable. The claim was made by some of the postal authorities that no records were kept which showed the color of the employees. However, some of the organizations of postal workers have partial data.[3] As far back as 1893 there were said to be 78 Negro postal employees in the city. By 1900 the number had increased to 135, by 1910 to 566, by 1921 to 1,400, and by 1930 to over 3,000.[4] In the last decade the ratio of the Negro employees to the total number of employees in the Chicago postal service rose from about 14 per

[1] *Congressional Record*, House, 70th Congress, 1st Session, Vol. 69, Part 3 (February 2, 1928), pp. 2390–92.

[2] A mass meeting was held in Chicago immediately after the Stevenson-Madden debate at which Madden's secretary spoke. Many Negroes were dissatisfied with Madden's reply because they felt it was too general.

[3] Washington Intercollegiate Club, *The Negro in Chicago, 1779–1927*, I, 177.

[4] The 1921 figure was found in the *Congressional Record*, *loc. cit.*, and the 1930 figure was given directly to the writer.

cent to 25 per cent.[5] The ratio among the skilled and unskilled laborers has been the highest and the ratio of clerks has been higher than that of carriers. According to the United States census figures the proportion of colored mail carriers was 4.4 per cent in 1910, 7.3 per cent in 1920, and 16.0 per cent in 1930.[6] All of these data show a rapid increase in the number of Negro employees and a relative position far in advance of the population ratio of 6.7 per cent in 1930. Table XV shows the situation as it existed in 1930.

REASONS FOR LARGE PROPORTION

The reasons for the large proportion of colored employees in the Chicago post-office are difficult to establish because the materials which might throw light upon the situation are lacking. It is not known how many white and black applicants there have been for postal positions at various times. The intellectual and physical equipment of the white and colored applicants is also an unknown quantity. The attitude of some of the Chicago postmasters toward Negro postal workers cannot now be ascertained because they are no longer living. The explanations which are offered below are tentative.

The Chicago postal service contains a larger relative number of Negro employees than some of the municipal services in the city because the federal civil service rules have been applied for a longer time than the city rules. Immediately after the merit system went into operation in the national service in 1883, a colored man took the examination for carrier and was appointed as a substitute.[7] The administration of the national civil service rules has been better, in general, than that of the local rules. Consequently, it became generally known that Negroes had a chance to enter the postal service if they had the proper qualifications. The service was attractive to some Negroes many

---

[5] Representative Stevenson in the speech referred to states that the ratio was 31 per cent in 1927. According to the figures which he furnished, Representative Stevenson's arithmetic is incorrect. He stated that there were 2,950 Negroes out of a total of 11,019. The ratio should be 27 per cent.

[6] See Appendix I.　　　　[7] Washington Intercollegiate Club, *op. cit.*, I, 177.

years ago and it has continued to be attractive in recent years.
A colored man who was appointed in 1890 said:

TABLE XV

PERSONS IN CHICAGO WORKING IN POSTAL SERVICE, BY
COLOR, SEX, AND OCCUPATION: 1930*

OCCUPATION	TOTAL WORKERS			NEGRO WORKERS			PER-CENT-AGE NEGRO OF TOTAL (4) of (1)
	Total (1)	Men (2)	Women (3)	Total (4)	Men (5)	Women (6)	(7)
Compositors, linotypers, and type-setters...................	11	10	1	3	3	......	27.3
Machinists....................	12	12	......	1	1	......	8.3
Mechanics (not otherwise speci-fied).......................	51	51	......	7	7	......	13.7
Chauffeurs and truck and tractor drivers....................	101	101	......	42	42	......	41.6
Foremen and overseers..........	133	133	......	6	6	......	4.5
Inspectors....................	27	27	......	1	1	......	3.7
Laborers.....................	531	530	1	369	368	1	69.5
Managers and officials.........	167	167	......	2	2	......	1.2
Guards, watchmen, and doorkeep-ers.........................	46	45	1	2	1	1	4.3
Charwomen and cleaners.......	13	3	10	9	1	8	69.2
Elevator tenders..............	14	13	1	12	11	1	85.7
Janitors.....................	40	29	11	35	25	10	87.5
Porters......................	24	24	......	23	23	......	95.8
Clerks.......................	6,512	6,246	266	1,825	1,764	61	28.0
Messenger, errand, and office boys	81	81	......	10	10	......	12.3
Stenographers and typists.......	47	14	33	2	......	2	4.3
Mail carriers..................	3,948	3,946	2	631	631	......	16.0
Other occupations.............	61	58	3	28	28	......	46.0
Pursuits in postal service in Chi-cago in 1930 in which there were no Negroes†.................	69	62	7	......	......	......	0.0
Total....................	11,888	11,552	336	3,008	2,924	84	25.2

* Figures furnished by the Director of the United States Census.

† Carpenters (3); electricians (5); engineers (stationary) (6); oilers of machinery (1); painters, glaziers, and varnishers (building) (1); apprentices, other transportation and communication (2); advertising agents (1); policemen (1); draftsmen (1); agents (not elsewhere classified) (6); accountants and auditors (7); book-keepers and cashiers (24); shipping clerks (1); weighers (3); housekeepers and stewards; office-appliance operators (7).

I had taken the civil service examination for the post-office. In those days
the salary was considered good. The fellows in the hotels were only getting
about twenty-five dollars a month and tips. The men on the road were making about the same. Then, too, the post-office was a more honorable kind of

work. When I went into the service I was supposed to get a letter from the superintendent of the "road" for recommendation. This man asked me why I was giving up the good "run" that I had to take a post-office job. I told him, "Anybody with common sense can be a porter. But a person must have a fairly good education to be a postal man." There were chances for advancement in the post-office, too. But if you stayed on the "road" for fifty years you would still be wearing lead buttons. At least in the post-office they gave you brass buttons.[8]

In recent times the examinations have been such that they could readily be passed by high-school graduates. One recent recruit pointed out how common it was for colored students to look to the post-office for their initial employment: "Just when I was graduating from Wendell Phillips High I found out that some of the boys were working their way through by working at the post-office. Some of them asked me why I didn't go down. I asked if I could get in before I was twenty-one and they told me that I could."[9] In 1925 and in 1928 salary increases were voted for postal workers and this placed them, according to one employee, "among the best livers of Chicago's south side."[10]

Assuming that the civil service examinations for postal workers were fair and open to all, then one explanation of the large proportion of colored employees would be that qualified colored persons applied in greater numbers than white persons. This view was expressed forcefully by one Negro postal worker:

I don't think that the percentage of Negroes in the population has anything to do with the number who are in the United States civil service in Chicago. At each examination they accept so many applications, and these applications are open to all who wish to apply. The examinations are competitive and the board is white. Don't forget that the board of examiners is white. Now if the whites aren't in the service in overwhelming numbers, whose fault is it? If they don't apply, that's their fault. And if they don't pass the examination, then it's because they aren't as good, because the white examiners are going to give them the break and that's sure. After all, aren't we all American citizens and aren't the examinations for American citizens? Well, how does it, at least hypothetically, make a damn bit of difference whether the man is white or black?[11]

[8] Interview, January 15, 1933.   [9] Interview, June 2, 1933.

[10] V. D. Bond, "Chicago Post Office," in Washington Intercollegiate Club, *op. cit.*, II, 62.

[11] Interview, June 2, 1933.

In theory, the color of an applicant should make no difference in applying for a civil service job, but it has been pointed out in connection with the city service that the practice of public personnel administration does not always conform with the abstract principles. If the appointing officers are prejudiced, they may refuse to accept colored applicants who have passed the examinations or, after accepting them, they may drop them during the probation period. In the postal service there is a board which investigates the character and fitness of applicants on the eligible list and makes a final decision regarding appointments. It has been shown that in the municipal service political pressure was sometimes used to prevent discrimination against colored applicants. Could Negroes have entered the postal service in as large numbers as they did without at least sympathetic treatment from the appointing authorities? In other words, why were the federal appointing officers less prejudiced than some of the city officers?

In the fifty-year period following the passage of the federal civil service law the Republican party controlled the presidency two-thirds of the time. During the same interval there were only two Democratic United States senators from Illinois, and their terms were not overlapping, so that until 1933 there was always at least one Republican senator from the state. Since postmasters are usually recommended by senators and appointed by the president, this meant that there were Republican postmasters in Chicago during Democratic city administrations. During his first administration President Wilson did not change the Chicago postmaster. As two of the Republican postmasters became candidates for mayor, it is clear that the position was not wholly removed from the field of party politics. A Republican postmaster could not afford to alienate such a large block of Republican voters as the Negroes constituted in Chicago. Postmaster Lueder was first appointed in 1921 by President Harding on the recommendation of Senator McCormick, and he served for twelve years. One of the older employees said that Negroes had made most progress in the post-office under Lueder's administration. Lueder had "bent backward" to be fair to

Negroes.[12] Another employee said that under his administration the Negroes got an almost 100 per cent square deal.[13]

Republican congressmen from Illinois went out of their way to see that Negroes were fairly treated in the Chicago post-office. It has already been indicated that Representative Madden's district happened to be in an area where the Negro population was rapidly increasing. When Madden first went to Washington he was put on the Committee on Post-Office and Post Roads, and it was said that here he saw that the Negroes in Chicago were not deprived of any opportunity to obtain post-office jobs. He also interceded on behalf of Negroes who claimed that they had been disciplined unjustly, and in this way he kept some from being separated from the service. It was said that he not only looked after Negroes in Chicago in the post-office, but he helped Negroes all over the country to get into the postal service.[14] Later, when he was on the powerful Appropriations Committee, he worked "long and hard" to secure the passage of his pet bill to increase the pay of all the employees of the postal service.[15] Senator Deneen was also active on behalf of Negroes seeking postal positions.

The way in which political influences operated in the recruitment of postal workers may be illustrated by individual cases. One Negro postal employee in a supervisory position said that after one got on the postal list for appointment help might be secured in getting appointed if one had a friend, such as a senator or representative.[16] One of the women employees made the following comment about her appointment.:

> One time I became tired of my trade (beauty specialist) so I decided to try for a job in the post-office. I took the examination and was called down in a group of five, three white girls, a Negro man, and myself. The three white girls were taken on. I then went to see the alderman who was a family friend. He wrote a letter and sent the Senator a wire. I was called and hired within a week.[17]

[12] Interview, July 16, 1931. For another view, see below, p. 316.

[13] Interview, July 17, 1931.

[14] Interview, November 16, 1931, with a prominent member of the Third Ward Republican organization.

[15] *Broad Ax*, October 23, 1926.

[16] Interview, July 9, 1931.   [17] Interview, October 20, 1930.

One young man, who is still in the service but who plans to leave as soon as he has obtained a law degree, was very frank about the influences which helped to secure his appointment:

As soon as I had passed the examination I sent word to my relative (a prominent Negro politician) who in turn wired to Congressman Madden. The examiners sent for me at once. They got me before three men who asked me some routine questions and I went to work. This board is supposed to have the final say on subs. Each member of the board knows before a call is sent out that a Negro applicant is coming. I think they have always maintained a proper proportion, proper in their minds anyway, between the number of entering white and colored.[18]

These cases do not establish any causal connection between political pressure and appointments in the postal service, but they raise a strong presumption in favor of such an interpretation. There has been no hint that any of the transactions were corrupt. No scandals arose like those in some of the southern post-offices, where it was alleged that jobs were bought and sold. It was simply a case of a friendly word from someone who had political power.[19]

There were some special reasons connected with general economic conditions which go part way to explaining the presence of so many Negro employees in the Chicago post-office. The postal service is like a public utility in that it has a very definite demand to satisfy. It must have sufficient man power to deliver letters and packages promptly. During the World War there was a shortage of labor in the postal service. Persons who might have sought to enter the service were in the military forces or in the highly paid war industries. Colored men and women who were discriminated against in industry took advantage of the openings in the post-office. In 1918 about one hundred colored women entered the service, nearly one-half of whom still remain.[20]

[18] Interview, December 28, 1933.

[19] Since the Democrats came to power in the state and nation in 1933, Ernest J. Kreutgen, a Democrat, has been appointed postmaster of Chicago. Before he was appointed there were drastic cuts in the total number of employees in the Chicago post-office. On July 21, 1931, there were 10,987 employees of whom 2,627, or 24 per cent, Negro. The Democrats have not lowered the ratio. See footnote 21 below.

[20] Bond, *loc. cit.*

During the upward trend of the business cycle from 1922 to 1929, comparatively few white persons thought of entering the postal service. In spite of the increases in the salaries of postal employees, there were many positions in private industry which appeared more attractive. The clerical positions open to Negroes in private industry were limited in number, so during this period the postal service again saw a great influx of colored employees. It was claimed by several that the number of Negroes who entered the service during these years was not unduly large. Most of the Negroes who became postal employees stayed, while many of the white employees left for more profitable positions in private industry. Since 1929 the recruitment of Negro employees along with all other employees in the post-office has fallen off sharply. However, the colored postal workers have managed to hold their relative position in the service.[21]

There is another reason why the postal service has been so attractive to some colored persons. It furnishes a very convenient transitional occupation. Negroes who are ambitious to complete their education, who wish to get started in some profession such as law or medicine, or who wish to accumulate a little capital to start a business, have found the post-office an excellent stepping-stone. However, in comparison with the total number of Negroes entering the service, the number of those who are looking forward to other occupations is not large.

There is no single reason for the relatively large number of colored postal employees. The civil service rules require the submission of a photograph by every applicant, so it would be easy enough for the officials concerned to determine the color of persons certified from the eligible list. If political influences

[21] Distribution of Employees of the Chicago post-office by color, August 16, 1934:

Classification	Total	Colored	Per Cent Colored
Clerks	5,490	1,224	22.3
Carriers	2,790	485	17.4
Skilled laborers	811	508	62.6
Spec. del. messengers	363	17	4.7
Cleaners	106	84	80.0
Total	9,560	2,318	24.2

have been used to prevent discrimination, there is no evidence of any corrupt bargains. Negroes argue that they have to fight prejudice with the weapons which are available and effective. When economic conditions produced some openings in the postal service, there were many Negroes who saw these opportunities and took advantage of them.

CONDITIONS OF WORK

As in the case of other civil service employees, the Negro postal workers had to face the possibility of unfair treatment in the service. The public was not as sensitive regarding the postal personnel as it was regarding the police or school personnel, but there were some white persons in supervisory positions in the service who held dogmatic views that were unfavorable to Negroes in general, and some of the public were conscious of the factor of color.

Many of the Negroes who qualified as postal clerks were assigned to the main post-office. Here there was a great mass of mail to handle. In the words of Kelly Miller, "The Negro is assigned in the federal service to the post-office, for the most part, for there the labor is not wholly clerical, but essentially manual."[22] An ambitious young high-school Negro graduate came to Chicago, took the examination for postal clerk, and then met the following situation: "I pictured myself at a desk doing clerical work and was very happy when I passed the examination, but I was soon bitterly disappointed. The work that was assigned to me was more fitting for a day laborer than for a clerk. I stayed there about three months."[23]

From time to time representatives of the Negro employees have complained about discrimination in the making of certain assignments. They called attention to the fact that only white persons were assigned as detail clerks and checkers in the various units of the mailing division, as armed guards in the motor vehicle service, and as window clerks. It was also pointed out that general work in the cashier's office, and assignments as

[22] Cited by C. S. Johnson, *The Economic Status of Negroes* (Nashville, 1933), p. 16.

[23] Interview, December 19, 1932.

carrier inspectors at various publishing houses were other details which were rarely given to colored employees.

Regarding the assignments given to colored clerks at the main office, one substitute clerk said:

> The substitute clerks are all mixed together, white and colored. You come in at a certain time and you all file in line after you punch the time clock. Then you go by the detail station and you pass in line and get detailed according to the whim and fancy of the detail clerk. There are no colored detail clerks. The clerks are usually impartial, but not always. A lot of the ganging together is the fault of the Negro clerks themselves. They will just stick together. Sometimes they will form half a line and the white clerks will pass by. We work around long tables with fourteen men at each table. Some of these tables, because of the colored clerks, have only colored and no whites.
>
> Something happened yesterday which I have not seen before in my four years of service. A printing company had need of so many men to do some clerical work which had to do with the mail. They sent over a request for so many men. When I came to work the majority of the colored had gone by. I don't line up with the colored clerks. The detail clerk was going by handing out slips to go over to the printing company to work. When he came to me, he said, "I will have to pass you up." One of my white friends came up and said, "I see that they are only taking white." But the detail clerk had handled the situation tactfully and I was not angry with him. I later was told that the large companies specify that they don't want colored when they ask for men to come over and work. The post-office could refuse to do this, but why don't they?[24]

It has been the policy of the post-office to assign clerks and carriers in the outlying business and residential districts to stations which were near their homes. As in the case of police officers and school teachers, the concentration of the Negro population has brought about a concentration of the postal employees. However, the colored postal workers have been so numerous that they have been assigned to stations in neighborhoods which are largely white but which happen to be near the main Negro community. The high schools in these neighborhoods have no colored teachers, but nearly half of the postal employees are Negro. In such a station the Negroes were more likely to be carriers than clerks. In the stations which were some distance from any of the Negro communities there might

[24] Interview, June 2, 1933.

be some colored laborers, a few colored carriers, but rarely a colored clerk.[25]

The efficiency records of the white and colored postal employees were not available. One of the high officials in the Chicago post-office said that the proportion of Negroes coming before the Efficiency Board was not unduly large. One of the station superintendents said that the Negro employees at his station did good work. There were a few lazy ones and a few excellent ones. One man consistently received the highest possible efficiency rating. The Negroes knew that they had good jobs in the post-office and they worked hard to keep them.[26] Administrative attitudes such as these offered no serious problems for the colored workers. On the other hand, one station superintendent said that the Negro workers were not up to the general efficiency level and that they required more supervision.[27] One high official said:

The Negroes in the service are fine men, many of them are college graduates. All race groups have characteristics peculiar to them. Up until now the Negro postal employees have been more easy going than the white ones. They don't think as far ahead. They will buy lots of stuff that they don't need or they'll go out and get married on $100 or $50. For this reason they have not been prompt in meeting their financial obligations, as have other groups. This becomes less and less true of them. When there is a complaint against some postal employee by a company that has sold him something on time, the employee is called in and questioned about the matter. If it's an honest, reasonable debt, the employee is advised to pay it. If he does not, disciplinary methods are used on him.[28]

The relations between the white and colored employees have been, in general, friendly. In the main post-office there is one rest room and one dining-room where all mix for their meals and pastime games. Negroes have been welcomed into the regular organizations of postal workers. Local No. 1 of the National Federation of Post Office Clerks has a colored membership of about 15 per cent. Colored members of this organization have from time to time represented the organization as delegates to various conventions.

[25] Nine selected postal stations were studied.

[26] Interview, July 21, 1931.

[27] Interview, July 21, 1931.

[28] Interview, July 9, 1931.

The Negro postal workers have also organized associations of their own which are devoted mainly to social and welfare activities. A local club, called the Phalanx Forum Club, was organized in 1911 for social, civic, and benevolent purposes. From time to time it has contributed money to the N.A.A.C.P., the Chicago Urban League, and to other community projects. In 1920 a branch of the National Alliance of Postal Employees was formed in Chicago. This organization, which is now the largest of the groups of its kind, is devoted to social affairs and to the safeguarding of the interests of its members.[29] Its representatives hold conferences with the postal authorities regarding such matters as sick-leave investigations, health problems, seniority rulings, and promotions.[30] A member of one of these organizations said that they did some good by agitating and that they knew just how far to go. The membership of the Alliance in 1933 was about 350, or some 12 per cent of the total number of Negro employees.

PROMOTIONS

Negroes have come into postal work in large numbers, but they have not been able to win many promotions to the higher positions in the service. In the post-office promotion is determined by seniority, efficiency records, and the discretion of the postmaster. The last two of these factors have presented the greatest difficulties to the ambitious colored employees.

One of the organizations interested in the welfare of the Negro postal workers charged that many Negro employees whose qualifications, seniority and otherwise, placed them in line for promotions were ignored or disregarded in some way and white employees advanced instead. It was claimed that colored clerks who received high ratings in their scheme examinations were not given the merits to which they were entitled while those who received low ratings were charged with demerits.[31] The section foreman who gave the efficiency ratings on which promotions were based was likely to give the efficient colored em-

---

[29] *Chicago Defender*, November 25, 1933. [30] *Ibid.*, February 21, 1931.

[31] The system by which mail is sorted is called a scheme. The accuracy with which this sorting is done is called a scheme examination.

ployees ratings just low enough to block their advancement. How were the Negroes to work around these difficulties?

One of the first Negroes to receive a promotion in the postal service was Major Robert R. Jackson, whose career has already been mentioned in another connection.[32] Major Jackson served as a stamping clerk, a letter distributor, and in several other capacities before he was promoted as foreman and later as assistant superintendent of a postal station. The same geniality that helped him in his military, fraternal, and political careers was of use in his civil service career. Below is a contemporary account of his success in the postal service:

It was on the 9th day of December, 1888, that Major Jackson entered the postal service of the United States, having passed the civil service examination for clerks with the unusual high average of 98.16. Since his entrance in the classified service he has maintained his record for high averages by defeating his white fellow-clerks in promotional examinations with averages of 99.40, 98.12, and 98.32, as many as 700 contesting for the honor in the same examination. During his fourteen years of service in the post-office he has worked in every branch of the service, at the present time being assistant superintendent of the Armour station.[33]

After Major Jackson left the service in 1909, other promotions of colored employees came very slowly. A Mr. Cummings was made a foreman about 1911, and for some time he was the only colored man in a supervisory position. It was not until Postmaster Lueder's administration that several Negroes were promoted at the same time. The colored men who were made foremen were usually those who had achieved positions of leadership and respect in their own communities. Family traditions, a light skin, an intense interest in his work, superior efficiency, and an affable personality were among the factors that contributed to the advancement described below:

My family were slaves in North Carolina a hundred years ago but they bought their freedom in 1832 and left their plantation. I still own their traveling papers. They drove to Ohio and later to Michigan where they acted as one station in the underground railroad system. My father fought in the Civil War with a regiment from Detroit. My mother had a rather good education which she received in Canada. Her mother was also educated.

[32] See above, p. 67.   [33] *Broad Ax*, December 27, 1902.

Many noted Negroes of the times were guests at our home. I was a small child, but I remember Mr. Pinchback and Mr. Frederick Douglass well. Mr. Douglass came to speak at my father's church. Before the meeting he had dinner with us. He wore a shiny Prince Albert coat and had very long white hair. He was generally looked down on by the members of the community, because he didn't work. The whole community worked very hard, and they considered that that was the way to help solve the problems, rather than by so much talk, as Mr. Douglass did.

I graduated from high school, here in Chicago, about 31 years ago. I got married immediately. I worked in my father's and brothers' catering business for awhile. I then began waiting table at a local club. Inside of a year, I was made steward. One day I took off an hour and a half to take the civil service examination. I did well enough on it to be appointed.

I've always worked hard. For example, once I watched the mechanic set-up the cancellation machine just from my interest. I learned to do the set-up. Later I was able to fill the vacancy when the mechanic failed to report on one day. This prevented the accumulation of mail and was a real help to the department. Another time I was assigned to sort mail with no instructions as to the technique. I got the instructions written out, memorized the processes at home that night, and surprized my superiors next day by my efficiency at the process. Once some friend of mine must have interceded for me. I am not sure. I was handling bags along with two hundred other men. One day the foreman asked me if I wouldn't like a more pleasant position and I was transferred to it. I was a tracer for six years and I have occupied most of the positions below my present one.[34]

The exact way in which political influences were brought to bear upon the various authorities to secure promotions for colored men in the postal service is shown by the following interview with a man who graduated from a leading Negro university and who entered the postal service after he had run up against obstacles to his advancement in private employment:

We have had a long tough fight to get colored men in responsible positions. The fight has been so tied up in politics that I don't know where to start in. We first started our fight in May, 1924. At that time, on the Saturday one o'clock set, there wasn't a white man working. They would move in white men from other sets to supervise us. The first time they did this I went home from work, it just made me sick. Finally after they had done it for several times a group of us decided to take the matter up. We formed a committee and started writing the postmaster. We wrote him every Thursday for a month. We never so much as received a statement that the letters had been received.

[34] Interview, July 16, 1931.

We finally decided to write to Martin B. Madden. In June, 1924, the committee was notified that Madden's son-in-law, Paul Henderson, the second assistant Postmaster General, would meet with us at the Appomattox Club. On the Sunday morning of the meeting, with all of the local politicians present, Mr. Henderson presented John Gainey with an appointment as assistant chief railway mail clerk at large. Mr. Henderson said on that occasion that he had made a start in the oldest, and though he didn't say it, the most exclusive branch of the entire service.

The thing I remember most about the meeting is not the speech of Mr. Henderson but the little speech that a local white politician made to me personally. I showed him some of the copies of the letters that we had sent Lueder which the Postmaster had not seen fit to answer. He swore and said that everybody should at least have a fair hearing. He got so mad that he arranged a personal hearing with the postmaster. Lueder made us wait and in the meantime sent for all of the superintendents on the floor. They weren't favorable to the appointment of a colored foreman. Lueder finally got us in his office and said that though he was for the colored people, they "didn't show good judgment in the last mayoralty election." He said that white men wouldn't work under colored men. He said further that they had too many colored men in the office as it was. After all this he did say that he would take the matter under advisement. We knew what that meant.

We went over to see Medill McCormick. The old man looked at us when we went over to the office and said, "Why in the hell do the colored people come to me when they want something but when Senator McCormick wants something they fight him?" We told him that we represented the National Alliance of Postal Employees and though some of the colored people had fought him in the past that we still had some votes. The senator thought over this and said that he would weigh the evidence and see that we got an equal opportunity. We knew what that meant too so we decided to put Henry Linc Johnson on the Senator's trail.

Things were still hanging fire until we went to see Ed Wright, who was on the Commerce Commission at that time, I think. After we had told Mr. Wright our story he said that he thought that the federal civil service was beyond all that and that he was glad to know that it wasn't. He told us that he would put over what we wanted. Wright went to Madden. Madden called a superintendent over to a hotel and told him that he wanted some colored foremen. That was all there was to it, there were some colored foremen. Lueder didn't want to appoint them and the superintendent said that Madden said to him one day, "God dammit, Arthur, if you don't, I'll have Harry (Harry New, Postmaster General) appoint them." Several were appointed.

Since most of the foremen have been retired lately, I think our day has passed in the office. The young men don't have the guts to make the fight we made. We got all kinds of discouragement even after we had the foremen appointed. Negroes kicked and didn't want to work under Negro foremen.

You have just got to get those jobs through politics. It will be some time before we have the connections we had then. We had a state senator, a congressman who had charge of the appropriations for the post-office work, four representatives, a commerce commissioner, and on top of that we had the Postmaster General pulling for us. When Archie Weaver of the N.A.A.C.P. wrote to Harry New congratulating him for confirming Lueder's appointments, New replied that he was the one that had made them.[35]

At the beginning of the year 1933 there were eleven colored foremen and one colored assistant superintendent of delivery. These officials constituted about 4 per cent of the some 300 supervisory officials in the Chicago post-office. According to one postal worker who was describing the National Alliance of Postal Employees and the Phalanx Club, "It is through these two organizations and the assistance of our friends, Senator Charles S. Deneen, the late Congressman Martin B. Madden, and Honorable Edward H. Wright, prominent Chicago attorney, that Chicago can boast of one assistant superintendent of mails and eleven foremen."[36] Another postal employee said: "There is no excessive amount of political activity within the department. Favors are usually given to friends, as also happens in the ordinary normal events of living."[37] During the first nine months of the Roosevelt administration five of the colored supervisory officers were retired, and since no new appointments were made, the number of colored supervisors was reduced to seven in 1934.

STATUS OF POSTAL WORKERS

The Chicago post-office has been the training ground for a number of colored leaders. The career of Major Jackson naturally comes to mind. After serving three terms in the state legislature, he was elected as alderman, in which capacity he has held office longer than any other colored man. George T. Kersey, who also served three terms in the state legislature, spent twenty-five years of his life in the postal service before he entered the undertaking business. A postal foreman who recently retired was a close adviser of the late Edward H. Wright.

[35] Interview, January 8, 1934.

[36] Bond, op. cit.   [37] Interview, July 17, 1931.

The iron master welcomed his advice because he was aloof from quarrels of partisan politics.

In the general life of the Negro community the postal workers have taken a prominent part. One is the leader of a famous choir which won prizes in a city-wide contest. Another was the president of the Appomattox Club, a social club which had a large following among the Negro professional and business men. Former postal employees are now found in many different lines of business. One is an ice-cream manufacturer, another runs a motion-picture house, and among the others are real estate agents, wholesale and retail merchants.

The Negroes in Chicago have found in the postal service one of their important occupational openings. About 3.4 per cent of all the male Negroes ten years of age and over gainfully employed in the city in 1930 were in the postal service. Many persons who were not interested in the protectional services of the city because of the hazards involved looked upon post-office positions as honorable, respectable, and reasonably remunerative. Whereas many white persons left the postal service for more lucrative positions, particularly during the upward trend of the business cycle, a large proportion of the colored employees remained. As in other civil service positions, so in the Chicago post-office the Negro employees have fought discrimination by modified trade-union methods, by political methods, and by other methods that suited their purposes.

CHAPTER XV

NEGROES AND COMMUNISM

The most dangerous menace to the peace of mind of Negroes has been economic insecurity. Uncertain employment, low wages, high mortality and morbidity rates, extortionate rents, overcrowded housing conditions, and recurrent police brutality have left a residue of discontent which has in some cases inspired open rebellion against conditions. The Republican and Democratic parties have neglected to take effective steps to end disenfranchisement, segregation, economic exploitation, and lynching in the South, and they have likewise been very slow in tackling such fundamental problems as trade-union discrimination, the organization of the public health services,[1] the provision of moderate-price housing, and unemployment.[2] Both of the traditional parties have more or less accepted the existing economic system and the somewhat inferior position which the system has accorded to Negroes.

In spite of the shortcomings of the old-line major parties, the Negroes in Chicago, as in the United States as a whole, have displayed very little tendency to listen to the political and economic appeals and symbols which have been presented by those who propose a radical alteration of the present order. The

---

[1] Regarding the failure of the Chicago Municipal Tuberculosis Sanitarium to deal with tuberculosis among Negroes, Robert F. Steadman, in his *Public Health Organization in the Chicago Region* (Chicago, 1930) said on page 113: "The Sanitarium has, obviously, located only a small number of the cases which exist among the Negro population. Under such conditions, one would expect the work of the Sanitarium to be redoubled in the Negro districts, especially since such huge additional funds have been made available to it. . . . . The effect of this general neglect of the Negro population seems to have had disastrous results. In 1915 the tuberculosis death-rate among Negroes was 363 per 100,000 . . . . and in 1925 the calculated rate for Negroes was 418 as compared with 65.4 among the whites. If the efforts against tuberculosis were concentrated in these sections, removing these foci of infection, Chicago's record of tuberculosis control might quickly alter." Since this book was published a calculation of rates for 1930 was made. They were 278 for Negroes and 41 for whites.

[2] See above, p. 186, for DePriest's attitude on federal relief.

leadership of the Negroes in Chicago has in the main been very conservative on economic questions. Bishop Carey expressed a typical bourgeois point of view in 1924 when he said, "I believe that the interest of my people lies with the wealth of the nation and with the class of white people who control it." A very similar attitude was expressed by the *Chicago Whip* in its campaign against the union of Negro sleeping-car porters in 1926: "The black people at large should align themselves as far as possible with the wealthier classes in America."[3] In general, those Negroes who had jobs in Chicago were afraid that they might lose them at any time on account of their color and they were not willing to run the additional risk of being classed as "red," "socialist," "Bolshevik," or "Communist." These symbols of radicalism have highly negative effect among the great masses in the United States as well as among the employers.[4] The rejection of them has been emphatic and persistent by a general public, which has long been conditioned by a conservative press and by an educational system which raises few questions about sanctity of the status quo. The Socialist and the Communist vote in the "Black Belt" of Chicago was practically non-existent prior to 1930.

The hostility which the Negroes displayed toward Marxian symbols was not the result of the fact that they failed to fit into the category of the exploited. A rough classification of the census data on occupations shows clearly that the Negroes in the city were more proletarian than the whites and that there were relatively fewer colored persons in occupations which tend to be capitalistic in their outlook.[5] According to the theory of the

[3] Cited by A. L. Harris and S. Spero in "Negro Problem," *Encyclopaedia of the Social Sciences*, XI, 348.

[4] H. Hart, "Changing Social Attitudes and Interests," in President's Research Committee on Social Trends, *Recent Social Trends* (New York, 1933), I, 429.

[5] The data for those gainfully employed in Chicago by color were classified according to Bukharin's categories. See Nikolai Bukharin, *Historical Materialism, A System of Sociology*, translated from Russian (New York, 1925), p. 276. This classification is applied to occupational statistics for the United States as a whole by A. N. Holcombe in his *The New Party Politics* (New York, 1933). Lack of space prevents the presentation of the tables which were compiled.

class struggle, the Negroes should have been a fertile field for Marxian propaganda.

The economic depression which started in 1929 greatly increased the insecurity of the Negroes in Chicago. According to the 1931 Unemployment Census there were no areas in the city which were harder hit than the sections inhabited largely by colored people. In one section of the Second Ward over 85 per cent of the persons ten years of age and over who had been gainfully employed in 1930 were unemployed a year later.[6] The relief agencies were not equipped or properly financed to meet the situation. Many colored persons faced the prospect of a cold winter without food, shelter, and proper clothing. Bank failures in the Negro Community were more complete and devastating than in other sections of the city and this meant that some of the middle-class Negroes who had raised their economic status at great personal sacrifices also became poverty-stricken. It was estimated that the Negroes constituted one-fourth of all the relief cases in the city. When the relief agencies ceased to pay rents there were many evictions, and when the funds of the United Charities ran low the allowances for food were drastically cut. Here were conditions which changed the prospects of economic radicalism. When a man is unemployed, he can risk listening to a Communist agitator. Even the conservative *Whip* recognized the seriousness of the situation:

The rottenness, the injustice, the grim brutality and cold unconcern of our present system has become too irksome to the man farthest down to be longer endured in silence and pacifism. It is high time that those who would stem a revolution busied themselves in sweeping and lasting cures to the cancerous sores which fester upon our body politic and fiercely competitive society. The Communists have framed a program of social remedies which cannot fail to appeal to the hungering, jobless millions, who live in barren want, while everywhere about them is evidence of restricted plenty in the greedy hands of the few. Safety and security, peace and plenty are the things most dear to the hearts of the inarticulate lowly, and these are the things which the radicals hold out as bait to the masses, white as well as black. To argue that they cannot give them but begs the question, for the obvious

[6] Census tracts, 535–38. The average for 147 districts covering the entire city except the Negro communities was 28 per cent.

answer is that our present systems HAVE not given them, and offer no promise of them.

If our two major parties would stem this rising tide of Communism, let
them take steps to provide for such immediate needs as are virtually hurling
the masses into the ranks of radicalism. Food, shelter and clothing, adequate
employment are the only answer to the challenge of communism, not mere
word of mouth denials. The demand among both black and white alike is
insisting for improvement—or change.[7]

The Socialist party of the United States made no concerted
effort to capitalize the discontent found among the Negroes as a
result of the relatively greater impact of the economic crisis
upon them. There were no Negro socialists in Chicago who
arose as leaders of the unemployed masses.[8] While the white
socialists made some verbal declarations of friendship toward
the colored citizens they did not follow up their words with
deeds. The national Socialist platform of 1932 merely said on
the race question: "The enforcement of constitutional guar-
antees of economic, political, and legal equality for the Negro.
The enactment and enforcement of drastic anti-lynching laws."
It did not mention the hardships of Negroes in the North, nor
did it appeal specifically to the white and black workers to get
together. In other words, it preached equality but it did not
state how this equality was to be secured. The nationally known
Negro socialist orator, Frank Crosswaith, came to Chicago from
time to time on his tours out of New York and presented the
case of the Socialist party to colored audiences, but there was
no person like him in Chicago who could keep hammering away
steadily on the Socialist objectives.

In contrast to the Socialist party, the Communist party has
worked out a distinct racial policy. One of the slogans of the
Russian revolution of 1917 was: "Peace without Annexations
and Idemnities, and on the Principle of the Right of Peoples

[7] *Chicago Whip*, August 1, 1931.

[8] Two Negroes took an active part in the work of the Chicago Workers' Committee
on Unemployment, the leaders of which were largely but not exclusively persons of
socialist leanings. This Committee on Unemployment was started a year after the
Communist Unemployed Councils. See R. E. Asher, *The Influence of the Chicago
Workers' Committee upon the Administration of Unemployment Relief* (University of
Chicago A.M. Thesis).

to Self-determination." When the Soviet system was set up the Communist leaders took great care to recognize the racial minorities which had been oppressed under the Tsarist régime. The Communist parties throughout the world have followed opportunistic policies, but since 1921 the Third International has emphasized the "united front" tactics which consist in putting forth concrete demands and slogans growing out of the everyday economic or political life of the country concerned. All workers, regardless of color, sex, or age, are then called upon to unite for the securing of these demands. The Sixth World Congress of the Third International, which was held in 1928, definitely recognized the Negro movement in the United States as an important link in its program of world-revolution. The Communists in the United States were to work for "self-determination in the black belt," a course of action which involved the setting-up of a Negro republic in the southern states composed of several hundred contiguous counties in which the colored people were in a majority. While this program was attacked as fantastic and unsuited to American conditions, and while it failed to meet the problems of the Negroes in the North, it nevertheless showed a willingness on the part of Communists to consider the special problems of the American Negroes.

The world-wide economic crisis which started in 1929 afforded the Communist party in the United States some special opportunities. Poverty, misery, hopelessness, insecurity, hunger, and exposure furnish a fertile soil for revolutionary doctrines. The Communist agitators proclaimed that the depression had come to stay and that the capitalistic collapse which Karl Marx had prophesied was on its way. A renewed drive was made upon the racial minorities in the United States. In accordance with tactics of the united front, the Communist leaders, white and black, looked around for some incident which would dramatize race discrimination in the United States. In 1931 an Alabama court furnished the now famous Scottsboro case, which was seized upon by the Communists and made the basis for a nation-wide agitation. Nine Negro boys who had been stealing a ride on a freight train were charged with raping two white girls who were found on the same train. Although the evidence was extremely flimsy, eight of the boys were sentenced to death by a hostile jury of white men. The International Labor Defense, a Communist affiliate, carried the case to the United States Supreme Court and secured a reversal in 1932 on the ground that the defendants were not permitted to have adequate counsel.[9] The cases were retried and for several years furnished an opening wedge to reach the Negro masses in the United States.

The 1932 presidential election offered another occasion on which the Communists could make a special appeal to Negroes. For a second time in the history of the United States a Negro was nominated for the vice-presidency. A leading American Communist has described the Chicago convention which took this bold step in the following words: "Fifteen thousand men and women waving red banners, singing, cheering. Brass bands, slogans, color, excitement, earthquake, sunrise, hope. Foster has just been nominated for President; Ford, for vice-president of these United States."[10] James Ford was a native of Georgia, where his father was a tenant farmer and where his grandfather had been lynched by a white mob because of a dispute over the ownership of a pig. The family moved to Alabama, where both father and son worked for the Tennessee Coal Company. After working his way through for three years at Fisk University, James Ford joined the army in 1917. After being denied admission into the United States army radio school because of his color, he entered the radio school of the French army and served at the front with distinction. When he left the army, he came to Chicago and entered the postal service, where he was active in the Postal Workers Union. In 1926 he joined the Communist party and rose rapidly because of his militant fight against segregation and his energy as a trade-union organizer.[11] Ford personified the grievances of the Negroes in the United States—lynching, the cropping system, discrimination, exploitation in southern industries, limited vocational opportunities in the North, and lack of recognition.

[9] *Powell* vs. *Alabama*, 287, U.S. 45 (1932).

[10] Michael Gold in the *Daily Worker*, June 1, 1932.

[11] *Chicago Whip*, May 7, 1932. See also *Chicago Daily News*, April 14, 1932.

COMMUNIST ACTIVITIES IN CHICAGO

In accordance with the international program of the party, the Communists in Chicago tried to apply the formula of the united front. Local as well as national incidents were seized upon to furnish the basis for concrete demands. When occasions presented themselves, the Communist leaders also tried what were called activist tactics, i.e., they backed up their words with deeds and showed an unexpected fearlessness toward the existing authorities and persons in positions of power. Each one of these occasions, some of which culminated in violence, was utilized to spread Communist ideas. All the available media were employed to disseminate the principles of the movement. The literature of the party was widely circulated, frequent meetings were held, elaborate demonstrations were staged, interracial dances were frequent, and strikes among Negro and white workers were fostered. To carry out this elaborate program the Communists created a large number of subsidiary organizations like the Unemployed Councils, the League of Struggle for Negro Rights, the United Front Scottsboro Defense, the Young Communist League, the Pioneers, and the Trade Union Unity League. While all of these organizations were not officially affiliated with the Communist party, they were controlled by party members. The party proper was composed of shop nuclei and of street units of at least three members each.

As early as 1924 Communist organizers had circulated throughout the Negro sections of Chicago issues of the *Daily Worker*, the central organ of the movement in the United States. They called attention to the articles denouncing the "firetrap" schools for Negro workers' children, the "vile Klan film" called the "Birth of a Nation," which the city permitted to be shown, the "railroading" of friendless Negroes to the gallows, and other alleged incidents of discrimination and mistreatment.[12] Street meetings were held during the warm months and continuous efforts were made to attract young Negroes to the movement. In order to show that the party was interested in the practical problems which confronted the community, a

[12] *Daily Worker*, January 24, 29, 30, 31; February 1, 6, 7, 9, 14, 18, 19; April 19, 1924.

Negro Tenants' Protective League of Chicago was formed to protest against the high rents and the lack of adequate housing for Negroes.[13] After circulating quantities of propaganda which showed that prominent Negro leaders were endorsing the idea, a meeting was held at one of the fraternal halls at which a white Communist agitator, Robert Minor, and a Negro journalist, Lovett Fort-Whiteman, made speeches denouncing the white and colored landlords, including Oscar DePriest. The League did not engage in any activities except the holding of meetings, the passing of resolutions, the signing of petitions, and the spreading of the gospel of the party.

In 1925 Lovett Fort-Whiteman and another Negro Communist were active in calling an American Negro Labor Congress in Chicago, which was made up of representatives from Negro labor unions, Negro farmers' organizations, and other Negro societies. With reference to the purpose of this Congress, Fort-Whiteman said in an interview with a correspondent of the *New York World:* "The fundamental aim of the Negro Labor Congress is to organize the industrial strength of the Negro as a fighting weapon. The Negro is essentially a worker-proletariat, as we would call it, suffering all the abuses of the working class in general, but in addition to that, racial discrimination and other racial oppression."[14] The comment of the *Chicago Tribune* on this Congress was: "Behind the conference is a plot of Red Russia to spread Communism among the colored people of the entire world. No attempt is made to hide the fact that it was financed and directed from Moscow, and that the aim was to stir up hatreds and disorder in the United States."[15] The definite accomplishments of the Congress were small, but the Communists looked upon it as the beginning of a movement which had far-reaching implications.

During the next four years there were no outstanding attempts made by the Communists to organize the Negroes in Chicago. At the celebration of the tenth anniversary of the

[13] *Ibid.,* March 1, 1924.

[14] *Literary Digest,* LXXXVII (November 21, 1925), 16.

[15] *Ibid.,* p. 15.

Russian revolution of 1917 an appeal was made to Negroes to join the Workers' Communist party. A contemporary account of the meeting in a Chicago bourgeois paper states that there was a sprinkling of Negroes in the audience and that pamphlets were distributed which declared that Negroes of America would never enjoy racial freedom until a soviet government was set up in the United States.[16] Meetings and interracial dances were held in the Chicago "Black Belt" from time to time, but no special preparations were made for the increased emphasis placed upon the Negro problem by the 1928 Congress of the Third International and for the impending economic crisis. According to one account there were thirty-five Negroes in the Workers' party in 1926 but only four or five Negro Communist party members in 1929 in the Chicago district.[17]

When the specter of misery resulting from unemployment, bank failures, and uncertain relief appeared in unmistakable outlines in the Negro community at the beginning of 1930, the Communists redoubled their efforts to attract the Negro masses. House-to-house canvasses, literature distribution campaigns, street-corner conversations, mass meetings, and demonstrations were conducted in order to reach the unemployed and those who were not sure of their jobs. At the end of two months of intensive work the claim was made that over a hundred new Negro Communist party members had been recruited in the city.[18] An unemployment demonstration in February, which culminated in a march on the city hall by white and black unemployed men, resulted in a mild clash with the police, but no one was seriously injured. The Industrial Squad of the Police Department (popularly called the "Red Squad") raided the meetings and headquarters of the party and its affiliates, but this application of force failed to prevent the holding of new meetings, many of which were organized to protest against the police brutality. The increased number of lynchings in various parts of the United States furnished additional ammunition for the

[16] *Chicago Tribune*, November 7, 1927.

[17] Edith Margo, "The South Side Sees Red," *Left Front*, June 1933, p. 3.

[18] *Daily Worker*, March 10, 1930.

Communist agitators. In the summer months huge open-air meetings were held in the northwest corner of Washington Park, where the unemployed, the curious, the homeless, and the militant were accustomed to congregate in order to exercise those basic rights of freedom of speech and assemblage which have been commonly associated with the American form of government.[19]

As the economic crisis deepened in 1931, the intensity of the Communist activity increased. The local party leaders were quick to recognize the possibilities of the Scottsboro case for their purposes. During the first three months which followed the famous trial over fourteen meetings were held in various parts of the Negro community under the auspices of such organizations as the League of Struggle for Negro Rights, the International Labor Defense, the Young Liberators of Chicago, and the United Front Scottsboro Defense. The last-mentioned organization enabled the Communists for the first time to get a hearing before Negro church congregations, Negro clubs, and trade unions. The colored ministers were afraid not to co-operate with a movement which aroused such deep-seated emotions among their followers. When some of the colored leaders at a meeting of the National Association for the Advancement of Colored People ventured to criticize the motives of the International Labor Defense, they were greeted with cries of "liar," "turncoat," "big faker," and "bully."[20] The disturbance was caused by some of the Communist agitators, but it had sufficient support to break up the meeting. The success of the Communists in seizing the leadership of the Scottsboro case defense furnished a basis for prolonged agitation among the Negroes.

In the summer of 1931 an incident occurred in Chicago which furnished an excellent local foundation for united front tactics in the Negro community. In order to understand the background of this event it is necessary to go back to the formation

[19] One of the local judges kept the South Park Police from breaking up these meetings.

[20] *Chicago Defender*, June 20, 1931; *Chicago Whip*, June 20, 1931.

of the Unemployed Councils in the fall of 1930 and to the policy of the relief organizations regarding the payment of rent. The Communists started a number of Unemployed Council branches in the Negro district with little difficulty because of the relatively greater amount of unemployment which they found there. At first these councils merely held demonstrations and meetings to protest against unemployment, but soon they began to concern themselves with the immediate problems of their neighborhoods. When the funds of the relief organizations began to run low, the policy was started of not paying rent. The result was a great increase in the number of evictions, particularly in the Negro community.[21] It was customary for a group of unemployed men to gather at the headquarters of the Unemployed Council and discuss conditions. At these informal assemblages the smoldering fires of resentment were nourished in such a way as to furnish the basis for militant group resistance and direct action. When the news of some eviction reached the group, the leaders would start out with the determination to put the evicted persons back in their homes. Here was open defiance of the court authorities, and there were many possibilities of friction with the police. Hundreds of evicted Negroes were restored to their homes by crowds which were led by members of the Unemployed Councils. Below is a description of these activities that appeared in one of the Negro bourgeois papers:

"REDS" RESTORE FAMILIES EVICTED BY LANDLORDS

Declaring their determination to defend the jobless and hungry families which abound on the south side, from eviction by landlords because of their inability to pay rent, a group of young colored radicals, affiliated with the Communist Party and operating under the title of the Unemployed Relief Council, restored seven jobless families in the community after they had been evicted by the bailiff's office and their belongings set out in the street.

The first of these cases occurred Wednesday when more than fifty of the group, most of them young men who are themselves sleeping in the Park, restored the belongings of Mrs. Katie Williams, a poverty-stricken widow with two small children, to the house at 734 East 45th Street, after she had been evicted by bailiffs at the order of her landlord. The woman, who had been out

---

[21] In the period from August 11 to October 31, 1931, there were 2,185 cases before the Renter's Court, 831, or 38 per cent of which were Negro cases.

of work since December, is five months behind in her rent, and had no place to go when she was moved by the officers. A short while after her furniture had been set on the sidewalk, a young radical appeared, and breaking the new lock on the front door, returned her furniture piece by piece, and ordered her to return to the house.[22]

The climax of the activities of the Unemployed Councils in eviction cases was reached on August 3, 1931, when a riot occurred at which three Negroes were killed by the police, three policemen were injured, and several bystanders were wounded. As in the case of many other evictions, a large number of persons started out to restore the furniture to the home. The crowd may have been a little larger on this occasion because the scene of the eviction was fairly close to the Washington Park forum. The first squad of police to appear on the scene arrested the men who seemed to be the ringleaders and left to secure reinforcements. The evidence is conflicting as to what happened next. The policemen who fired the fatal shots claimed that they acted in self-defense and that the Communist leaders were armed with guns.[23] At the coroner's inquest eye-witnesses testified that the Negro victims were not armed and were not resisting arrest.[24] It is indisputable that three policemen were badly injured, but it is not clear as to whether they were attacked before or after the shooting. We are primarily interested in the use made of this incident by the Communists in spreading their views. The event was referred to as the "Chicago massacre" and it furnished the basis for mammoth meetings and demonstrations. The *Daily Worker* issued the following plea: "The barbarous murder of our 3 class comrades by the Chicago bosses, Negro and white, must be answered by the sternest pledge of revolutionary solidarity and fighting strength; by the mobilization of large masses of Negro and white workers who must take the streets in tremendous solidarity demonstrations.[25]

The immediate result of the riot was the temporary suspension of evictions and a careful consideration of the available

[22] *Chicago Whip*, July 25, 1931.   [23] *Chicago Tribune*, August, 4, 1931.

[24] *Chicago Whip*, October 24, 1931; *International Labor Defense News Release*, August 4, 5, 7, 1931.

[25] *Daily Worker*, August 6, 1931.

sources for additional relief funds. This the Communists regarded as a great victory, as is shown by the following comment
made by a Communist speaker at an enormous open-air meeting
in Washington Park:

> For the past ten weeks we have been fighting for just this thing, but not
> until this violent clash occurred have the city and county officials taken proper
> notice of the suffering caused among jobless families by landlords who put
> them out into the streets because they cannot pay their rent through no fault
> of their own. With the suspension of eviction orders, hundreds of poverty
> stricken families, white and black, in all parts of the city are now relieved of
> the spectre of being heartlessly shoved out into the streets.[26]

For two of the victims, Abe Gray and John O'Neal, the Communists staged a mass funeral which attracted crowds which
were said to be from twelve to fifteen thousand strong.[27]   The
funeral was an occasion at which thousands of Communist
leaflets were distributed and at which the Communist flags,
emblems, and symbols were displayed.

The riot did not stop evictions nor did it stop the Unemployed
Councils in their efforts to block evictions. When the situation
became less tense, the bailiff's office began to serve writs again.
However, the police were more cautious in their handling of
crowds and more ruthless in their attacks upon the headquarters
of the Unemployed Councils and upon persons who were suspected of being Communists. As late as May, 1933, the League
of Struggle for Negro Rights was instrumental in stopping evictions by moving furniture back into homes.[28]

Another one of the activities of the Unemployed Councils in
the Negro district was the staging of demonstrations in front of
the relief stations. These mass protests were held when complaints came to the attention of the councils regarding the slow-
ness, the insufficiency, or the lack of relief. At some of the relief
centers the representatives of the Unemployed Council would
present the demands of their clients in a very vigorous fashion
and claim the credit for whatever action was taken. In January,
1932, attention was called to this type of activity on the part

[26] *Chicago Daily News*, August 4, 1931.

[27] *Ibid.*, August 8, 1931.   [28] *Daily Worker*, May 31, 1933.

of the Communists by a riot which occurred in front of a relief
station located in the center of the Negro community. In spite
of the presence of some thirty-five policemen in front of the
relief center, a crowd gathered to protest a proposed cut in
relief. A soap-box orator urged the crowd to storm the building
and to strike the superintendent who had treated an applicant
for relief in a rough manner. Among the ringleaders of the
crowd were two white Communist agitators who were later
arrested by the police. When the crowd crashed an entrance
to the building, the policemen were met with a bombardment
of bricks, milk bottles, and stones. Three policemen, a girl, and
a number of others were injured before order was restored.[29]
The police arrested forty-one persons and then wreaked their
vengeance upon the headquarters of the Unemployed Council
which was near by. The temper of the Negro community is
clearly shown by willingness of many who were in the direst
straits to follow the leadership of those who advocated a show
of resistance.

Among the employed Negro workers the activities of the
Communists were concentrated upon the formation of trade
unions affiliated with the Trade Union Unity League. District
conferences were held by the League and attempts were made
to establish contacts in the meat-packing, electrical, steel, and
other industries. The aim of the Communists was to establish
trade unions of their own and at the same time to organize
"revolutionary opposition within the American Federation of
Labor unions." In carrying on this work the Communists organized demonstrations against wage cuts and planned a number of strikes.

Because the meat-packing industry was looked upon as a key
industry the Communists made a special effort to organize what
they called a Packing House Industrial Union. In accordance
with the Communist ideology, the organizers appealed to white
and colored workers to unite in their struggle against the hated
"bosses." When the packing houses announced a wage cut in
April, 1932, the Communist union and the Stockyards Un-

[29] *Chicago Tribune*, January 12, 1932.

employed Council held mass meetings and distributed leaflets
calling for a huge demonstration to protest against the pending
wage cut. The demonstration took the form of a parade which
ended at the stockyards gates where a meeting was held and a
committee presented a series of demands to the companies.[30] The
Communists claimed that they held up the wage cuts for a
period of two months but at the end of that time their protests
were ineffective in preventing the wage reductions.

The weakness of the trade-union work of the Communists in
the meat-packing industry was revealed by the stockyards
strike of 1933. A strike of the live-stock handlers was organized
by unions affiliated with the American Federation of Labor
which were dissatisfied with the working of the labor provisions
of the Blanket Code which was worked out in July by the
National Recovery Administration. The Communist union
issued leaflets calling upon the workers in the stockyards to
spread the strike to all stockyard workers. In this the Communists were unsuccessful. A caustic criticism of the failure of
the party to function in this situation appeared in the *Daily
Worker* for December 4, 1933:

> First and foremost there stands out the isolation of our Party from the
> main body of the workers in Chicago. The strike took our Party by surprise.
> We have in the city of Chicago a membership of 2,500 in the Party, but yet
> such an important struggle could develop without our Party in any way being
> prepared for it. That this is so can be seen from the participation of the Chi-
> cago comrades in the National Packing House Conference and the meeting
> of the District Bureau immediately following it. This results from the follow-
> ing facts: The Party is not yet composed of the decisive sections of the Chi-
> cago proletariat, it has not yet drawn the membership into the trade unions
> (only 20 to 25 per cent are in unions and these are in the lighter industries);
> the leadership is not sufficiently a driving force for trade union work and the
> Party although recognizing the growing radicalization of the workers in resolu-
> tions does not draw the proper conclusions from this growing radicalization
> of the workers especially in the basic industries which include large sections
> of Negro workers. . . . .
> Without doubt the situation revealed in the stockyard strike is charac-
> teristic of the whole trade union work in the District. The slight progress
> made recently in the trade union work has been limited almost entirely to a

[30] *Daily Worker*, April 12, 1932.

few of the lighter industries both as far as the T.U.U.L. unions are concerned, as well as to the work in the A.F.L. We remain isolated and have made no progress among the basic sections of the unorganized and the more important industries among the workers organized in the A.F.L. unions. The leadership does not steer a decisive course in the trade union work and only a small section of the Party is taken up with trade union work.

As the foregoing article indicates the Communists have achieved their greatest successes in the lighter industries in Chicago. The outstanding event of their labor activities during the first four years of the economic depression was the strike maneuvered by the Needle Trade Workers Industrial union in the six apron and house dress shops owned by B. Sopkins. The wages paid in these shops were literally starvation wages and many of the employees received supplementary aid from the relief agencies. All work in the shops was on a piece-rate basis and the average earnings of the colored women employed ranged from two to six dollars a week. The Communists obtained the nucleus of an organization in these shops and started an agitation for a strike in June, 1933.[31] The preliminary work of organization for the strike was carried on entirely by word of mouth under the leadership of a woman organizer who understood factory conditions and who had been trained in a workers' school. Sopkins knew of some of the meetings but he did not take them seriously. The conditions in the shop were obviously contrary to the spirit of the "New Deal," which President Roosevelt was just introducing into industry, and consequently it was possible to make the stoppage of work quite complete. The Sopkins shops were successfully picketed in spite of the fact that the police brutally clubbed some women, and it was apparent to South Siders that it was wise to do something about the situation even before the national textile codes went into effect. Several conferences were held at which representatives of the union, the Urban League, the company, and city labor arbitrators were present. Congressman DePriest also took a hand in the settlement of the strike. It was urged by the labor arbitrators that a compromise settlement should be accepted

[31] *Chicago Defender*, June 24, 1933.

and the strike ended on the ground that the national textile code would soon go into effect. The Communists wished to hold off in order to secure recognition of the union, but in this purpose they were thwarted at the last minute by Congressman DePriest. Their anger at him knew no bounds, but they were realistic enough to see that further resistance would have been futile upon their part. The comment of the bourgeois Negro press upon this strike reveals a change in attitude toward Communist activities as compared with the early days of the economic crisis.

The attempt of certain leaders to handle the sweatshop case of the Bernard Sopkin & Sons factory without first studying the cause and effect resulted in a debacle for all parties concerned. Both employee and employer must realize that a new day has arrived. Mr. Sopkin represents an age and an idea that is rapidly fading, and a new conception of industrial ideals is taking form.

Institutions that pay women starvation wages are contributors to prostitution and vice. They are enemies to society and to law and order. These women are entitled to just compensation for their services. This is not a political football, it is an industrial question. They don't need speeches, they need a sound and constructive program worked out whereby their pay will be raised in proportion to the work they do.

It is not the duty of the police to settle strikes; they are to preserve law and order. Many of them seem to think they are to take sides with sweatshop keepers. At the time those women were assaulted by the police they were only peacefully walking the streets. There is no crime in peacefully walking on the street, yet these women were brutally clubbed by the police.

The police are attempting to smoke-screen the issue by calling these women Communists. Suppose they are! Take some of these same policemen off of the pay roll for six months and they will be Communists too. This nation is dedicated to the principle of free speech, and it is not up to the police to change the Constitution.[32]

From the standpoint of the workers, the Communists could claim that the strike in the Sopkins shops was a success. The wages, rates of some 1,600 women workers in the shops, were raised 17 per cent and improvements were made in some of the working conditions. A partial victory was won, but on the crucial point of the recognition of the union the Communists

---

[32] *Chicago Defender*, July 1, 1933. After the strike was settled with an increase in wages, some favorable articles on the Sopkins factories appeared in the columns of this paper.

had to admit defeat. In commenting upon "Mistakes in the Sopkins Strike," the *Workers Voice* said:

> The outstanding weakness in the Sopkins Dress strike is that the Party and the Young Communist League were not built sufficiently. Only a handful of workers were recruited in the Party and YCL and only so far one shop nucleus of the Young Communist League has been organized. This in spite of the fact that there are large numbers of Negro women who are ready for the Party and about 30 of them filled out application cards to join the Party.
> . . . . The task confronting the Party is to consolidate organizationally in the shops, Needle Trades Industrial Union: by building shop nuclei of the Communist Party and the Young Communist League.[33]

Encouraged by the results in the Sopkins strike, the Communists endeavored to foment strikes in other industries employing white and colored workers at very low wages. In August, 1933, fifty-three women workers in the Stetson China Company and some two hundred and fifty women nut pickers in the National Pecan Products Company went on strike.[34] These strikes did not end as successfully as the dress-shop strike, but they furnished material for continued Communist agitation.

The various Communist activities in the Chicago "Black Belt" were designed to win as many new party members as possible. The Unemployed Councils, the International Labor Defense, the trade unions, and the Young Communist League were all ultimately interested in converting people to the program of the party. It is probable that around five hundred Negroes joined the party during the period of the intensive drive.[35]

COMMUNIST SYMBOLISM AMONG THE NEGROES

The Negroes in Chicago could see and appreciate many of the Communist activities, but it was quite a different problem to bring them to react favorably to the symbolism of the Communist movement. While they hailed with joy the restoration

---

[33] August 15, 1933. In an interview with one of the organizers of the strike, it was brought out that the Sopkins shops were hit hard by the textile code brought in by NRA. However, in order to get around the minimum wage scales Sopkins organized an apprentice shop which was made up in fact of old workers.

[34] *Daily Worker*, August 7, 14, 1933.   [35] *Ibid.*, February 18, 1932.

of evicted families, the defense of the Scottsboro boys, and the successful dress-shop strike, they still had feelings of distrust and uncertainty toward such symbols as the red flag, the internationale, the revolution, the dictatorship of the proletariat, the Soviets, Lenin, Stalin, and the Third International. These symbols were not directly related to Negro experience, and if they were to become potent factors in guiding Negro action it was necessary that they be associated with aims and ideals of the Negro world.

In trying to introduce their master symbols into the Negro community the Communists were confronted with a number of serious obstacles. During the days of slavery the symbolism of Protestant Christianity became firmly rooted in the folk culture of the American Negroes. These symbols furnished an important escape or release for the sufferings, humiliation, and restraints which were the common lot of most Negroes. After the Civil War these symbols continued to play an important rôle in Negro life because the actual economic and social emancipation of the Negroes fell far short of their idealistic longings. The doctrines of Christianity have been and still are powerful stabilizers of Negro life. In slavery times and since the masses of Negroes have interpreted the Bible to mean that they should suffer their economic and social woes of this life in silence and to look to a better world hereafter. Their experience in their struggle to gain an education and an opportunity to work has led them to rely on the bourgeoisie rather than the proletariat.

In conformance with the international policies of the movement, the Communists who were working among the Negroes in Chicago felt that it was necessary for them to attack the religiosity of the masses. The open-air meetings would very frequently be devoted to the making of jibes at the Negro ministers and at slavishness of the Christian bigots. One speaker in the Washington Park forum said: "If heaven is such a fine place, why didn't the people who thought so go there? If the Bible was such a fine book, why were there so many vile pages in it?"[36] In an interview one of the Negro Communist leaders

[36] Report of political meeting, August 5, 1931.

explained that the majority of Negroes they dealt with were very religious and they didn't make a broad-sided attack on religion. The Negroes didn't know that religion was just a drug, an opiate. He organized them on the basis of the economic struggle and he felt that in the struggle the worker would see the part the capitalistic church played.[37] The Communist daily showed how the party used old familiar religious tunes to direct the intense longings of the Negroes.

On the south side the old slavish spirituals are being rewritten by a new race. The deep yearning that once turned to a mythical heaven for freedom now fights for a real and wonderful future on this earth.

"THAT NEW COMMUNIST SPIRIT"

"Gimme That Old Time Religion, it's good enough for me," they used to sing at their prayer meetings. Now I heard them sing it fervently:

"Gimme that new Communist spirit,
(two repeats),
It's good enough for me.
It was good for Comrade Lenin,
(two repeats),
and it's good enough for me.
(And so on—dozens of verses.)

Many such new songs and singers. At mass meetings their religious past becomes transmitted into a Communist present. They follow every word of the speaker with real emotion; they encourage him, as at a prayer meeting, with cries of "Yes, yes, comrade," and often there is an involuntary and heartfelt "Amen!"[38]

The Communists also had to combat the symbolism of the ethnocentric movements among the Negroes. Important among these was the Garvey "Back-to-Africa Movement" which reached its peak in the early twenties but continued to attract Negroes after the exile of its leader.[39] The Garvey movement, with its gorgeous uniforms, regalia, decorations, insignia, court etiquette, African Legion, and Black Cross nurses made an extraordinary appeal to the American Negroes. Garvey created the vision of a utopia which was particularly attractive to dark-skinned Negroes. The first Communist meetings which were

[37] Interview, February 9, 1934. [38] *Daily Worker*, September 30, 1932.
[39] J. W. Johnson, *Black Manhattan* (New York, 1930), pp. 251–59.

held in Chicago hit at the Back-to-Africa Movement. At one
of these a Negro speaker brought with him a large map of the
African continent which he put to good use in trying to explode
the Garvey Back-to-Africa panacea. He explained that all
workers must unite since the problems and interests of the
Negro workers were identical with those of white workers.[40] In
a series of articles on Negro Communists in Chicago, Michael
Gold stressed the fact that many of them had deserted the
Garvey movement for the Communist party.[41]

Bourgeois symbolism also had a firm hold upon the imagination of nearly all of the Chicago Negroes. The most successful
colored political leaders of the traditional parties were those
who had achieved some pecuniary independence. Outstanding
among them was Congressman DePriest, who symbolized the
political and economic ambitions of Negroes not only in Chicago but generally throughout the United States. He was
"Congressman" DePriest, wealthy real estate owner, the fearless fighter for Negro rights who had achieved some economic
independence and who could talk to the white political leaders
in their own language. He could bring home the bacon from
the white politicians. The Communist leaders saw that
DePriest must be discredited at all costs. He was pictured as
the "Negro misleader," the "millionaire landlord who evicted
his hunger-stricken tenants," "the traitor to the Negro people."[42]
Derogatory references were made to his speech in Congress
against unemployment insurance, his "Uncle Tom" record in
Congress, and his support of "Jim Crow" legislation.[43] One of
the most bitter attacks was delivered upon him immediately
following the Sopkins fight during which his intervention
blocked the efforts of the Communist trade union to secure
recognition.

    . . . . Further, it is of tremendous importance to concentrate to attack the
betrayal of the Negro masses by Oscar DePriest, whose rôle as an arch enemy
of the Negro people and lackey of the white ruling class is known. During the
August days of 1931, when the three Negro workers were killed on the south

---

[40] *Daily Worker*, October 15, 1924.   [42] *Ibid.*, June 1, 1932.

[41] *Ibid.*, October 1, 3, 1932.   [43] *Ibid.*, July 14, 1932.

side of Chicago in the eviction struggles, DePriest was behind it. DePriest is behind terror that rages against the Negro masses on the south side of Chicago and now he openly robbed the Negro women of their victories in the Sopkins Dress. He stabbed Negro women in the back.[44]

It was not sufficient for the Communists to attack the symbols that had been significant and meaningful to the Negroes. It was their task to substitute for these symbols the Communist slogans, catch-words, emblems, and insignia. The Communist orators and journalists searched for phrases which would have a powerful appeal to the Negroes during the economic crisis. They had to show the Negroes that there was a place for them in the Communist utopia. In place of the uncertainty, want, and deprivation of the capitalistic régime their program called for unemployment and social insurance at the expense of the state and employers, a wide united front struggle in every locality, in every street and block, of employed and unemployed workers for relief and against wage cuts. In the hunger march on the state capitol which was called in April, 1933, the demands made to the Governor included "cash relief" to all unemployed workers, moratorium on the debts and taxes of all small-home owners, unemployment insurance, withdrawal of the troops from the coal fields, and no discrimination against Negroes."[45] In a local hunger march the demands included "better housing," immediate resumption of work on Wendell Phillips school, clean streets and new lights for the Negro neighborhoods, the immediate abolition of police terror, right of Negro workers to all jobs—municipal, civil service, construction, and on public utilities—the right to live in all neighborhoods, prohibition of the dumping of the worst qualities of meat and vegetables in the Negro neighborhoods, no foreclosures for taxes or mortgages on the property of Negro small-home owners, and a resolution of the city council demanding the release and safe conduct of the nine innocent Scottsboro boys.[46] All of these symbols of demand were closely related to the needs and yearnings of the Negroes in Chicago.

[44] *Workers Voice*, August 15, 1933. See also *Daily Worker*, July 4, 1933.

[45] *Daily Worker*, April 4, 1933.   [46] *Ibid.*, April 13, 1933.

On the race issue the Communists went the whole length in recognizing the demands of the Negro. "Complete equality" in all matters, economic and social, was the slogan of the Communists.[47] Whenever any sign of race prejudice ("white chauvinism") appeared among persons in any way connected or affiliated with the Communist movement it was stamped out immediately. When a white party member slapped the face of a Negro member in an argument about the circulation of leaflets, he was tried before a jury of one hundred and fifty workers, suspended from the party for two months, and pledged to action in behalf of the struggle for Negro rights.[48] The bourgeois Negro press recognized that the Communist party took the most advanced stand of all groups on the question of interracial relations. In commenting on a trial of a Communist for "white chauvinism" in Milwaukee, the *Chicago Defender* said:

WHY WE CAN'T HATE "REDS"

And the cause for which he was expelled was that he had made some uncomplimentary remarks about workers of the Race. He didn't call us criminals, thugs or rapists. . . . . He said merely that we are "dumb, cowardly and can't be organized." And for those words, things which we have said about each other numbers of time, he was expelled from the organization to which he belonged and for which he had a high regard.

But a white man made that statement, and for it he was penalized. How, under such circumstances, can we go to war with the Communist Party? Is there any other political, religious or civic organization in the country that would go to such lengths to prove itself not unfriendly to us? Is there any other group in the country that would not applaud the sentiments as expressed by the man who was ousted in this instance?

We may not agree with the entire program of the Communist party, but there is one item with which we do agree wholeheartedly and that is the zealousness with which it guards the rights of the Race.[49]

The ultimate goal of the Communist party in the United States is revolution brought on by the masses and resulting in the establishment of a dictatorship of the proletariat. On every possible occasion the Negroes were reminded that they had rev-

[47] William Z. Foster, head of the Communist party in the United States, in his testimony before the Fish Committee. Cited in the *Chicago Bee*, February 8, 1931.

[48] *Daily Worker*, March 14, 1933.   [49] January 14, 1933.

olutionary traditions. On the one hundredth anniversary of the death of Nat Turner the Communists held a big rally in an old church in order to extol the heroism of the man who was looked upon as a martyr. "The capitalists and their historians," said one Communist orator at the meeting, "have tried to establish the fact that Negroes have always been docile and subservient. The life of Nat Turner and many others proves this is a lie. We must be like him. We must struggle, fight, and even die. But we must not be slaves."[50] Another speaker said: "Nat Turner would not stand for the oppression of his people, and revolted. Now today we need a revolution just as badly. The Nat Turner spirit has not died but is alive today in the hearts of the Young Communists, and when the time comes we will fight and die just as he did." The modern Chicago Negro martyrs were the men who were killed in the eviction riot of August, 1931. At the funeral of these men placards were displayed carrying the slogans: "*They Died for Us! We Must Keep Fighting! Fight Against Lynching. Equal Rights for Negroes.*" Red flags were conspicuous in the parade and the Young Communists appeared in their red shirts. Judging from the size of the crowd which watched the funeral procession it appeared that the Communists were making some headway with their master symbols.

SOME TYPICAL NEGRO COMMUNISTS

In carrying on the activities which have been described above it was necessary for the Communists to recruit and train persons for quite different rôles. To lead the militant resistance against court bailiffs, policemen, and the strong-arm men of various employers, it was necessary to have men with powerful physiques, boundless courage, and great determination. To organize the unskilled workers in the sweatshop trades it was necessary to have persons who were trained in the techniques of

---

[50] Report of meeting held November 18, 1931. Nat Turner led an armed insurrection of Negroes against whites in Southampton County, Virginia, in 1831. Sixty white people were killed before the state militia and United States troops captured Turner and his confederates. Turner believed that he was ordained to liberate his people. He was tried and hanged for his part in the insurrection.

persuasion, bargaining, and collective action. To spread the Communist propaganda among the Negroes it was necessary to have persons who understood the longings of the Negro race, could make them articulate, and who understood the ideology of Communism. Some of the agitators were expected to run the risk of personal injury, arrest, and persecution; others were expected to keep out of the way of the public authorities and those who were hostile to the movement in order that they might direct the work of others even under the most unfavorable circumstances.

"Comrade" X was one of the first Negroes in Chicago to join the Communist party. He has the reputation for being one of the best-grounded Negroes in the country in the theory of Communism. In conversation he showed great familiarity with the Soviet leaders and with the more important works on the theory of the Communistic state. He is married to a young white woman and their daughter was given the name, "Michele," after a heroine of the French revolution.[51] Comrade X was a short, slight individual so he could not be expected to take a leading part in riots, but he was prominent as a speaker on many crucial occasions. He was one of the leaders of a demonstration which was held in front of DePriest's real estate office, but he managed to escape arrest. He was the hero of the famous tree episode in Ellis Park. As the *Daily Worker* expressed it: "That brave and sensitive young leader was speaking when the thugs arrived. He climbed into an old oak tree and went right on talking from its branches. Some of the uniformed killers tried to climb up after him, but their graft-swollen bellies interfered. It was comical, and the crowd laughed."[52] When the police began to fire their guns in the air the discreet comrade came down so as to avoid unnecessary casualties. He was also one of the hecklers in a DePriest meeting at a colored church, and here again his name did not appear among those

[51] While the interview was being conducted, his wife played the "Internationale" over on the phonograph. She was bathing her baby and explained that she wanted to give the child the proper background.

[52] September 29, 1932.

who were arrested for inciting a riot.[53] Regarding his start in the Communist movement he said:

I was born in Boston, Massachusetts, in 1904. My parents were both from Virginia and they were of slave ancestry. My family was composed of two sisters, both older than myself and one brother, a meek Baptist mother and a discontented father who had to turn to waiting table in a hotel because of the inability to find work at his trade, house-painting. He was Jim-Crowed and forced to become a laborer. My family was never close in the sense of having strong ties of affection binding them. I never got along with my sisters, one of whom is at present teaching in the Boston schools. I never saw much of my brother.

After finishing public and high school in Boston, I was nipped by a wanderlust and traveled to Chicago by a devious route that took me through most of New York state. I arrived in the city of Chicago in 1925, groping for work. I sought to find employment in my trade, which was printing. I had been a printer's devil in Boston. After looking vainly for work, I joined the Communist party in 1926.

I knew something was wrong. I had been groping ever since I finished school. I just couldn't seem to fit in. I was an agnostic. This made things pretty hard for me around the house because both of my parents were hardshell Baptists. I had always attended church and Sunday School. When I was 13 or 14 I read Ingersoll and Paine and have never been the same since. I turned atheist after joining the party.

As a result of my party activity I went to the Soviet Union in 1927, where I stayed for 18 months as one of the leaders of the textile industry. My official title was a leader of the proletariat. In the unit where I worked there were 40,000 workers. I am at present a member of the district and the central committees of the party. I have never been a member of the Unemployed Council but have always been a member of the party.[54]

Comrade Y was a tall, dark, muscular Negro weighing about 195 pounds. He has been in the thick of most of the riots and fights between the Communists and the police on the South Side of Chicago. So fearless and reckless was his behavior that he was sent as an example of militant leadership to Minneapolis, Milwaukee, Indianapolis, and other centers in the middle west. He started trouble at a Chicago meeting of the National Association for the Advancement of Colored People; he fought the police at a DePriest meeting until he was knocked unconscious;[55]

[53] Chicago Defender, October 29, 1932; Daily Worker, October 28, 1932.

[54] Interview, February 9, 1934.   [55] Chicago Defender, October 29, 1932.

he led the early eviction riots; he took part in the demonstrations before the relief stations that ended in violence and police oppression. He was arrested at least fourteen times and, as he explains below, his last charge is a very serious one. His face was scarred as a result of rough handling by the police, but his spirit was unbroken. He was clearly a masochist type seeking martyrdom, since most of the injuries which he received might have been avoided if he had been less hot headed. He thought that he did his best work in the Washington Park forums and in the Unemployed Councils. Part of his story is given below:

I was born in Montgomery County, Tennessee, on November 30, 1903. I had two brothers older than myself and my father was a farmer who was rather well off when I was a kid. I went to the public and high schools there in Montgomery and also attended Fisk University from 1921 to 1923. Between 1923 and 1927 I did quite a bit of traveling around, working at one time on the railroad as a Pullman porter. I came to Chicago to live on July 6, 1927.

When I first came here, I got a job in the stockyards without any trouble at all. I only worked there for a few months, though, and went to the Illinois Steel Company out in Gary where I got better pay. I lived in Chicago all the time I was working in Gary. I worked in Gary for a year and a half, a good Baptist just like my folks, worrying not about the revolution but about my pay and an occasional spree.

I joined the ranks of the unemployed in 1929 confident that the Lord would take care of me as I still prayed every night. I used to hang around the Illinois Free Employment agency there on Thirty-fifth Street. We organized a forum, and because I could talk pretty well, they made me the leader. This forum was the indirect cause of my joining the party, as you will see.

I first heard of the Unemployed Council in 1930 when they called a meeting in the Third Ward to ask Bob Jackson to endorse the unemployed insurance bill in the city council. The police broke up the meeting and I remember the talk we had about it afterwards. I remember that I argued that the cops should have broken the thing up. In the argument we had at the time somebody asked why we didn't carry the question to our own people who might do us some good. Somebody suggested the National Baptist Convention. I wasn't so much in favor of the idea but I was the leader so I fell in with the idea. We pitched in our little pennies and made up a lot of crude signs. We talked around a little and raised each other's hopes. Somebody said they were spending $35,000 for the convention so they would surely help us poor workers.

The next day when we went down there wasn't a Red among us. We got to the Coliseum and I didn't know where to go to see about presenting our request. I bet we certainly looked funny, about 150 of us with our signs, "A Christian Is a Good Samaritan," "The Lord Loveth A Cheerful Giver." . . . . My old Nashville minister sent me over to see a big man who must have thought we were Communists, because when we asked him for permission to speak he said, "Nothing doing." We felt pretty bad and we didn't have sense enough to insist so we went back up to listen to the convention. We found out later that they were supposed to have the election of officers that day, and such carryings-on I had never thought existed in the church. . . . .

A few days later one of the fellows that used to hang around the agency came up to me and said the Communists were giving me hell, calling me a "tunist" and all kinds of names. He went on to tell me that the *Chicago Tribune* had put my name in the paper as having led a Communist demonstration at the Baptist meeting. I don't to this day know where they got my name for nobody had asked me at the Coliseum anything at all. I went to one of the meetings and found that Sol Harper of New York was my chief criticizer. He was here doing some organizing work. It just happened that he criticized me again that night, so I arose and defended myself. Harper felt as though I were some cheap politician who had cashed in on the Communist name. He explained why the attack was made. I joined the Negro Labor Congress that evening, the Unemployed Council the next week, and the party the week after that.

Soon after I joined the party I lost what little deep religious feeling I had. I had an ability to speak and there were only four Negro members of District 8, comprising Missouri, Wisconsin, Illinois, and Indiana. There were many members of the Unemployed Council, so I saw a chance to do some real work.

As you have heard, hell began popping loose very soon. I had gotten in just in time. I remember one of the first assignments I had was to go to the city hall with a committee of the Unemployed Council and sit with the City Council about Unemployed Insurance, etc. When we went down there were only two Negroes with the group, Don Sikes and myself. I was the leader. We marched up to the chambers only to find out that the council was not in session that day. Our old friend, the Red Squad, was out though, and was waiting for us. They met us in front of the chambers and told us to get the hell out. When the group turned to go that meant that I as leader was in the rear. We were leaving peacefully until I noticed two coppers that had grabbed a little white 135-pound comrade. They were beating him about the face something terrible. I turned loose on the first one. . . . .

Soon after this I had quite a run in at the LaSalle Hotel. The governor, Emmerson at that time, was holding his Emergency Relief meeting there sitting in with various trade groups and leaders. Our party hadn't been invited but we determined to go. I was the only Negro in the picked group. . . . We pulled on the door and gave an expectant rush only to find out that we had broken into an ante room and more than that right in the arms of the red squad. We saw then we weren't going to get in the meeting so we raised hell

there in the ante room. They shushed us out of the room into the hall. There
were a lot of nice respectable people sitting around and these coppers were
trying to shut us up and rush us out. We were yelling and raising hell. These
cops were really sore and the one that had my arm whispered to me, "You
black bastard if you don't shut up I'll shoot you right here in the hall." That
was all I wanted. I stopped and yelled, "Shoot me! Go ahead, kill me. When
I ask for bread you give me bullets. Shoot me when I ask for coal for my
family." They all turned red and mumbled and the good people around the
walls raised their eyes and looked horrified. They finally got us out and kept
us in the can for three days. We were dismissed with a warning. . . . .

There were about 350 evictions a day at this time. The first major case
that the council took part in was an eviction at 4618 Calumet Avenue. A
former steel worker and his family were put out by a Negro landlord. We got
a message at 11 o'clock and rushed right over with 20 men and put the furniture back. We were being very sentimental. We were righting a great wrong.
Well, the family was put out a second time two weeks later. . . . .

Meanwhile the second eviction took place. I had decided to improve on the
previous bungling methods that we had used. I knew all twenty men running
out would certainly be flirting with a jail sentence. So instead of having our
twenty put the furniture back, I had them go around to all of the houses in the
neighborhood telling the neighbors what was happening to a friend and
neighbor. Charles Ranks and I were together and we had to hang back a
little because we were known to the police. Well, the landlord meanwhile had
turned in a riot call and a cruising car saw Ranks and myself and picked us up.
We were disheartened because we thought surely the thing would fail without
somebody there to talk to the crowd. We heard afterward that 350 people
from the neighborhood came in. A white worker named Tabert who just
happened along climbed up and spoke. The crowd took in the furniture and
the police didn't bother them. They did arrest the ringleaders though.

We did some of our best work through the unemployed councils. Soon after
Horner came in they stopped recognizing the councils at the relief stations.
Things were drawn to a head on January 20, when we had a demonstration at
the station on Fiftieth Street. The demonstration was set for 11 o'clock.
When we arrived there were 400 policemen around. . . . . The cops clubbed
everybody, women and kids too. Somebody grabbed me off the chair back-
wards and dragged me across the street. I thought I was pinched and started
fighting. I found I was in the hands of two comrades who had heard the
police instructed to get me whatever happened. They had planned to finish
me that day. They had even released a story to the *Times* (*Daily Times*) that
I had been fatally injured. They missed. They did almost kill a fellow they
thought was me. They even tried to make him admit in the Bridewell hospital
that he was me. After this fight, they smashed up everything. They broke up
the councils.

All this time they had not stopped looking for me. About three weeks

later a squad came in the Alvin looking for me. We were having a dance up
there that night. My wife was at the door and I was in a meeting at the back
of the hall in a little room. The first thing I knew was that somebody had
opened the door where we were having our meeting and all the noise from outside was coming in. I yelled, "For God's sake close that door." I looked up
in the face of a big cop. Middleton came back, identified me and took me
over to Forty-eighth Street, where I was placed in a cell with two murderers.
When they took me over to the Criminal Court building for trial, my counsel
greeted me with a "good morning murderer" and laughed. I didn't know
what it was all about. I learned later that I was charged with assault with
intent to commit murder on an officer by the name of McGuire (same man
who cursed me in station at a previous date) with a brick at the Fiftieth Street
demonstration. I had to post a $25,000 bond and am out on that now. I've
been indicted by the grand jury and my case is to go before Judge Reinberg
on April 2.

An examination of the characteristics of several other active
Negro Communists shows that for the most part the movement
attracted the young men and women in their twenties or thirties, the unemployed, and those who had become disillusioned
about Christianity. Among the recruits were a young woman
who had been active in the industrial Young Women's Christian
Association and a former Mohammedan. The latter said of
Mohammedanism, "It appealed to me on race grounds. I had
seen so much of the brutality and hypocrisy of white Chris-
tians. . . . . But one day I started to read the Koran. It was the
same old Bible bunk, Adam and Eve, and the rest of it. I quit."[56]
A number of the Negro Communists were former Garveyites
and the collapse of this movement left them with unsatisfied
yearnings. "Whatever the crimes and mistakes of this misleader Garvey," said one of them, " I learned a lot about organization from him."[57] Some were World War veterans who
were embittered by the indifference and hostility of the white
public on their return to the United States. A few had organized resistance during the race riots of 1919. A World War
veteran said: "I fought in the riots; some of us captured guns
from the lynchers and barricaded this street."[58] This man
joined the party in the Spring of 1929 because he was attracted

[56] *Daily Worker*, October 1, 1932.
[57] *Ibid.*, October 1, October 3, 1932.   [58] *Ibid.*

by the stand of the movement on lynching. When employed the Communists had been largely unskilled or semi-skilled workers in the steel, the meat-packing, and the construction industries.

In educational experiences the Negro Communist leaders were above the average of the Negro community. Most of them had gone to high school for at least two years. After they joined the Communist party all of them attended for a time the Chicago Workers' School, and a few of them were sent to the Soviet Union to study and observe.

COMMUNIST ELECTION ACTIVITIES

According to the theses of the Third International Communist parties in all democratic countries were to engage in electioneering activities as a means of preparation for the world-revolution. In the United States it has not been possible for Communist candidates to secure positions on the ballot in every one of the forty-eight states, but in Illinois such candidates have appeared on the ballot ever since the formation of the American branch of the party. The votes received by these candidates at different elections are a very rough measure of the popular support which the party has been able to secure at different times. It is notorious that in Chicago fraud and error have frequently distorted the official election returns.[59] It is probable that the error in the case of the Communist candidates is much greater than it is where candidates of the two major parties are involved. The election machinery is in the hands of representatives of the Republican and Democratic parties who usually show scant sympathy for radical movements. Furthermore, the Communists have failed to develop an efficient organization of their own which would safeguard their election interests. The official returns, then, constantly underestimate the actual voting strength of the Communist candidates.

Beginning with the election of 1924 the Communists have put

[59] D. M. Maynard, "Fraud and Error in Chicago Referendum Returns," *National Municipal Review*, XIX (1930), 164–67.

up colored candidates for congressmen in the First Congressional District at least once every four years. The candidate in 1924 was Gordon Owen, who was reported to have spoken at a number of street-corner meetings in the heart of the Negro community.[60] In the final election Owen was accorded some 32 votes out of a total of 59,768.[61] Four years later the candidate of the party, Edward L. Doty, ran against Oscar DePriest and William H. Harrison. While the 1928 election marked the beginning of an intensive drive on the part of the Communists to attract Negroes, Doty received on the official count only 100 votes out of a total of 51,227. When the party again put up a candidate for this office in 1932, conditions were more propitious for a larger vote. The Communist activities during the economic crisis furnished a basis for many appeals to the Negro voters. The Scottsboro defense, the anti-eviction demonstrations, the demands for more adequate relief, and the stand of the party on racial questions were all used effectively by Herbert Newton, who in his campaign against Oscar DePriest led a demonstration in front of DePriest's office and took part in the heckling at DePriest meetings.[62] The official returns gave Newton 843 votes out of a total of 61,467.

Communist candidates were also put up for some of the municipal and state elective positions. The petitions of the Communist candidates for aldermen in wards that contained a large Negro population were rejected by the Board of Election Commissioners during the period under discussion because of technical and other alleged defects. In 1931 the actions of the election authorities were used as the basis for extensive agitation. It was said that the Chicago bosses deprived the workers of their candidates by "fascist rulings."[63] The case of Wella Clinton, Negro candidate for alderman in a West Side ward, was particularly featured. "Comrade" Clinton was a scrubwoman in a hotel who supported her mother, and the protest

[60] Daily Worker, September 9, 1924.
[61] Figures are compiled from the Daily News Almanac.
[62] Daily Worker, July 18, October 28, 31, 1932.   [63] Ibid., February 13, 1931.

meetings, which were organized as a result of her exclusion from the ballot, emphasized her working-class origins.[64] When the Negro Communist candidates for aldermen received the same treatment in 1933, the cry again went up that the workers were barred from the Chicago ballot, and the charge was made that violence and corruption characterized the city administration.[65] The Communist voters were urged to write in the names of the working-class candidates who had been ruled off the ballot, and it was recorded in the election books that some 168 voters wrote in the name of Brown Squire in the Second Ward.

While the Communists have urged their supporters to vote a straight ticket for all the Communist candidates who are running for elective office, in practice the candidates for president and vice-president receive a larger vote than the other candidates on the ticket. In recent presidential campaigns several Negro delegates have been sent to Communist nominating conventions and in the 1932 convention one of these delegates was an outstanding orator. Laura Crosby, a Chicago stockyards worker, stirred her audience profoundly with the following words:

Comrades and fellow-workers:

I represent Chicago, a great big beautiful city of starvation. Here in Chicago, when the workers come out in demonstration, we are lined up against the walls at the point of machine guns, and that isn't low and dirty enough to do to the working class. The dicks took baseball bats and whips to use against our comrades.

First of all I want to speak to the Negro people most especially because we have been the most oppressed nationality in the world. We get the lowest pay, the worst jobs. Never before in history can any of us look back and see where a Negro had the privilege and the opportunity to run for vice-president. . . . .

Fellow-workers, you understand we are not only fighting for that little lousy amount of $15 a week. We are fighting for equal rights and social equality for all Negroes. Fellow-workers, we have a party by the name of the Communist party, which is the only party in the world that fights for the working class, the only party that organizes the Negro workers with the white

[64] *Ibid.*, February 16, 1931. See also *Chicago Daily News*, January 27, 1931.

[65] *Daily Worker*, February 20, 1933.

workers. Fellow-workers, the Communist party has got the world of workers stirred up and don't forget it.[66]

After the convention, which nominated Foster and Ford, was over, strenuous efforts were put forth to attract the Negro voters in Chicago. Frequent mass meetings and demonstrations were held at which the candidacy of Ford for vice-president was featured. At the final Communist election rally in Chicago Ford was the principal speaker and the question of Negro equality was stressed. The gains made by the party in the Negro community as reflected in the official returns for the 1932 election were considerable when compared with the 1928 returns, but small when considered in relation to the total vote. The Second and Third wards were the banner wards for the Communist party in the entire city, with a vote which was slightly under 3 per cent of the total vote cast in the wards. In some of the precincts, which were inhabited largely by Negroes, between 5 and 6 per cent of the total votes recorded went to Foster and Ford. These precincts were located in neighborhoods where the rents were low and the unemployment rates were high.[66a]

COUNTER-ACTIVITIES AND PROPAGANDA

The election returns and the available figures for party membership show that the Communist movement failed to spread very widely among the Negroes of Chicago. In the early years of the economic depression the movement attracted a higher ratio of Negroes than of whites, but this ratio was a very small one. In spite of heroic efforts only some five hundred Negroes became party members, and as the economic crisis continued the numbers declined rather than increased. Apparently, conditions were not favorable for the rapid development of Communist doctrines among the colored workers, and the counter-movements had ample powers of resistance against the most militant of the Communist attacks.

Among the most active of the anti-Communist organizations

[66] *Ibid.*, June 3, 1932.   [66a] Heavy lines in Fig. 2 are ward lines.

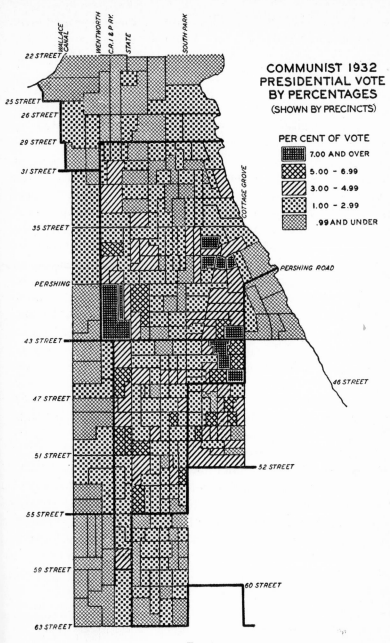

FIG. 2

were the religious bodies. The Communist doctrines were first brought in by whites who were not only strange to the Negro community but in some cases foreign to America. On the other hand, the Negro churches belonged to the Negroes and were a product of the life of the group in the United States. During the first intensive drive of the Communists a Negro minister had two white agitators arrested for distributing anti-lynching leaflets in front of his church.[67] These foreign atheists were not to undermine the faith of his flock by appearing to defend the Negroes against the lynch terror. The Communists would increase, not diminish, the danger from mob violence. After the famous eviction riot of August 3, 1931, a number of prominent colored ministers held a meeting at which they accused Communist agitators, white and colored, of fomenting the riot in which three Negroes were slain and three policemen slugged. "The trouble is caused by Russian Communist propaganda," said one of the ministers. "It is a challenge to the law-abiding people and should be handled by the United States government. The hungry, homeless Negro is being used as a tool."[68] Since the great mass of the colored people still clung to the symbolism and ideology of religion, these words from the church leaders carried great weight.

The Communist activities were such that the leaders of the movement were brought into conflict with the authorities charged with maintaining law and order. The police, the deputy bailiffs, and the deputy sheriffs used the coercive power of the community to frustrate and destroy the movement. From the very beginning of the intensive drive of the party for recruits the police centered their attention on repressive measures. A special industrial Squad (the "Red Squad") sent police spies into the Communist meetings and watched developments closely. Some of the new Negro party members became "stool pigeons" for the police. Communist meetings were broken up,

[67] *Ibid.*, July 30, 1930.

[68] *Chicago Whip*, August 8, 1931; *Chicago Tribune*, August 4, 1931; *Chicago Daily News*, August 4, 1931.

demonstrations were forbidden, literature was confiscated, the party headquarters were raided, and the leaders were beaten up and arrested.[69] Real estate men were warned not to rent halls and rooms for the Communist activities. The police were particularly severe upon the white Communist leaders who tried to organize the Negro community. In any crowd which the Communists collected the white leaders were pounced upon first, but soon some of the Negro Communist leaders were also made the brunt of many attacks. With the most active Negro leaders in jail or out on bond it became more and more difficult for the party to function in an effective fashion in the community. No sooner would one of these leaders get out of one encounter with the police and the courts through the agency of the International Labor Defense than he found himself in another legal tangle. Negro police officers were assigned to the work of liquidating the Negro Communists and some of them performed their work in an efficient fashion. The white officers on the Red Squad, who had strong religious convictions and deep prejudices against the mingling of whites and blacks, were particularly ruthless in their handling of the Communists.

The inauguration of the Roosevelt administration further complicated the development of the movement. The party had based its propaganda on the failure of the capitalistic system in the United States to provide the elementary necessities of human existence to all who were willing to work. The Roosevelt government undertook huge expenditures for relief and for public works. The codes adopted under the National Recovery Act eliminated the worst sweatshops. The feeling of confidence which was brought in by the administration proved to be a stumbling-block for the Communists. The attack made by the party on the inflationary policies of the "New Deal" and the scorn which it poured upon the labor policies of the National Recovery Act could not offset the new hope which came to

[69] *Chicago Defender*, October 17, 1931; *Daily Worker*, April 14, July 19, September 6, 25, October 20, 1930; November 16, 1931; March 28, 1932; February 11, May 30, June 23, August 14, 1933.

many Negroes that the employment situation would soon be better.[70] Relief was already more adequate and the federal expenditures appeared to be increasing business activity.[71]

In general, it must be said that Communism did not take very deep root in the Chicago "Black Belt." However, that success which came to the party in the Negro community in the years immediately following the 1929 crash left a residue in the minds and hearts of the race which has been traditionally classed as submissive.

[70] *Stockyard Worker*, March, May, 1933 (mimeographed paper of Communist Party Stockyard units).

[71] One of the Negro Communists obtained a CWA job and during the noon hour he spoke on conditions and tried to organize a union among the CWA workers. In a short time this man was told that he did not earn enough money on CWA work to support his family and he was put back on the relief rolls.

CHAPTER XVI
SUMMARY: NEGROES AS A POLITICAL POWER

The Negroes in Chicago constituted a racial minority which entered the struggle for political power with many initial handicaps. Success in politics in a metropolitan community like the city of Chicago ordinarily depends upon access to large campaign funds, upon the support of some of the metropolitan dailies, upon a certain measure of social prestige, and upon political experience and acumen. The colored citizens who came streaming to the city in ever increasing numbers in the period following the collapse of reconstruction in the South were not in possession of the elements which go to make up a powerful political group. For the most part they were poor and propertyless, and even those who managed to achieve a certain economic independence did not feel that their position was secure enough to warrant the risk of great outlays in the form of campaign contributions. The incidence of the economic depression, which began in 1929, showed that these Negro business and professional leaders had been wise in not pouring out their small resources for such purposes. Not only were the Negroes unable to finance political activities by themselves, but they also were at a disadvantage in securing publicity. Since the Negroes were not merely a minority but an unpopular one, the great white daily newspapers were prone to stress the unfavorable aspects of the political behavior of the group. Furthermore, the colored people have had comparatively little opportunity to acquire training and experience in politics. In a northern urban center like Chicago the ambitious Negroes who aspired to political influence had to compete with native white and with foreign-born white politicians who had been in the game for many years and who thoroughly understood the tricks of the trade.

Another obstacle which stood in the way of Negroes, who

357

were anxious to acquire a position of political importance for the group, was the lack of confidence which the rank and file had in their own leaders. Bitter complaints were heard about the lack of colored leaders. Those who called themselves leaders were sometimes looked upon by other members of the group as self-seeking, corrupt, and treacherous persons who sold out the race and were responsible for the fact that the Negroes were getting pushed farther and farther back in political matters. A few of the rank and file trusted white leaders more than they trusted their own leaders. The distrust which the Negro voters had of their own leaders may be traced in part to the rôle which fear plays generally in the life of a submerged group which is not sure of its position. The Negroes in America have been uncertain as to their jobs, their personal safety, and their very lives. A few of them have compensated for these feelings of anxiety by over-assertiveness. This occasional aggressiveness has further complicated the pathway of the race to political success.

In the last analysis the peculiar difficulties which confronted the Negroes in their struggle for political power can in some way be related to the factor of color. If the group was not conspicuous, if the identifying mark of color was not present, then individual members would be able to compete with members of other groups on a more or less equal basis. Many foreign-born white persons have come to the United States without wealth, without social prestige, and with little educational equipment and they have achieved positions of economic, social, and political power. The ruling élite in America has accepted the leaders of immigrant groups with comparatively little hesitation. With the acquisition of wealth and some social polish, outstanding men from alien countries have been able to move to high places without attracting any special attention. On the other hand, the Negroes have been handicapped from the start. In searching for economic opportunities, in trying to learn the ways of business, in seeking to run for city-wide elective offices, and in endeavoring to secure key positions in the party organizations, the Negroes had to face the obstacle of color.

They were compelled to live in a world which set them apart because the mark of their racial origin made them too obvious.

The difficulties which faced the Negro group in its struggle for political influence were considerable and might have discouraged a minority which had been less inured to disappointments. However, the Negroes in America have displayed remarkable capacities for adjusting themselves to changing circumstances, and they met each obstacle in one way or another. If they lacked money to spend for political purposes they were not slow in getting in touch with white persons who were willing and anxious to contribute to campaign chests. The utility magnates, the real estate barons, the liquor dealers (before, during, and after prohibition), and other important business men, found that they could reach understandings with the colored leaders. One Negro legislator was proud of the fact that he had sponsored certain bills for the utilities and thereby opened a few jobs for Negroes and acquired some help in political campaigns.

If the group lacked support from the daily press, it could start weekly papers of its own; it could hold great mass meetings where first-hand contacts were established between the rank and file and the leaders, and it could develop a canvassing technique that reached most of the potential voters. If the group lacked political experience there was still the will to learn, and in the northern city there were opportunities for political training which were open to those who were alert enough to seize them. If the rank and file lacked confidence in their own leaders at first, years of success in office gradually tended to diminish this distrust.

In the eyes of many whites the Negroes occupied an inferior position in the social hierarchy, and this attitude might have blocked Negro political advancement. However, Negroes refused to accept any caste status, and when the color line was drawn against them they fell back upon themselves and developed the doctrine and practice of race solidarity. If the whites acted together against them, they would act together to secure recognition for themselves. Voting on candidates fol-

lowed racial lines and woe to the white candidate in a close
primary or election who antagonized this particular racial
minority. The votes on propositions also showed that the Negroes had developed considerable group cohesion. On bond
issues, on the wet issue, and on local transportation issues the
colored voters were more united than other groups, usually on
the side favoring change. This tendency to vote "yes" on
measures was utilized by the Negro leaders in bargaining for
favors. In general, the morale of the Negro voters was good.

The Negroes had practically no leisure class so it was not
possible for them to recruit leaders from an educated and
wealthy élite. Several of the earliest Negro leaders were former
waiters or porters. These occupations gave them experience in
dealing with whites at a time when the Negroes were such a
small minority that they had to depend upon white support
for political advancement. When the equilibrium between the
races was disturbed by a great influx of Negroes from the South,
the growing antagonism of the whites and the developing race
consciousness of the Negroes demanded a new type of colored
leader. Following the World's Fair of 1893 a new group of more
aggressive leaders came to the front. County Commissioner
Edward Wright, a lawyer by profession, was so aggressive in his
demands for his race during the late nineties that he was
shelved by the white politicians for a period of fifteen years,
during which time the colored population increased slowly. At
the end of this time the migration from the South was well on
its way and the Negro minority could support a leader of
Wright's type.

Congressman DePriest was also a product of the new mold.
A former decorator, a successful contractor and real estate
dealer, DePriest was noted for his fearlessness and gruffness in
the presence of whites. While the Negro community in Chicago
has the beginnings of a Negro "society" or a four hundred, and
while ancestry, education, and cultural opportunities are important in the Negro community, the question most frequently
asked of prospective political leaders is not from what did they
arise but how far they have gone and in what direction. Mu-

lattoes, educated business and professional men, appear to be coming to the top, but there is no bar to the black man who is courageous, intelligent, and persistent.

Some of the Negro political leaders came from the ecclesiastical group. The colored churches were at once the rivals and the helpers of the political organizations. A few of the ministers competed with the professional politicians for preferment and prestige but at the same time they worked along with the organization in its main objectives. The Negro churches took a more active part in politics than most of the white churches because religion has played and still plays a more important rôle among Negroes than it does among whites. Religion has furnished to the colored race in the United States both an outlet for gregarious tendencies and an escape for humiliations and hardships suffered in this world. An institution which is vitally concerned with the social life of the group could hardly keep out of the struggle for political power and influence. The church was a forum, the ministers were campaign orators, the church members were precinct workers, and the church conventions were schools for the seekers of power.

From time to time the leaders of the colored underworld entered the political arena. Of all the contestants, the gambling kings, the vice lords, and the liquor magnates were most likely to have political funds of their own which they could invest in politics. These elements had a block of votes at their beck and command as their most bitter rivals soon discovered. They also had a code of their own which in general was on a higher level than the codes of their white contemporaries in similar activities. A Negro gambling king might exploit the poor people in his area, but if he wasn't there a white man would be there. The most trusted of the colored gambling kings did not cheat their customers; they were men of their word and they kept the earnings of the business within the community. Furthermore, these men were interested in the advancement of the race and they financed Negro theatricals, Negro motion-picture companies, and Negro musicians, as well as Negro candidates for elective office. While the prostitutes, pimps, and lesser employees of the gambling houses were frequently unreliable as political workers, the leaders of the underworld could not all be ignored by an aspiring faction.

The relations between the Negro political leaders were by no means harmonious all the time. The battles between rival factions were waged with a bitterness that would be hard to equal elsewhere. While the gulf between the ministers and the gambling kings was wide, individual colored leaders might enlist the support of the church elements at one time and the support of the underworld at another. By and large the open-town interests tended to gravitate to the faction which was in power, while the religious leaders rallied to the side of the opposition which could make vocal complaints regarding moral conditions in the Negro community. Ministers who were with the dominant faction had to meet many harsh criticisms. In times of crisis, when the safety of the entire group was at stake, all the diverse elements would be temporarily welded together.

The techniques employed by the Negroes who rose to positions of power in one or the other of the two major parties in Chicago were borrowed from the whites who devised and practiced them. The colored leaders had to adapt these techniques to the characteristics of their followers. They had to show a sensitivity in race matters, a thoroughness in the details of organization, and a superior skill in the distribution of patronage.

In the manipulation of symbols and the art of propaganda there were some of the group leaders who became experts. They learned how to select the symbols which would arouse the sentiment of the masses for or against given candidates. They came to understand the value of repetition, identification, and substitution. If the masses heard it said often enough that Mayor Thompson was a second Lincoln, they would come to believe it. If the rank and file were made to feel that a certain party was their party and their candidates were the candidates of that party they would act accordingly. If the man in the street could be convinced that his status was linked up with the success of his group leaders, he would stand by those leaders through thick and thin. When the colored leaders determined to cut a given white candidate they could marshal a set of negative symbols which nearly wiped out the chances of this candidate with the colored voters. These symbols might and often did give an unfair picture of the candidate concerned. However, Negro politicians were not bothered about such nice questions as to who introduced the practice of humbuggery in American politics. They followed the rules of the game as it was played in Chicago in the whoopee twenties and the dismal thirties. When two Negro leaders were fighting for the same position they selected symbols which exaggerated each other's weak points. In such campaigns they put into practice current mud-slinging techniques with due allowance to faults which were held to be most grievous by the general Negro public.

The successful Negro politicians were tireless organizers. It almost appeared that they would rather speak than eat and that they would rather attend political conferences than sleep. They made a business of politics three hundred and sixty-five days out of the year. Political meetings, canvassing, collecting signatures, checking on potential voters, manning the polls, watching the count, and listening to the returns were their meat. In no part of the city were more enthusiastic and inspiring political meetings held. In no section where the mobility of the population was equally as high was there a larger poll of the eligible voters. The obstacles of illiteracy, ignorance, timidity, and indifference were met wherever they were encountered, and the organization usually came off victor. The leaders knew how to hire workers on election day to the greatest advantage to the faction which furnished the money. They also knew how to instruct their followers to vote the most complicated of ballots.

Patronage or expectation of patronage was an important component of the cement which held the Negro political or-ganization together. More than any other minority group in the city the Negroes were in need of jobs which would not only give economic security but furnish recognition for the group as well. If race prejudice blocked the way for Negroes seeking employment in private industry in clerical, managerial, and

professional positions, then they must turn to political pressures
to open opportunities for them in the public service. Among the
governmental positions were many very desirable posts which
were exempt from the operation of the merit system. As the
Negroes gradually developed political power they began to demand more and more of these appointments. Gradually the
tradition grew up that certain appointments were to be allotted
to the group regardless of party or factional changes. A new
administration would change the personnel but the new men
appointed to the posts vacated would be Negroes. Generally
speaking, the Negroes fared better in such appointments under
Republican administrations than under Democratic, but the
Democrats in the past forty years have always had some
Negroes in conspicuous positions.

In addition to the prominent appointive positions which were
given to the sub-leaders of the political organization, the Negro
machine was interested in many lesser positions which were not
under civil service or were filled by temporary appointments or
were filled on the basis of merely nominal physical examinations.
In the last-mentioned group came numerous jobs as common
laborers, which were welcome to many Negroes who had just
come recently from the South. While the Negro political
leaders could not always secure as many important appointive
posts as they wished, they could bargain for a larger share of
the lesser positions on this account. If they could not have
more legal positions they would strive for more jobs as street-
cleaners, road-repairers, janitors, and ditch-diggers. All of the
political appointees were expected to engage in election campaign activities, and many of them were precinct captains.
When the dominant faction to which they were attached was in
power, their organization was a very smooth-running mecha-
nism.

The political organizations of the group were not in a position to benefit from the most lucrative varieties of political
graft that have been common in Chicago. There were no great
Negro contracting firms, no Negro banks that did a city-wide
business, no Negro real estate men that operated on a county-

wide basis, and no Negroes in the administrative posts that furnished the greatest opportunities for spoils. However, the organizations came in for their share of the graft connected with the police, the administration of criminal justice, and the political manipulation of various public agencies. The colored leaders took a very realistic view of current practices. The daily press and the common talk of white politicians were full of allusions to the raising of campaign funds by tribute levied upon the underworld and upon businesses which were anxious to avoid the too rigid enforcement of governmental regulations. These references were taken at their face value and put into practice. If the political game was a corrupt one, they would play it according to the rules. The reform movements did not interest them particularly. Reformers were always drawing a color line somewhere while the realistic politicians and rulers of the underworld would recognize any group that was of use to them.

The greatest contribution which the rank and file of the Negro group had to offer to the white political leaders was personal loyalty. The politician who won their confidence could count on their support even in the most adverse of circumstances. It was common belief among certain white politicians that the Negro vote was influenced primarily by large expenditures of money. It is true that colored party workers demand compensation for their services on behalf of given candidates. Other things being equal, the colored voters, like the white voters in many parts of the United States, support the candidates who spend the most money. However, these candidates had to measure up to given standards of acceptability if the money spent was to yield the best returns. In other words, money, jobs, and other rewards might not influence the Negro voters to support a candidate who was regarded as hostile to the interests of the race in preference to one who had a reputation of fair dealing in race matters. This is not to say that the favored candidate, if he wanted a large vote, could neglect to spend the money that was commonly put into districts of the same economic status. Another evidence of the loyalty of the colored voters was their behavior when the political fortunes of their favorite candidates were sinking. The Negroes, like other minority groups, do not enjoy supporting losing causes, but when their friends are going down they stick with them to the last.

Many of the Negro voters were also loyal to a political party which they felt had their interests at heart. This party might desert them in other parts of the country, some of its leaders might fail to recognize the group, and it might refuse to take a militant stand on behalf of Negro rights. However, it was still the party which had traditionally stood for the protection of the Negro and as compared with its chief rival it was regarded as having more to offer. While political landslides, economic depressions, and the breaking of political scandals might cause the voters in other groups to shift their party allegiance, many members of this minority group remained in the party fold. Only continued failures to win the important elective offices tended to weaken this loyalty. Those most likely to waver under these circumstances were on the outskirts of the main Negro community or in isolated communities which were subject to group disciplines. They were also likely to be those whose economic position was the most insecure.

Although Negroes have been denied in practice many of the benefits of democracy in the United States, they have been very loyal to the ideals of democracy. The democratic dogmas of equality, universal adult suffrage, universal free education, freedom of movement, freedom of speech, freedom of assembly, and equality of candidacy have inspired hope and helped to maintain the morale of the group. These symbols were associated with emancipation and the early opportunities of the reconstruction period. In the southern states they had a revolutionary significance since the Negroes who insisted upon their democratic rights were attacking the social order. In the northern states the democratic slogans meant an improved social status. The faith of the group in democratic ideology was strengthened by the fact that the anti-democratic movements were usually hostile to demands of the group. Movements like the Ku Klux Klan were violent in their opposition to efforts of the Negroes to advance their position. Voting was an important ritual which enabled minority groups to defend themselves against some forms of oppression. Education held a promise of emancipation of a part of the group from the less desirable forms of labor.

Has the loyalty which the Negroes have displayed toward the democratic process been well placed? Does the experience of the group in Chicago show that a minority group without economic power can gain material and psychological advantages by the method of political action? The changes which have taken place in the economic and social status of the Negroes have been the result of so many complex factors that it is impossible to isolate any one factor. However, some inferences may be made as to the rôle of political methods in the life of a conspicuous minority group.

Participation in politics has brought a certain number of more or less desirable jobs to the group. Of all the governmental services in the city, whether national, state, or local, the postal service has offered the greatest opportunities. At the very beginning of the Negro migration this service was under the spoils system, but since 1883 it has been under the civil service rules. The increase in the openings for Negroes in this service has been less the result of specific political pressures than it has been the product of the general participation of Negroes in local politics. Negroes applying for postal positions were given fair treatment and the penetration into the service was rapid. Of all the departments in the municipal government of Chicago, the Negroes have fared best in the public library, the health department, and the water bureau. In absolute numbers they have secured more positions in the police department than in any other American city. Colored women have made notable strides in securing positions in the public-school system. While the progress in the fire department, the controller's office, and in other branches of the local governments has been snail-like, it has been steady. Political pressures have sometimes been effective in preventing discrimination on account of color. Where partisan connections have been used to secure special favors for Negroes in the civil service, the results have been uncertain. A change in adminis- tration sweeps away temporary employees and endangers those who have secured advancements by political pull.

The governmental jobs secured by Negroes in Chicago have not only meant a livelihood for an important fraction but they have also brought prestige to the entire group. The presence in the city of a Negro ward superintendent, Negro principal clerks, Negroes in charge of branch libraries, Negro police lieutenants and sergeants, a Negro fire captain, a Negro school principal, Negro high-school teachers, and Negro postal fore- men meant that the group was getting on. The occupation of these offices indicated that the group was bearing some of the responsibilities of the government. While some white people did not like the situation, they could not deprive the group of the ground that had been won.

Even greater prestige was attached by the group to certain elective positions than to the appointive and civil service posi- tions which were secured. The Negro elective officers were more independent of the white politicians because in most cases they owed their position to black voters. These officers could cham- pion the interests of the race in the legislative halls of the city, the state, and the nation. The continued representation of the race in these bodies was one of the fruits which the group en- joyed because of its loyalty to a given party. That party was willing to support colored candidates for these positions and, although it might lose national and city elections, it won many of the district elections. The Negro representatives came from those districts which loyally supported the Republican party in the days of its adversity. These representatives were symbols of Negro political achievement. The Negro Congressman from the Chicago community was the sole representative of a group of some eleven million people in the national legislative body. In the minds of some white people a seat in the United States House of Representatives is not highly prized. In the minds of persons who are engaged in a bitter struggle to improve their status and security such a seat is a glorious indication of the passing of another goal post.

An unpopular minority which is increasing in size and political importance develops antagonisms in the majority. The Negroes in Chicago had to pay a high price for their political gains. The race riot of 1919 was the product of many complex factors, but among them was the feeling of resentment among some Democratic politicians of foreign extraction that the Negro migration had weakened the position of their party in local politics. During the riot the friction was most acute along the line that divided the "Black Belt" from "Canaryville," a settlement made up of Irish Democrats. Following a number of unsuccessful election campaigns Democratic politicians relieved their feelings of frustration by making the Negro a scapegoat. The race issue became the leading issue of some local campaigns. Mayor Thompson was pictured as a "nigger lover" who kissed Negro babies, and his black cohorts were blamed for the decline of South Side real estate values, for putting white men out of jobs, and for the deterioration of South Side schools. Negro infiltration in certain areas was marked by bombings of buildings and personal intimidation. While the "Negro menace" never became as overwhelming a specter as it is pictured by bourgeois groups in the southern states, it furnished an escape for some middle-class antagonisms. The Negro voters in the isolated West Side communities were terrorized around election time by gangster politicians of Jewish or Italian origin who wished to prevent the Negro domination that characterized certain South Side wards.

All over the entire city the white voters became more race conscious as a result of the growing political power of the Negroes. Guided by white politicians and by the white press, the Caucasian voters cut candidates of African origin. Before the Negro migration it was easier for a colored man to be elected to a county-wide position than it has been since. In some appointive and civil service positions it is now harder for Negroes to get ahead than it was before the whites became so aware of Negro competition. As the group has increased in size and in-

fluence, it has become more localized. It has been thrown back
upon itself and it finds it harder to win offices on a city-wide
ticket. DePriest would find it more difficult now to win once
more a seat on the county board than to be re-elected to Congress from the First Congressional District.

Elective offices, appointive positions, civil service posts, and
seats in the party councils are for the few; the many are in need
of police and fire protection, adequate public schools, clean and
well-paved streets, expert medical care and preventive health
measures, relief in times of unemployment, recreational facilities, pure water supply, and other services that can be rendered
by an efficient and well-ordered government. With higher
burglary rates, more retardation in the schools, higher morbidity and mortality rates, higher delinquency rates, a greater
number of arrests, and more carelessness on the part of the gov-
erning agencies in the Negro community than in other parts of
the city, it might appear that political action had failed to bring
many benefits to the Negro masses.

The Chicago Commission on Race Relations, which investigated the race riot of 1919, brought out very clearly in its
elaborate report that political action on the part of Negroes had
failed to protect them against mob violence, against bombings,
and against vice resorts and that it had failed to provide for all
homes that were fit to live in, clean streets and alleys, sufficient
recreational facilities, adequate school accommodations, and
the necessary public welfare services. This report came out
after the Negroes had been engaged for eight years in intensive
political organization and it appeared that they had made gains
in securing appointments, civil service jobs, and teaching positions. The first two Thompson administrations, which the
Negroes largely supported, were not primarily concerned with
increasing the efficiency of the city services. However, the Negroes were probably no worse off than other minority groups
which had supported Thompson and his associates for reasons
best known to them. Whites as well as blacks failed to see in
the report of the Commission a condemnation of machine politics in Chicago.

Thirteen years have now gone by since the Commission on Race Relations made its recommendations to the police, the city council and administrative boards, the park boards, the civic organizations, and the white and colored public. While the bombing of Negro homes has greatly decreased and there have been no race riots, the Negro politicians have been unable or unwilling to prevent police brutality, to check crime conditions in the Negro community, to insist upon adequate recreational and educational facilities, to provide the best possible health services, and to secure sufficient housing at reasonable rentals. During this time Thompson was mayor for five years and Democratic mayors were in office for eight years. Over the entire period complaints were common regarding vice and crime in the "Black Belt," discrimination against Negroes in the parks and the public schools, and the failure of the government to protect the health, the safety, and the security of the Negro minority. Some of the colored police officers, instead of protecting their own people, took over the exploitive patterns of behavior found in the department. It was charged that the colored people sold their birthright for a mess of gambling privileges and petty jobs. In the meantime, in the areas of Negro concentration, the schools were greatly overcrowded, the bathing beaches and other recreational centers were lacking or insufficient, many poorly paid workers were dissipating their meager earnings in gambling, and the general economic insecurity of the masses was greater than in other parts of the city. The Negro politicians were not prepared to meet the economic crisis which began in 1929. They were too closely attached to the political party which was soon to be swept from power, they were too closely allied with the robber barons of business, and they were lacking in social outlook. At the beginning of the depression Congressman DePriest, the sole representative of the Negroes in the national law-making body, talked against federal aid to states for relief purposes. A year later, when his race in Chicago was more dependent than any other minority upon the federal public relief funds, he was compelled to swallow his words.

What account do the Negro politicians have to make for themselves? What have they done for the public in general and for their race in particular? The voting records of the Negro legislators show that they have been opposed to efficiency methods in government, in favor of overloading the city and state budgets, opposed to laws strictly regulating the liquor traffic, and amusement places, and in favor of laws which aided the white political bosses without appearing directly to work to the disadvantage of the colored people. On the one hand they voted against the council-manager plan, the extension of civil service, the adoption of business methods for hauling ashes and garbage, and the investigation of city or school board finances, and, on the other, they voted for extravagant budgets, the repeal of prohibition, and the pet measures which the white machine leaders needed to consolidate their power. Although they represented constituencies which were largely working class, they opposed bills fostered by the trade unions, such as the anti-injunction bill and the eight-hour law for women. On these and on other questions they explained their votes on the ground that they wished to punish certain groups for discrimination against Negroes. In fact, their entire records were defended on racial grounds. They felt that it was necessary to go along with the white leaders in power in order that they might protect their own people against attacks on the Civil Rights Act and against intolerant movements. White reform organizations might criticize their behavior, but the essence of representative government is that each group must be the judge of its own best interests.

At the time that the malfunctioning of the governmental services was most pronounced, the Communist agitators spread the view that the Negroes were oppressed and exploited by their political "misleaders" and the white bosses. Economic crises bring out in sharp relief the shortcomings of a given political order and make it possible for revolutionary propaganda to be spread among persons who are ordinarily regarded as complacent. Unemployed Negroes, who had no assurance that the fundamental human needs of shelter, food, and clothing would be supplied, were willing to listen to agitators who dramatized their plight. In contrast to the religious utopias pictured by the colored ministers and the African utopias painted by the followers of Garvey, the Communists pointed to the classless American society of the future which would be part of a world-order in which there would be self-determination for all minorities. In order to prepare their listeners for the Marxian ideology, they took advantage of concrete grievances which could be used for purposes of propaganda. From these Communists the Negroes learned what a few determined men could accomplish in securing more adequate relief, in slowing up the eviction process, and in organizing the most exploited workers. In actual numbers the Communist movement declined among Negroes after the governmental machinery began to function more effectively. Nevertheless, the movement has left a residuum of distrust in the present order and of hope in a remote system which is based upon equality of races and the sanctity of toil.

From another viewpoint the balance sheet of political action of the sort possible for a racial minority in a bourgeois democracy does not appear as unfavorable as it is made out to be by radical groups. What would have happened to the governmental services given to this minority if it had had no political power at all? The services secured were short of what might have been obtained had the community been consciously organized to seek social ends. However, the Negro politicians took over the general pattern of behavior which was common among the white politicians, and this pattern did not call for great concern about the efficiency with which the government ran the social services. Under the existing political system the Negroes secured about as many concrete benefits from the government as most other minority groups. However, because their needs were greater, these benefits were not sufficient. Inadequate as they were, these services came nearer to meeting the needs than in areas where the Negroes have not developed some political power.

APPENDIX I

TABLE XVI

PROPORTION OF ADULT CITIZENS AND ELIGIBLE VOTERS REGISTERED
IN SECOND WARD AND IN CITY OF CHICAGO, 1920 AND 1930

	CITY		SECOND WARD*	
	1920	1930	1920	1930
Total adult citizens..............	1,367,515	1,906,366	50,185	31,947
Estimated eligible voters†..........	1,331,000	1,858,000	45,000	29,000
Percentage of adult citizens registered.	64.7	66.3	64.7	71.4
Percentage of estimated eligible voters registered....................	66.4	68.1	71.6	77.4

* 1921 ward lines. Census figures as given by census tracts were fitted to ward lines as closely as possible.

† In C. E. Merriam and H. F. Gosnell, *Non-Voting* (Chicago, 1924), p. 37, it is stated that 7.6 per cent of the non-registered adult citizens interviewed lacked the legal residence qualifications. A non-published tabulation for this study showed that 27.4 per cent of the non-registered adult Negroes lacked the residence qualifications. These ratios were used to estimate the number of eligible voters, i.e., adult citizens who fulfilled the residence qualifications.

TABLE XVII

REASONS FOR NOT VOTING GIVEN BY HABITUAL FEMALE NON-VOTERS
OF SPECIFIED COLOR AND NATIVITY: PERCENTAGE
DISTRIBUTION*

	Native White	Negro	Foreign-Born White
Number..................................	297	276	712
Per Cent.................................	100.0	100.0	100.0
Loss of business or wages.....................	1.3	3.2	2.5
Disbelief:			
Women's vote...........................	26.6	14.8	20.1
Objections of husband.....................	2.4	2.2	2.9
One vote counts nothing...................	1.7	1.5	1.8
Disgust with politics......................	3.7	8.7	2.8
Disgust with party........................		0.7	
Ballot box is corrupted....................	1.0	1.1	0.6
Disbelief in all political action..............	1.0	0.7	1.0
Inertia:			
General indifference.......................	48.3	36.6	45.8
Indifference to particular election...........	1.0		0.6
Neglect.................................	2.7	2.2	2.9
Ignorance or timidity.....................	10.3	27.2	18.0
Failure of party workers...................		1.1	1.0

* Unpublished figures collected in connection with the study of *Non-Voting* (Chicago, 1924).

374

TABLE XVIII

COLORED MEMBERS OF ILLINOIS HOUSE OF REPRESENTATIVES,
1876–1934

Year Elected	Number of General Assembly	Number of Senatorial District	Name of Representative	Order of First Appearance	Occupation	Birthplace
1876.....	30	2	John W. E. Thomas	1	Teacher	Alabama
1882.....	33	3	John W. E. Thomas	......	Teacher	
1884.....	34	3	John W. E. Thomas	......	Teacher	
1886.....	35	3	George F. Ecton	2	Waiter, baseball club owner	Kentucky
1888.....	36	3	George F. Ecton	......	Same as above	
1890.....	37	3	Edward H. Morris	3	Lawyer	Kentucky
1892.....	38	3	James E. Bish	4	....	
1894.....	39	5	John C. Buckner	5	Major in Nat. Guard	Illinois
1896.....	40	5	John C. Buckner	......	Same as above	
1898.....	41	5	William L. Martin	6	Lawyer	Missouri
1900.....	42	5	John G. Jones	7	Lawyer	
1902.....	43	1	Edward H. Morris	......	Lawyer	
1904.....	44	1	Edward D. Green	8	State office-holder	Pennsylvania
1906.....	45	1	Alexander Lane	9	Physician	Mississippi
1908.....	46	1	Alexander Lane	......	Physician	
1910.....	47	1	Edward D. Green	......	State office-holder	
1912.....	48	3	Robert R. Jackson	10	Postal employee	Illinois
1914.....	49	1	Sheadrick B. Turner	11	Editor, business man	Louisiana
....	......	3	Robert R. Jackson	......	Printing and publishing	
1916.....	50	1	Benjamin H. Lucas	12	Insurance	Illinois
....	......	3	Robert R. Jackson	......	Printing and publishing	
1918.....	51	1	Sheadrick B. Turner	......	Editor	
....	......	3	Adelbert H. Roberts	13	Lawyer	Michigan
....	......	3	Warren B. Douglas	14	Lawyer	Missouri
1920.....	52	1	Sheadrick B. Turner	......	Editor	
....	......	3	Adelbert H. Roberts	......	Lawyer	
....	......	3	Warren B. Douglas	......	Lawyer	
1922.....	53	1	Sheadrick B. Turner	......	Editor	
....	......	3	Adelbert H. Roberts	......	Lawyer	
....	......	3	George T. Kersey	15	Undertaker	North Carolina
1924.....	54	1	Sheadrick B. Turner	......	Editor	

TABLE XVIII—*Continued*

Year Elected	Number of General Assembly	Number of Senatorial District	Name of Representative	Order of First Appearance	Occupation	Birthplace
1924.....	54	1	Charles A. Griffin	16	Real estate and insurance	Ohio
....	......	3	Warren B. Douglas	......	Lawyer	
....	......	3	William E. King	17	Lawyer	Louisiana
1926.....	55	1	Sheadrick B. Turner	......	Editor	
....	......	1	Charles A. Griffin	......	Real estate and insurance	
....	......	3	George T. Kersey	......	Undertaker	
....	......	3	Warren B. Douglas	......	Lawyer	
1928.....	56	1	George W. Blackwell	18	Lawyer	Virginia
....	......	1	Harris B. Gaines	19	Lawyer	Kentucky
....	......	3	George T. Kersey	......	Undertaker	
....	......	3	William E. King	......	Lawyer	
....	......	5	William Warfield	20	Real estate appraiser	Illinois
1930.....	57	1	George W. Blackwell	......	Lawyer	
....	......	1	Harris B. Gaines	......	Lawyer	
....	......	3	William E. King	......	Lawyer	
....	......	3	Charles J. Jenkins	21	Lawyer	Texas
....	......	5	William J. Warfield	......	Real estate appraiser	
1932.....	58	1	Harris B. Gaines	......	Lawyer	
....	......	3	William E. King	......	Lawyer	
....	......	3	Charles J. Jenkins	......	Lawyer	
....	......	5	William J. Warfield	......	Real estate appraiser	

TABLE XIX

PERSONS IN CHICAGO IN PUBLIC SERVICE (NOT ELSEWHERE CLASSIFIED)
BY OCCUPATION, COLOR, NUMBER, AND PERCENTAGE, 1930*

OCCUPATION	TOTAL WORKERS	NEGRO WORKERS	
		Number	Per Cent
Carpenters..................................	125	1	0.8
Electricians.................................	491	3	0.6
Engineers (stationary)........................	513	9	1.7
Firemen (except locomotive and fire department)	211	20	9.5
Mechanics (not otherwise specified)............	87	10	11.5
Oilers of machinery..........................	51	1	2.0
Plumbers and gas and steam fitters.............	182	8	4.4
Chauffeurs and truck and tractor drivers.......	616	35	5.7
Draymen, teamsters, and carriage drivers.......	245	13	5.3
Firemen, fire department.....................	2,674	27	1.0
Guards, watchmen, and doorkeepers...........	527	20	3.8
Laborers, public service:			
Garbage men and scavengers...............	359	42	11.7
Other laborers...........................	4,021	384	9.5
Marshals, sheriffs, detectives, etc.:			
Detectives...............................	699	13	1.9
Marshals and constables...................	42	3	7.1
Probation and truant officers..............	194	17	8.8
Sheriffs..................................	455	14	3.1
Officials and inspectors (city)..................	1,954	48	2.5
Officials and inspectors (county)...............	362	3	0.8
Officials and inspectors (state)................	273	6	2.2
Officials and inspectors (United States)..........	824	43	5.2
Policemen...................................	7,214	152	2.1
Soldiers, sailors, and marines..................	251	4	1.6
Chemists, assayers, and metallurgists...........	71	6	8.5
Lawyers, judges, and justices..................	253	9	3.6
Cranemen, derickmen, hoistmen, etc...........	30	1	3.3
Civil engineers and surveyors..................	479	5	1.0
Trained nurses..............................	107	8	7.5
Social and welfare workers....................	42	5	11.9
Charwomen and cleaners......................	28	3	10.7
Housekeepers and stewards....................	61	2	3.3
Elevator tenders.............................	61	5	8.2
Janitors and sextons.........................	429	116	27.0
Porters and cooks............................	24	16	66.6
Agents (not elsewhere classified)................	203	14	6.9
Accountants and auditors.....................	215	3	1.4
Bookkeepers and cashiers.....................	243	7	2.9
Office appliance operators....................	42	1	2.4
Clerks......................................	3,795	185	4.9
Messenger, errand, office boys and girls..........	46	8	17.4
Stenographers and typists....................	1,059	29	2.7

TABLE XIX—*Continued*

OCCUPATION	TOTAL WORKERS	NEGRO WORKERS	
		Number	Per Cent
Other public service pursuits and advertising agents..................................	1,083	43	3.9
Teachers (school)............................	19,425	452	2.3
Mail carriers...............................	3,948	631	16.0
Street cleaners.............................	652	8	1.2
Public service occupations in which there were no negroes in Chicago in 1930†.................	621		
Total.................................	55,287	2,433	4.5

* Information furnished by the Director of the United States Census. The figures were given by sex but the original table was too long to present here. The important groups of Negro women workers were: probation and truant officers, 7; trained nurses, 8; janitresses, 18; clerks, 32; stenographers and typists, 24; teachers, 392; others, 28; total, 509.

† Blacksmiths (31), boilermakers (6), builders and building contractors (8), cabinet-makers (1), coopers (1), machinists (176), millwrights (2), painters, glaziers, and varnishers (building) (58), pattern and model makers (1), structural iron workers (12), canvassers (2), salesmen and saleswomen (11), designers (2), draftsmen (108), photographers (15), electrical engineers (63), mechanical engineers (69), mining engineers (including chemical and metallurgical engineers) (14), waiters (4), collectors (10), credit men (2), purchasing agents (15), shipping clerks (5), weighers (5). All the above were men except 1 woman draftsman and three waitresses.

TABLE XX

EMPLOYEES OF SELECTED COOK COUNTY OFFICES BY COLOR, 1932

	TOTAL EMPLOYEES*	NEGRO†	
		Number	Per Cent
Sheriff—County Building............	206	13	6.3
Sheriff—General Offices.............	314	2	0.6
Sheriff—Criminal Court and Jail......	201	11	5.5
Assessor...........................	134	1	0.7
County Treasurer...................	173	4	2.3
Recorder...........................	355	3	0.8
Clerk of Superior Court.............	59	1	1.7
Clerk of Probate Court..............	65	1	1.5
Coroner............................	37	5	13.5
State's Attorney....................	145	8	5.5
Oak Forest institutions..............	295	4	1.4
County Hospital....................	596	50	8.4
Bureau of Public Welfare............	1,797‡	102	5.7
Juvenile Detention Home............	95	4	4.2
Adult Probation Office..............	25	4	16.0
Juvenile Court Probation Office.......	139	13	9.4
Total selected offices.............		226	

* County Appropriation Bill, 1931.

† Information not obtained regarding all county offices. Since the figures given were obtained by interviews with persons in the offices concerned, their accuracy is not vouched for.

‡ Figures furnished by the Bureau.

TABLE XXI

SOUTH PARK BOARD EMPLOYEES, BY COLOR, 1931*

OFFICE OR DIVISION	TOTAL NUMBER OF EMPLOYEES	NEGRO EMPLOYEES	
		Number	Per Cent
Playground and sport	260	18	6.9
Police	300	1	0.3
Mechanical and electric division	136	4	2.9
Maintenance and repairs:			
Grant Park	200	75	37.5
Jackson Park	75	10	13.3
Washington Park	115	6	5.2
Laundry	53	11	20.8
Others	11	1	9.1
Offices in which there were no Negroes†	126	0	0.0
Total	1,276	126	9.9

* Figures furnished by South Park Board employee.
† Accounting Department, Purchasing Department, Engineering and Construction, Special Assessment Office, Civil Service Office.

APPENDIX II

SELECT BIBLIOGRAPHY

DOCUMENTS

Chicago. Board of Election Commissioners of the City of Chicago. Records (unpublished).

———. *Council Proceedings.*

———. Police Department, Records (unpublished).

Chicago Crime Commission. Records (unpublished).

Cook County Commissioners. *Official Record of Proceedings*, 1896–1900, 1904–10, 1929–34.

Democratic National Convention. *Official Report of the Proceedings*, 1920, 1924, 1928, 1932.

Illinois, *Illinois Blue Book*, 1877–1933.

———. *Journal of the House of Representatives.*

———. *Laws of Illinois.*

Republican Campaign Textbook, 1900, 1920, 1924, 1928, 1932.

Republican National Convention. *Official Proceedings*, 1868–1932.

United States Bureau of the Census. *Fifteenth Census: Occupation Statistics: 1930.*

———. "Negroes in the United States." Washington: Government Printing Office, 1915.

———. "Negro Population 1790–1915." Washington: Government Printing Office, 1918.

———. *Religious Bodies: 1926.*

———. *Thirteenth Census, 1910: Population.*

United States Bureau of Education Statistics. "Statistics of Education of the Negro Race, 1925–26." Washington: Government Printing Office, 1928.

United States Congress. *Congressional Record, 56th, 71st, 72d, 73d Congresses.*

United States Congress, Senate. Hearings before a Special Committee Investigating Campaign Expenditures in Senatorial Primary and General Elections, 1926, 69th Congress, 1st Session, Part II (Reed Committee).

———. *Positions Not Under the Civil Service*, Document No. 173, 72d Congress, 2d Session.

———. Select Committee on Senatorial Campaign Expenditures, 71st Congress, 2d Session, Part 2, Illinois (Nye Committee).

United States Congress. Senate Subcommittee of the Committee on Post Offices and Post Roads, 70th Congress, 2d Session, Influencing Appointments to Postmasterships, Hearings. Washington: Government Printing Office, 1929.

United States Department of Labor. "Negro Migration in 1916–1917." Washington: Government Printing Office, 1919.

United States Women's Bureau. *Negro Women in Industry.* Washington: Government Printing Office, 1922.

NEWSPAPERS

Illinois:

Broad Ax, 1897–1927.

Chicago Bee, 1930–34.

Chicago Daily News, 1905–34.

Chicago Daily Times, 1929–34.

Chicago Defender, 1914–34.

Chicago Evening American, 1922–34.

Chicago Herald and Examiner, 1920–34.

Chicago Journal, 1922–28.

Chicago Record Herald, 1907.

Chicago Review, 1931–33.

Chicago Tribune, 1876–1934.

Chicago Whip, 1919–32.

Chicago World, 1930–33.

Maryland:

Afro-American, 1929, 1932.

New York:

Amsterdam News, 1932.

Daily Worker, 1924–34.

New York Age, 1929–32.

New York Times, 1928–29.

New York World, 1907, 1928.

Ohio:

Cincinnati Union, 1931–32.

Oklahoma:

Oklahoma Eagle, 1932.

Pennsylvania:

Pittsburgh Courier, 1928–32

Tennessee:

Nashville Globe, 1929.

Washington, D. C.:

Washington Tribune, 1928–29.

BOOKS AND PUBLICATIONS

ANDREAS, A. T., *History of Chicago from the Earliest Period to the Present Time.* Chicago: A. T. Andreas, 1884–86.

Annals of the American Academy of Political and Social Science, 1928. "The American Negro" (Donald Young, ed.). Philadelphia, 1928.

ASSOCIATED NEGRO PRESS. *Annual,* 1919-20. Chicago: Associated Negro Press, 1920.

AYER, N. W. AND SONS. *Directory of Newspapers and Periodicals,* 1880-1934 (title varies). Philadelphia: Ayer & Sons.

BANCROFT, FREDERIC A. *A Sketch of the Negro in Politics, especially in South Carolina and Mississippi.* New York: J. F. Pearson, printer, 1885.

BINDER, CARROLL. *Chicago and the New Negro.* Chicago: Chicago Daily News, 1927.

BOGARDUS, EMORY S. *Immigration and Race Attitudes.* Boston and New York: D. C. Heath & Co., 1928.

BOND, HORACE M. "An Investigation of the Non-intellectual Traits of a Group of Negro Normal School Students." University of Chicago (A.M. Thesis). Chicago, 1926.

BOWEN, L. DE K. *The Colored People of Chicago: An Investigation Made for the Juvenile Protective Association.* Chicago, 1913.

BOWERS, CLAUDE G. *The Tragic Era.* Cambridge, Mass.: Riverside Press, 1929.

BRAWLEY, BENJAMIN GRIFFITH. *Social History of the American Negro,* Being a History of the Negro Problem in the United States. New York: Macmillan Co., 1921.

BRECKINRIDGE, SOPHONISBA P. "Housing Conditions in Chicago, Illinois. Back of the Yards," *American Journal of Sociology,* XVI (Chicago, January, 1911), 433.

BRIGHT, JOHN. *Hizzoner Big Bill Thompson.* New York: Jonathan Cape & Harrison Smith, 1930.

BUNCHE, R. J. "The Thompson-Negro Alliance," *Opportunity,* VII (March, 1929), 79.

BURGESS, ERNEST W., AND NEWCOMB, CHARLES (eds.). *Census Data of the City of Chicago: 1930.* Chicago: University of Chicago Press, 1933.

CHESNUTT, CHARLES WADDELL. *Frederick Douglass.* Boston: Small, Maynard & Co., 1899.

CHICAGO COMMISSION ON RACE RELATIONS. *The Negro in Chicago.* Chicago: University of Chicago Press, 1922.

Chicago Daily News Almanac and Year Book, 1886-1934.

CHICAGO VICE COMMISSION. *The Social Evil in Chicago.* Chicago: A report submitted to the Mayor and City Council of Chicago. 4th ed. Republished by Vice Commission of Chicago, Inc., for distribution by American Vigilance Association, 1912.

COUNTS, GEORGE SYLVESTER. *School and Society in Chicago.* New York: Harcourt, Brace & Co., 1928.

DE SAIBLE ASSOCIATION, CHICAGO. *Souvenir of Negro Progress, Chicago, 1779-1925.* Chicago, 1925.

DETROIT MAYOR'S COMMITTEE ON RACE RELATIONS. *Report*, 1927. Detroit: Detroit Bureau of Governmental Research, 1927.

DETWEILER, FREDERICK GERMAN. "The Negro Press in the United States." University of Chicago (Ph.D. Thesis). Chicago, 1922.

DOUGLASS, FREDERICK. *Life and Times of Frederick Douglass*. Hartford, Conn.: Park Publishing Co., 1882.

DOWD, JEROME. *The Negro in American Life*. New York: Century Co., 1926.

DREWRY, WILLIAM SIDNEY. *Slave Insurrections in Virginia (1830–1865)*. Washington: Neale Co., 1900.

DuBois, WILLIAM EDWARD BURGHARDT. *The Philadelphia Negro*. Publications of the University of Pennsylvania. Philadelphia, 1899.

———. *The Souls of Black Folk: Essays and Sketches*. Chicago: A. C. McClurg & Co., 1904.

DUKE, CHARLES S. *The Housing Situation and the Colored People of Chicago*. Chicago, 1919.

DUNCAN, HANNIBAL GERALD. The Changing Race Relationship in the Border and Northern States. University of Pennsylvania (Ph.D. Thesis). Philadelphia, 1922.

DUTCHER, DEAN. "The Negro in Modern Industrial Society." Columbia University (Ph.D. Thesis). Lancaster, Pennsylvania, 1930.

EMBREE, EDWIN R. *Brown America*. New York: Viking Press, 1931.

FARLEY, JOHN WILLIAM. *Statistics and Politics* (2d ed.). Memphis, Tennessee: Saxland Publishing Co., 1920.

FELDMAN, HERMAN. *Racial Factors in American Industry*. New York and London: Harper & Bros., 1931.

FERGUSON, GEORGE OSCAR. "The Psychology of the Negro; An Experimental Study. Columbia University (Ph.D. Thesis). New York, 1916.

FISHER, MILES MARK. "The History of the Olivet Baptist Church of Chicago." University of Chicago (A.M. Thesis). Chicago, 1922.

———. *The Master's Slave, Elijah John Fisher*. Philadelphia: Judson Press, 1922.

FRAZIER, E. FRANKLIN. *The Negro Family in Chicago*. Chicago: University of Chicago Press, 1932.

GIBSON, J. W., AND GROGMAN, W. H. *The Colored American*. Atlanta: J. L. Nichols & Co., 1903.

HARRIS, A. L., AND SPERO, S. "Negro Problem," *Encyclopaedia of the Social Sciences*, XI, 335–56.

HARRIS, H. L., JR. "Negro Mortality Rates in Chicago." *Social Service Review*, I, (March, 1927).

HARRIS, NORMAN DWIGHT. *The History of Negro Servitude in Illinois and of the Slavery Agitation in that State, 1719–1864*. Chicago: A. C. McClurg & Co., 1904.

HERRICK, MARY JOSEPHINE. "Negro Employees of the Chicago Board of Education." University of Chicago (A.M. Thesis). Chicago, 1931.

HERSHAW, L. M. "The Negro Press in America," *Charities*, XV (1905), No. 1.

HERSKOVITS, MELVILLE J. *The American Negro*. A Study in Racial Crossing. New York: A. A. Knopf, 1928.

HOLLAND, F. M. *Frederick Douglass, the colored orator*. New York, 1891.

HOWARD, OLIVER OTIS. *Autobiography of Oliver Otis Howard, Major General, United States Army*. New York: Baker & Taylor Co., 1907.

JOHNSON, CHARLES S. *The Economic Status of Negroes*. Nashville: Fisk University Press, 1933.

———. *The Negro in American Civilization*. New York: Henry Holt & Co., 1930.

JOHNSON, CLAUDIUS O., *Carter H. Harrison I*. Chicago: University of Chicago Press, 1928.

JOHNSON, JAMES WELDON. *Black Manhattan*. New York: A. A. Knopf, 1930.

JONES, JOHN G. *The Black Laws of Illinois and a Few Reasons Why They Should be Repealed*. Chicago: Tribune Book and Job Office, 1864.

KINGSBURY, J. B. "The Merit System in Chicago from 1915 to 1923," *Public Personnel Studies* (November, 1926).

LANGSTON, JOHN MERCER. *"From the Virginia Plantation to the National Capitol*. Hartford, Conn.: American Publishing Co., 1894.

LEGISLATIVE VOTERS LEAGUE OF ILLINOIS. *Assembly Bulletin*, 1911–1934.

LEWINSON, PAUL. *Race, Class and Party*. London: Oxford University Press, 1932.

LEWIS, LLOYD, AND SMITH, HENRY JUSTIN. *Chicago: The History of Its Reputation*. New York: Harcourt, Brace & Company, 1929.

LOCKE, ALAIN LEROY. *The New Negro. An Interpretation*. New York: A. and C. Boni, 1925.

LOGGINS, VERNON. *The Negro Author*. New York: Columbia University Press, 1931.

LYNCH, JOHN ROY. *The Facts of Reconstruction*. New York: Neale Publishing Co., 1913.

MARK, MARY LOUISE. *Negroes in Columbus*. Columbus: Ohio State University Press, 1928.

MASON, M. C. "Policy of the Segregation of the Negro in the Public Schools of Ohio, Indiana, and Illinois." University of Chicago (A.M. Thesis). Chicago, 1917.

MAYS, BENJAMIN ELIJAH AND NICHOLSON, JOSEPH WILLIAM. *The Negro's Church*. New York: Institute of Social and Religious Research, 1933.

McLEMORE, FRANCES WILLIAMS. "The Rôle of the Negroes in Chicago in the Senatorial Election 1930." University of Chicago (A.M. Thesis). Chicago, 1931.

MECKLIN, JOHN MOFFATT. *Democracy and Race Friction: a Study in Social Ethics*. New York: Macmillan Co., 1914.

MERRIAM, CHARLES E. *Chicago: A More Intimate View of Urban Politics*. New York: Macmillan Company, 1929.

MERRIAM, CHARLES E., AND GOSNELL, HAROLD F. *Non-Voting: Causes and Methods of Control.* Chicago: University of Chicago Press, 1924.

MILLER, HERBERT ADOLPHUS. *Races, Nations and Classes.* Philadelphia: J. B. Lippincott Co., 1924.

MORTON, RICHARD LEE. *The Negro in Virginia Politics, 1865–1902.* Charlottesville, Virginia: University of Virginia, 1919.

MOTON, ROBERT RUSSA. *What the Negro Thinks.* New York: Doran, Doubleday, Page & Co., 1928.

MUNICIPAL VOTERS' LEAGUE OF CHICAGO. *Reports, 1915–1933.*

Negro Yearbook and Annual Encyclopaedia of the Negro. Nashville, Tenn.: Sunday School Union Print., 1912.

NOWLIN, WILLIAM F. *The Negro in American National Politics.* Boston: Stratford Company, 1931.

OLBRICH, EMIL. *The Development of Sentiment on Negro Suffrage to 1860.* Madison, Wisconsin: University of Wisconsin, 1912.

PARK, ROBERT E. "Mentality of Racial Hybrids," *American Journal of Sociology,* XXXVI (January, 1931), 534–51.

———. "Methods of a Race Survey," *Journal of Applied Sociology.* X (May, 1925), 410.

———. "Negro Race Consciousness as Reflected in Race Literature," *American Review,* I (1923), 505–517.

———. "Racial Assimilation in Secondary Groups," *Publications of the American Sociological Society,* VIII (1913), 75–82.

PENDLETON, MRS. LEILA (AMOS). *A Narrative of the Negro.* Washington, D.C. Press of R. L. Pendleton, 1912.

PENN, IRVINE GARLAND. *The Afro-American Press and Its Editors.* Springfield, Mass.: Willey & Co., 1891.

PENNSYLVANIA DEPARTMENT OF PUBLIC WELFARE. *Negro Survey of Pennsylvania.* Harrisburg, 1928.

PIDGEON, MARY ELIZABETH. *Negro Women in Industry in 15 States.* Washton: Government Printing Office, 1929.

QUAIFE, MILO MILTON. *Checagou.* Chicago: University of Chicago Press, 1933.

RECKLESS, WALTER. *Vice in Chicago.* Chicago: University of Chicago Press, 1933.

REUTER, EDWARD BYRON. *The American Race Problem; a Study of the Negro.* New York: T. Y. Crowell Co., 1927.

———. *The Mulatto in the United States.* Boston: R. G. Badger, 1918.

Rhea's New Citizen's Directory of Chicago, Illinois and Suburban Towns. Chicago: Press of W. S. McCleland, 1908.

ROBINSON, GEORGE F., "The Negro in Politics in Chicago," *Journal of Negro History,* XVII (April, 1932), 180–229.

ROOD, ALICE QUAN. "Social Conditions among the Negroes on Federal Street between 45th Street and 53rd Street." University of Chicago (A.M. Thesis) Chicago, 1924.

SANDBURG, CARL. *The Chicago Race Riots, July 1919.* New York: Harcourt, Brace & Howe, 1919.

SCOTT, EMMETT JAY. *Negro Migration During the War.* New York: Oxford University Press, 1920.

SIMKINS, F. B. AND WOODY, R. H. *South Carolina during Reconstruction* Chapel Hill: University of North Carolina Press, 1932.

SPERO, STERLING D., AND HARRIS, ABRAM L. *The Black Worker.* New York: Columbia University Press, 1931.

SUTHERLAND, ROBERT LEE. "An Analysis of Negro Churches in Chicago." University of Chicago (Ph.D. Thesis). Chicago, 1930.

TAYLOR, ALRUTHEUS AMBUSH. *The Negro in the Reconstruction of Virginia.* Washington: Association for the Study of Negro Life and History, 1926.

———. *The Negro in South Carolina during the Reconstruction.* Washington: Association for the Study of Negro Life and History, 1924.

THOMAS, WILLIAM HANNIBAL, *The American Negro.* New York and London: Macmillan Co., 1901.

WALLACE, JESSE THOMAS. "How and Why Mississippi Eliminated the Negro from State Politics in 1890. University of Chicago (A.M. Thesis). Chicago, 1923.

WALLACE, JOHN. *Carpetbag Rule in Florida.* Jacksonville, Fla.: Da Costa Printing and Publishing House, 1888.

WASHINGTON, BOOKER TALIAFERRO. *Frederick Douglass.* Philadelphia and London: G. W. Jacobs & Co., 1907.

———. *My Larger Education; Being Chapters from My Experience.* Garden City, New York: Doubleday, Page & Co., 1911.

———. *The Story of the Negro, the Rise of the Race from Slavery.* New York: Doubleday, Page & Co., 1909.

WASHINGTON INTERCOLLEGIATE CLUB OF CHICAO. *The Negro in Chicago, 1779–1927.* Chicago: Washington Intercollegiate Club, Vol. I, 1927; Vol. II, 1929.

WELLS-BARNETT, IDA. *How Enfranchisement Stops Lynching.* New York: Original Rights Magazine, Charles Lenz, 1910.

———. *Southern Horrors: Lynch Law in All Its Phases.* New York: New York Age Print, 1892.

WHITE, L. D. *Prestige Value of Public Employment.* Chicago: University of Chicago Press, 1929.

Who's Who in Colored America. New York: Who's Who in Colored America Corporation, 1927.

WILSON, EDWARD E. "The Responsibility for Crime," *Opportunity,* VII (March, 1929), 95–97.

WINSTON, SANFORD. "Studies in Negro Leadership; Age and Occupational Distribution of 1,608 Negro Leaders," *American Journal of Sociology*, XXXVII (January, 1932), 595.

WOOD, JUNIUS B. *The Negro in Chicago*. Chicago: Chicago Daily News, 1916.

WOODDY, CARROLL H. *The Case of Frank L. Smith*. Chicago: University of Chicago Press, 1930.

WOODSON, CARTER GODWIN. *A Century of Negro Migration*. Washington: Association for the Study of Negro Life and History, 1918.

———. *Free Negro Heads of Families in the United States in 1830*. Washington: Association for the Study of Negro Life and History, 1925.

———. *History of the Negro Church*. Washington: Associated Publishers, 1921.

———. *Negro Orators and their Orations*. Washington: Associated Publishers, 1925.

———. *The Negro as a Business Man*. Washington: Association for the Study of Negro Life and History, 1929.

———. *The Negro in Our History*. Washington: Associated Publishers, 1922.

WOOFTER, THOMAS JACKSON (ed). *Negro Problems in Cities*. Garden City: Doubleday, Doran & Co., 1928.

WORK, MONROE NATHAN. *A Bibliography of the Negro in Africa and America*. New York: H. W. Wilson Co., 1928.

———. "Negro Real Estate Holders of Chicago." University of Chicago (A.M. Thesis). Chicago, 1903.

———. *Negro Year Book* (eighth edition), 1931–32. Tuskegee: Negro Year Book Publishing Co., 1932.

WRIGHT, RICHARD ROBERT. "The Industrial Condition of Negroes in Chicago," University of Chicago (D.B. Thesis). Chicago, 1901.

YOUNG, DONALD R. *American Minority Peoples*. New York and London: Harper & Bros, 1932.

INDEX

INDEX

Abbott, Robert S., editor of *Defender*, 102–3, 105–6

Adjustments made by Negro civil service employees, 240–43, 272–79

African Methodist Episcopal Church, 95, 98, 170

Alabama: Negroes in Chicago from, 17, 27, 66, 128, 164; attitude of whites in, toward DePriest, 185; administration of justice in, 323–24

Aldermen, influence of, in politics, 73, 285, 307

American citizenship of Negroes, 65, 305; *see also* Patriotism of Negroes

American Federation of Labor, 332–34; *see also* Labor unions

American Negro Labor Congress, 326, 346

Anderson, Alderman Louis B.: on Hoover, 30; and Dever, 44; candidate for alderman, 75–77, 171; primary candidate for congressman, 88, 98, 103; as a journalist, 104; and Henry Jones, 130; and DePriest, 171, 175–77, 181–82, 187–90; ward committeeman, 187 n.; assistant corporation counsel, 199

Anti-Communist organizations, 352–56

Anti-lynching laws, 26, 37, 322; *see also* Lynching

Appeal, colored weekly, 105

Appointive positions, Negroes in, 7–8, 196–218

Appomattox Club, 111, 316, 318

Ashton, H. M., legislative candidate, defeat of, 68

Assignment of Negro policemen, 257–60, 265–66

Atlanta bond issue election, 10

Austin, J. C., Negro minister, and Thompson, 51–52

Australian Ballot Act of Illinois, and Negro candidates, 67; *see also* Straight votes

Ayer's *Newspaper Annual*, cited, 101

"Back to Africa" movement; *see* Garvey, Marcus

Bailiff, Negroes as deputies of, 204

Baker, Harry, candidate for Congress, 81 n.

Ballot, as a symbol, Negroes on, 18, 26; *see also* Democracy, Negro suffrage

Bank failures, and Negroes, 321

Barnett, Ferdinand L.: candidate for municipal judge, 85, 105 n.; lawyer, 123 n.; assistant state's attorney, 155, 206

Barnett, Mrs. Ida Wells: career of, 25–26; and Thompson, 50; as a social worker, 204

Barrett, Judge George F., and Negro politicians, 207

Beliefs concerning Negroes: as voters, xi, 3–7, 17; as politicians, 71 n., 75 n., 79, 86, 125, 145, 162 n., 163, 192; in public employment, 254, 266, 299, 312

Benvenuti, Julius, alleged gambling operator, 134 n.

Bibb, Joseph: editor of the *Whip*, 105 n.; member of Library Board, 201

Biblical language used by Negro politicians, 148–49

"Big Fix," 57, 115

Binga, Jesse, banker, 107

Bipartisan deals, and Negro candidates, 84

Biracialism, 218, 241–42

"Birth of a Nation" film: and Thompson, 57; and Communists, 324

Bish, James E., state representative, military record of, 112

Black, Julian, alleged gambling operator, 134

"Black Belt" in Chicago, defined, 19

Black-and-tan cabarets, 120, 172

Blackwell, George, member of Illinois legislature, 73 n., 113, 376

Blaine, James G., on Negro congressmen, 6–7

Blanton, Thomas, congressman from Texas, and DePriest, 188, 190

Blease, Senator Cole, from South Carolina, on DePriest, 185

Board of Education: demand for Negro member of, 55 n., 202, 281; Negro employees of business department, 197, 224, 228; educational department, 280 ff.; policies of, 287, 295; *see also* Teachers

391

Wilson, Edward, lawyer, 168, 206–7
Wilson, President Woodrow: and Negro appointments, 28; at Put-in-Bay, 73 n.
Woman suffrage, and Negro voters, 111
Women High School Teachers' Federation, 298
Worker's Voice, cited, 336
World-revolution, Communist program of, 323
World War veterans, 72, 112–13, 348
Wright, Edward H.: Republican ward committeeman, 44, 51, 55, 71, 86–87, 132, 153–62, 210–11, 214; quoted, 64–65, 79, 158–59, 161, 360; candidate for

alderman, 74; county commissioner, 82–83, 154–55, 206; lawyer, 108; founder of club, 111; sketch of, 153; president pro tem of county board, 155; state central committeeman, 156; assistant corporation counsel, 157, 199; member of Illinois Commerce Commission, 159, 215; and Thompson, 160; and DePriest, 167–68, 170, 175–76, 178; state employee, 213; and Negro postal employees, 316–17

Yarros, Victor S., cited, 40 n.
Young Communist League, 325, 336, 342
Young Liberators, 328